SIERRA NEVADA NATURAL HISTORY

BERKELEY, LOS ANGELES, LONDON

SIERRA NEVADA
NATURAL HISTORY

An illustrated handbook

BY TRACY I. STORER
AND ROBERT L. USINGER

UNIVERSITY OF CALIFORNIA PRESS

University of California Press
Berkeley and Los Angeles, California
University of California Press, Ltd.
London, England
© 1963 by The Regents of the University of California
ISBN: 0-520-01227-5
Library of Congress Catalog Card Number: 63-12681
Printed in the United States of America

16   17   18   19   20

The paper used in this publication meets the
minimum requirements of American National Standard
for Information Sciences—Permanence of Paper for
Printed Library Materials, ANSI Z39.48–1984. ∞

PREFACE

THIS HANDBOOK is planned for people who wish to identify the common plants and animals of the Sierra Nevada and to learn something of where and how they live. The subject matter relates mainly to inhabitants of the mountains but includes some found in the western foothills and others living along the east side. The introductory sections provide a background about the Sierra—its physical features, climate, waters, geological history, and the ways in which the mountain areas are affected by human occupancy. The section on distribution indicates some of the factors that determine where plants and animals can live and, in general terms, the kinds of environments in which the common representatives can be sought. The lists of references (p. 358) include publications for general reading and books or manuals that supply more detailed information than can be given in this handbook.

The plant accounts include a selection of fungi, lichens, ferns, wildflowers, many shrubs, and most of the trees, but only examples of the grasses, sedges, and rushes. The sections on animals omit various small creatures that are rarely seen, most of the water birds that are merely migratory visitants, and a few lesser mammals. Some of the accounts of insects deal only with the "order" or "family," but for the butterflies and moths and a few others the commoner species are described. The book contains descriptions of more than 750 species or groups, most of which are illustrated.

Because of space limitations it is impossible to deal with every plant or animal known in the Sierra Nevada. Those of common occurrence that are readily identified are included. Where a group is represented by several kinds that cannot be distinguished from one another except by a trained person using a technical book, a single account is provided. Examples are the willows and the shrews and bats. In other cases the commonest and most widely distributed one is described, with brief mention of others.

Each account of a plant or animal starts with the accepted common name (boldface type), followed by the scientific name (italics). Where several members of a group are mentioned, only the genus name is used (*Ceanothus, Peromyscus,* etc.). Biologists have an international system of two-part scientific names in Latin—genus and species—by which each kind of plant or animal is known. There is general but not universal agreement on the name to be used. In some instances, therefore, the scientific name for a species in this handbook differs from that in some of the reference works. Reasons for these differences cannot be discussed here for lack of space.

Technical workers also give scientific names to local geographic races or subspecies in certain cases. Thus, the Steller Jay (*Cyanocitta stelleri*) as a species ranges from southeastern Alaska to Nicaragua; 6 subspecies are distinguished in the United States. That in the Sierra Nevada is *Cyanocitta stelleri frontalis*, sometimes called Blue-fronted Jay. In like manner botanists designate varieties or subspecies in many plant species. For simplicity in this handbook we omit mention of subspecies or varieties and also omit the name of the "author," the person who first described a species. Subspecies, varieties, and author names are given in many of the reference books.

To assist the reader, the text account and the illustration of a species bear the same number. Plants and animals in each section (trees, birds, etc.) are numbered in sequence, each with a prefix (T-, B-, etc.), and the scientific name is followed by the number of the plate containing its illustration. Thus for mammals the text headings are: **M-1. Shrews.** Genus *Sorex* (pl. 61); to **M-50. Mountain Sheep.** *Ovis canadensis* (pl. 65). Plates also are numbered in sequence; for example, Plate 61. Mammals, has pictures of 1. Shrew, 2. Mole, and several others. The abbreviation "col. pl." refers to the colored plates, which are numbered in a separate sequence and bound together between pages 182 and 183. Reference to a color plate is thus: **B-49. Red-shafted Flicker.** *Colaptes cafer* (col. pl. 19). If a species is shown in both black and white and color, reference is made to two plates: **WF-33. California Poppy.** *Eschscholtzia californica* (pl. 9, col. pl. 6). All other illustrations, including sections across the Sierra, structure or work of animals, and bark of trees, are numbered consecutively as text figures.

Before using the handbook to identify a plant or animal, the reader should consult the introductory paragraphs at the head of the appropriate section because these contain suggestions for assisting in identification and some include a special figure and a table to aid in the process.

Tracy I. Storer
Robert L. Usinger

August, 1962

ACKNOWLEDGMENTS

THE AUTHORS are grateful to many persons and several organizations for much generous coöperation in producing this handbook—selecting lists of species to include, reviewing manuscript, and lending or permitting use of illustrations. Full citations of books mentioned are given in the References at the back of the book.

Geological history: C. G. Higgins (review).

Weather data on plant belts: P. A. Munz and D. D. Keck.

Fungi: R. T. Orr (list, review, photographs); Univ. Calif. Herbarium, Berkeley (Elizabeth Morse negatives).

Lichens: J. W. Thomson, Isabelle Tavares (identifications).

Ferns: Figures from Leroy Abrams. 1926–1960. Illustrated Flora of the Pacific States. Stanford, Calif., Stanford University Press.

Wildflowers and shrubs: J. T. Howell (lists); J. M. Tucker (review); June McCaskill (identifications); figures from L. Abrams and R. S. Ferris. Flora. 1926–1960; a few from N. L. Britton and Addison Brown. 1913. An Illustrated Flora of the Northern United States. . . . 2nd ed. By permission of New York Botanical Garden; color slides (besides those of the authors): California Academy of Sciences (Charles Webber collection); Sierra Club; Yosemite National Park Museum; E. O. Essig; T. H. Jukes.

Trees: Figures from W. L. Jepson. Trees of California. 1923. Berkeley, Calif.: Sather Gate Bookshop; G. B. Sudworth. 1908. Forest Trees of the Pacific Slope; and L. Abrams and R. S. Ferris. 1926–1960. Flora.

Miscellaneous animals: Some figures from T. I. Storer and R. L. Usinger. 1957. General Zoology. 3rd ed. New York, McGraw-Hill Book Co., by permission of the publishers.

Mollusks: Allyn G. Smith (list, review, specimens for figures).

Insects: Arthur C. Smith and Jerry Powell (review); Frieda L. Abernathy, Celeste Green, and other persons in Dept. of Entomology, Univ. Calif., Berkeley; T. I. Storer and R. L. Usinger, 1957. General Zoology; and R. L. Usinger. 1956. Aquatic Insects of California. Berkeley and Los Angeles, Univ. Calif. Press; some photos of insect work from Pacific Southwest Forest and Range Experiment Station, Berkeley.

Fishes: W. I. Follett (list, distributional data, review); Calif. Dept. of Fish and Game (3 color plates); other figures from scientific papers.

Amphibians and reptiles: R. C. Stebbins (list, review, figures from his Amphibians and Reptiles of Western North America. 1954. New York, McGraw-Hill Book Co., by permission of the publishers.

Birds: R. T. Orr (list); L. H. Miller (review); Yonekichi Makino (line figures); Museum of Vertebrate Zoology, Univ. Calif., Berkeley, owl figures and color plates from J. Grinnell and T. I. Storer. 1924. Animal Life in the Yosemite. Berkeley, Univ. Calif. Press; Edward Spaulding color plate of red finches and leucosticte used in Ralph Hoffman. 1927. Birds of the Pacific States. Boston, Houghton Mifflin Co., by permission.

Mammals: R. T. Orr (list); L. P. Tevis, Jr. (review); Museum of Vertebrate Zoology, Univ. Calif., Berkeley (color plate of chipmunks); plate of mammal tracks adapted in part from W. H. Burt and R. P. Grossenheider. 1964. A field guide to the mammals. 2d edition, by permission of W. H. Burt; Emily E. Reid, Don G. Kelley, Julia P. Iltis (line figures).

Other drawings made by Emily E. Reid, Julia P. Iltis, Barbara Daly, Paul Catts, and Petr Wygodzinsky.

Cover illustrations: Sierra Nevada (W. H. Wright, Lick Observatory); animals and trees (Dave Brower and Joseph Leconte, Sierra Club; National Audubon Society).

CONTENTS

INTRODUCTION

1. MAN AND THE SIERRA NEVADA

THE SIERRA NEVADA, with its rugged topography, varied resources, and superb flora and fauna, is a dominant feature of California. During centuries of pre-history, Indians had their rancherias on its lower flanks; they foraged in its higher parts during the summer, and some crossed to trade with tribes beyond. Spanish occupants of the coastal hills and valleys thought of it as a *terra incognita,* distant and foreboding, and considered it a barrier to invasion from the east—although later that proved otherwise.

Discovery of gold in the western foothills, the Mother Lode, stimulated the spectacular settlement of California by Americans in the mid-nineteenth century. This commanding range with its feed and water and game was a haven of refuge to westbound pioneers after the rigors of parched deserts in Utah and Nevada. Crossing of the Sierra with wagons, however, before roads were built, was a herculean task for both men and animals.

For several decades after the gold rush the major enterprises in the Sierra were mining, timber production, and livestock grazing. Meanwhile discovery of Yosemite Valley in 1851 and of the giant sequoias the next year gave hints of the recreation values present. The building of a railroad across the range and a connecting narrow-gauge line from Truckee to Lake Tahoe led to the establishing of early resorts and summer homes in that area. Mountain climbers and campers pushed into various parts of the range to scale the peaks, to enjoy the rugged scenery, and to hunt and fish. Throughout the "horse and wagon" days an outing in the mountains demanded time, effort, and perseverance, but brought rich rewards. The automobile and improved roads have spread opportunities for outdoor enjoyment so that now thousands of people use the mountains for a wide variety of interests and some portions are available at all seasons.

Because of its geographic position and topographic features, the Sierra Nevada has a wide variety of climatic conditions and biological features—equivalent to a spread from northern Mexico to the fringe of the American Arctic. A trip on any cross-mountain highway between the Great Valley and Great Basin reveals a diversity in plant and animal life scarcely equaled by a journey of similar length anywhere else. In two or three hours during summer one goes from the shimmering heat of the Sacramento–San Joaquin plains to cool elevations under pines and firs. There are changes in the flora and fauna every few miles. From the lowland valleys that never experience snow, the roads cross summit passes where winter drifts may exceed 20 or 40 feet in depth. Each elevation and each season has its sequence of change in weather and floral pattern. The lower western flats and slopes become green with winter rains and colorful with wildflowers in spring, but by mid-summer their ground cover is parched, tinder dry, and yellow. The mountain valleys and slopes, by contrast, are snow-blanketed for months during the winter, but from May or June to August are green parks bright with wildflowers.

Recorded history of these mountains began precisely on April 2, 1772. The missionary, Pedro Font, while in the western edge of the San Joaquin Valley saw, about 40 leagues (120 miles) to the east, a great snowy range. In his diary he sketched the mountains and termed them *una gran sierra nevada*—a great snowy range; today we use his name. The lower reaches of the larger rivers—Sacramento, San Joaquin, Feather (Las Plumas), Merced, and Kings—were visited and named in the early 1800's, but neither the Spaniards nor Mexicans went farther. First to cross the range, from the west, were Jedediah Smith and two companions, in October, 1827, through snow, probably in Ebbetts Pass. In October, 1831, Joseph Walker and a party of fifty struggled up the east slope and descended, presumably between the Merced and Tuolumne rivers, being the first to glimpse Yosemite Valley and perhaps giant sequoias. The explorer John C. Fremont and his party, with Kit Carson as guide, saw Lake Tahoe on February 14, 1844, and in the ensuing month forced their way over what is now Carson Pass and on to Sutter's Fort. A few years later, with the discovery of gold, crossings became common.

The California State Geological Survey in 1863–1864 made the first scientific studies in the Yosemite region and southward, and in 1875 members of the federal Wheeler Survey examined the Lake Tahoe region. The intrepid John Muir began his visits to the mountains in 1869, and his pleasant accounts of the scenery, geology, plants, and animals did much to inform the public about the wonders of the Sierra Nevada. Before 1900 professional and amateur naturalists had started to collect, study, and describe the native plants and animals. Such work has proceeded with increasing tempo until there is now a fairly large literature on the subject, both technical and popular.

There are many subjects of interest for both laymen and scientists in the natural features and denizens of the Sierra Nevada. These include:

the rocks and minerals and the evidence of many geological processes, including much on the work of glaciers; the differing types of weather at various elevations and in the many unlike parts of the range; the water cycles of snow, ice, and rain, the varied kinds of lakes and streams, and the work of water in modifying the landscape; the diverse belts of plant cover, and the many adjustments made by plants with differing requirements as to temperature, moisture, soil, sunlight, and shade; the responses of plants to natural environmental changes by erosion, landslides, drought, or lake filling; the sequences of changes in plant cover following man-made disturbances by lumbering, fire, or overgrazing; and the animals of many kinds, both large and small, each of which has distinctive requirements for food, shelter, and nesting places. The varied aspects of the Sierra Nevada offer much to those who find "books in the running brooks, sermons in stones," and in the other elements of nature.

2. PHYSICAL FEATURES

Topography. The Sierra Nevada is a unified mountain range that extends about 360 miles from near Mt. Lassen at the north to the edge of Walker Pass, east of Bakersfield. It varies from 60 to 80 miles in width and trends roughly from northwest to southeast. All of it, except the Carson Range, lies within California. The Sierra consists essentially of a massive granite block that is tilted so that the western side, 50 to 65 miles broad, has a gradual slope of only 2 to 6 per cent. The spectacular eastern side, however, rises abruptly from the flattish bordering valleys that are 4000 feet or more in elevation. At the north the escarpment rises only 2000 to 3000 feet, but at the south it ascends 7000 feet in a horizontal distance of 5 miles along Owens Valley. The crest of the range consequently is near the eastern border. The summits increase gradually in altitude from north to south, being 6000 to 8000 feet in the Feather River country, about 10000 feet west of Lake Tahoe, 13000 in the Yosemite region, and even higher near Mt. Whitney, where there are twelve peaks more than 14000 feet above sea level. The entire range includes fully 500 peaks that exceed 12000 feet in altitude.

The term High Sierra applies properly to the alpine region above the main forest (about 8000+ ft.), where peaks, lake basins, and other rock structures carved by glaciation are conspicuous. It extends about 150 miles from north of Yosemite down to Cottonwood Pass and spreads on both sides of the crest, with an average width of about 20 miles. Between the peaks there are extensive highlands that are relatively flat and open. This is the land of the hiker and the pack train, accessible only in summer.

The western slopes of the range are dissected by many deep stream

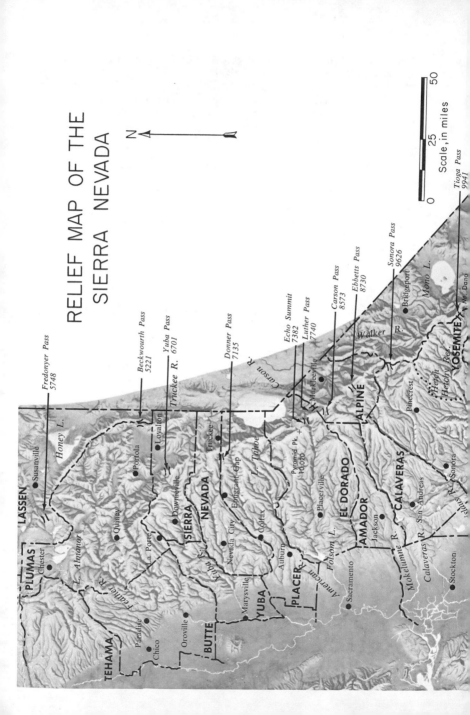

RELIEF MAP OF THE SIERRA NEVADA

N

Scale, in miles
0   25   50

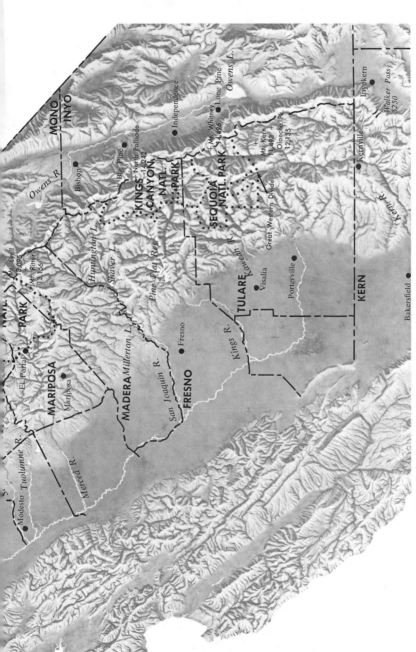

Map 1. Relief map of the Sierra Nevada. (U. S. Geological Survey photo.)

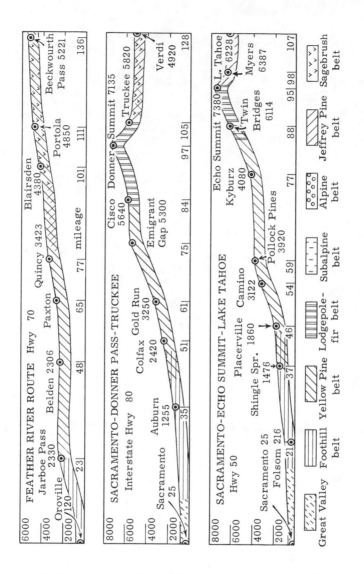

Figure 1. Sections across the Sierra Nevada showing elevations, distances, and plant belts. Elevations are given (in feet) below each place named; mileage is from city named at left side; plant belts are as on map 2 but with the Boreal Region subdivided.

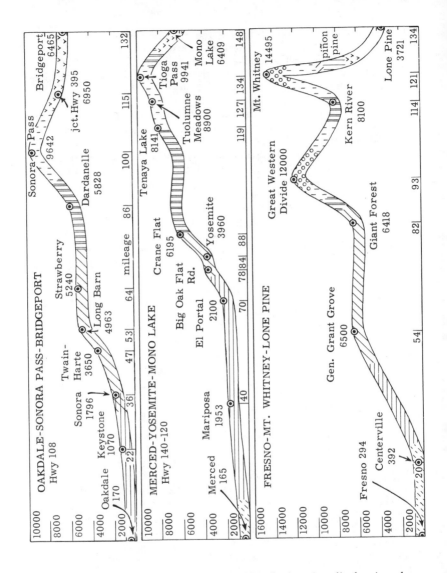

Figure 2. Sections across the Sierra Nevada (continued) showing elevations, distances, and plant belts. (See fig. 1 for symbols indicating plant belts.)

7

valleys with steep slopes. The lower foothills, however, grade insensibly into the Great Central Valley, where the flat agricultural lands on both sides of the Sacramento and San Joaquin rivers are only 500 to less than 50 feet above sea level. East of the range the plateau of the Great Basin extends across Nevada to western Utah and the first ranges of the Rocky Mountains.

Only a few portions of the Sierra Nevada are named as distinct ranges. These are the Diamond Mountains in eastern Plumas County, the Carson and Crystal ranges on the east and west of Lake Tahoe, and the Greenhorn Mountains at the far southern end. The eastern part of Sequoia National Park contains the Great Western Divide, a huge north-south ridge with 14000-foot peaks, that separates the Kern River system from the Kings and Kaweah drainages.

The crest is broached by a succession of passes, earlier used by Indians and pioneers and now crossed by motor highways in the northern and central parts of the range. Fredonyer Pass (5748 ft.) to Susanville marks the northern limit of the Sierra Nevada. Next in turn the chief routes are: Beckwourth Pass (5221 ft., Western Pacific R.R. and Calif. Highway 70) from Quincy; Yuba Pass (6701 ft.); Donner Pass (7135 ft., Southern Pacific R.R. and Interstate Highway 80); Echo Summit (7380 ft., U.S. 50); Carson Pass (8573 ft., Calif. Highway 88) from Jackson; Ebbetts Pass (8730 ft., Calif. Highway 4); Sonora Pass (9642 ft., Calif. Highway 108) from Sonora; and Tioga Pass (9941 ft., Calif. Highway 120) from Yosemite. Highways 70, 80, and 50 are kept open in winter. Other passes, to the south of Tioga, are usable only in summer by hikers and horses, mules, or burros. Walker Pass (5250 ft., Calif. Highway 178) from Bakersfield, open all year, marks the southern border of the range.

The topography and rock architecture of the Sierra Nevada are too diverse and huge for description in words. They must be experienced—visited and explored repeatedly, especially on foot—to obtain an appreciation of their grandeur. Tapered peaks, jagged crests, and massive mountains surround valleys and rock basins, wide or narrow, of every shape and kind. The High Sierra has the most spectacular panoramas, but there are many other places with notable scenery, including some on highways and lesser roads. The Carson Pass highway is especially attractive because much of it is on the summit of a ridge, affording wide vistas of the surrounding mountains.

Waters. High in aesthetic appeal are the Sierran waters—streams, falls, lakes, snow, ice, and glaciers. In their many and varied forms they add immeasurably to the pictorial beauty. Less evident but important is their role in the erosive forces that gradually modify the landscape. These actions vary from the slight expansion of seepage freezing in a rock crevice to the powerful transport of a fast stream or the colossal forces in a slow-moving glacier.

The most conspicuous waters are those of the major river systems. On the precipitous eastern flank there are a few short but turbulent rivers such as the Truckee, Carson, Walker, and Owens, together with some lesser creeks. After leaving the mountains they all either disappear into the Great Basin desert or form alkaline lakes.

On the broad western slope, where most of the rain and snow fall, the situation is quite different. There ten large river systems have cut deep canyons. From north to south these master streams, each with many tributaries, are the Feather, Yuba, American, Mokelumne, Stanislaus, Tuolumne, Merced, San Joaquin, Kings, and Kaweah. Their general trend is southwesterly. An eleventh, the Kern River system, flows southward out of the southern Sierra, then westward. The waters of the first eight join the Sacramento–San Joaquin system in the Great Valley and discharge into San Francisco Bay. The output of the Kern formerly fed the Buena Vista Lakes west of Bakersfield, and that of the Kings and Kaweah formed Tulare Lake, all in the San Joaquin Valley. The lakes are gone because the supplying waters now serve local communities or are used for irrigation.

The upper valleys of some of the big rivers were scoured by glaciers into gorges that rival the Grand Canyon of Arizona in depth. Yosemite Valley (Merced River) is 3000 feet deep, the "grand canyon" of the Tuolumne is 4000 to 5000 feet, Kern Canyon has a depth of 6000 feet, and part of Kings Canyon is a stupendous 7000 to 8000 feet from stream to summit. The lower unglaciated canyons of these rivers are deeply V-shaped, with long steep slopes.

Sierran streams fluctuate widely in volume. Late spring rains and snow melt yield maximum runoff, often with heavy flooding of bordering meadows and some dry areas. Formerly when these waters reached the Great Valley they covered vast areas and did much damage to crops and towns. Control by check dams in the mountains and by levees in the lower elevations now reduces this hazard. Further protection results from dams that impound water for hydroelectric power and irrigation, making many artificial lakes at middle elevations. By autumn many mountain streams carry little water. Besides seasonal variations there are lesser daily fluctuations because of the alternate freezing and thawing of sources at high altitudes. Not all the streams flow throughout the year. On both east and west slopes many of the smaller ones are intermittent, flowing during periods of rain or snow melt and then declining. Some become entirely dry in late summer, and others flow then only near their sources.

Cascading and falling waters are never-ending attractions, and the several high falls of Yosemite Valley are the most famed in the Sierra. The narrow Nevada Fall (594 ft.) and the broad Vernal Fall (317 ft.) flow over huge steps of massive granite planed bare by glaciers on the upper Merced River. The Bridal Veil Fall (620 ft.), the majestic two-part Yosemite Falls (total 2565 ft.), and some lesser ones pour from high hanging side valleys where the former hill slopes and stream beds were stripped away during the Ice Age. Other falls, less renowned, occur in Tenaya Canyon and the Hetch Hetchy Valley (both in Yosemite National Park), and on the upper San Joaquin River near the Devil's Postpile. Cascades of white, turbulent, speedy water are present on the upper reaches of many rivers and creeks.

There are fully 1500 lakes in the Sierra, varying from rock pools 20 to 50 or more feet across to the great "lake of the sky," Lake Tahoe. Scouring by ice and accumulations of rock debris have made the high country a land of lakes. The scooping by glaciers near their origins left many shallow basins (tarns) that became lakes with narrow sandy beaches. Their waters freeze and thaw repeatedly throughout the year. After ice forms, a sharp drop in temperature causes it to contract and split. The crevices in the ice fill with water which freezes and expands, forcing the margins of the ice out on the shores. Rocks and sand from the bottom and sides thereby are gradually pushed out to form a surrounding beach ridge or rampart. The sandy and rocky shores are relatively barren. The "pure" water of these lakes lacks the minerals essential for growth of algae, diatoms, and the minute animals in the food chains for fish; in consequence, few of them contain trout. High-altitude lakes are catchment basins for rain and snow melt which overflows to cascading brooks; these join to form upper tributaries of the large rivers.

Below the high country there are fewer lakes. Some in and below the Lodgepole—fir belt are of water dammed behind glacial moraines; Fallen Leaf Lake of the Tahoe region is an example. The floor of Yosemite Valley resulted from filling of a post-glacial lake basin. Best known and largest of all is Lake Tahoe, 21 by 11 miles in extent. Because of its great depth (1685 feet), the surface waters never cool to 32°F. and so it remains ice-free at all seasons.

Peat (compacted sphagnum moss) is rare in the Sierra; two examples are: Bog Lake in the Yosemite region and a meadow on Sagehen Creek north of Truckee. The latter is a "hanging bog" composed of water-soaked sphagnum.

Rocks. Mountain ranges in other regions are often hidden under forest or lesser vegetation. In much of the Sierra, with sparser plant cover, the rock masses often are dominant in the landscape. The topography, coloration, and other features of a mountain range result from the kinds of rock present and the ways they have been altered by erosion and other geological agencies. Rocks in the Sierra Nevada are of three major groups, granitic, volcanic, and sedimentary (see Geological History, p. 17).

Sparkling white granite is exposed over much of the range. Granite is a crystalline mixture composed chiefly of two light-colored minerals, quartz (silica or SiO_2) and feldspar (aluminum silicates), with lesser amounts of dark-colored hornblende and mica. Some varieties of granite have higher proportions of the latter materials which make them darker in over-all color. The granitic domes of the Sierra are an outstanding feature, seldom found elsewhere in the world. These are of unjointed massive rock with smoothly rounded contours. In size and shape they vary from low eminences that rise only slightly above their surroundings to the enormous Half Dome dominating the eastern end of Yosemite Valley. They are most numerous in the Yosemite region, but some occur to the north and south. Domes owe their form to slow loss (exfoliation) of curving shells or scales, somewhat akin to the peeling of the layers of an onion. The shells vary in thickness from 6 inches to 10 feet on different domes. The manner of their formation is not fully known (fig. 3).

On either side of the Sierran block there are somber red, brown, green, gray, and black rocks, some derived from sedimentary deposits of the ancient mountains and others erupted from volcanoes. The former, originally laid down in water and later elevated, have been metamorphosed into slates and schists containing pyrite (iron sulfide, etc.) that colors the outcrops. Slate forms the summit of numerous peaks, including Mt. Tallac, Mt. Lyell, Mt. Goddard, Mineral King, and the Kaweahs. Mt. Dana is mostly of slate and altered lava, capped by limestone, and untouched by the glaciers that flowed around its lower slopes. Ancient slates (such as the nearly upright "Mariposa gravestones") and other nongranitic rocks are exposed at many places on the lower western slopes.

Another type of rock is rough brown or blackish basalt and andesite from relatively recent lava flows. Basalt occurs from Plumas to Tulare counties. One flow, at the outlet of Lake Tahoe, slightly raised the lake level and that of its drainage, the lower Truckee River. Later this obstruction was broached, and exposures of the lava can be seen on the highway to Truckee. The Devil's Postpile, about 300 feet long and 200 feet high, near Mammoth Lakes, is of huge five- or six-sided basaltic columns of volcanic origin; the tops are scored where overridden by glacial ice. From Mammoth Mountain to Mono Lake there is a line of fully 30 post-glacial volcanic craters, some 2000 feet high, that showered out pumice (steam-shredded lava) to cover areas near Mammoth Pass deeply. Volcanic rocks—pinkish, reddish, dark gray—cover areas around Soda Springs, at the west and southwest of Lake Tahoe, and parts of the east slope near the origin of Owens River. There are also volcanic cones scattered from the Mono Craters (near Mono Lake) northward to Mt. Lassen. Hot springs, indicative of subsurface heat, are common along the eastern base of the Carson Range and elsewhere.

Over much of the Sierra rocks of all three types are marked by joints or fractures in one or more planes. These permit water to seep in, freeze, and expand. This action contributes to breakage and disintegration and ultimately produces sand and soil. Rock crevices are the places where many rock-dwelling plants—from herbs to trees—get started. Growth of their roots later aids fracture and disintegration. As the crevices become enlarged they serve as daytime and winter retreats for various animals.

Limestone (calcium carbonate) is rare in the crest region but present at lower altitudes on the west slope. As a result of water action caves have developed, principally in two areas. In the Mother Lode are Bower Cave, east of Coulterville, and Moaning and Mercer caves near Murphys. The Sequoia–Kings Canyon region includes Church, Crystal, and Soldiers caves; Boyden Cave in Kings Canyon is fully 800 feet long. Marble (metamorphosed limestone) is quarried at several places, notably near San Andreas, for manufacturing cement.

From the lower parts of the conifer forest down into the foothills, flat upland surfaces are covered by a deep powdery red soil. Travel there in the dry season on unimproved routes envelops man, beast, or vehicle in suffocating dust and blankets the roadside vegetation. This is the Mother Lode—from Plumas County to Mariposa County— where the "forty-niners" found gold-bearing quartz in modern and ancient stream beds and recovered $500 million in gold. Gravels and sands in the beds of west slope streams still yield small nuggets sparingly to amateur prospectors who pan for gold.

3. CLIMATE

The pattern of weather in the Sierra Nevada results from the physical form and the geographic position of the range in relation to the Great Valley, Coast Ranges, and Pacific Ocean. There are many local climates in the Sierra because of its diverse topography and wide span in latitude and altitude. The exact weather at a particular place and time is not easy to predict, but for the entire range there is an over-all seasonal character that makes the Sierra an ideal recreation area. The dry cool summers provide a pleasant change from the hot lowlands on either side and from the foggy coast, and the relatively warm winters with record snow packs at middle altitudes are ideal for winter sports. Such a combination is rare among mountain ranges elsewhere in the world.

The climate affects the economy and well-being of people living in the Sierra and of all who dwell in adjacent parts of California and Nevada. Water from Sierran storms accumulates in the winter snow pack, then melts slowly to fill streams and reservoirs that sustain the vast needs of lowland agriculture and communities. These waters, when they reach the valleys, help to refill underground water storage spaces. A wet year means prosperity, but a series of dry years is disastrous.

A summer cold spell in the mountains drives out visitors and causes resort owners to lose money, but an early snowfall followed by well-spaced storms brings profits to ski resorts and stores a maximum of water.

Weather records in the Sierra began in 1870 with completion of the first through railroad (now the Southern Pacific) having stations at Folsom, Auburn, Colfax, Cisco, Norden, Truckee, and Boca. This transect, paralleled by U.S. Highway 40, is fairly central. A second follows the Western Pacific (and U.S. Highway 40A) along the Feather River from Oroville through Las Plumas, Stanwood, Bucks, Quincy, and Portola. A third road is from Red Bluff through Westwood to Susanville. There are few climatic records for the southern Sierra, where elevations are higher and all the passes are closed in winter. Throughout the range there are practically no weather stations above 8000 feet and so the record is far from complete.

The annual cycle of seasons follows the familiar pattern of the Northern Hemisphere, but the position of the Sierra near the western coast of the continent determines the type of climate for both summer and winter. Ordinarily, there is a low-pressure area over the North Pacific Ocean throughout the winter and a high-pressure area there in the summer. The reasons for this shift are complex, involving the alternate cooling and warming of Arctic land masses and the rise of the warm, moisture-laden air over the ocean in winter. The rotation of the earth sets the prevailing winds from west to east and carries storms across California. The Coast Ranges catch some of the resulting rain, especially in the north, but there is no barrier at the Golden Gate and the heaviest precipitation occurs to the east and north of that gap as the air ascends the gradual western slope of the Sierra. Often a high-pressure area over central California in winter deflects the storms northward so that the weather is "fine" (except for farmers).

In general, temperature decreases 1° F. for each 300 feet of rise in altitude, and the air, thus cooled, drops its moisture as rain or snow. Precipitation increases 2 to 4 inches for each 300-foot rise, reaching a maximum at about 5000–6000 feet elevation in the central part of the range. Most of the moisture in the air having fallen, the amount of precipitation declines above that altitude. The east side of the Sierra is definitely in a "rain shadow" where little rain or snow falls and desert conditions prevail.

A typical Sierran winter storm starts a series of events unnoticed and unsuspected by the traveler, who seems merely inconvenienced by having to add antifreeze to his radiator and to put on tire chains. First, weather warnings alert snowplow crews and men who service electric power lines. When the storm strikes hundreds of people steel themselves for a battle with the elements—local residents, travelers, truck drivers, railroad crews, highway patrolmen, and even physicians. Then there are innumerable small dramatic events until the winds abate, the sun breaks through, and another hard but much needed storm has passed. An average storm lasts 5 to 6 days, during which the temperatures are moderate because of the incoming maritime air. Afterwards the temperature drops.

Temperature. Sierran temperatures are generally warm in summer with maxima of 80° to 100° F. and minima of 15° to 37° F., depending on altitude. In winter the maxima range from 55° F. to 70° F. and the minima from about 0° to more than minus 30° F. Some examples of extremes are Folsom (elevation 216 ft.), 119°F. in July and 22°F. in January; Yosemite Valley (3960 ft.), 90°F. in July and 22°F. in January; and Lake Tahoe on the east side (6239 ft.), 93° F. in July and minus 15° F. in January.

Temperatures at middle elevations on the west slope (Cisco, 5939 ft.) and east side (Truckee, 5820 ft.) are similar, the mean being about 62° F. in July and 30° F. in winter. The extremes, however, are much greater at Truckee (+100° F. and −30° F.) than at Cisco (+94° F. and −6° F.). Temperature zones rise gradually from north to south. Alpine temperatures doubtless will show the widest extremes when data become available. On the summit of Mt. Whitney, during a brief period in September, the daily maxima averaged 62.5° F. and the minima 22.5° F. The coldest part of the day was between 3 A.M. and 6 A.M.

Precipitation. The total precipitation includes both rain and snow; about 10 inches of snow equals one inch of rain. In the Sierra more than half the total falls in January, February, and March (with a curious lesser amount in February), but less than 3 per cent is received in summer. Precipitation decreases steadily from north to south —thus, at 5000 feet, it is 90 inches in Plumas County but only 55 inches in Mariposa County. In general a map showing precipitation, like temperature, conforms to the altitude contours, increasing to about 6500 feet on the west slope of the central Sierra. However, the contrast in rainfall between the west (75 in.) and east (20 in.) sides at 5500 feet elevation is striking.

Summer showers are of increasing frequency at higher elevations, and correspondingly there are more cloudy days. This trend is typical of high mountains and results from local increases in humidity and movements of air (winds) up the slopes and canyons during the day and downward at night. As the air moves up slope it cools and moisture condenses to form rain, often with hail, thunder, and lightning. Such thundershowers are usually of short duration and make little impression on the predominantly dry summer season, but the lightning causes many forest fires.

Snowfall. Snow is one of the most spectacular features of the Sierra. Increasing with altitude in much the same pattern as rainfall, it starts with an ill-defined "snowline" at about 2000–3000 feet on the west slope. In the central Sierra the annual average increases steadily from about 2 feet at Colfax to 34 feet at Norden, near Donner Summit. At the latter station 86 per cent of the total precipitation falls as snow. The total seasonal fall there, however, varies within wide limits, from 13 feet in 1880–1881 to 65 feet in 1951–1952. The greatest annual fall ever recorded in the Sierra was at Tamarack, Alpine County (8000 feet)—73½ feet during the winter of 1906–1907. The pattern of high and low years is believed to follow certain cycles which have been used as a basis for predictions.

Such heavy snowfall and the resulting pack is equaled only in a few places in the Pacific Northwest. Yet the winter climate in the Sierra is comparatively mild, and all but about sixty small glaciers and snow patches in northern exposures at high elevations evaporate or melt by midsummer. At Donner Summit melting proceeds at about 4 inches per day in mid-May. The snow naturally persists longer at high elevations or during unusually cool summers. The ground is again usually blanketed with snow by the middle of November. Snow melt during warmer spells in winter results in waterlogged snow—a 14-foot pack at Donner Summit, for example, increases in weight from 10 pounds per cubic foot at the surface to 28 pounds at the bottom. A special feature of the Sierra snow pack is its persistence in spite of warm air temperatures (40° to 60° F.) during the day and only moderately low temperatures (20° to 32° F.) at night. The reasons for this involve both reflection of sunlight from the surface of the snow and the capture of much of the sun's heat by the coniferous forest canopy. Thus at Tahoe City in one year all snow had melted on a treeless meadow by April 10, but 1.3 inches remained in a pine–fir forest and 7.1 inches in a fir forest on April 20.

Snow falls as flaky crystals which have innumerable surfaces that reflect (rather than absorb) heat from the sun. Then the alternate daytime melting and nighttime refreezing change its character. Melt water trickles down and freezes to form hard-packed granules. A new crust forms each night on the surface. Early storms build the snow pack, the later layers protecting those beneath from melting. As winter ends the character of the surface changes. It becomes granular and pitted (by rain), and receives a scattering of needles and other plant debris. By mid-March the once crystalline top has become an irregular, heat-absorbing surface. Thenceforth melting increases, and three-fourths of the total pack melts in April, May, and June. In spring, therefore, waterfalls are at their best, rivers are in flood, and snow-melt streams and pools pass through their ephemeral existence. In the aggregate the runoff, in wet years, is sufficient to fill all reservoirs and also send much water down in lowland streams.

Winter conditions in the High Sierra were recorded on a trip near the crest from Cottonwood Pass to Yosemite between December 25, 1928, and April 3, 1929, mostly above 9500 feet (O. Bartholomew. 1930. Sierra Club Bull. 15 [1]:69–73). In a protected flat (at 10300 ft.) night temperatures were $+12°$ to $-14°$ F., but on ten nights in more open places at 11000 feet or higher none was below 0° F.; elsewhere the night minima were up to 32° F. Daytime maxima were 22° to 50° F. The average snow pack was 4 feet or less; southern exposures in canyons often were bare. Mt. Tyndall and Mt. Whitney had bare summits and little snow on the slopes. Many streams, even above 10500 feet, were flowing, with little snow or ice. Most lakes had both ice and snow, two being solidly frozen. Sierran hares were out on wind-swept summits and chickadees were ever present in trees, but nutcrackers and chickarees were seen mostly below 10000 feet; martens raided unguarded food bags at night. Other animals seen were conies, mice, weasels, grouse, and porcupines—even frogs and flies. This was a year of average snowfall as indicated by records at five west slope stations (4900–8000 ft.) in Fresno and Tulare counties.

Streams and Lakes. Sierran streams usually flow throughout the winter but are impeded during freezing weather. Year-long records for Sagehen Creek (at 6337 ft., 12 mi. north of Truckee) show average water temperatures (high vs. low) of 67°–45° F. in July and 40°–32° F. in January. Winter snow usually covers part of the stream. Each night in the coldest period small masses of white anchor ice form on the bottom and on immersed objects. This slows the flow, causing pools along the stream to rise in level. Anchor ice melts by day, and normal flow is resumed. If the night temperature drops to 32° F., small crystals of frasil ice form in the stream water.

The situation is different in lakes. Some of the smallest freeze solid. Those of moderate size become ice-covered; Lower Echo Lake (at 7450 ft., near Highway 50) is an example. The water freezes to a depth of about 8 inches, and a 7-foot surface blanket of snow persists for about 6 months. The bottom water in winter is about 40° F. (temperature of greatest density), and that close under the ice is 32° F. After the spring melt, wind-driven waves circulate the entire water mass, which becomes uniform in temperature (e.g., 40° F., June 13, 1951). As summer sun heats the surface portion, a stratification results, with warmer and lighter water above (surface 63° F., July–Sept., 1949) and colder heavier water (45° F.) below, there being an abrupt change (thermocline) about 40 feet down. In autumn the surface waters cool and circulate until the whole lake again is of uniform temperature.

Lake Tahoe never freezes, being large and deep (to 1685 ft.). Sierran winters are not long or cold enough to lower the entire water mass to 40° F. Hence cooling and lightening of surface water to 32° F. does not occur. The bottom water is always near 40° F.; the surface varies from 40° F. in March to 68° F. in August.

Unlike waters in lower altitudes, few Sierran lakes are comfortable for bathing. The surface portion in a protected cove may reach 70° F. on a sunny afternoon, and then be quickly chilled as a breeze causes circulation of colder deeper water.

4. GEOLOGICAL HISTORY

The area now occupied by the Sierra Nevada has had a long and complex history. The Calaveras formation in the central foothills includes slates, marbles, and greenstones derived from rocks fully 200 million years old (late Paleozoic era). Rocks of that time were eroded to a flattish surface, sank, and became covered by the sea. Then a thick sequence of both volcanic and sedimentary materials was deposited (Mesozoic era: Triassic and Jurassic periods). Subsequently these marine beds, formed into rock, were folded up into parallel northwest-trending mountainous ridges and valleys. Thereupon streams, flowing either northwesterly or southeasterly, began to erode.

Later (Middle Cretaceous, 100 million years ago), vast amounts of molten granite were injected, as many small intrusions, into and under the overlying folded strata. This material crystallized as a huge mass of solid rock. Along with these intrusions, rocks of the central Sierra and foothills received their content of minerals such as gold, copper, and tungsten. Subsequent erosion (Late Cretaceous) began to expose the granite and reduced the landscape to one of broadly rolling form, covered by deep residual clay soil, but the original trends of hills and valleys persisted. Throughout this time interval the sea reached inland to about the eastern border of what is now the Sacramento Valley.

In the next epoch (Eocene, 70 to 60 million years ago) the Coast Ranges were folded up, and the ancestral Sierra tilted so that it sloped westward. Streams began to remove the deep covering of clay and carry it into the sea, then near the western side of the Great Valley. Other uplifts followed (Oligocene and Miocene epochs), and in the north floods of volcanic mud from craters and fissures buried valleys and lower ridges on the west slope. There were only local flows in the central and southern portions. About 12 million years ago (end of Miocene) the range was bowed up to a height of several thousand feet. It stood well above lands to the east because of faults (vertical slippages) along parts of its eastern flank. The epoch that followed (Pliocene: 11 to 1 million years ago) was quiet at first, but toward its end the final and greatest uplift took place, bringing the range to about its present height.

Long ago, as the Sierran mass began to rise and tilt to the west, a new series of streams began to flow southwesterly down the slope. With each uplift their grade and erosive action was increased. Eventually they cut broad but deep valleys down the western slope. As their headwaters extended backward into gaps of the older northwest-trending crests, they captured streams there which had maintained their directional courses since ancient times. In consequence, the headwaters and many upper tributaries of major west-slope rivers today flow either northwesterly or southeasterly whereas their lower valleys align with the existing southwestward slope of the Sierra.

Throughout the last million years (Pleistocene epoch), preceding the Recent time in which we live, two processes were at work that produced much of the spectacular scenery of today. The high country, pushed above the snow line, acquired glaciers and was sculptured by them. Concurrently, there was repeated local faulting along the east base of the range. The Sierra Nevada, in consequence, now has the form of a tilted block with an abrupt escarpment on the east and a long gradual western slope which has been dissected by streams of water and ice.

The latest conspicuous faulting was in the Owens Valley during 1872, when an earthquake destroyed the town of Lone Pine and killed many of its people. Two fault scarps were formed, 6 to 20 feet high, and the land between sank. Evidence of many other faults can be found all along the eastern base, varying in length from a few yards to several miles. Lake Tahoe, 1685 feet deep, probably derives from subsidence (perhaps piecemeal) of a huge block between the Sierran mass and a great splinter, the Carson Range. Other northern ranges on the east side also have splintered off; they are bounded by faults and small fresh scarps. The eastern base of the Carson Range near Genoa, Nevada, has cliffs 40 to 50 feet high with vertical grooves and polish, attesting relatively recent slips under great pressure. In this manner the bold towering eastern escarpment of the Sierra evolved over many millennia.

Glaciers form in high latitudes or altitudes where the climate is such that the annual total of snow received exceeds that lost by melting and evaporation. (Decrease in average annual temperature of only a few degrees probably would result in large Sierran glaciers.) Snow intercepted and accumulated on a high mountain gradually compacts into ice. Because of its weight the ice mass, a glacier, begins moving slowly down slope, usually in a preëxisting stream valley. Several years later its front melts at some lower elevation. (There is also some melting along its sides.) From the sides and floor of its path the great forces of the huge, slowly flowing ice mass pluck rocks. As these are carried along they cut and scour the surfaces over which the glacier moves. Gradually the original V-shaped stream valley is converted into a U-shaped glacial valley. Lateral tributaries whose lower portions are removed by a glacier become hanging valleys that end high on the walls

a. Lyell Glacier (white), moraine (blackish), and tarn (lake; lower right)

b. Erratics and glacial smoothing; Tioga Road near Olmsted View

c. Glacial polish; Desolation Valley

d. Exfoliation near Tenaya Lake

e. Exfoliation on Turtleback Dome west of Wawona Tunnel

Figure 3. Glaciers and granite in the Sierra Nevada.

of the broadened and deepened gorge. After the ice disappears their waters descend as speedy cascades or falls. The area below a peak, where a glacier starts, becomes scooped out as a bowl-like depression or cirque. At the opposite end of a glacier, where the ice finally melts, the rocks and soil it carried are deposited in a transverse ridge of debris or terminal moraine. As a glacier recedes it usually forms a succession of these moraines. Debris deposited along the side of a glacier's path makes a lateral moraine (fig. 3).

During the Ice Age (Pleistocene) there were four lengthy glacial stages, separated by even longer warm interglacial intervals. In the Sierra there is good evidence for three of them. Here, however, instead of one huge undivided ice cap—such as covered much of northeastern North America—glaciers and ice fields were discontinuous. Some parts of the range had none. At the northern end (elevation about 7000 feet) there were only small "cirque" glaciers nestled in declivities on the taller peaks. But from Donner Pass south to the upper Kern River Canyon there were, in different stages, individual ice fields of a few to many square miles. From each of these there were trunk glaciers that flowed down valleys, both east and west.

The region between Lake Tahoe and Yosemite, with peaks up to 13000 feet, received great supplies of moisture-laden air through the Golden Gate. A true ice cap developed, 80 miles long by 40 miles wide, above which only a few peaks projected. From it, among others, came the Tuolumne Glacier that scoured Hetch Hetchy Valley and was 46 miles long. At another time its length was 60 miles. The Yosemite Glacier, formed of ice flows in Tenaya Canyon and the upper Merced drainage, at one stage reached slightly below El Portal, for a total length of 36 miles. The San Joaquin River drainage had an ice field and glaciers, as did the Kings and Kaweah basins. Southernmost of the trunk glaciers was that in Kern Canyon.

The first Yosemite Glacier submerged much of Half Dome (but the now absent front "half" disappeared because of erosion from a joint plane, not by glaciation). This glacier was 3000 feet deep opposite Glacier Point. The second was not quite so thick, and the third, largely responsible for the valley's present appearance, reached just above the Royal Arches. A terminal moraine of the last glacier lies across the valley near El Capitan. As the ice melted back, this moraine served as a dam to impound waters that formed a Lake Yosemite of prehistoric times. Now it is breached by the Merced River (at El Capitan bridge) and by two roads; a cross-valley road runs on top of it. Other moraines are to be seen on the valley floor. The unglaciated lower canyon of the Merced River resulted entirely from stream cutting, whereas the upper part through the Little Yosemite and Yosemite valleys, once of stream type, was scoured out by glaciers. Several falls and cascades in Yosemite now emerge from hanging valleys.

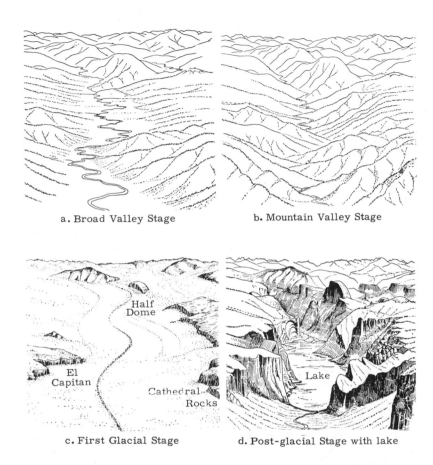

a. Broad Valley Stage   b. Mountain Valley Stage

c. First Glacial Stage   d. Post-glacial Stage with lake

Figure 4. Four stages in geological evolution of Yosemite Valley. (After François Matthes, 1930.)

An example of geological evolution in Sierran landscape is provided in sketches by F. E. Matthes (1930) of Yosemite Valley (fig. 4). During the broad valley stage (a) the Merced River was 500 to 1000 feet below the forerunners of El Capitan and Sentinel Rock. Some six million years later Yosemite had become a mountain valley 1600 feet deep (b), and Little Yosemite was 1200 feet deep. In the canyon stage, after another estimated one million years, El Capitan was 2400 feet high and Glacier Point 2000 feet above the river. Through all these stages the valley was broadly or narrowly V-shaped. Then the glaciers

(c) gouged Yosemite into the broad U-shaped form seen today. The post-glacial lake (d) on the valley floor has disappeared.

The Ice Age ended perhaps 10000 years ago, being followed by climate warmer than the present when there probably were no glaciers in the Sierra. Today, however, there are about sixty "glacierets," thought to have formed not more than 4000 years ago. The largest are on Mt. Lyell and Mt. Maclure and on the Palisades farther south. None is a mile long, most of them are half this size, and some are even smaller. These little glaciers can be distinguished from snow fields by the presence of crevasses on the upper surface and the whitish water emerging below them.

The Sierra Nevada shows much evidence of glacial action (fig. 4). There are moraines of various sizes and ages and scattered hanging valleys. Many massive rock surfaces were planed and polished, some to mirror brilliance by sand particles, or scored with parallel grooves by harder materials carried in the ice. Boulders weighing hundreds or thousands of pounds were transported from higher regions by glaciers and later stranded where the ice melted; they are the "glacial erratics," now resting on surfaces of different rock composition. Finally there is "glacial milk," the melt water issuing from beneath existing glaciers, which is whitened by its content of finely ground "rock flour."

Scenic features and biological environments of today are the products of various geological processes. Angular peaks derive from "rock plucking" by glaciers once under their summits. Many cirques and other rock basins scooped out by moving ice became lakes, with little or no organic debris and thus biologically poor. A stream entering a glacial lake will carry gravel, sand, and soil which accumulate at its mouth or outlet. With gradual filling, plants begin to grow on the surface and the area in turn becomes a marsh, a meadow, and ultimately land invaded by forest. Many mountain meadows are filled lake basins. At each stage in the succession from wet to dry environment various species of plants and animals occupy the area in turn, according to the kind of habitat each requires.

From steep-sided canyon walls scoured by glaciers other environments evolve. Exposed rocks develop cracks into which water seeps, freezes, and expands, eventually loosening the outer portions. Angular pieces, small or large, later slide or fall down the slope, aided by avalanches and frost action, to accumulate below as jumbles of steep talus rock. Spaces within talus cones and aprons serve as shelters for many kinds of animals from insects and small reptiles or mice to bigger carnivores. In time, plants of successively larger size colonize the slides. The great talus slopes of Yosemite Valley now support a forest of golden oaks affording acorns for band-tailed pigeons, woodpeckers, and squirrels, together with food for many insectivorous birds.

Other geological processes yield soil where forest trees grow, gravelly slopes which are the sites for certain kinds of flowering plants and shrubs, and exposed masses of partly fractured granite that support Jeffrey pines, junipers, and other "rock-loving" plants. The segregation of animals by habitats stems back through the types of plant cover that can grow on different kinds of substrate. These in turn result from the kinds of rock present and the ways in which they have been weathered through time. Geological materials and processes, together with climate, thus are the ultimate bases for animal and plant distribution.

5. PLANT AND ANIMAL DISTRIBUTION

Living plants and animals are not of uniform occurrence. Instead, each species is limited to a definite area, large or small (geographic distribution), within which it is further restricted to a type of environment where its essential needs for life are available (ecologic distribution). Most kinds of animals can live only in certain kinds of plant cover so that their occurrence depends also on conditions that regulate plant distribution. In general, plant and animal distribution is controlled by annual and seasonal patterns of temperature, precipitation, and other climatic factors and by the type of ground surface (substrate). In mountainous country climate is influenced by altitude (see Climate, pp. 12–17).

The distribution of plants and animals, however, is not infinitely varied. Some kinds of both are commonly found together so that it becomes possible to group them in larger and smaller units, each with certain member species. Several plans have been proposed for describing distributional assemblages—biotic provinces, life zones, plant–animal communities or associations, and others. These systems are not altogether in agreement because the subject is complex and the controlling factors are not fully understood.

Geographic Distribution. The fauna and flora of California can be divided broadly into five major biotic provinces: (1) Northwest Humid Coast; (2) Californian, west of the Sierra Nevada and southern mountains; (3) Sierran, from the lower conifer forest to the summits; (4) Nevadan, largely in the Great Basin; and (5) Southern Deserts. This handbook deals mainly with no. 3 but includes some plants and animals in nos. 2 and 4.

Many biologists describe distribution in terms of a system of life zones (proposed 1898 by C. H. Merriam). These are (1) Lower Sonoran (much of Great Valley; southeastern deserts); (2) Upper Sonoran (foothill region; also Sierran east side sagebrush and piñon–juniper areas); (3) Transition (yellow pine belt; also coast redwood belt); (4) Canadian (lodgepole pine–red fir belt); (5) Hudsonian

Map 2. Plant belts of the Sierra Nevada. (Adapted from various sources.) The Lodgepole–fir, Subalpine, and Alpine belts are grouped as a "Boreal Region." They are shown separately on the sections of the Sierra (figs. 1 and 2). The area marked Jeffrey Pine is distinct on the east slope of the southern Sierra but intermingles with Yellow Pine north of Lake Tahoe.

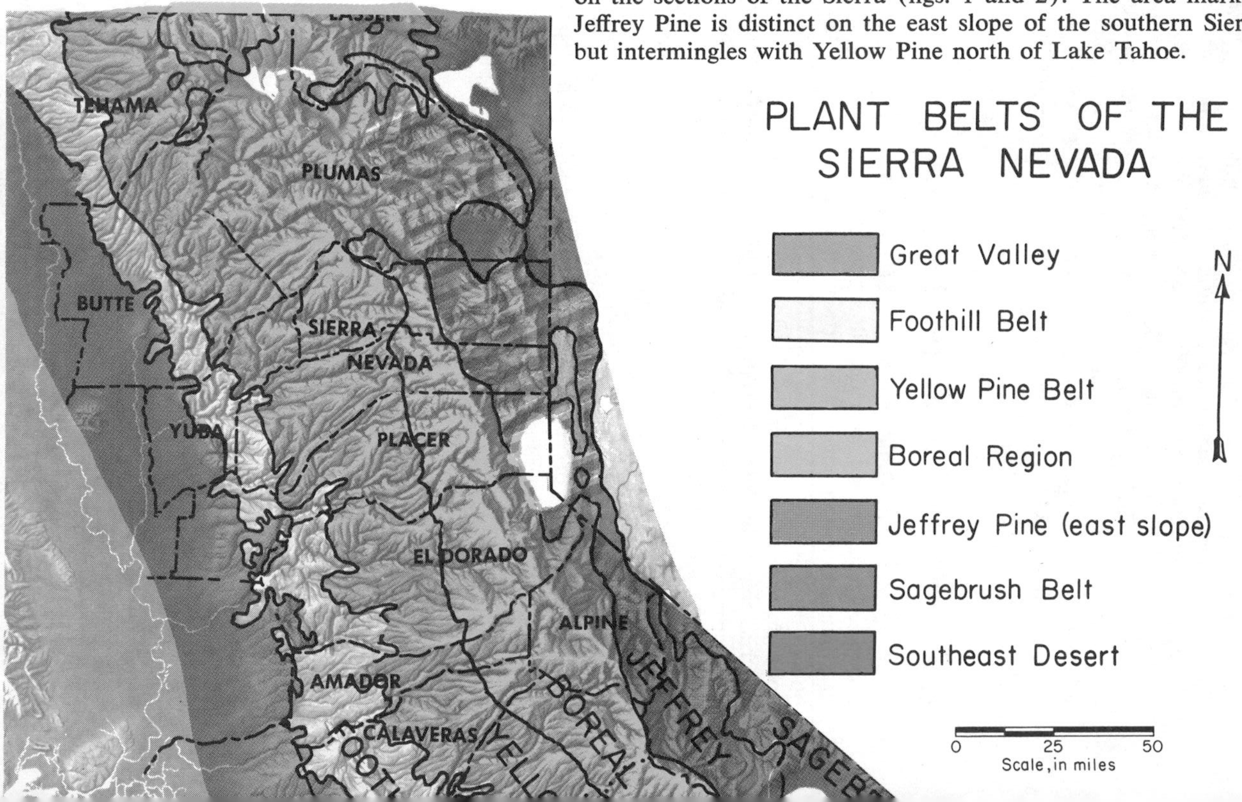

PLANT BELTS OF THE SIERRA NEVADA

N

- Great Valley
- Foothill Belt
- Yellow Pine Belt
- Boreal Region
- Jeffrey Pine (east slope)
- Sagebrush Belt
- Southeast Desert

0   25   50
Scale, in miles

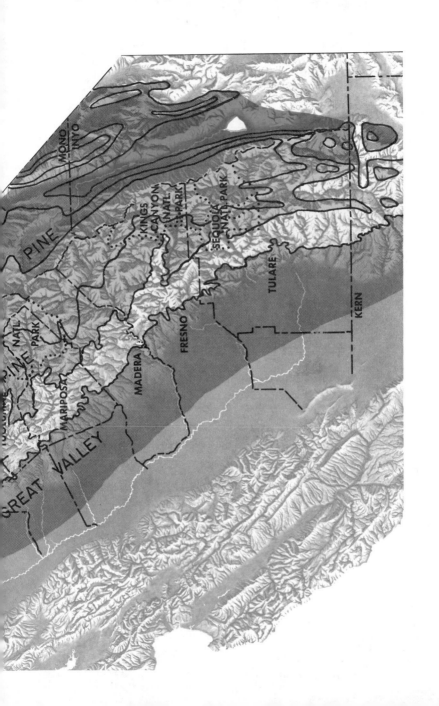

(subalpine or whitebark pine–hemlock belt); and (6) Arctic–Alpine (above timberline). This pattern is satisfactory on the west slope of the Sierra Nevada but not on the east side, where "Upper Sonoran" meets "Canadian" in some places with no "Transition" between. Also, some animals that occur separately in "Upper Sonoran" and "Transition" on the west are mixed together on the east side. Almost all the plants of these zones are different on the two slopes of the range. For these reasons, this handbook uses plant belts to indicate distribution.

On the Sierra Nevada the plants (flora) and animals (fauna) are distributed in a series of lengthwise belts. The boundaries of each rise in elevation from north to south, and those present on both slopes are at relatively higher altitudes on the east than on the west. Some of these belts, with changes in plant and animal components, also are present in the Cascade and Rocky Mountains, and the higher ones reach into Canada and Alaska.

The boundary between two belts is seldom sharp or straight; instead the belts interlace slightly. The lower extends upward on warm south-facing slopes, and the higher descends on cooler or moister sites. On the western flank, sun-facing hillsides with digger pines and associated plants thus stand opposite shadier slopes with yellow pines and Douglas firs in places where the two belts meet; the one will have California jays, the other Steller jays. In a valley near a boundary, the cooler air and greater soil moisture bordering a river or creek often results in a downstream tongue of the higher belt. Scattered yellow pines and their plant companions thus become established and grow down at a slightly lower altitude where digger pines clothe the adjacent slopes.

Among both plants and animals, some species are restricted to a single belt (black oaks only among yellow pines), others occupy two or three belts although not always in equal numbers, and a few are present in any belt where their particular habitat (ecologic) needs are available. The belts, their climatic features, and some characteristic plant and animal inhabitants of each are as follows:

I. GREAT CENTRAL VALLEY (mainly Lower Sonoran Zone). West of and not part of the Sierra Nevada. Flat, elevations to 300 or 400 ft. at north and south ends, about 50 ft. at center; 375 miles long by 40 to 60 miles wide; original native bunchgrass cover replaced by annuals; former extensive marshes and overflow areas along rivers mostly reclaimed by levees; now largely agricultural and irrigated. Summer hot, rainless, av. maxima 88°–101° F.; winter cool, av. minima 34°–38° F., often with low (tule) fog; rainfall 6–20 in.; growing season 7–11 months.

Fremont cottonwood, T-22	wood duck, B-9	yellow-billed magpie, B-74
misc. willows, T-24	red-bellied hawk	cottontail, M-8
valley oak, T-31	Calif. horned lark, B-67	golden beaver, M-22

II. Foothill or Digger Pine–Chaparral Belt (Upper Sonoran Zone) (col. pl. 1b, c, fig. 5). Western valley margins and foothills at 500–3000 feet (north), 800–4000 feet (center), and about 1250–5000 feet (south); extends lower along major streams. Of two unlike parts, often intermingled: pine–oak woodland and brushlands or chaparral (see Shrubs, p. 114). Summer rainless, hot, av. maxima 75°–96° F.; winter moderate, av. minima 29°–42° F.; rainfall 15–40 in., little fog; growing season 6–10 months.

digger pine, T-9	Calif. buckeye, T-38	Calif. thrasher, B-94
interior live oak, T-30	redbud, S-27	brown towhee, B-142
blue oak, T-32	red-legged frog, A-11	brush rabbit, M-9
chaparral (chamise,	striped racer, R-12	gray fox, M-38
S-19; ceanothus, S-34;	Calif. jay, B-73	ring-tail, M-40
yerba santa, S-48;	plain titmouse, B-80	spotted skunk, M-45
etc.)	wrentit, B-86	
	canyon wren, B-91	

III. Yellow Pine Belt (Transition Zone) (col. pls. 1d, 2a, fig. 5). Main timber region. Along western slope at 1200-5500 ft. (north), 2000–6500 ft. (central), and 2500–9000 ft. (south). Extended eastward in lower northernmost part of Sierra. Summer warm, dry, av. maxima 80°–93° F.; winter cool, av. minima 22°–34° F.; precipitation 25–80 in., some snow, little summer rain; growing season 4–7 months.

yellow pine, T-6	kit-kit-dizze, S-17	spotted owl, B-38
sugar pine, T-2	prostrate ceanothus,	pygmy nuthatch, B-84
Douglas fir, T-12	S-34	Swainson thrush, B-97
white fir, T-13	western azalea, S-40	orange-crowned war-
incense cedar, T-16	rubber boa, R-8	bler, B-110
black cottonwood, T-23	mountain king snake,	Nashville warbler,
black oak, T-29	R-15	B-111
broadleaf maple, T-36	band-tailed pigeon, B-30	
Calif. dogwood, T-40	pygmy owl, B-36	

IV. Lodgepole Pine–Red Fir Belt (Canadian Zone) (col. pl. 2c, d, fig. 6). Lower part of "boreal region," at 5500–7500 ft. (north), 6500–8000 ft. (central), and 8000–10000 ft. (south); on both slopes; higher altitudinally on east side. Summer cool, av. maxima 73°–85°F.; winter cold, av. minima 16°–26° F.; precipitation (total water) 35–65 in., heavy persistent snow (hence winter sports area), some summer showers; growing season 3–4½ months (40–70 frost-free days).

lodgepole pine, T-8	bush chinquapin, S-5;	Hammond flycatcher,
silver pine, T-1	snowbrush, S-34c;	B-64d
Jeffrey pine, T-7	green manzanita,	green-tailed towhee,
red fir, T-14	S-45c, etc.)	B-140
Sierra juniper, T-17	goshawk, B-12	fox sparrow, B-153
aspen, T-21	Williamson sapsucker,	Lincoln sparrow, B-154
mountain chaparral	B-54	varying hare, M-6
(huckleberry oak, S-4;		Allen chipmunk, M-15f

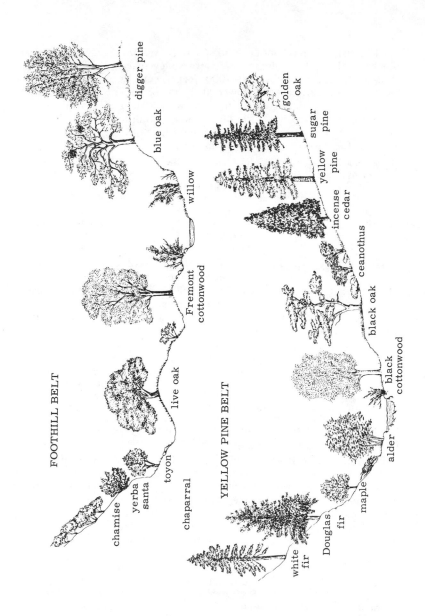

Figure 5. Principal trees and shrubs of the Foothill and Yellow Pine belts.

Some east slope areas have Jeffrey pine with little or no lodgepole pine or red fir, but including scattered piñon pine, Utah juniper, mountain mahogany, etc. (Jeffrey Pine area on map 2).

V. SUBALPINE BELT (Hudsonian Zone) (col. pl. 3a, b). Includes much of sparsely forested High Sierra on both slopes near summit of range. On Mt. Lassen above 7000–8000 ft. and a few other northern peaks; above Donner Pass and on Crystal Range w. of Lake Tahoe; thence of wider occurrence at 7500–10000 ft. (central) and 8000–11000 ft. (south). Summer days warm, nights cold; winter minima unknown; precipitation 30 to 50 in. (15 in. on east slope); heavy persistent winter snow, some summer rain; growing season 7–9 weeks (killing frosts in any month).

whitebark pine, T-3	white heather, S-43	rosy finch, B-136
foxtail pine, T-4	three-toed woodpecker,	wolverine, M-42
lodgepole pine, T-8	B-59	mountain sheep, M-50
mountain hemlock, T-11	pine grosbeak, B-135	(in south)
red heather, S-42		

VI. ALPINE BELT (Arctic–Alpine Zone) (col. pl. 3c). Above timberline (some summits treeless due to scant soil and force of wind). At north chiefly on mountaintops: Mt. Lassen, above 8000 ft.; Mt. Rose, 10000 ft.; Pyramid and Dicks Peaks, 9900 ft. w. of Lake Tahoe; thence on summit areas from 10300–11000 feet upward on Mt. Dana, Mt. Lyell, and others in Yosemite region and south to Kings–Kern Divide and Mt. Olancha, Tulare County. Extreme sunlight exposure at all seasons, cool or cold in summer because of upmountain winds, lightning strikes common, precipitation scant, some summer thundershowers, much of winter snow evaporated by wind. Few climatic records.

Flora includes more than 40 grasses, sedges, and flowering plants, all of low or creeping growth form. The alpine willow (*Salix petrophila*) with irregular branches on ground has flowering shoots only 1 to 6 inches high. Some animals stray up to forage in Alpine fields.

VII. SAGEBRUSH BELT (col. pl. 3d, fig. 6). On east side at 4200–5600 feet (north) and 6000–7000 ft. (south); also over much of Great Basin. Summer dry, hot, average maxima 82°–89° F.; winter cold, average minima 10°–20° F.; precipitation 10–30 inches, mostly as snow; growing season 2–5 months. Soil rocky or sandy, scattered trees 10–60 feet tall, shrubs between.

piñon pine, T-10	black-billed magpie,	Brewer sparrow, B-150
Utah juniper, T-18	B-74	desert jackrabbit, M-7
mountain mahogany,	piñon jay, B-77	Nuttall cottontail, M-8
S-18	sage thrasher	pocket mice, M-20
bitterbrush, S-20	vesper sparrow, B-144	kangaroo rats, M-21
sagebrush, S-60	Bell (sage) sparrow,	grasshopper mouse,
sagehen	B-147	M-25
		short-tailed vole

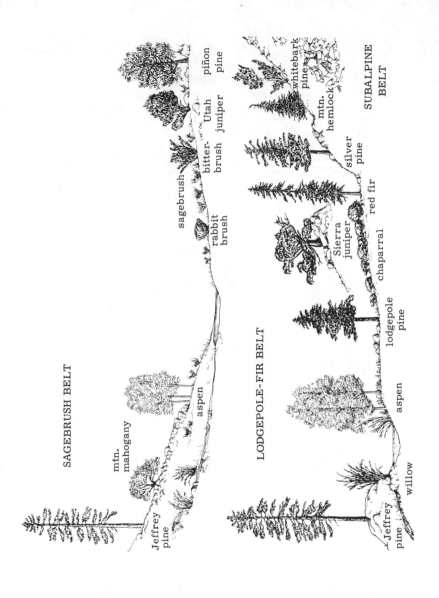

Figure 6. Principal trees and shrubs of the Lodgepole–fir and Sagebrush belts.

Ecologic Distribution. Habitat restriction for plants depends on the nature of the soil or other surface covering (substrate), seasonal moisture supply, and other factors. Most willows, for example, need fine moist soil, manzanitas do best on well-drained slopes which may be rocky, and sagebrush is found chiefly on coarse, sandy dry sites. Animals are regulated by the availability of suitable food, shelter, and places for rearing young according to the manner of life of each species. The robin in summer can live wherever there are trees (for nest sites) close to damp ground (for foraging)—from the Great Valley up into the Subalpine belt and on the east side. In winter it needs berry-producing shrubs or trees as food supply. By contrast, the ousel lives only along and in cool rapid streams.

Some habitat types and plant–animal associations such as lakes and meadows are present in several belts, from the edge of the Great Valley up into the Subalpine belt. Others are more restricted; the rockslide–pika–bushy-tailed woodrat complex is found only at rather high elevations. The principal ecologic environments of the Sierra Nevada and some plant and animal inhabitants of each are the following:

1. STANDING WATERS (lakes, ponds, reservoirs, backwater pools of quiet streams). Surface usually free of vegetation; often bordered by shrubs or trees in lower belts (see no. 4).

OPEN WATER		MARGINS	
beaver, M-22	cormorant, B-5	herons, B-6	garter snakes, R-9
muskrat, M-31	fishes	shore birds,	frogs, A-11 to
ducks	gnat larvae,	B-26 to B-28	A-14
	I-140	kingfisher, B-48	dragon-flies, I-40
			damsel flies, I-41

2. FLOWING WATERS (rivers and creeks, fast or slow) (col. pl. 1a). Shores and bottom of rock, sand, or mud; bordered by marsh, grassland, trees or shrubs.

fishes	water ousel, B-87	larvae of
herons, B-6	garter snakes, R-9	stone-flies, I-10
ducks	frogs, A-11 to A-14	may-flies, I-42
spotted sandpiper, B-27		caddis-flies, I-44

3. MARSHES. Growths of grasses, sedges, and other concealing vegetation over standing water or mud.

Pacific treefrog, A-10	larvae of
garter snakes, R-9	crane flies, I-138
meadow mice, M-30	mosquitoes, I-139

4. STREAMSIDE WOODLAND (col. pl. 1a). On bottomlands with good supply of subsurface water near streams and some lakes. Broad-leaved deciduous trees 15–100 feet high in rows or clumps, often closely

spaced and with thickets of shrubs; vegetation lush, much "edge" bordering other environments.

aspen, T-21	wood duck, B-9	song sparrow, B-155
cottonwoods, T-22, 23	flycatchers, B-62 to B-66	shrews, M-1
willows, T-24	some warblers, B-110 to	cottontail, M-8
alders, T-26, 27	B-119	white-footed mice, M-24
sycamore, T-35	goldfinches, B-138	raccoon, M-41

5. GRASSLAND. Surface covered mainly by grasses with some herbaceous plants, and occasionally scattered shrubs; of several types.

   a. Dry grassland. Soil moisture declines rapidly after growing season; plants grow, produce seeds or fruits, and then dry out.

racer (snake), R-11	savannah sparrow,	Calif. ground squirrel,
gopher snake, R-13	B-143	M-13
meadowlark, B-121		pocket gopher, M-19

   b. Meadow. Sufficient moisture so that plants remain green until autumn frosts.

garter snakes, R-9	white-crowned sparrow,	Belding ground squirrel,
sparrow hawk, B-21	B-151	M-12
robin, B-95 (foraging)	mole, M-2	pocket gopher, M-19
meadowlark, B-121		meadow mouse, M-30

   c. Subalpine and alpine. Under snow until early summer; short growing season; often more sedges than grasses.

rosy finch, B-136	Belding ground squirrel, M-12
marmot, M-11	mountain sheep, M-50

6. CHAPARRAL. Of multi-stemmed woody perennial shrubs 2–12 ft. tall, often closely spaced and forming covered lanes beneath; ground litter usually scant (see Shrubs, p. 114).

   a. Foothill chaparral (west slope) (col. pl. 1c).

scrub oak, S-3	yerba santa, S-48	brush rabbit, M-9
spice bush, S-7	roadrunner, B-32	white-footed mice,
bush poppy, S-8	wrentit, B-90	M-24 (3 or 4 sp.)
chamise, S-19	Bewick wren, B-90	dusky-footed wood rat,
chaparral pea, S-28	Calif. thrasher, B-94	M-26
ceanothus, S-34 (2+ sp.)	crowned sparrows,	gray fox, M-38
manzanita, S-45 (3 sp.)	B-151 (winter)	

   b. Mountain chaparral (both slopes, mainly in upper Yellow Pine and Lodgepole–fir belts) (col. pl. 2a, b).

huckleberry oak, S-4	manzanita, S-45 (2 or 3	green-tailed towhee,
bush chinquapin, S-5	sp.)	B-140
ceanothus, S-34 (2 or 3	alligator lizard, R-7	fox sparrow, B-153
sp.)	mountain quail, B-24	chipmunks, M-15 (2+
	dusky flycatcher, B-64c	sp.)

7. PINE–OAK WOODLAND (west slope) (col. pl. 1b). Scattered trees, some with branches touching; grasses or occasional shrubs below.

digger pine, T-9
interior live oak, T-30
blue oak, T-32
alligator lizard, R-7
common kingsnake, R-14
rattlesnake, R-16
Calif. quail, B-23

mourning dove, B-31
screech owl, B-34
Calif. woodpecker, B-51
Nuttall woodpecker, B-57
Calif. jay, B-73
plain titmouse, B-80
mockingbird, B-93

western bluebird, B-98
brown towhee, B-142
Calif. ground squirrel, M-13
Calif. gray squirrel, M-16
pocket gopher, M-19
skunks, M-45, M-46

8. MOUNTAIN CONIFEROUS FOREST (col. pls. 1d, 2a, c, d, 3a, b). Evergreen coniferous trees 30–200 ft. tall, in open (sometimes dense) stands; ground strewn with needles and with sparse cover of grasses or low shrubs, dry in summer, snow-covered in winter.

sugar pine, T-2
yellow pine, T-6
Jeffrey pine, T-7
lodgepole pine, T-8
Douglas fir, T-12
white fir, T-13
red fir, T-14
big tree, T-15 (locally)
incense cedar, T-16
madrone, T-41
currants, S-10

gooseberries, S-10
kit-kit-dizze, S-17
ceanothus, S-34 (2 or 3 sp.)
manzanita, S-45 (2 or 3 sp.)
pygmy owl, B-36
spotted owl, B-38
woodpeckers, B-49 to B-59
flycatchers, B-64 to B-66

Steller jay, B-72
mountain chickadee, B-79
kinglets, B-102, B-103
warblers, B-110 to B-116, B-119
chipmunks, M-15
gray squirrel, M-16
red squirrel, M-17
porcupine, M-35
marten, M-42

9. SUBALPINE FOREST (col. pl. 3a, b). Only in High Sierra. Trees scattered, few shrubs.

whitebark pine, T-3
lodgepole pine, T-8

mountain hemlock, T-11
Clark nutcracker, B-78

pine grosbeak, B-135
marten, M-42
weasels, M-43

10. ROCKY AREAS (cliffs, talus slides, local outcrops). Foothills to mountain summits; plants few.

rock wren, B-92
cony, M-4

marmot, M-11
bushy-tailed wood rat, M-27

11. SAGEBRUSH (col. pl. 3d). Mainly on east side, locally on west slope at higher altitudes (and in Kings River Canyon). Often mixed with open coniferous forest or piñon–juniper woodland. Multistemmed shrubs 2 to 5 feet high, spaced 2 to 6 feet apart.

sagebrush, S-60
bitterbrush, S-20
rabbit brush, S-58
sagehen
black-billed magpie, B-74

sage thrasher
vesper sparrow, B-144
Bell (sage) sparrow, B-147

Brewer sparrow, B-150
Nevada cottontail, M-8
chipmunks, M-15
pocket mice, M-20
kangaroo rats, M-21

12. JUNIPER WOODLAND. East side only. Trees 10–35 feet high, spaced out, with scattered grasses and brushy plants of arid Great Basin; in upper part of no. 11.

piñon pine, T-10   black-billed magpie, B-74
Utah juniper, T-18   piñon jay, B-77
mountain mahogany, S-18

Beyond the general limitations of geographic range and habitat already described, each species of plant or animal is further restricted to a small local environment called its *ecological niche*. A pine tree, for example, offers a variety of niches for different kinds of birds—and insects—trunk, twigs, or foliage, low or high (fig. 19). Other sorts of niches are the rock slides used by conies (fig. 23), the dead wood used by termites (fig. 15), or the spaces amid rocks in a stream used by caddis-fly larvae. The distinctive requirements for each species of animal as to food, shelter, and breeding places are to be found in its niche.

All the plants and animals at any one spot are interrelated members of a *biological community,* as may be seen in a fallen log, willow thicket, or meadow. The members are specialized for various "jobs": producers, consumers, or scavengers. Plants are the *primary producers*. From soil minerals, water, and sunlight they manufacture the complex substances of their roots, stems, leaves, flowers, and fruits. This is the ultimate source of food for animals, which are diverse as to diet. Some, like bears or ground squirrels, eat a variety of foods, but others take only certain kinds—hummingbirds use nectar and small insects from flowers, termites eat only wood, beavers the inner bark of softwood trees, and so on. Many kinds of animals prey and feed solely on other animals. The plant feeders are *primary consumers,* the predators are *secondary consumers,* and any that eat dead plants or animals are *scavengers.* Thus in any community the organic materials move along in a *food chain* or *food web:* plants → plant eaters (insects, rodents, deer) → predaceous insects or flesh eaters (hawks, wildcats), and so on. Viewed in another way the member animals form a *pyramid of numbers* in which those at the base are abundant but small and those at the top are few but large. In a deciduous woods the aphids and other minute plant-feeding insects may be enormously abundant, spiders and insect-eating beetles that prey on them fairly common, insectivorous birds that eat spiders or beetles fewer, and hawks or weasels that capture the birds rather scarce.

Here, then, is the basis for differences in numbers between the various kinds. The shifting fortunes and thereby the populations of some member species in a community may rise or fall, and such change can affect other parts of the community. These and other factors bring about the alterations in local populations and distribution of plants or animals from year to year. A conspicuous case is that of the population of Tortoise-shell Butterflies (I-101), which periodically "erupts." Huge numbers of the caterpillars strip the leaves of Tobacco Brush (S-34d). Thereby other animals are deprived of using that shrub for food or cover, but birds of several species from other habitats concentrate there to feed on the resulting abnormal food supply—the larvae and later the butterflies. Meanwhile various parasitic insects such as Ichneumon Wasps (I-162) and others multiply and destroy many caterpillars, thereby helping to restore the usual "balance."

The "web of life" in nature is complex and only partly known, so that much further study is needed for better understanding. Interested amateurs can contribute usefully to the subject by making careful observations and keeping records in natural history.

6. MODIFICATIONS BY MAN

Indians, because of their small numbers, had no permanent effect on the Sierran flora or fauna. They used fire to clear brushlands and grasslands so that brodiaeas and other bulbous-rooted and seed-bearing plants useful for food would grow more abundantly. Also they set fire to chaparral as a means of forcing out rabbits and other small animals in order to capture them for their flesh and pelts. Certain flat forest areas were fired at intervals to destroy small trees and brush and leave open stands of the larger trees. This was to lessen the chance of surprise attacks by enemy tribes. The well-spaced forest on the floor of Yosemite Valley which was to be seen until the early 1900's resulted from this practice. Today this forest is choked with innumerable small trees of all ages and some beautiful vistas are obscured—a result of rigid fire exclusion.

Gold mining from 1849 onward made the first changes in Sierran landscape. The early hydraulic mining used high-pressure streams of water in hoses to sluice down hillsides and expose gold-bearing quartz. Scars of this destructive practice still show along Interstate Highway 80 near Gold Run and in places bordering California Highway 49. In placer mining gravel from creek beds or small excavations was washed in wooden troughs to recover the gold. Small pits and heaps of rock discarded from this work are still evident along stream bottoms in the Mother Lode—the main gold-bearing region. Later large dredgers were floated in artificial ponds of broad stream valleys and flat lands bordering the western foothills to excavate gravel below the surface. When the "washings" emerged from the dredgers (after separating out the gold), the soil particles went to the bottom and huge mounds of large creek-worn boulders were piled on the surface of the land. These disfigurements are present in many places. Several decades are required for enough air-borne soil to accumulate on the boulder heaps so that plants and trees can take root and grow. The mounds will be evident for several centuries. Modern deep mining for various minerals in shafts and tunnels results in large surface piles of rock debris that are only slowly invaded by plants.

Before the settlement of California by Americans, the Sierran woodlands and forests were affected only by lightning fires, native insects, and plant diseases, and by local snowslides or avalanches. The axes and saws of the pioneers began a levy on the trees that has been continuous and ever-accelerating. Miners needed timber to construct their buildings, to reinforce their shafts, and to use as fuel. The needs of ever-growing towns and cities fostered a lumber industry. The latter has evolved from much hand effort in felling trees to the use of power-driven saws, and from the transport of logs or lumber by ox teams, flumes, and mountain railroads to that by the large automotive trucks of today.

The most accessible forests on the lower western slopes were logged a century ago, but vehicular roads and railroads have since permitted cutting in practically all Sierran areas where there are suitable lumber trees. The trees most in demand are yellow or ponderosa, Jeffrey, and sugar pines, together with some incense cedar and white fir; formerly giant sequoias were cut in a few places. Much of the present forest of the first three species is of second- (or third-) growth timber. Virgin timber is scarce in the Sierra. Many areas denuded of forest, when few or no "seed" trees were left, have reverted to seemingly permanent chaparral where newly started conifers are few or none. Efforts at reforestation by planting seeds or seedlings are rarely successful. Rodents of several kinds dig up and eat the seed, and young trees are damaged or destroyed by these animals and by rabbits, deer, and insects. Moisture conditions—the amount and timing of rain or snow melt—may be such that new trees can start and survive only in occasional favorable years. Much logging on state or federal lands now is by selective cutting which takes out only a limited number of mature trees, leaving space and sunlight for the smaller ones to grow.

The original cover of oaks on the western foothills and stream valleys was far greater and more extensive than today. For more than 100 years they have been cut for firewood and, in some places, removed to increase range and pasture lands. Young trees, sprouted from naturally planted acorns, are relished by livestock, so that oak woodlands that are heavily grazed contain few or no replacement trees. Some foothills now covered entirely by grassland formerly supported blue and live oaks.

The foothill chaparral, a distinctive Californian plant complex, has evidently experienced fire for millennia and become adapted to it. Even severe burns that consume leaves, branches, and trunks are not entirely fatal. Some species of chaparral plants produce abundant new shoots from the root crowns, and the seeds of others germinate successfully only after a fire! The chaparral, therefore, tends to succeed itself as a type of cover. Modern man, however, has learned that certain kinds of soil covered by chaparral can be converted to grassland for grazing of livestock. Some areas have been cleared by burning or chemical treatment and then seeded to grasses to yield forage.

Much vegetation in the main timber belt and foothills becomes tinder-dry in the long hot rainless summer. Fires start easily, burn fiercely over large areas, and are difficult and costly to extinguish. In the prehistoric period some resulted from lightning and others were set by Indians. Such fires burned until ended by natural barriers or rain. Early white travelers in the mountains saw much evidence of fire in scars on trees, many charred trunks, and areas denuded of forest. As Americans began to occupy the Sierra, damage increased from other causes—sparks from untended campfires or wood-burning locomotives, slash burns that went out of control, and malicious efforts of "firebugs." Lightning, careless campers and smokers, and maliciousness are the main causes today.

Efforts at fire prevention and control by state and federal foresters during the last half-century have reduced the damage, although there still are numerous fires, small and large. The fire suppression program, however, has resulted in accumulation of much ground litter, so that when fires do start they are increasingly difficult to stop. "Controlled burning" to clear selected foothill brushlands has become a well-organized procedure directed by state forestry employees. Under appropriate weather conditions, trained personnel can start, guide, and extinguish chaparral fires. Foresters in charge of mountain timberlands need to learn and practice controlled burning of ground trash to reduce the summer fire hazard. When a severe fire destroys the entire forest cover on an area, it soon becomes densely clothed with brush which may persist for several decades before the first trees start. A century or more may pass before the area again is well forested.

Grazing resources in the Sierra were early recognized and used. Some Swiss dairymen took their cattle up in the spring, made cheese from the milk in summer, and returned to the western lowlands in autumn. Mountain meadows and their bordering slopes were used by beef cattle, and drier areas served for sheep. Great herds and flocks were slowly driven up mountain in spring to successively higher levels as feed became available and brought down only when forage was far reduced or at the first hint of winter. Mountain roads became ankle-deep with dust created by hooves of migrating livestock.

For years there was no regulation; many areas were heavily overgrazed and seriously affected. Then grazing came under regulation by the U. S. Forest Service and permittees were limited as to numbers of livestock and the season of use. Reduction, however, was slow, and further injury to vegetation resulted. At present most or all of the cattle and sheep are transported by motor truck—to lessen herding labor and also the losses in weight of livestock on the long migrations. The number of animals now permitted is a small fraction of those in the mountains in earlier years. Even national park lands were grazed for years.

Mountain plants and grasses, because of the short growing season, are easily damaged and slow to recover. Evidence of early abuse is still to be seen. Severe overgrazing by sheep in parts of the southern High Sierra denuded some areas of vegetation, and the damage is all but permanent. On many oaks and conifers in the foothills and mountains, livestock have chewed off the lower leaves and twigs to leave a "browse line" at the upper limit of their reach. At higher elevations some stream banks of fine gravelly soil are eroding badly where stripped of vegetation by overgrazing.

Logging, fire, and brush removal all affect native animals. Species adapted to living in conifer forests or oak trees or amid chaparral lose their homes and food sources when these types of plants are destroyed. With total removal of timber, for example, conifer dwellers such as tree squirrels, woodpeckers, chickadees, nuthatches, creepers, and Steller jays disappear and are replaced later by brush-inhabiting ground squirrels, chipmunks, fox sparrows, green-tailed towhees, and the like. Parallel results follow removal of other types of cover. Each animal species adheres to its "trade"—its place and manner of life. When the environment to which it is adapted is eliminated, it cannot go elsewhere because the "elsewhere" of that habitat already is fully occupied by individuals of its own kind. When forest is replaced by chaparral, however, species adapted to the latter have opportunity to increase in numbers. Changes in plant cover on the Sierra over the past century favored chaparral dwellers at the expense of those suited to life in trees; both, however, are still common.

Use of toxic chemical sprays and dusts to control certain grasses, herbs, weeds, and insects affects various animals. Sparrow hawks, kingbirds, and shrikes use roadside trees, poles, and fences as perches whence they swoop down to catch insects for food in the vegetation below. Chemical weed control along lowland roads has been followed by reduction or disappearance of these birds. Dead vegetation means few or no insects, and hence no birds—or the poison may pass from plant to insect to bird. Some tree toad populations (and possibly other amphibians) also are affected. Fortunately there is as yet little of this control in the foothills or mountains. Spraying of waters with various chemicals to control mosquito larvae, which is done commonly in the lowlands and some mountain resort areas, may affect other kinds of aquatic animals.

Native species of currants and gooseberries are intermediate hosts for a disease, white pine blister rust, that affects silver and sugar pines. To protect forest growths of these trees a campaign to eradicate the shrubs has been in progress for years, first by uprooting and later by chemicals. The shrubs are now scarce or lacking in many places, and their fruits no longer are available as food for various birds, squirrels, and chipmunks.

Populations of several game, fur, and predatory animals have been changed by man. The grizzly bear, native to the western slope, became extinct in 1924. Mountain sheep, originally common on much of the High Sierra, were early reduced to very small numbers by overhunting. The wolverine, fisher, and marten have been almost exterminated by trapping. Reduction of coyotes and wildcats, to lessen losses among flocks of domestic sheep, has been followed by an increase in mule deer. In some places deer are now so abundant that they overbrowse shrubs they use as food. Destruction of the two carnivores also is believed to have permitted porcupines to increase, with consequent greater damage by these rodents to timber pines. In past years ground squirrels and even pocket gophers were poisoned on mountain meadows in a misguided effort to enhance the amount of forage for domestic livestock, but there was no lasting effect on the rodents. The only addition to the Sierran mammals has been the introduction of beaver into several streams having growths of willows and aspen. The beavers have built ponds and harvested trees, but it is uncertain whether tree replacement growths will be adequate for their needs.

The Sierra originally had three species of native trout distributed in separate drainage systems. Natural propagation kept their populations up to provide excellent sport for a moderate number of fishermen. For years there was no legal restriction; then early in this century a legal limit of 50 per day was set but seldom enforced. Adventurers in the high country often transplanted trout into lakes and streams previously barren. Then artificial propagation in hatcheries and fish planting began under state auspices. Through the years this program has increased greatly. Brown trout and eastern brook trout were brought in and native species were moved about so that now there is a mixture in streams and lakes of the Sierra Nevada. With the great increase in number of fishermen the daily limits have been reduced. Some remote streams, accessible only to enthusiastic hikers, still afford good sport, but those close to roads are fished out almost as soon as planted— commonly with trout of "legal" size. Many waters of the latter sort now are paralleled by a beaten trail made by a succession of ardent but often unsuccessful fishermen.

Making roads and highways in the mountains has had varied biological effects. Opening up a road through dense forest lets in more direct light and warmth from the sun so that plants needing these conditions are favored at the expense of species adapted to greater shade. Scraping the sides of a roadway may remove plants already present, whereupon other species that succeed in disturbed soil will grow and thrive. The runoff water from a road often provides the bordering soil with more than a normal amount of moisture, thereby inducing germination of seeds already present. At middle altitudes the roadside scrapings (often ridged up to regulate the runoff of snow melt) become populated by dense assemblages of young pines and firs or by flowering plants.

Cut banks, resulting from the grading of a road, are favored by various grasses and plants—prostrate ceanothus, gilias, etc.; they also provide places into which ground squirrels and chipmunks burrow, and small depressions where juncos, Townsend solitaires, and other ground-nesting birds produce their broods. These and other plants, animals, and birds consequently come to live where people who are traveling slowly along roadways can see them readily. It is thought that the California ground squirrel was originally confined to the lowlands and foothills, but as man cleared roadways it moved up to occupy places in the higher mountains—chiefly near roads.

Back roads, when unsurfaced, are good places for nature study. By sitting quietly in an automobile at the side of a minor road, the senior author of this book has had many unusual glimpses of animals—once he watched a cony on a rock nearer than 10 feet for several minutes. High-speed modern highways, however, confer little benefit on the native plants and animals, and interested persons have little opportunity to study those that live along such routes. There are ever-present hazards to personal safety for anyone who wishes to drive slowly or stop. A straight highway slashed through forest and hillside has the single virtue of providing for rapid transit; it is without aesthetic appeal. Clearings for pole lines and ski lifts are other intrusions on the primeval.

A mountain cabin (not too close to others) is an excellent place for watching native animals. Many of the smaller species soon accept the structure as part of their environment—and some even find it an added facility for food and shelter. Squirrels, chipmunks, and mice may make nests in the foundation or interior, sometimes to the distress of the owner. There is indeed *some hazard* because these rodents carry certain diseases (plague, tularemia, spotted fever) transmissible to man. However much these visitors and boarders are enjoyed, their close presence involves a risk.

Summer resorts and communities, now increasing rapidly in the mountains, have some adverse effects on the local plant and animal life. The much-used ground, repeatedly trodden, soon loses the small vegetation. Both trees and shrubs may be disfigured or killed by the activities of unthinking people. Close placement of buildings and aggregations of people discourage some of the shier mammals and birds. Disposal of garbage, especially tin cans, bottles, and other unburnable trash, leads to disfigurement of the landscape. Inadequate control of sewage wastes from large mountain settlements contaminates waters once crystal clear and pure. With more people comes more littering of roadsides, camping and lunching places, even of foot trails, with waste metal, glass, and paper—cans last for years in the dry summers and cold winters. Large numbers of dogs at homes and camps means more ground-dwelling native animals are killed.

High Sierran meadows represent a transitional stage in landscape evolution. They occupy glacial-scoured basins that have filled with sand and gravel. When undisturbed they slowly progress from wet to dry conditions and eventually are captured by forest. The change is greatly hastened under heavy grazing by pack and saddle animals; many have deteriorated seriously from this cause in recent years. The native grasses, eaten down in the short growing season, do not recover as do those of a lowland pasture. Decline begins when the meadows are used every year by only a limited number of animals. In succession, bare areas appear and are captured by ferns or unpalatable weeds, the bared soil is removed by wind and water erosion, stream channels are cut where once there was sod, and invasion of the drained soil by shrubs and conifers is hastened. No effective plan of management to offset this decline has been developed. Many attractive meadows are doomed as summer visitors on horseback with pack stock increase.

A century and more of increasing use and occupancy of the Sierra by modern man has led to various changes from primeval conditions. The rock masses show little change save where blasted and graded for roads. Waters of many streams in the middle and lower elevations have been diverted or stored in reservoirs for power, irrigation, or domestic use. The forests are far different in extent and size of trees, although still beautiful and inspiring over much of the range. Some ferns and other attractive plants, in demand for home gardens, have been taken in such quantities that they now are scarce in well-visited places. Many alien grasses and weeds have invaded the mountains on wagon roads and become established members of the flora. Some of the larger mammals have declined and populations of smaller birds and animals have been affected by alterations in tree and shrub cover. The most pronounced change of all is the human invasion with homes, summer cabins, and stores being built at an ever-increasing rate. Only by careful and intelligent planning and management will some features in these mountains remain attractive in the face of continuing modification.

7. OWNERSHIP AND MANAGEMENT IN THE SIERRA

Anyone may travel freely over much of the Sierra Nevada, but there are some restrictions that must be kept in mind. These result from the varied pattern of ownership and management of the lands, forests, and waters. Much of the area has been and still is the property of the United States government, but there are many private holdings. These were acquired long ago for timber, mineral, or water rights or as homesteads for ranches or homes. Other portions belong to the state of California and some to counties or cities. Ownership and use privileges therefore are complex and sometimes controversial.

Yosemite Valley and the Mariposa [Wawona] Big Tree Grove were transferred from federal to state jurisdiction in 1864 but were returned in 1906. Federal forest reserves were set aside in the 1890's and became national forests in 1907, with some subsequent additions. San Francisco acquired Hetch Hetchy Valley in 1909 as a source of water, and Oakland obtained rights to Mokelumne River water in 1929. Los Angeles did similarly with many waters on the east slope south of Mono Lake from 1913 onward. Irrigation districts and electric power companies have been granted rights to gather water of many west slope streams and have built numerous storage reservoirs—the artificial lakes now at various elevations. State and federal agencies have constructed dams to impound waters as a measure of flood control and to conserve water supplies for power generation, irrigation, and other purposes.

National parks were established to conserve and maintain, for public enjoyment, the natural scenery, fauna, and flora, of certain outstanding areas. Sequoia National Park (established 1890; 385,178 acres) contains groves of giant sequoias, the world's largest and nearly oldest living things, together with Mt. Whitney (alt., 14495 ft.), the highest U. S. peak outside of Alaska. Kings Canyon National Park (1940; 453,655 acres) includes two great canyons of the Kings River, many High Sierra summits, and the former General Grant National Park with sequoias. Yosemite National Park (1890; 757,617 acres) has Yosemite Valley with spectacular waterfalls, much High Sierra, and 3 big tree groves: Wawona, Merced, and Tuolumne. In national parks *no flowers, plants, or animals may be taken* (except under permit for scientific use). Camping, the making of fires, and the speed of automobile travel are regulated. Visitors are advised of other regulations upon entering a national park.

Each national park has a museum with exhibits of plants, animals, geology, Indian materials, and local history. Trained naturalists give frequent lectures on these subjects, answer questions, and conduct field trips for interested persons to learn about the flora and fauna and other natural features. An independent Natural History Association, associated with each park, publishes special booklets on birds, wildflowers, etc.

The Devil's Postpile National Monument on the east side near Mammoth Lakes includes a display of 60-foot vertical basaltic columns. Two state parks now include the north and south groves of Calaveras

Big Trees on the Ebbetts Pass road. (Calif. Highway 4). Other state parks, especially at Lake Tahoe, provide public recreation areas in a region largely in private ownership.

The national forests include practically all tree-producing lands (and some that have no trees) in the Sierra Nevada except those in private ownership or in national parks. The nine forests from north to south are: Lassen, Plumas, Tahoe, Eldorado, Stanislaus, Toiyabe, Sierra, Inyo, and Sequoia. Each has an administrative staff, rangers on patrol, and lookouts at high places to watch for fires during the dry season. Many public campgrounds are maintained in the forests, each with piped water supply, fireplaces and tables, garbage disposal, and toilets. Visitors are urged to use these facilities for their convenience and to lessen the hazard from campfires elsewhere. Permits are required to build campfires in the forests. Grazing and timber cutting in national forests also are regulated by the U. S. Forest Service.

Four parts of Sierran national forests have been designated as wilderness areas where roads, buildings, and other forms of permanent occupancy are prohibited. These are: Desolation Valley (41000 acres, west of Lake Tahoe in Eldorado N. F.); Emigrant Basin (98000 acres, from Kennedy Meadows to Yosemite N. P. and Stanislaus N. F.); Dana-Minarets (82000 acres, between Tioga Pass and Devil's Postpile in Inyo and Sierra N. F.); and High Sierra (394,000 acres, along crest from Mammoth Lakes to Mt. Whitney in Inyo and Sierra N. F.).

Hunting is permitted in national forests, but not in national parks. It may be prohibited when the fire hazard is excessive. Fishing is allowed in both national parks and forests. In general, the laws of the California Game Code and regulations of the California Department of Fish and Game apply to all lands and waters in the Sierra Nevada.

On all state and county roadsides (rights of way) it is illegal—a misdemeanor—to pick or remove flowers, ferns, plants, trees, or shrubs. The same applies to plant materials on private land except with written permission of the owner (Calif. Penal Code, sec. 384a).

There are many maps for the Sierra Nevada. Oil companies provide free road maps showing main highways and lesser roads, mileage between places, and other details. The California State Automobile Association and Automobile Club of Southern California print large maps, free to members, which include roads, towns, mileages, most streams, and the principal mountains. The U. S. Geological Survey issues a series of topographic maps covering the entire range (and other parts of California). Topography is shown by brown contour lines, lakes and streams are in blue, and human "culture"—political boundaries, cities and towns, roads, etc.—in black. Special maps are available for the national parks and some other areas. These large-scale and highly detailed maps are sold in stationery stores in the larger cities. The U. S. Forest Service produces free maps for each national forest with some of the same information and other roads and trails shown (but no contours). Some books and articles (see References, p. 358) contain regional maps. Finally there are many decorative maps on sale that picture the features or history of parts of the Mother Lode and other local areas.

8. GOOD CONDUCT IN THE SIERRA

It is a privilege to enjoy the natural features of our great mountains. Visitors in the Sierra should be well behaved and not abuse the scenery, plants, or animals, leaving them for others to enjoy. Pioneer travelers and early residents had a simple unwritten code of good manners that should be followed by all who now find pleasure in the mountains.

Streams. Keep them clean. Do not use them for laundry, garbage, or human bodily wastes. Bury garbage in the ground at some inconspicuous place away from roads or trails. When no toilet is available, take to the woods, well away from streams or lakes.

Fires. Build fires only when and where permitted, in an open dry place where there is no dry grass or ground litter. Do not start an open fire if there is strong wind. Never leave a fire unattended. Always quench a fire thoroughly with water—then add one more bucket of water for safety. Do not discard burning matches or cigarettes on the roadside. If you see a fire, report it to the nearest forest ranger or office.

Trees. Leave them as they are. Initials cut in the bark remain as scars for years and serve no useful purpose.

Picnic Sites. After enjoying an outdoor meal at the roadside or in the woods, pick up all papers, cans, and other debris and carry them until you find a trash can. The pleasant place you enjoyed will remain attractive for the next visitors.

Camps. Wherever you stop, even overnight, leave the site clean. *Do not add trash to the landscape.* If there is no refuse can nearby, bury fresh garbage, paper, and cartons, etc. Take metal or glass to the nearest place where such waste is collected.

Livestock. If you meet riding or pack animals on a trail, step aside far enough to let them pass easily.

Wild Animals. It is dangerous to offer food to deer or bears that seem "tame." Deer can strike quickly and severely with their front feet, and a bear's paw, with its claws, delivers a powerful stroke. Many persons have been severely injured by animals that frequent roadsides or camps for gifts of food. Squirrels and chipmunks carry diseases transmissible to man. Do not feed them.

THE PLANTS

9. FUNGI

THE FUNGI, unlike the higher plants, lack green chlorophyll and feed on complex substances drawn from living or dead plants and animals. Some kinds cause serious diseases in live plants, animals, and man. Others, such as baker's yeast and the molds used to produce antibiotics, are highly beneficial. The bracket fungi and mushrooms (club fungi, Class Basidiomycetes) described here include some that damage live or dead trees and lumber. In nature their role is to decompose woody materials. Along with many sorts of bacteria, molds, and insects, they are "sanitary agents" that consume and thereby dispose of dead organic matter.

The fungus starts as a microscopic spore that develops a network of thread-like parts (*hyphae*). These penetrate dead plant tissue in or above the ground to obtain nutriment. Later growth yields the larger and exposed spore-producing stage (*sporophore*). In mushrooms this comprises an upright stalk (*stipe*) covered by a cap (*pileus*), either dome-shaped or flat. Under the cap are many thin, plate-like, radiating vertical gills that carry the spore-producing organs. Bracket fungi lack gills, the spores coming from many small tubes opening as pores on the under surface of the bracket-shaped cap or fruiting body. Spores differ in color, size, and form according to the species of fungus. They are produced by the millions and distributed by wind, water, or animals.

Some mushrooms and other fungi are edible and tasty. A few kinds, however, are dangerously poisonous, causing severe illness and even death if eaten. There is no quick, easy, and certain way to distinguish a presumably safe and edible "mushroom" from an unpalatable or dangerous "toadstool" or other fungus. Accurate identification requires some experience and careful study of fresh entire specimens using descriptions and figures in a reliable reference book (such as Krieger, 1947). *The brief accounts given here must not be depended upon for this purpose.*

Fu-1. Saddle Fungus. *Helvella lacunosa* (pl. 1). Cap 1″–2″ dia., shape irregular, lobed, and inflated, lobes bending outward, grayish black; stem

1½"–4" high, ¾"–1½" dia., usually tapering upward, deeply ribbed and pitted, hollow, white at first, graying with age. DISTR. On ground, usually under or near conifers, in spring and autumn.

Fu-2. Narrow-headed Morel. *Morella angusticeps* (pl. 1). Cap 2"–4" tall, to 1" dia.; bluntly conical, whole surface with large dull brown pits, ridges darker, brown to black; stem 2"–4" long, ¾"–1¼" dia., tapered or cylindrical, often furrowed at base, dingy cream to buff. DISTR. Under conifers (esp. white fir), often common after a fire.

Fu-3. Cup Fungus. *Sarcosphaera coronaria* (pl. 1). Cap dia. to 3", at first globular and buried in soil, later partly exposed and splitting downward to yield a cup margined with 7–10 pointed rays, lavender-brown inside, whitish outside; stem short, thick. DISTR. In coniferous woods under humus on forest floor.

Fu-4. Indian Paint Fungus. *Echinodontium tinctorium.* Cap large, hoof-shaped, black, perennial; lower surface with many large, hard spines or teeth pointing downward; interior bright rust-red. DISTR. Common on white fir, also Douglas fir, occasionally on red fir.

The fungus starts on dead roots or wounds in bark, producing a destructive heartwood rot in white fir throughout California. It ends with a cavity containing stringy growths inside the undamaged cylindrical shell of sapwood. In the Pacific Northwest it attacks standing hemlocks. The caps (fruiting bodies) grow well up on a tree. Indians powdered the interior of caps to prepare red war paint.

Fu-5. Man's-Hair or Cepe. *Boletus edulis* (pl. 1). Cap 4"–6" dia., convex to flat, smooth, moist, grayish or brownish red or yellowish brown, margin paler; flesh white to yellow, compact then soft; tubes (pores) on under surface nearly free from cap, round, minute, changing from white to yellow to greenish; stem 4"–7" high, dia. 1"–2¼", stout, often bulbous, surface finely net-veined, white to brownish. DISTR. On ground in woods, summer and autumn.

Fu-6. White-pouch Fungus. *Cryptoporus volvatus* (pl. 1). Cap small, about 2" across, hoof-shaped, smooth, light yellow-brown, later white, interior corky or hard; under surface hidden by thick leathery skin, the pink spores escaping through a hole; produces superficial gray rot on dead timber. DISTR. On conifers except junipers and big tree.

Fu-7. Red-belt Fomes. *Fomes pinicola* (pl. 1). Form variable; on standing trees cap often hoof-shaped, to 8" wide, margin rounded, surface often resinous; under side flat, blackish above, creamy below, with reddish band above lower pale-colored edge; pores minute, white to yellow; flesh layered, corky to woody, light brown. DISTR. Common on conifers except incense cedars, junipers, big tree.

This commonest of timber-destroying pore fungi in the Sierra pro-

1. Saddle Fungus   5. Man's Hair   2. Narrow-headed Morel

3. Cup Fungus   7. Red-belt Fomes

6. White-pouch Fungus   9. Incense Cedar Dry-rot

Plate 1. Fungi   47

duces a red-rot of heartwood in fallen logs and some live trees. On the under side of downed logs the cap may be knob-like, and on the upper side the fungus may be a stemless toadstool.

Fu-8. Sulfur Bracket Fungus. *Polyporus sulphureus* (pl. 2). Bracket (cap) to 24″ wide, ½″–1½″ thick, of several fan-like layers, flattish, wavy-edged; upper surface smooth to woolly, lemon-yellow to orange; under surface flat, silky-surfaced, pores minute, light sulfur-yellow; flesh spongy-textured, juicy, yellow, later white, splitting but not hardening with age; usually no stem (or a short and lateral one); spores white. DISTR. On decaying logs or stumps and living tree trunks.

Shelf-like caps of this large, brilliant fungus often overlap one another in clusters. When mature they become dry and crumbling, and in early decay are phosphorescent. Some bracket fungi damage both forest trees and timbers in mines or buildings.

Fu-9. Incense Cedar Dry-rot. *Polyporus amarus* (pl. 1). Cap knob-shaped at first, later bracket-like with rounded top, like a bell cut in half; above smooth, tan-colored, below bright sulfur-yellow, later brown; interior fleshy; produces narrow oblong pockets ½″ to several feet long in heartwood, filled with charcoal-like mass. DISTR. On incense cedar, usually of 24″ dia. or larger, mainly in heartwood.

The channeled surfaces of incense cedar boards, sought for decorative interior walls of buildings, result from attacks by this "dry-rot" fungus. Fruiting bodies (caps) on trees start from knotholes in summer and autumn. Being fleshy they are eaten by tree squirrels and invaded by insect larvae. Woodpeckers seek the larvae, leaving cup-like depressions in the bark with "shot-hole" patterns where the larvae tunneled.

Fu-10. Shelf Fungus. *Ganoderma lucidum* (pl. 2). Cap 2″–8″ wide, irregular, kidney-shaped, wrinkled, margin often notched, color successively yellowish, red, then chestnut-brown, becoming shiny; flesh woody, tough; stem lateral, irregular, shiny brown, well anchored; pores grayish brown, later tan. DISTR. On pine (and hemlock?) in damp woods.

Fu-11. Rainbow Shelf Fungus. *Polyporus versicolor* (pl. 2). Cap ¾″–4″ wide, thin, many in shelf-like layers above one another, velvety- or leathery-surfaced, zoned in various colors; pores small, round, white to gray or yellowish; stalk short. DISTR. Common on stumps and trunks, both conifers and deciduous trees.

This varicolored fungus "decorates" trees especially after fire. It does much damage in eastern deciduous pulp and hardwoods. Besides subsisting on heartwood, it may also be a parasite on the living sapwood.

Fu-12. Ring-scale Fungus. *Trametes pini.* Cap to 8″ dia., irregular, hoof-shaped, rough, dull, often cracked in crosswise furrows, above dark grayish, lower margin light brown, under surface light grayish brown; flesh

8. Sulfur Bracket Fungus

10. Shelf Fungus

13. Honey Mushroom

14. Orange-milk Mushroom

16. Scaly Lentinus

17. Fawn-colored Pluteus

11. Rainbow Shelf Fungus

19. Sulfur-top Fungus

20. Sierra Puffball

Plate 2. Fungi

corky, rusty brown; pores irregular, large or small. DISTR. On mature pines and firs, also cut lumber; attacks softer (spring-growth) wood of some annual rings.

Fu-13. Honey Mushroom. *Armillaria mellea* (pl. 2). Cap dia. 1″–6″, convex or spread, often with fine tufts of brown or black hairs, pale to dark brown, edge finely furrowed with age and yellow; flesh whitish, browning with age; gills attached to stem, white, browning with age; spores white, stem 1″–6″ x ¼″–¾″, of variable dia., firm and fibrous, spongy within, often a prominent ring above middle, upper part pale, lower part honey-colored to brown, darkening with age. DISTR. Common in woods or cleared land, on ground or decayed wood, summer and autumn.

Dense clusters of this mushroom appear on stumps, logs, and buried roots (rhizomorphs) of both conifers and deciduous trees in autumn. Within the wood are the shining brown hyphae. Known also as oak fungus, it does damage in California peach orchards.

Fu-14. Orange-milk Mushroom. *Lactarius deliciosus* (pl. 2). Cap 2″–5″ dia., circular, flat but later funnel-shaped, smooth, slightly sticky at times, distinctly zoned, reddish yellow, orange, or brick-red, aging to green; stem 2″–4″ high, dia. ⅓″–⅔″, smooth, solid but later hollow, colored like cap or paler; gills narrow, crowded, orange; spores spiny. When bruised all parts become orange, then green; fluid orange-colored, fragrant; flesh and fluid acrid-flavored. DISTR. On ground in woods in moist duff.

Fu-15. White Russula. *Russula brevipes.* Cap 3″–8″ dia., circular, deeply depressed in center, margin rounded, white, ageing to dingy buff or brown; stem 1″–3″ long, ¾″–1″ dia., thick, dull white ageing to brown. DISTR. On ground under needles in conifer woods, esp. in autumn.

Fu-16. Scaly Lentinus. *Lentinus lepideus* (pl. 2). Cap 3″–10″ dia., curved, irregular, with darkened brownish scaly patches, white to yellow; stem 1″–2½″ high, dia. ¼″–½″, sometimes off-center and irregular, scaly, solid; gills broad, crowded, inner ends curving and extending down stem, whitish. DISTR. On wood of conifers, causing decay of fence posts, bridge timbers, and untreated railroad ties.

Fu-17. Fawn-colored Pluteus. *Pluteus cervinus* (pl. 2). Cap 2″–4″ dia., convex or flat, smooth margined, top more or less hairy, sometimes sticky, yellowish-, grayish-, or blackish-brown; stem 2″–6″ high, dia. ¼″–½″, solid, smooth or black-haired, brownish; gills free of stem, broad, whitish to pink; spores pink. DISTR. Common on stumps and logs, sometimes on sawdust.

Fu-18. Cobweb-gilled Fungus. *Cortinarius* sp. Cap 2″–5″, thin or thick, dryish to sticky surfaced, bright yellow to reddish; flesh yellowish to white; gills thin, yellow to pale cinnamon, aging to dull yellow or brown; stem 1″–6″ long, dia. to ¾″, often hollow, whitish to brownish; spores rust-colored. DISTR. In woods or partly cleared areas.

There are many species in this group, but few are readily identified. The description above is therefore rather general. The generic name refers to cobwebby threads hiding the gills of young plants.

Fu-19. Sulfur-top Fungus. *Naematoloma fasiculare* (pl. 2). Cap 2″ (to 3″) dia., bluntly conical to flat, thin, smooth surfaced, above tan-orange aging to brown, margin yellow; flesh yellow; gills many, narrow, pale yellow, later greenish; stem 2″–4½″ high, dia. to ⅜″, hollow, sulfur-yellow, darkening later; spores purplish brown. DISTR. In clusters on decaying logs, spring or autumn.

Fu-20. Sierra Puffball. *Calbovista subsculpta* (pl. 2). Fruiting body (cap) to 6″ dia., spiny-topped when young, becoming a flattened globe, the surface with both raised and depressed triangular patterns, white; stem short, large; interior at first soft, white, later a mass of spores. DISTR. Formerly common, now rare in coniferous forests on both slopes of Sierra above 2500 ft.

Other kinds of puffballs when dry and touched emit a cloud of white spores. Insects and rodents eat puffballs and probably carry spores on their bodies or hair by which they become distributed. The decorative Sierra Puffball has become scarce as summer visitors have picked and removed it. Smoother puffballs of other species occur in the Foothill belt.

10. LICHENS AND MOSSES

Lichens are small colored plants that grow on the surface of rocks and trees, often making decorative patterns. Most lichens consist of a fungus body combined with colonies of microscopic one-celled algae. The combination is an example of mutual benefit, called *symbiosis.* The fungus affords shelter, absorbs moisture from the air, and derives mineral salts from the surface on which it grows. The algae contain *chlorophyll,* the green substance which by the action of sunlight manufactures complex food for both members. The thread-like parts (*hyphae*) of the lichen produce strong acids that decompose rocks, even granite, to obtain needed minerals, and hence these plants aid in soil formation. Lichens are highly resistant to cold, drought, and strong sunlight. Their growth is exceedingly slow. They reproduce in three ways. The fungus produces microscopic spores (like those of a mushroom) that are scattered by the wind and combine later with the algae, which are of wide occurrence. Lichens also produce tiny packets (*soredia*) containing both hyphae and algae. Broken pieces of lichens, spread by storms, begin growth if they fall on suitable surfaces.

Crustose lichens (Lecideaceae and others) are tightly attached to rock surfaces, forming thin patches that are black, gray, brown, dark green, yellow, orange, or white in different species. The Map Lichen

(*Rhizocarpon geographicum;* Li-1, pl. 3) is common on Sierran granite.

Foliose lichens (Parmeliaceae, etc.) grow as green, flat, leaf-like lobes, plates, or rosettes that are attached to tree bark or rocks by tough black fibers. An example is the flat *Parmelia flaventior* (Li-2, pl. 3).

The erect or hanging fruticose lichens (Usneaceae, etc.) are the most advanced types, with a stalk bearing branches that sometimes are coral-like. Some have cup-shaped fruiting bodies. The Staghorn or Wolf Lichen (*Letharia vulpina;* Li-3, pl. 3) of pale yellow-green color abounds on trunks of firs and other conifers in the Sierra. The Horse-hair Lichen (*Alectoria*) grows in dense, dark-colored tufts, commonly on conifers.

Mosses are primitive green plants, small but conspicuous and attractive, that grow on wet stream banks and, in moist weather, on rocks, trees, and buildings. A moss begins as a microscopic spore. On a damp surface it germinates and grows into a branching chain of cells (*protonema*) from which buds develop into shoots bearing small spirally arranged green leaves. These make the familiar moss plant. In time the tops of the shoots produce organs bearing egg cells and others bearing sperm cells. In wet weather (or under melting snow) the motile sperms swim and fertilize the egg cells. From each union a spore-bearing plant grows up from the leafy shoot. It consists of a wiry upright stalk (*seta*) topped by a cup-shaped capsule in which thousands of spores are grown and later scattered by wind.

Upwards of forty kinds of mosses occur in the Sierra, but little has been published about them. Identification requires specimens with capsules, a hand lens or microscope, a manual with keys (see References), and some experience. Because of these needs, no accounts of mosses are included here.

11. FERNS

The ferns (Pteridophyta) are green plants that lack flowers and seeds; the life cycle comprises two distinct phases. The larger (*sporophyte*) is the familiar "fern." It has a creeping stem or rootstock (*rhizome*), with roots, and one or many upright leaves or *fronds*. Each frond starts from the rootstock on a short *stalk* which continues upward as the central support or *rachis* of the frond (fig. 7). A young frond is tightly spiraled and uncoils as it grows. The full-sized frond (in Sierran ferns) is cut almost or entirely to the rachis. The divisions are called *pinnae*, and the frond is termed pinnate. If a pinna is divided the frond is 2-*pinnate* (further subdivision results in 3-pinnate, even 4-pinnate fronds); the final subdivision is a *segment*. The under surfaces of all or

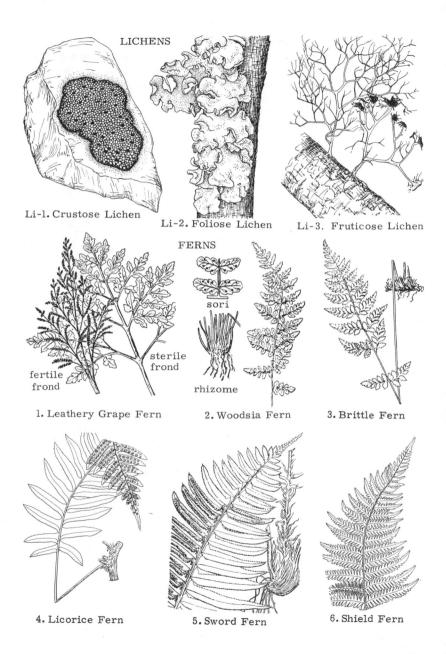

LICHENS

Li-1. Crustose Lichen

Li-2. Foliose Lichen

Li-3. Fruticose Lichen

FERNS

sori

fertile frond

sterile frond

rhizome

1. Leathery Grape Fern

2. Woodsia Fern

3. Brittle Fern

4. Licorice Fern

5. Sword Fern

6. Shield Fern

Plate 3. Lichens and ferns

some segments bear small "fruit dots" (*sori*). Each sorus includes many stalked spore cases (*sporangia*) that produce microscopic spores. The sporangia may have special coverings (*indusia*), sometimes formed of the curved margin of the frond segment. When spores are mature they shower out as fine dust if a frond is touched. In moist ground a spore grows into the inconspicuous second phase (*gametophyte* or *prothallium*), about ¼″ wide. In turn this produces male and female sex cells that join and grow to become a new fern.

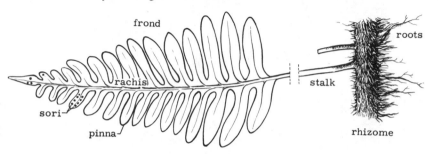

Figure 7. Structure of a fern.

Fe-1. Leathery Grape Fern. *Botrychium multifidum* (pl. 3). To 18″ high; rhizome short, with many corrugated roots; fronds stout, to 12″ wide, pinnately divided; spore-bearing stalk stout, long, branched, with large green sporangia clustered like grapes. DISTR. Yellow Pine and Lodgepole-fir belts, 3000–10000 ft., on moist meadows and open areas in forest.

Fe-2. Woodsia Fern. *Woodsia scopulina* (pl. 3). Rhizome erect, short, with thin pale brown scales; stalks densely clustered, straw-like, 1″–5″ long; fronds many, 5″–10″ high, lance-shaped, dark green, 1- or 2-pinnate, with scattered short hairs; sori near margin, indusia cup-like. DISTR. At 4000–12000 ft. in rocky places; not common.

Fe-3. Brittle Fern. *Cystopteris fragilis* (pl. 3). Rhizome slender, creeping; stalks clustered, fragile, 1¼″–12″ long; fronds break off easily, broadly lance-shaped, 2″–12″ long, bright green, 1- or 2-pinnate, segments round-edged, varying in shape; sori on little veins, small and black when young, later brown; indusia hood-like. DISTR. At 2000–10000 ft. on stony stream banks or in sheltered moist woods. Resembles no. 2 but larger, paler, and more delicate.

Fe-4. Licorice Fern. *Polypidium vulgare* (pl. 3). Rhizome to ¼″ thick, covered with short brownish papery scales; fronds 8″–18″ tall, narrow, segments oblong, cut almost to stem, edges smooth or slightly toothed; sori about ⅛″ dia. near ribs of segments, yellow, turning brown. DISTR. Foothill and Yellow Pine belts to 4000 ft. on canyon banks or in rock crevices with seepage, as near bases of falls in Yosemite Valley.

Fe-5. Sword Fern. *Polystichum munitum* (pl. 3). Rhizome woody, very scaly; fronds many, in dense clumps, dark green, shiny, 12"–48" high, gently tapered, cut nearly to stem; segments to 4" long, tapered, edges toothed; sori many, round, in rows along margins of segments. DISTR. From upper foothills into Lodgepole-fir belt at 7000 ft., in canyons; smaller varieties to 15" tall on some talus slopes.

Fe-6. Shield or Wood Fern. *Dryopteris arguta* (pl. 3). Rhizome stout, woody, with thin brown scales; fronds several, close, erect, 12"–30" high by 10" wide at base, tapered, 2-pinnate, segments with spiny teeth, dark, evergreen; indusia kidney-shaped. DISTR. Foothill and Yellow Pine belts at 2000–6000 ft., often under shelter of logs or overhanging rocks.

Fe-7. Woodwardia or Giant Chain Fern. *Woodwardia fimbriata* (pl. 4). Rhizome stout, woody; scales glossy, bright brown; fronds to 6 ft. or more, almost erect; pinnae to 15" long, lance-shaped, cut almost to midrib; edges of segments toothed, slightly scalloped; sori oblong in a "chain" each side of midvein on segment. DISTR. Mainly near lower border of Yellow Pine belt, locally where continuing seepage is present.

This is the largest and most spectacular of our ferns, common in the coast redwoods but restricted in the Sierra to areas of constant wet soil bordering some of the larger rivers—Kaweah, Merced, etc. Indians used fibers of the rachis dyed red by juice from elder bark in weaving baskets and textiles.

Fe-8. Lady Fern. *Athyrium filix-femina* (pl. 4). Rhizome stout, erect, scales thin, dark brown; fronds to 48" or more by 18" broad, mostly erect, thin, and soft, 2- or 3-pinnate, segments angled on midrib; fronds and segments varied in form; sori at angle to midrib; indusia flap-like, attached along 1 side. DISTR. Yellow Pine and Lodgepole-fir belts, 4000–8000 ft. or higher, along creeks or ravines.

Vase-like clumps of this fern inhabit rich soil that is moist throughout the growing season. Another species (*A. alpestre*), of lesser height and with narrower fronds, reaches Subalpine forest areas at 7000–11000 feet.

Fe-9. Gold Fern. *Pityrogramma triangularis* (pl. 4). Rhizome stout, scales brownish to blackish; fronds many in cluster, to 12" long or more, triangular in shape, mixed pinnate and 2-pinnate, upper surface dark green, lower surface covered with yellow or white powder; sori oblong, covering most of under surface at maturity. DISTR. Foothill and Yellow Pine belts, to 5000 ft., in sun or shade on soil or in crevices of rocks.

Fe-10. Parsley Fern or Rock Brake. *Cryptogramma acrostichoides* (pl. 4). Rhizomes in chaffy clumps; stalks densely clustered, straw-like; fronds 2"–9" long, 2- or 3-pinnate, and of 2 kinds: sterile fronds (no sori) shorter and broader, segments rounded, rachis with narrow ridge on each side; fertile fronds (with sori) taller, segments slender, pod-shaped; sori close

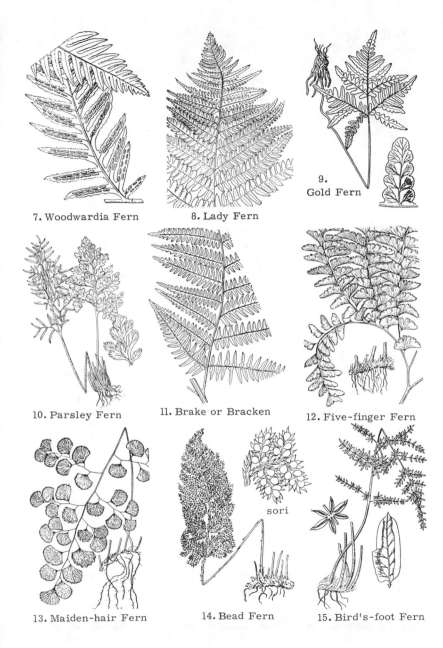

7. Woodwardia Fern

8. Lady Fern

9. Gold Fern

10. Parsley Fern

11. Brake or Bracken

12. Five-finger Fern

13. Maiden-hair Fern

14. Bead Fern

sori

15. Bird's-foot Fern

Plate 4. Ferns

together on veins, covering back of segment. DISTR. Upper coniferous forest, at 5000–10000 ft.; in crevices of granite.

Fe-11. Brake or Bracken. *Pteridium aquilinum* (pl. 4). Rhizomes underground, long, much branched, hairy; stalks scattered, erect, rigid, to 12" long; fronds 2–5 ft. long and same in width at base, triangular in outline, 2- to 4-pinnate, basal pinnae large, outermost pinnae undivided, hairy beneath; sori on veins along margins of segments; indusium continuous. DISTR. Foothill and Yellow Pine belts, especially on acid soils.

The Brake, commonest of all our ferns, sometimes covers whole hillsides or valley bottoms with its large fronds. Often it grows abundantly where fire has destroyed other ground cover. Indians used the rootstock and young tender fronds for food, and they wove baskets and textiles from the slender rhizomes. Early white settlers thatched summer shelters with the fronds.

Fe-12. Five-finger Fern. *Adiantum pedatum* (pl. 4). Rhizome thick, short; stalks shiny black or brown, thin, forked at top, bearing 3–8 pinnae; fronds to 30" high, pinnae delicate, to 9" long; segments with upper edge lobed, lower edge straight, entire; sori along upper curved edge of pinnae. DISTR. At 3000–10000 ft., in moist cool sites.

The Five-finger lives only in cool, damp, and protected rock crevices having much moisture. Originally it abounded near waterfalls in Yosemite Valley, but so many of the plants were removed that it became scarce by the early 1900's.

Fe-13. California Maiden-hair Fern. *Adiantum jordani* (pl. 4). Rhizome slender, creeping; stalks fine, blackish, shiny, pinnately branched at top; fronds to 24" high; segments thin, to 1" wide, on delicate stalks, fan-shaped, lower margins straight, upper edges toothed or lobed; sori near upper curved edge of some segments. DISTR. Local in central Sierra at 2000–3000 ft., in moist sites.

The Maiden-hair is common in damp situations of the Coast Ranges, but rather rare in Sierran foothills, where it may be in evidence from February to June.

Fe-14. Bead Fern. *Cheilanthes covillei* (pl. 4). Rhizome short, creeping; fronds to 8" x 1½"; narrow, 3- or 4-pinnate, upper surface smooth and green, under surface and rachis with scales; segments many, crowded, beadlike; sori on margins of segments, nearly hidden by scales. DISTR. At 2500–6500 ft., on dry slopes, ridges, and peaks.

The densely grouped, bead-shaped segments make this species unlike any other Sierran fern. The related Lace and Lip ferns (*C. gracillima,* and others) have narrow or rounded frond segments. In time of drought the fronds of these and some others roll up and become dry, but open up when moisture again is available.

Fe-15. Bird's-foot Fern. *Pellea mucronata* (or *ornithopus*) (pl. 4). Rhizome thick, long, woody, with toothed scales; stalks clustered, stout, rigid, shiny dark brown; fronds to 18″ high by 5″ wide at base, tapered, 2- or 3-pinnate near base; segments to 3/16″ long, sharp-tipped, edges rolled, often in 3's suggesting a bird's track; sori near ends of veins under rolled edge of segment. DISTR. At 400–5000 ft., in dry gravelly or rocky sites.

Miwok Indians used the long rhizomes of this fern for brown fibers in their baskets. When sheep or goats eat the wiry stalks these break into sharp pieces that pierce the intestinal wall and result in death (hence called "poison fern"). The Bird's-foot is one of several "cliff brakes" noted for their ability to grow in dense clumps on rocks or cliffs exposed to the glaring summer sun. One species (*P. breweri*), 3 to 6 inches high, occurs under rocks at 7000 to 11000 ft., in the High Sierra.

12. FLOWERING PLANTS

The Sierra Nevada, with varied topography and climate, has a large flora, about 2000 species of ferns and flowering plants. In the "boreal region," above the Yellow Pine belt, 633 have been listed (Smiley, 1921). Yosemite National Park has fully 955, exclusive of grasses, sedges, and rushes. This handbook includes about 275 of the commoner kinds.

The flowering plants here are divided into three groups according to growth form: section 13, Wildflowers (WF) or herbs with little or no woody tissue and usually small; section 14, Shrubs (S) with several woody stems; and section 15, Trees (T) with one woody trunk. Grasses, sedges, and rushes are flowering plants with small blossoms of special form, difficult to identify. Examples of these and a few other types are described below in the subsection on Miscellaneous Plants. The sequence throughout is that of Jepson (1925); some changes in scientific names are from Munz and Keck (1959).

Instead of botanical keys, other aids for identification are provided.

1. The Guide to Families of Flowering Plants (table 1) directs the reader to the family in which a plant belongs.

2. The characteristics of each species as to plant, flower, and fruit are given in a simplified description (small type).

3. Each is shown in a line figure, often with details of flower or fruit.

4. There are color illustrations of many wildflowers and shrubs.

5. The wildflowers and shrubs are listed in tables by color of blossom and number of petals.

6. Each species bears the same number throughout: the Corn Lily (wildflower) is no. 2 in description, line figure, color plate, and table.

Individual plants of a species vary in size and form depending on the soil, seasonal amounts of moisture and sunlight, degree of shading,

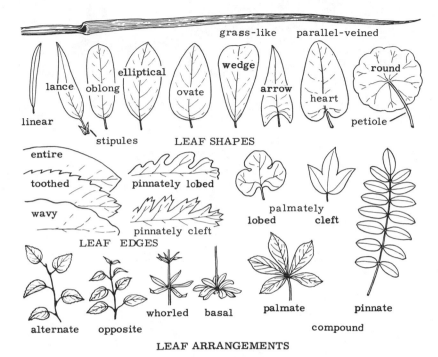

grass-like   parallel-veined

elliptical

wedge

lance   oblong

ovate   arrow

round

heart

linear

stipules

petiole

LEAF SHAPES

entire

toothed   pinnately lobed

wavy

palmately

pinnately cleft   lobed   cleft

LEAF EDGES

whorled   basal   palmate   pinnate

alternate   opposite   compound

LEAF ARRANGEMENTS

Figure 8. Leaf shapes and arrangements.

and other factors. Structural details as to leaf shape, manner of branching, numbers of flower parts, etc., are more constant. Learning some common terms used in describing plants, leaves, and blossoms (figs. 8 and 9) will help when seeking to identify a specimen by comparing it with descriptions and pictures.

A leaf comprises a flat blade, a stalk or *petiole,* and often two small leafy *stipules* where the petiole joins the plant stem. Leaves are *simple* when of 1 blade. *Compound leaves,* of 2 or more *leaflets,* are *pinnate* when the leaflets are along the sides of the petiole but *palmate* if all leaflets fan out from the end of the petiole. Figure 8 shows other details of leaves—their shapes and edges, and whether they are lobed, parted, whorled, etc.

Flowering plants (Angiosperms) and cone-bearing trees (Gymnosperms) reproduce by means of seeds, whereas the lower plants (fungi, lichens, mosses, ferns) do so by spores. Seeds of conifers (pines, firs,

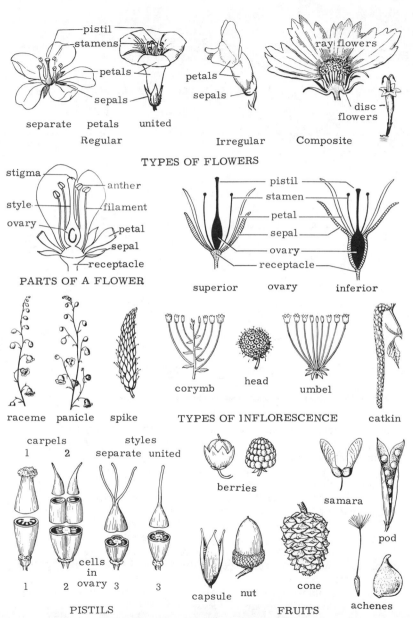

pistil
stamens
petals
sepals

separate   petals   united
Regular

petals
sepals

Irregular

ray flowers

disc
flowers

Composite

TYPES OF FLOWERS

stigma
style
ovary

anther
filament
petal
sepal
receptacle

PARTS OF A FLOWER

pistil
stamen
petal
sepal
ovary
receptacle

superior   ovary   inferior

raceme panicle spike

corymb   head   umbel

TYPES OF INFLORESCENCE

catkin

carpels
1   2

styles
separate united

berries

samara

1   2   cells
in
ovary 3   3

capsule nut

cone

pod

achenes

PISTILS

FRUITS

Figure 9. Parts of flowering plants.

60

etc.) at first are naked and exposed to the air but later are tightly enclosed by the cone and scales. In flowering plants the seeds develop within an ovary which ripens to become the fruit.

Typically a flower has four circular rows of parts: *sepals* (outermost), *petals, stamens,* and *pistils;* its base is the *receptacle* or enlarged end of a stem (fig. 9). The sepals together form the *calyx,* and the petals the *corolla;* one or the other is lacking in some plants. In many flowers all sepals and petals are *separate;* in others they are partly or completely joined or *united.* The stamen has a slender base or *filament* topped by an expanded pollen-producing *anther* (= male part; ♂). Filaments usually attach to the receptacle but sometimes to the corolla, and occasionally are united into a tube. The *pistil* (= female part; ♀) has the egg-producing *ovary* at its base and a slender vertical *style* supporting the *stigma,* which receives pollen brought by wind or insects from other blossoms to fertilize the eggs. Some flowers have 1 pistil; others (roses, buttercups) have many separate pistils. More commonly, however, the pistils are somewhat joined; when completely united a *compound pistil* results (each element is a carpel); a cross section of the ovary usually will show 2 or more compartments indicating the number of carpels of which the pistil is composed. Willows and a few other plants have male and female (staminate, pistillate) flowers on separate plants.

A flower is *regular* when the parts are in circular pattern (radially symmetrical) and each petal or sepal is of the same size and shape (fig. 9); otherwise it is *irregular* (pea, etc.). The ovary is *superior* when above and free from the calyx, but *inferior* if somewhat below and joined to the calyx. If a single flower is at the top of a stem it is *solitary* and *terminal,* but if at the base of a leaf it is *axillary.*

When flowers grow in clusters, each usually is borne on a short stem-like *pedicel.* Clusters are named as follows: *raceme* (flowers along an axis, pedicels of about equal length); *panicle* (a branched raceme); *spike* (like raceme but flowers lack pedicels); *corymb* (like raceme but lower pedicels longer so cluster is flat-topped); *umbel* (all pedicels arise from one point, like ribs of an umbrella, cluster flat-topped); *catkin* (a hanging spike with or without a leaf-like bract at each flower); *head* (flowers without pedicels on spherical receptacle).

In the Sunflower Family (Compositae) the individual flowers are grouped into a *composite head* that can be mistaken for an individual blossom. Actually the flowers are of two types: in the outermost or *ray flowers* the upper part of the united corolla is flared out on one side to resemble a "petal"; the central or *disc flowers* are small and tubular; some composites lack ray flowers.

Dry fruits are of several kinds: *achene* (small, hard, 1-seeded, nonsplitting; buttercup); *capsule* (splitting, of more than 1 carpel; ceano-

TABLE 1. Guide to Families of Flowering Plants in This Handbook

When trying to identify a flower or plant, this table (with figs. 8 and 9) will help the reader to find the family in which the plant belongs and thereby reduce the amount of searching necessary. Often it will serve for species related to those included in the handbook.

Leaves are always alternate unless marked *op.* (opposite), and simple unless marked *com.* (compound). The ovary is superior unless marked *ov. inf.* (inferior). For the "pistil" the number is either of the free parts (carpels) or of the cells in the ovary (as seen in a cross-section). Other abbreviations: 0 = none; m = many; WF, wildflower; S, shrub; T, tree. Less common numbers of parts are shown in parentheses.

Families	Leaves	Sepals	Petals	Stamens	Pistil
LEAVES PARALLEL-VEINED					
Lily, WF-1 to -11; S-1; corolla regular		3	3	6	3
Iris, WF-12, -13; corolla regular (*ov. inf.*)		3	3	3	3
Orchid, WF-14 to -16; corolla irregular (*ov. inf.*)		3	2+1	1+2	1
Flowers in catkins; No petals					
LEAVES NET-VEINED					
Willow, T-21 to -24; seeds with tufts of hair in catkins		0	0	1–m	1
Birch, T-25 to -27; fruit a cone		4–6	0	1–6	1–2
Hazel, S-2; fruit a nut		0	0	4	2
Oak, S-3 to -5; T-28 to -33; fruit an acorn		4–6	0	4–12	1
Silk Tassel, S-37; young branchlets 4-sided; fruit a berry	op.	4	0	4	1
Corolla regular — Stamens free from corolla — Petals separate					
Buttercup, WF-26 to -31; (no. 28 flower irreg.); S-6 (leaves op.)		3–m	0–m	m	m
Rose, WF-43, -44; S-11 to -26	some com.	5	5	10+	5+
Mistletoe, WF-17; flowers minute; fruit a berry	op.	2–5	0	2–5	1
Birthwort or Ginger, WF-18 (*ov. inf.*)		3	0	6–12	6
Buckwheat, WF-19 to -21; sepals often petal-like		5–6	0	4–9	1
Purslane, WF-22, -23; leaves succulent		2(8)	5(6)	5	1
Pink, WF-24; stem nodes swollen	op.	5(4)	5(4)	5(4)	1(3)
Water Lily, WF-25; aquatic		5–12	12–18	m	m
Sweet Shrub, S-7; bracts, sepals, and petals alike	op.	m	m	m	m
Laurel, T-34; leaves aromatic; fruit a berry		6	0	9	1
Poppy, WF-32, -33; S-8; juice colored		2,3	4,6	m	1
Fumitory, WF-34; corolla heart-shaped, irregular	com.	2	2+2	3+3	1
Mustard, WF-35 to -39; taste pungent		4	4	4+2	2(1)

TABLE 1. Guide to Families of Flowering Plants (*Continued*)

			Families	Leaves	Sepals	Petals	Stamens	Pistil
Corolla regular	Stamens free from corolla	Petals separate	Stonecrop, WF-40; leaves succulent		5	5	10	5
			Saxifrage, WF-41, -42; S-9, -10		5	5(4,8)	5,10+	2
			Plane, T-35; outer bark peels; flowers in balls		0	0	3–8	1
			Geranium, WF-51; leaves lobed, divided; fruit 1-seeded with coiled "tail" (style)		5	5	10,5	5
			Meadow Foam, WF-52		5	5	6,10	5
			Sumac, S-31; juice oily		5	5	5,10	1
			Maple, T-36, -37; leaves 5- or 3-lobed; fruit a 2-winged samara	op.	5	5	4–10	2
			Buckeye, T-38; leaflets 5–7; fruit a large seeded capsule	op. & com.	4,5	4,5	5–7	3
			Buckthorn, S-32 to -34; T-39		5(4)	5(4)	5(4)	3(2)
			Vine, S-35; tendrils for climbing		4(5)	5	5	2
			Mallow, WF-53; stamens united into a tube		5	5	m	m
			Sterculia, S-36; stamens united into a tube at base; sepals petal-like		5	0	5	5(4)
			St. John's Wort, WF-54; leaves black-dotted	op.	5(4)	5(4)	m	1,3
			Violet, WF-55; flower slightly irregular, 1 petal spurred at base		5	2+2+1	5	1
			Loasa, WF-56; stinging hairs on leaves		5	5	m	1
			Evening Primrose, WF-57 to -62; pollen cobwebby (*ov. inf.*)		4	4	8	4(2)
			Parsley, WF-63 to -65; stem hollow; flowers in umbels (*ov. inf.*)	com.	5,0	5	5	2
		Petals united	Dogwood, S-38; T-40 (*ov. inf.*)	op.	4	4	4	2
			Heath, WF-66 to -68; S-39 to -46; T-41; petals separate or united		5(4)	5(4)	10(8)	4–10
			Bellflower, WF-105; juice milky		5	5	5	2–5

TABLE 1. Guide to Families of Flowering Plants (*Continued*)

Families	Leaves	Sepals	Petals	Stamens	Pistil
Primrose, WF-69, -70; capsule 5-valved		5	5	5	1
Storax, S-47; stamens united into a tube		4(5)	4–8	10–16	1(3)
Ash, T-42; fruit a 1-winged samara	op. & com.	4	2	2	2
Gentian, WF-71; corolla funnel-like; capsule 2-valved	op.	4–5	4–5	4–5	1
Dogbane, WF-72; juice milky	op.	5	5	5	2
Milkweed, WF-73; juice milky; pollen in minute waxy masses	op.	5	5	5	2
Morning Glory, WF-74, -75; twining vine; corolla funnel-like		5	5	5	2
Gilia, WF-76 to -80	some op. or com.	5	5	5	3
Phacelia, WF-81 to -83; S-48; seed coat pitted		5	5	5	2
Borage, WF-84 to -88; herbage hairy; flowers on spiral spike; 4 nutlets		5	5	5	2
Nightshade, WF-96, -97; S-49; corolla funnel-like		5	5	5	2
Madder, S-51; flower heads spherical	op.	4	4	4	2
Pea, WF-45 to -50; S-27 to -30; stamens united into a tube but free from corolla; petals mostly free	com.	5	1+2+2	10	1
Mint, WF-89 to -95; stems square; herbage aromatic	op.	5	2+3	4(2)	4
Figwort, WF-98 to -104; S-50	some op.	5(4)	2+3	2+2(5)	2
Honeysuckle, S-52 to -56; fruit a berry (*ov. inf.*)	op.	5(4)	5(4)	5(4)	2–5
Lobelia, WF-106; corolla 2-lipped; stamens not on corolla		5	2+3	5	2
Sunflower, WF-107 to -123; S-57 to -60; flowers in heads surrounded by leafy bracts				5	1

Left margin groupings: Corolla regular — Stamens on corolla, Petals united; Corolla irregular — Stamens on corolla.

thus); *follicle* (pod formed from 1 carpel, splitting on 1 edge; delphinium); *pod* (thin, flat, splitting on 2 seams; pea); *samara* (1 or 2 wings, non-splitting; maple); *nut* or *acorn* (like achene but larger; oak). Fleshy fruits include: *drupe* (1 central seed; cherry); *single berry* (pulp contains 1 or more seeds; currant, grape); *aggregate berry* (from many carpels on 1 receptacle; blackberry).

MISCELLANEOUS PLANTS

Between the ferns and wildflowers in botanical classification there are several types of plants that are common and widespread but have inconspicuous flower parts. Examples are included in this section. There are many species of grasses, sedges, and rushes, but to name them correctly requires complete specimens with both flowers and seeds, a magnifier, a technical manual, and some experience.

MP-1. Common Horsetail. *Equisetum arvense* (pl. 5). Rootstock jointed, branched, roots in whorls at nodes; stems erect, rigid, jointed, hollow; leaves reduced and united as a sheath at nodes; sterile stems 12″–18″ high, green, branches 3- or 4-angled, sheaths 4-toothed; fertile stems 4″–7″ high, whitish, unbranched, ending in cone-like spore-producing body. DISTR. Up to 8000 ft. in open sandy wet soil or swamps.

The rush-like Horsetail (neither a fern nor flowering plant) occurs over much of the Northern Hemisphere. Related species formerly served for scouring pots and kettles because of the abrasive silica present in parts of the stem.

MP-2. Cat-tail. Genus *Typha* (pl. 5). Rootstock creeping in mud below water or in wet soil; stem 3½–6 ft. high, round, solid, jointless; leaves long, to 1″ wide, sheathing the stem at base; flowers minute in dense cylindrical hairy brown spike, 7″–13″ long, at top of stem; male flowers above, female below. DISTR. Common in marshes.

Cat-tails fill many quiet backwaters and marshes at low to middle altitudes. Muskrats eat the rootstocks. Red-winged and tricolored blackbirds suspend their nests on the stems or leaves. Various other marsh dwellers find shelter among the leaves and stems.

MP-3. Pondweeds. Genus *Potamogeton* (pl. 5). Water plants with stems simple or branched, round or flattened; leaves often of 2 kinds: floating leaves broad, oval, submerged ones grass-like; flower parts small, all in 4's—calyx, corolla, stamens, and ovaries. DISTR. In fresh or brackish ponds and slow creeks.

Pondweeds of several species grow from low altitudes to 9000 ft. in quiet Sierran waters. The submerged leaves and stems afford shelter for aquatic insect larvae and other small animals. The pea-sized tubers on the roots of Sago Pondweed (*P. pectinatus*) are eaten by some ducks.

MP-4. Water Plantain. *Alismo triviale* or *plantago-aquaticum* (pl. 5). Ht. 2–4 ft.; rootstock surrounded by long petioles holding erect oval pointed leaves 2″–6″ long; flower cluster a panicle of branches each with umbel of flowers; petals minute, white; stamens 6. DISTR. Margins of rivers, lakes, and ponds, in shallow water or damp ground, to 5000 ft.

MP-5. Arrow-head. *Sagittaria latifolia* (pl. 5). Rootstock with tubers, fibrous roots, and milky juice; leaf blade resembling arrow point, variable in outline, 2″–12″ long, nerves connected to many small veins; blossom stalk (scape) 3″–3 ft. high, flowers near top in 3's; fruit head spherical, dia. to 1″. DISTR. Stream margins, marshes, and meadows up to 6000 ft.

The tubers, called wappato, were food for Indians. Later the Chinese on islands of the Sacramento–San Joaquin delta cultivated the plants and ate the tubers under the name of tule potato.

MP-6. Grasses. Family GRAMINEAE (pl. 5). Usually with round, hollow stems, closed at nodes; leaves parallel-veined, in 2 rows; each leaf of 2 parts, a sheath around the stem and a narrow linear blade; junction of sheath and blade with soft tissue (ligule) usually around stem; flowers minute, in groups or spikelets, base of each spikelet with 2 leaf-like bracts (glumes) that often enclose the flowers.

Grasses are the commonest of flowering plants. There are dozens of species that vary in structure, growth form, and distribution. Some kinds cover flat lands of the Great Valley and rolling western foothills, and other assemblages carpet the pleasant green mountain meadows. Still others grow sparingly in the big conifer forests, in gravelly or rocky places, above timberline, or among east side junipers and sagebrush.

Grasses and grasslands (with some associated herbaceous plants) serve many roles in the complexities of nature. Grasses are the staple foods for grasshoppers and many other insects, ground squirrels, marmots, meadow mice, and rabbits. Grass seeds are eaten by various insects, mourning doves, many sparrows, chipmunks, and other animals. Horned larks, meadow larks, savannah sparrows, and other birds find both food and cover in grasslands. Carnivorous animals that prey on grass- and seed-eaters are supported indirectly by the grasses. Grasslands afford pasturage for man's domestic animals, and aesthetically they contribute to many scenic views. Live or dead grasses and their roots serve as soil binders to lessen erosion by wind or water. Many alien grasses have spread widely in California, and some native species have become extinct.

MP-7. Sedges. Family CYPERACEAE (pl. 5). Grass- or rush-like; roots fibrous, often on long rootstock; stem solid (rarely hollow), often triangular (some round, 4-sided, or flat); leaves in 3's, mostly basal, narrow, with closed sheath around stem; flowers in spikes, solitary or densely clustered; 1 bract per flower; calyx and corolla of bristles or lacking, stamens 1–3, ovary 1-celled; fruit an achene.

Different kinds of sedges (*Cyperus, Scirpus, Carex,* etc.) grow in various sorts of soil, fertile or alkaline and soggy to dry, from the Great Valley lowlands to Sierran peaks. Some are of wide occurrence and others local in distribution. The achenes are sought by seed-eating birds and mammals.

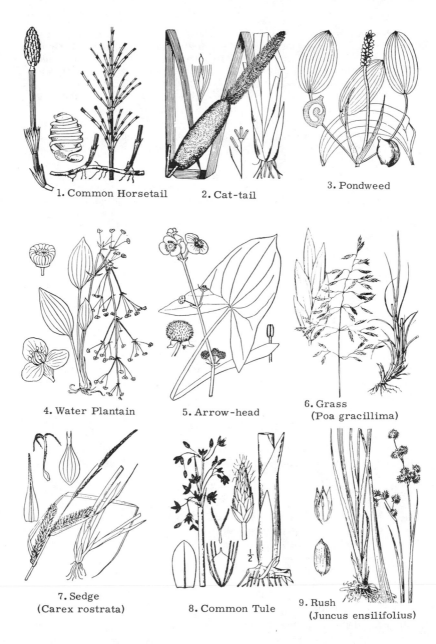

1. Common Horsetail   2. Cat-tail   3. Pondweed

4. Water Plantain   5. Arrow-head   6. Grass
(Poa gracillima)

7. Sedge
(Carex rostrata)   8. Common Tule   9. Rush
(Juncus ensilifolius)

Plate 5. Miscellaneous plants   67

MP-8. Common Tule or Bulrush. *Scirpus acutus* (pl. 5). Rootstock creeping; stem 3–9 ft. high, round or bluntly triangular above; a short rounded leaf or none; blossom head 1″–5″ long with stout short bract at base, spikelets ¼″–½″ long. Distr. Salt and freshwater marshes up into Yellow Pine belt; widespread.

Lowlands along the major Great Valley rivers originally had huge tule swamps (perhaps 250,000 acres), now mostly reclaimed for agriculture. The stems were used by Indians to build small rafts bound together with stems of wild grape. For Americans they served to pack nursery stock or to thatch haystacks.

MP-9. Rushes. Family Juncaceae (pl. 5). Herbaceous, grass-like, often in clumps; stem 3″–4 ft. tall; simple, round, with spongy pith or hollow, leafy or leafless; leaves stiff and round or flat, narrow, sheathing at base; flowers in heads, spikes, or panicles, minute, green or brown, lily-like in structure, sedge-like in form with 6 similar narrow segments; stamens 6 (or 3); ovary 3- (or 1)-celled, fruit a 3-valved capsule.

The round wiry stems of rushes formerly served as binding material. Different species live from the lowlands to the mountain flats at 11000 ft., mostly in wet places.

13. WILDFLOWERS

This chapter includes the commoner herbaceous plants having showy, attractive blossoms. Usually only one species of a group (genus) is described. Related forms often can be recognized from the description of the commoner one. Where many species are present, as with the lupines, the account is of the genus, with mention of a few conspicuous species. Characters given under the plant families are usually not repeated in species accounts. The blossoming period is indicated by months: Jan.– Apr., etc.

In general, wildflowers should be enjoyed in their natural setting and not picked (never in national parks). For careful identification blossoms must be examined closely; sometimes a flower must be cut vertically to show whether sepals or petals are partly united or separate, how the stamens are attached, and whether the ovary is superior or inferior (fig. 9). When a specimen must be picked and carried for later identification, it should be wrapped in paper with damp soft paper around the stem. Botanists take plants as records and for later study, pressing them to dry in half folded sheets of newspaper between blotters. The pairs of blotters are separated by layers of corrugated cardboard and cinched tightly in a plant press with wooden frames and straps. Full data as to locality, habitat, altitude, height of plant, date, and name of collector are written on the margin of the paper. Specimens so prepared are later mounted on stiff white paper and filed in a school or museum herbarium.

TABLE 2. Wildflower Color Chart

White, Cream, or Green	Yellow, Orange, or Brown	Red, Pink, or Rose	Blue to Purple
A. FLOWER PARTS IN 3'S OR 6'S; LEAVES PARALLEL-VEINED			
1. Death Camas			
2. Corn Lily			
3. Camas			3. Camas
4. Soap Plant		5. Swamp Onion	
	6b. Brodiaea	6e. Brodiaea	6a, c, d. Brodiaea
7. Mariposa Lily	7. Mariposa Lily	7. Mariposa Lily	7. Mariposa Lily
8. Fawn Lily	8. Fawn Lily		8. Fawn Lily
9. Fritillaria			9. Fritillaria
10a. Washington Lily	10b. Small Tiger Lily		10a. Washington Lily
11. False Solomon Seal			
12. Iris (Blue Flag)	12. Sierra Iris		12. Iris (Blue Flag)
14. Rein-orchis			13. Blue-eyed Grass
15. Ladies Tresses			
16. Coral Root			
(all below have leaves net-veined)			
B. NO PETALS; SEPALS VARIOUS, NOT PETAL-LIKE			
17. Mistletoe (sepals 3)			18. Wild Ginger (calyx 3-lobed)
19. Knotweed (calyx 5-lobed)		19. Knotweed (calyx 5-lobed)	
20. Western Dock (sepals 6)			
21. Buckwheat (calyx 6-parted)	21. Buckwheat (calyx 6-parted)	21. Buckwheat (calyx 6-parted)	
C. PETALS 4, SEPARATE TO BASE			
22. Pussy Paws		22. Pussy Paws	28. Larkspur (irregular)
	33. Calif. Poppy		
	35. Streptanthus		35. Streptanthus
37. Rock Cress	36. Mustard	37. Rock Cress	37. Rock Cress
	38. West. Wall Flower		
58. Fireweed	39. Draba	58. Fireweed	58. Fireweed
59. Clarkia		59. Clarkia	59. Clarkia

TABLE 2. Wildflower Color Chart (*Continued*)

White, Cream, or Green	Yellow, Orange, or Brown	Red, Pink, or Rose	Blue to Purple
		60. Farewell-to-spring	60. Farewell-to-spring
61. Evening Primrose	61. Evening Primrose	61. Evening Primrose	
62. Gayophytum		62. Gayophytum	

D. PETALS 4, MORE OR LESS UNITED

White, Cream, or Green	Yellow, Orange, or Brown	Red, Pink, or Rose	Blue to Purple
34. Bleeding Heart		34. Bleeding Heart	34. Bleeding Heart
		57. Fuchsia	
		69. Shooting-star	69. Shooting-star
102. Paintbrush (calyx petal-like)	102. Paintbrush (calyx petal-like)	102. Paintbrush (calyx petal-like)	71. Gentian
	103. Owl Clover	103. Owl Clover	103. Owl Clover
104. Lousewort	104. Lousewort	104. Lousewort	104. Lousewort

E. PETALS 5, SEPARATE TO BASE; FLOWERS REGULAR

White, Cream, or Green	Yellow, Orange, or Brown	Red, Pink, or Rose	Blue to Purple
23. Miner's Lettuce		23. Miner's Lettuce	
		24. Indian Pink	
	27. Columbine	27. Columbine	
30. Anemone (sepals 5–6, petal-like; no petals)			30. Anemone (sepals 5–6, petal-like; no petals)
41. Saxifrage			
42. Alum-root		42. Alum-root	
43. Strawberry			
44. Cinquefoil	44. Cinquefoil		44. Cinquefoil
51. Wild Geranium		51. Wild Geranium	
52. Meadow Foam		52. Meadow Foam	
	54. St. John's Wort	53. Wild Hollyhock	53. Wild Hollyhock
63. Queen Anne's Lace	55. Violet		55. Violet
64. Cow Parsnip	56. Blazing Star		
65. Swamp Whiteheads			65. Swamp Whiteheads
66. Wintergreen			

TABLE 2. Wildflower Color Chart (*Continued*)

White, Cream, or Green	Yellow, Orange, or Brown	Red, Pink, or Rose	Blue to Purple
		F. PETALS 5, SEPARATE TO BASE; FLOWERS IRREGULAR	
29. Monkshood			29. Monkshood
45. Lupine	45. Lupine	45. Lupine	45. Lupine
46. Clover	46. Clover	46. Clover	46. Clover
47. Hosackia	47. Hosackia		
48. Rattleweed			48. Rattleweed
50. Shrub Pea	50. Shrub Pea		49. Vetch
		G. PETALS 5, MORE OR LESS UNITED; FLOWERS REGULAR	
40. Stonecrop	40. Stonecrop	40. Stonecrop	
67. Pine-drops		68. Snow Plant	
		69. Shooting-star	69. Shooting-star
		70. Sierra Primrose	70. Sierra Primrose
72. Mtn. Hemp		72. Mtn. Hemp	
74. Morning Glory		73. Milkweed	73. Milkweed
75. Dodder			
77. Collomia	77. Collomia	77. Collomia	76. Polemonium
78. Phlox		78. Phlox	78. Phlox
79. Gilia	79. Gilia	79. Gilia	
80. Mustang Clover		80. Mustang Clover	81. Baby Blue Eyes
82. Phacelia			82. Phacelia
			83. Draperia
		84. Forget-me-not	84. Forget-me-not
87. Cryptantha	86. Fiddleneck		85. Mtn. Bluebell
88. Pop-corn Flower	98. Common Mullein		
		H. PETALS 5, MORE OR LESS UNITED; COROLLA IRREGULAR	
			89. Blue Curls
			90. Skull-cap
		91. Giant Hyssop	91. Giant Hyssop
		92. Self-heal	93. Sage, Chia
94. Pennyroyal		94. Pennyroyal	94. Pennyroyal
		95. Mint	95. Mint
96. Tolguacha			96. Tolguacha
97. Nightshade			97. Nightshade
99. Collinsia			99. Collinsia

TABLE 2. Wildflower Color Chart (*Continued*)

White, Cream, or Green	Yellow, Orange, or Brown	Red, Pink, or Rose	Blue to Purple
100. Pentstemon	100. Pentstemon 101. Monkey- flower	100. Pentstemon 101. Monkey- flower	100. Pentstemon 101. Monkey- flower 105. Harebell 106. Downingia

I. PETALS MORE THAN 5

White, Cream, or Green	Yellow, Orange, or Brown	Red, Pink, or Rose	Blue to Purple
26. Marsh Mari- gold (sepals 6–9, petal-like; no petals)	25. Pond Lily (sepals and petals many, alike)	25. Pond Lily (sepals and petals many, alike)	26. Marsh Mari- gold (sepals 6–9, petal- like; no petals)
31. Buttercup (petals 9–16)	31. Buttercup (petals 9–16) 32. Cream Cups (sepals 3, petals 6)		

J. FLOWERING HEADS COMPOSITE, OF FEW TO MANY INDIVIDUAL FLOWERS; MARGINAL (RAY) FLOWERS PETAL-LIKE, CENTRAL (DISC) FLOWERS SMALL, TUBULAR

White, Cream, or Green	Yellow, Orange, or Brown	Red, Pink, or Rose	Blue to Purple
108. Hawkweed	107. Sow Thistle 109. Goldenrod		110. Lessingia (no rays)
	111. Mtn. Aster (disc) 112. Fleabane (disc)		111. Mtn. Aster (rays) 112. Fleabane (rays)
113. Rose Everlasting (no rays)	114a. Black-eyed Susan (rays)	113. Rose Everlasting (no rays)	
	114b. Cone Flower (rays) 115. Mule Ears 116. Tarweed		
117. Tidy Tips	117. Tidy Tips 118. Woolly Sunflower 119. Sneezeweed		
120. Yarrow Milfoil 123. Sierra Thistle (no rays)	121. Groundsel 122. Arnica	123. Sierra Thistle (no rays)	123. Sierra Thistle (no rays)

LILY FAMILY (LILIACEAE). Leaves parallel-veined; "petals" (= sepals + petals) 6; stamens 6 (or 3 without anthers).

WF-1. Death Camas. *Zygadenus venenosus* (pl. 6, col. pl. 4). Stem 8"–24"; bulb ovate, to ¾" broad; leaves shorter than stem, to ½" wide, folded, mostly basal; racemes 3"–10" long, flowers many, erect, dia. to ⅜", greenish-white, 3 styles; May–July. DISTR. Foothills to Lodgepole–fir belt at 8200 ft. in moist places, also rocky slopes; uncommon.

Leaves of young plants resemble grass and are poisonous to sheep. The bulbs are safely eaten by hogs, hence called "hog potatoes."

WF-2. Corn Lily. *Veratrum californicum* (pl. 6, col. pl. 4). Stems 3–6 ft., stout, leafy, resembling cornstalk; rootstock short, thick, fibrous; leaves 6"–12" x 4"–8", oval, tip pointed, sheathing stem at base, upper leaves narrower, shorter; flower panicle 12"–16" long, woolly, flowers many, to ¾" long, white, greenish at base, 3 styles; July–Aug. DISTR. Yellow Pine and Lodgepole–fir belts at 4500–8500 ft. or higher; in wet meadows and along stream banks.

This plant resembles but is not related to the eastern skunk cabbage (*Symplocarpus*); it is also called "false hellebore" from its resemblance to *Helleborus* of Europe. The shoots are poisonous to livestock but they seldom eat it.

WF-3. Camas. *Camassia quamash* (pl. 6, col. pl. 4). Stem 12"–30", from an onion-like bulb; leaves basal, grass-like, shorter than stem; raceme of 5–25 flowers ¾"–1" long, blue (rarely white), style 1, 3-cleft at tip. DISTR. Upper Yellow Pine and Lodgepole–fir belts, at 4500–6500 ft. in wet meadows.

Indians cooked and ate quamash bulbs, but carefully avoided those of death camas.

WF-4. Soap Plant. *Chlorogalum pomeridianum* (pl. 6). Stem 2–5 ft., nearly leafless; leaves many, basal, 9"–24" x ½"–1½", with keel, wavy-edged; flowers few in long spreading cluster, narrow-petaled, ¾" long, white, purplish-veined, style 1, 3-cleft at tip; bulb 3"–4" long, dia. to 2", with dense coat of coarse brown fibers; May–Aug. DISTR. Foothill belt to 5000 ft. on dry, open, and stony ground.

The delicate flowers open only in the afternoon. Scales of the bulb form a lather with water. Indians roasted the bulbs for food and used its fibers for brushes.

WF-5. Swamp Onion. *Allium validum* (pl. 6, col. pl. 4). Stem 1–3 ft., stout; bulb to 2" long, on creeping rootstalk with coarse roots, bulb scales white or red-tinged; leaves 3–6, basal, grass-like, 12"–24" long; flowers in dense head, many, petals to ½" long, pink or rose-purple, style 1; July–Sept. DISTR. Lodgepole–fir and Subalpine belts, at 4000–11000 ft. in high wet meadows, often in small beds.

Several species of wild onion grow in the Sierra. This, the common-

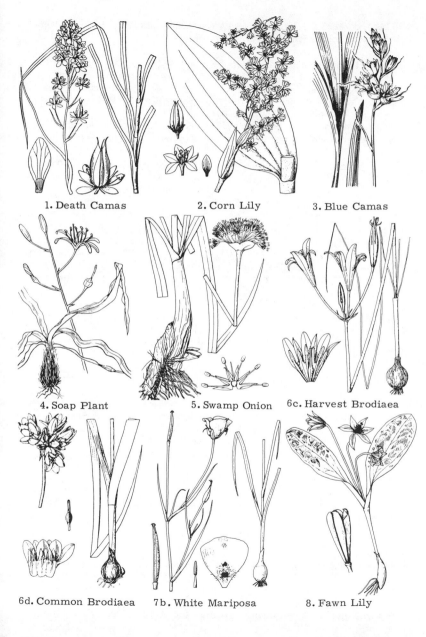

1. Death Camas   2. Corn Lily   3. Blue Camas

4. Soap Plant   5. Swamp Onion   6c. Harvest Brodiaea

6d. Common Brodiaea   7b. White Mariposa   8. Fawn Lily

Plate 6. Wildflowers

est, has a strong garlic odor. The fibrous bulbs may be used to flavor hearty camp soup or stew.

WF-6. Brodiaea. Genus *Brodiaea*. Stem erect or long and twining; leaves few, grass-like, dying early; flowers terminal, in open umbels on long pedicels (*a, b, c*) or in dense head (*d, e*), sepals + petals united in tube at base, tips spread, blue, violet, pinkish, white, or yellow; stamens with anthers 6 (*a, b*) or 3 (*c, d, e*).

a. Grass Nut. *B. laxa.* Stem 12″–28″, rigid; flowers violet-purple, 8–48 in loose open umbel, pedicels 2″–3½″, flowers 1¼″–1¾″ long; Apr.-June. DISTR. Foothill belt at 500–4600 ft. on adobe soil; bulbs eaten raw by Indians.

b. Golden Brodiaea. *B. ixioides.* Stem 6″–18″; flowers salmon yellow with dark vein on each segment, 16–40 in loose umbel, pedicels 1″–4″, flowers ½″–¾″ long; May-July. DISTR. Foothill belt and up to 8000 ft. on sandy soil.

c. Harvest Brodiaea. *B. coronaria* (pl. 6). Stem 7″–20″, erect; flowers blue or violet, 3–11 in open umbel, pedicels 1″–3½″, flowers 1¼″–1¾″ long; Apr.-July. DISTR. Foothill belt and up to 7000 ft.

d. Common Brodiaea or Blue Dicks. *B. capitata* or *pulchella* (pl. 6). Stem 6″–15″, erect; flowers to ⅔″ long, deep blue, 4–10 in dense head; Mar.-May. DISTR. Foothill belt of w. slope and on e. side amid piñon and juniper.

e. Twining Brodiaea. *B. volubilis* (col. pl. 4). Stem to 3 ft. high and erect or twining over bushes for 7–8 ft.; flowers 18–30 in dense head, dia. to 6″, rose-red or pinkish, pedicels ½″–1″, flowers ½″–⅔″ long; Apr.-July. DISTR. Foothill belt, Butte to Tulare Co., at 500–2500 ft. on open brushy slopes.

WF-7. Mariposa Lilies, etc. Genus *Calochortus*. Stem from a bulb; leaves narrow, 1 or 2 at base, few on stem; sepals small, leaf-shaped, green or colored; petals usually large, showy, and broadly wedge-shaped, each with large glandular pit (often dark) near base and few or many hairs; stamens 6.

a. Yellow Mariposa. *C. luteus.* Stem 6″–24″; petals yellow to orange with dark lines on center, ¾″–2″ long and wide; May-June. DISTR. Foothill belt at 150–2500 ft. in open on heavy soil.

b. White Mariposa. *C. venustus* (pl. 6, col. pl. 4). Stem 4″–10″ (to 48″); flowers 1–4; petals white with red-brown spot, to 2½″ long; June-July. DISTR. Foothill belt to 2000 ft. or higher on sandy soil.

c. White Globe Lily. *C. albus.* Stem 12″–24″; 1 basal leaf, 12″–24″ long; flowers several, white to pale rose, globe-shaped, petals 1″–1¾″ long, folded over each other; Apr.-June. DISTR. Foothill belt, Butte to Madera Co., up to 5000 ft. in shady brush or woods, often in rocky soil.

d. Yellow Star Tulip. *C. monophyllus.* Stem 9″–12″; petals yellow to brown, ½″–¾″ long, hairy; Apr.-May. DISTR. Foothill and lower Yellow Pine belt, s. to Tuolumne Co. at 1200–3600 ft.

e. Sierra Star Tulip. *C. nudus.* Stem 2″–6″; 1 basal leaf 3″–10″ x ⅓″–1½″; flowers in cluster; petals white to pale lilac, ⅓″–½″ long, with few hairs; June. DISTR. On w. slope up to 7500 ft. in moist meadows.

f. Sego Lily. *C. nuttallii.* Stem 3″–17″; flowers 1 or several in umbel;

petals white to purple, 1"–1¾" long; May-Aug. DISTR. E. slope at 4000–10000 ft. on dry sites (e. to Utah).

WF-8. Fawn Lily. *Erythronium hartwegii* (pl. 6). Stem 4"–8", erect, from narrow bulb; leaves 2, basal, to 10" long, tapering to bottom; flowers 1–5, ¾" long, white or cream, orange or yellow at base; stigma 3-lobed; Mar.-May. DISTR. Foothill belt s. to Mariposa Co. on brushy hillsides.

A purple-tinged species (*E. purpurascens*) occurs in the Yellow Pine belt at 4000 to 8000 ft.

WF-9. Fritillaria. *Fritillaria parviflora* (pl. 7, col. pl. 4). Stem 1½–3 ft., erect, from a bulb; leaves 3"–5" long, narrow, alternate or in whorls; flowers 3–20 in a cluster, each to ½" long, purple or greenish-white, mottled; styles 3; Apr.-June. DISTR. Foothill and Yellow Pine belts, at 1500–3900 ft., often in woods; several other species of various colors.

WF-10. Lilies. Genus *Lilium.* Stem 1½–7 ft., erect, from a bulb; leaves 3"–5" long, narrow, scattered or in whorls; flowers large, showy, 1 or few in raceme; stigma 3-lobed.

a. Washington Lily. *Lilium washingtonianum* (pl. 7). Stems 4–6 ft.; flowers 3"–4" long, pure white, often purple-dotted, aging purplish, fragrant; July-Aug. DISTR. Yellow Pine belt at 3000–6000 ft. in forest or thickets on dry slopes.

b. Small Tiger Lily. *Lilium parvum* (pl. 7, col. pl. 4). Stems to 7 ft.; flowers 1"–1¼" long, orange-yellow spotted with purple; July-Sept. DISTR. Lodgepole–fir and Subalpine belts, at 6000–9000 ft. in boggy places or near streams.

The larger Leopard Lily (*L. pardalinum*) grows at 3000 to 6000 feet, blooming May to July.

WF-11. False Solomon Seal. *Smilacina amplexicaulis* (pl. 7). Stem 1–3 ft. from horizontal rootstalk; leaves alternate, 3"–5½" long, broad, clasping stem at base, tip pointed, rough with short hairs; flowers in 2"–4" panicles, small, white; stigma 3-lobed; berry-red, 1-seeded; Mar.-May. DISTR. Shaded woods below 6000 ft.; a smooth-leaved variety occurs up to 8500 ft.

IRIS FAMILY (IRIDACEAE). Leaves parallel-veined, mostly basal; "petals" 6, stamens 3, ovary inferior.

WF-12. Sierra Iris. *Iris hartwegii* (pl. 7, col. pl. 4). Stems 6"–12", several, from stout, creeping rootstock; leaves many, ¼" wide; flowers commonly in pairs on pedicel ½"–3¾" long, petals 1½"–2" long, yellow with lavender veins or pale lavender with deeper-colored veins and yellow at middle; May-June. DISTR. Yellow Pine belt, 2500–6000 ft. in dry open forest.

The Western Blue Flag (*I. missouriensis*) with whitish or pale blue flowers grows in moist meadows at high elevations, mainly on the east slope.

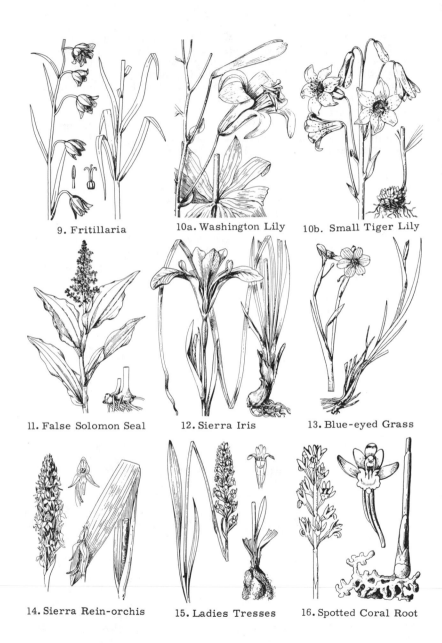

9. Fritillaria   10a. Washington Lily   10b. Small Tiger Lily

11. False Solomon Seal   12. Sierra Iris   13. Blue-eyed Grass

14. Sierra Rein-orchis   15. Ladies Tresses   16. Spotted Coral Root

Plate 7. Wildflowers

WF-13. Blue-eyed Grass. *Sisyrinchium bellum* (pl. 7, col. pl. 5). Stems 6″–24″, 2-edged, from fibrous roots; leaves grass-like; blossoms on short pedicels projecting from 2 green sheathing bracts; flower ⅔″ long, "petals" blue, yellow at base, end with a sharp tip in a notch; stamens united, their anthers alternating with the 3 stigmas; Mar.-May. DISTR. Foothills and lower forest belt, on grassy slopes and in meadows.

ORCHID FAMILY (ORCHIDACEAE). Leaves parallel-veined, sheathing stem or scale-like; flowers irregular; "petals" 6, one (the "lip") unlike others; stamens 1–2, united with pistil; ovary inferior.

WF-14. Sierra Rein-orchis. *Habenaria leucostachys* (pl. 7, col. pl. 5). Stem 9″–30″, base thick, leafy, from a tuber; leaves 4″–9″ x ½″–1″; blossom spike 4″–8″ long, dense; flowers white, ½″ long; May-Aug. DISTR. From middle altitudes to 11000 ft. in moist places.

WF-15. Ladies Tresses. *Spiranthes romanzoffiana* (pl. 7). Stem 5″–16″, leafy, from tuberous roots; leaves 3″–7″ long, narrow, tapering; flower spike 1½″–5″, dense, twisted; flowers ¼″–½″ long, dull or greenish white; June-Aug. DISTR. Higher forest to 10000 ft. on wet banks and meadows.

WF-16. Spotted Coral Root. *Corallorhiza maculata* (pl. 7). A root parasite, no green foliage; roots branching, coral-like; stem 8″–13″, erect; leaves small, scale-like; flower cluster terminal, 2″–7″ long, flowers about ¼″ long, lower petal (lip) 3-lobed, white, purple spotted; June-Aug. DISTR. Coniferous forest at 3000–9000 ft. among pine needles and humus.

The Striped Coral Root (*C. striata*, col. pl. 5) has larger flowers with purple stripes.

MISTLETOE FAMILY (LORANTHACEAE). Leaves opposite, ♂ and ♀ flowers on separate plants; regular; sepals 3; no petals; stamens 3; ovary inferior.

WF-17. Mistletoe. *Phoradendron villosum* (pl. 8). Evergreen, bush-like, parasitic on trees; stem 1–3 ft. long, hairy; leaves many, thick, oval, ½″–1½″ long; flowers small, greenish on fleshy, jointed short spike; berry round, pulpy, pink. DISTR. Foothills to middle altitudes, chiefly on oaks.

Other species with scale-like leaves include *P. juniperinum* on Sierra juniper and *P. libocedri* on incense cedar. The related Pine Mistletoe (*Arceuthobium campylopodum*), with scale-like yellowish or brownish leaves and flattened berries, lives on pines and firs.

BIRTHWORT FAMILY (ARISTOLOCHIACEAE). Calyx bell-shaped, 3-lobed; no petals; stamens 12; styles 6; ovary inferior.

WF-18. Wild Ginger. *Asarum hartwegi* (pl. 8). Flowers and leaves rising directly from fragrant, creeping rootstock; leaves 2″–5″ wide, mottled, heart-shaped, on petioles 3″–7″ long; flower close to ground, on short stalk; sepals

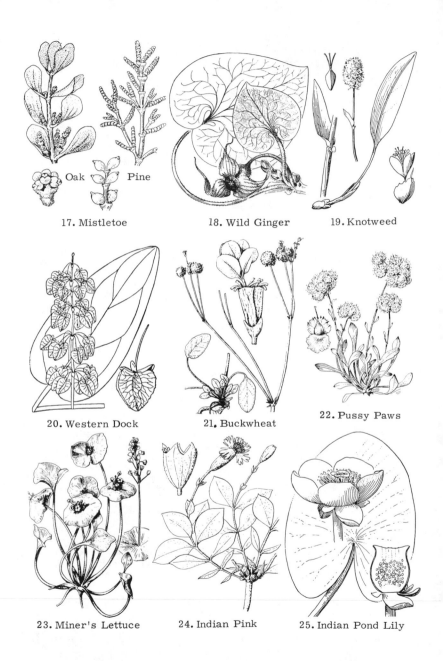

Oak   Pine

17. Mistletoe   18. Wild Ginger   19. Knotweed

20. Western Dock   21. Buckwheat   22. Pussy Paws

23. Miner's Lettuce   24. Indian Pink   25. Indian Pond Lily

Plate 8. Wildflowers   79

to 1¼" long, brownish-purple, spreading, hairy, tips long and tapered; May-June. DISTR. Yellow Pine and Lodgepole–fir belts, at 2500–7000 ft., in shaded places.

BUCKWHEAT FAMILY (POLYGONACEAE). Calyx 5- or 6-parted; no corolla; stamens 4–9.

WF-19. Knotweed. *Polygonum bistortoides* (pl. 8, col. pl. 5). Stems 6"–24", several, root woody; basal leaves 3"–5" long, narrow, upper leaves smaller; flowers ⅙"–⅓" long, white, in dense cylindrical raceme, ¾"–1½" long; calyx 5-lobed; stamens 8; June-Aug. DISTR. Yellow Pine to Subalpine belts, in wet meadows.

P. californicum, with white sepals and a rose-colored midvein, occurs in the dry foothills; several High Sierran species have greenish white or reddish flowers.

WF-20. Western Dock. *Rumex occidentalis* (pl. 8). Stems 3–6 ft., stout, smooth; leaves mostly basal, 6"–16" long, lance-shaped; flower panicles 1–2 ft. high, erect, dense, with few leaves; flowers to 3/16" long, green; sepals 6, inner 3 larger, persist around achene; stamens 6, styles 3; whole plant maturing cinnamon brown; Aug.-Sept. DISTR. In high valleys on marshy land.

Among the several other species the introduced weedy Sheep Sorrel (*R. acetosella*) is common at low elevations.

WF-21. Buckwheat. *Eriogonum nudum* (pl. 8, col. pl. 5). Stems 1–3 ft. high, erect, smooth, spreading into an open cluster; leaves 1"–2" long at base, from woody tap root, oblong-oval, hairy below; flowers on slender pedicels, 2–6 in ball-shaped head; calyx shiny, 1/12"–⅛" long, usually white, sometimes rose-colored or yellow, 6-parted; stamens 9, styles 3; July-Aug. DISTR. At all elevations in dry, usually rocky, places.

Of many other Sierran species, the Sulfur Flower (*E. umbellatum*) is most conspicuous. Its stems are 3" to 12" high, and the sulfur yellow flowers in dense heads. It blooms from June to August on dry slopes and ridges at 2500 to 10000 ft.

PURSLANE FAMILY (PORTULACACEAE). Leaves succulent; sepals 2 (to 8); petals open only in sunshine.

WF-22. Pussy Paws. *Calyptridium umbellatum* (pl. 8, col. pl. 5). Stems 3"–15", several from a dense basal rosette of spoon-shaped leaves 1"–2" long; flowers in dense terminal heads; sepals 2, papery; petals 4, pink or white; stamens 3; May-Aug. DISTR. Yellow Pine to Subalpine belts at 2500–11000 ft. in sandy or gravelly soil.

WF-23. Miner's Lettuce. *Montia perfoliata* (pl. 8). Stems 4"–10" (or 16"), several, erect, bare except for 2 leaves united into disc of ½"–2" dia. just below flower cluster; other leaves ½"–2" long, basal, narrow; flowers in a raceme, in 2's, 3's, or bundles; petals white to pinkish, ¼" long, sepals 2, petals 5, stamens 5; Feb.-May. DISTR. Below 5000 ft. in shady moist places. The basal leaves and stems were eaten as greens by Indians and miners.

PINK FAMILY (CARYOPHYLLACEAE). Nodes of stem usually swollen; leaves opposite; sepals and petals 5.

WF-24. Indian Pink. *Silene californica* (pl. 8, col. pl. 5). Stems 6"–12" (or to 3½ ft. among bushes), 1 or more, leafy; leaves 1"–3" long; narrow to broadly oval, tapering to tip; calyx tubular, 5-cleft; corolla crimson, dia. to 1", petals bent outward, deeply 4-cleft; stamens 10; styles 3–4; Mar.-Aug. DISTR. Foothill and Yellow Pine belts up to 5000 ft. in open woods of canyons.

WATER LILY FAMILY (NYMPHAEACEAE). Leaves floating or erect; flowers large.

WF-25. Indian Pond Lily. *Nymphaea polysepala* (pl. 8, col. pl. 5). Rootstock in water; leaves 7"–14" x 6"–11"; floating, heart-shaped; flower dia. 3"–5", calyx yellow or brownish-red, sepals petal-like, 9–12; petals 12–18, to ½" long, hidden under many stamens with dark red anthers; fruit dia. to 1½", ovate; Apr.-Sept. DISTR. Yellow Pine belt and higher, from Mariposa Co. n. at 4500–7500 ft. in ponds and slow streams.

BUTTERCUP FAMILY (RANUNCULACEAE). Leaves mostly palmately divided or lobed; flowers of varied forms.

WF-26. Marsh Marigold. *Caltha biflora* (pl. 9). Stems 4"–12", from fibrous rootstock; leaves roundish, 2"–4" wide, basal, on long petioles; flowers regular, white (or bluish on back); sepals 6–9, petal-like, ½" long; petals none; stamens many; pistils 5–10+; May-July. DISTR. W. slope n. to Plumas Co. at 4500–10500 ft. on wet meadows or marshy slopes.

WF-27. Red Columbine. *Aquilegia truncata* (pl. 9, col. pl. 5). Stems 1½–3½ ft., several, branching, smooth; basal leaves on long petioles, twice alternately compound, leaflets ¾"–1¾" long, deeply lobed; flowers regular, scarlet, center yellow; sepals 5, flat; petals 5, formed as hollow backward-pointing spurs; stamens many; pistils 5; Apr.-Aug. DISTR. Up to 8000 ft. in moist shaded sites.
The alpine *A. pubescens* is smaller and minutely hairy, with yellow flowers; it occurs from Mariposa to Tulare County at 9000 to 12000 feet in rocky places, blooming from June to August.

WF-28. Tall Larkspur. *Delphinium glaucum* (pl. 9). Stem 3–6 ft., stout, leafy, from root cluster; leaves 3"–5" wide, smooth, deeply 5–7 palmately parted, raceme 6"–18" long, flowers irregular, blue or purplish, many; sepals ½" long, colored, base of uppermost formed as a backward-pointing spur;

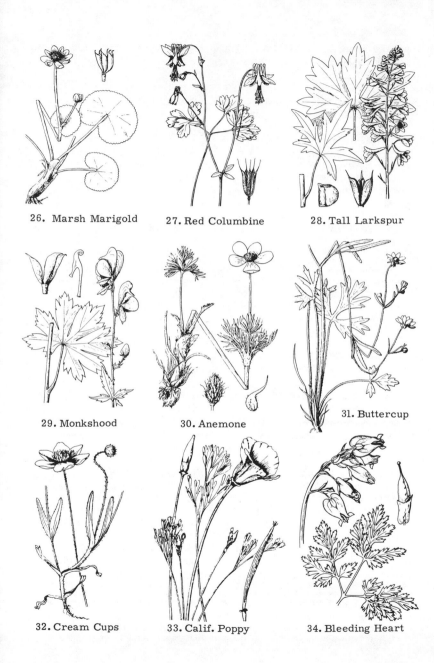

26. Marsh Marigold

27. Red Columbine

28. Tall Larkspur

29. Monkshood

30. Anemone

31. Buttercup

32. Cream Cups

33. Calif. Poppy

34. Bleeding Heart

Plate 9. Wildflowers

petals 4, the lower ones cleft to middle; stamens many; pistils 3; July-Sept. DISTR. Yellow Pine to Subalpine belts at 5000–10600 ft. along streams or in wet meadows.

The smaller *D. decorum* (col. pl. 6) with deep blue flowers blossoms in May and June; it is found in the Foothill and Yellow Pine belts at 2000 to 7000 feet.

WF-29. Monkshood. *Aconitum columbianum* (pl. 9). Stems 1½–3 ft., from thick roots; leaves roundish, 2″–3″ wide, palmately 5-lobed and subdivided; flowers in racemes, blue (rarely white or cream), irregular; sepals 5, upper one ½″ long, hooded; petals 2, hammer-shaped, hidden by hood; stamens many; pistils 3–5; July-Aug. DISTR. Mainly in Yellow Pine belt at 4000–8000 ft. in moist places, especially willow thickets.

WF-30. Anemone. *Anemone occidentalis* (pl. 9, col. pl. 6). Stems 4″–24″, hairy; leaves 5-parted and further subdivided into narrow lobes; flowers regular, white or purplish; sepals 5 (6), petal-like, oval, 1″ long; petals none; stamens many; achenes several, each with 1″ feathery tail; July–Aug. DISTR. Yellow Pine to Subalpine belts at 5500–10000 ft. on dry rocky slopes.

WF-31. Buttercup. *Ranunculus californicus* (pl. 9, col. pl. 6). Stems 9″–18″, branching, from fibrous roots; leaves with long petioles, deeply divided into many lobes, upper ones entire or with fewer lobes; flowers many, regular, dia. ¼″–½″, sepals usually 5, greenish yellow; petals 9–16, yellow, shiny; stamens 30–60; Feb.-May. DISTR. Foothill belt to 3000 ft. on moist slopes and meadows.

R. occidentalis at 2500 to 4500 feet has only 5 or 6 petals. The water buttercup (*R. aquatilis*) grows in ponds and slow streams up to 6000 feet. Its flowers, from April to July, are white with yellow centers, having 5 sepals and 5 petals.

POPPY FAMILY (PAPAVERACEAE). Sepals 2 or 3 dropping early; petals 4 or 6 (usually); stamens many.

WF-32. Cream Cups. *Platystemon californicus* (pl. 9, col. pl. 6). Stems 3″–12″, few to many, hairy, spreading from base; leaves ½″–1″ long, linear, mostly basal, opposite; flowers cream-yellow, dia. 1″; sepals 3, petals 6; Mar.-May. DISTR. Great Valley and Foothill belt, up to 5000 ft. in open grassy places.

WF-33. California Poppy. *Eschscholtzia californica* (pl. 9, col. pl. 6). Stems 9″–24″, leafy, erect or spreading; leaves 4″–12″ long including petioles, of many linear segments; flowers deep orange to pale yellow, dia. ½″–2″, petals fan-shaped, usually 4; sepals 2, united as a cap that falls when flower opens; Feb.-Sept. DISTR. Great Valley into Yellow Pine belt, up to 6500 ft. on open or grassy sites.

California's golden state flower sometimes covers whole hillsides with its bright blossoms. The scientific name honors J. F. Eschscholtz, a Rus-

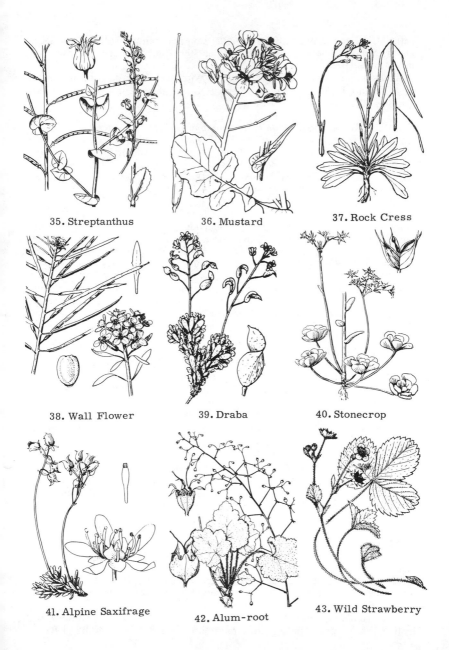

35. Streptanthus

36. Mustard

37. Rock Cress

38. Wall Flower

39. Draba

40. Stonecrop

41. Alpine Saxifrage

42. Alum-root

43. Wild Strawberry

Plate 10. Wildflowers

sian naturalist who visited California on Kotzebue's ship in 1824 and collected the first herbarium specimens of this flower.

FUMITORY FAMILY (FUMARIACEAE). Leaves alternate, compound; flowers irregular; sepals 2, small; petals 4, of 2 unlike pairs; stamens 6.

WF-34. Bleeding Heart. *Dicentra formosa* (pl. 9, col. pl. 6). Stems 8″–18″ high; leaves from creeping rootstock, compound, many-lobed, 3″–9″ long, petioles 4″–12″ long; flower cluster at tip of stem, flowers rose-purple, to ¾″ long, heart-shaped, petals joined to above middle, flared at ends; Mar.-July. DISTR. On w. slope into Yellow Pine belt at 7000 ft. in shady places; a variety growing at 7500 to 10000 feet has yellow-tinged flowers.

MUSTARD FAMILY (CRUCIFERAE). Sepals and petals 4; herbage with pungent taste.

WF-35. Streptanthus or Jewel Flower. *Streptanthus tortuosus* (pl. 10, col. pl. 6). Stems ½–4 ft., high, many-branched; leaves ½″–1½″ long, mostly oblong-ovate, clasping stem; flowers along tops of stems, pale yellow or purplish, ¼″–½″ long; May-Aug. DISTR. Foothill and Yellow Pine belts at 1000–6500 ft. on dry rocky slopes.

Small bushy varieties with purplish or yellow sepals grow at 7000 to 11500 feet.

WF-36. Mustard. *Brassica campestris* (pl. 10). Stems 1–6 ft., branched, smooth; leaves clasping stem, lower ones commonly pinnately lobed, upper leaves smaller, toothed or entire; flowers large, yellow, petals ⅜″ long; pods smooth, 1½″–2½″ long, slender, end tapered to a point; Jan.-May. DISTR. Great Valley into Subalpine belt, widespread on cleared land. An introduced weed.

No other flowering plant adds more bright color to the lowlands and hills than this showy mustard. In "black" mustard (*B. nigra*), of the lower elevations, the upper stem leaves are not clasping and the pods are conical at the end.

WF-37. Rock Cress. *Arabis holboellii* (pl. 10). Stems 1–2½ ft., simple or branched; basal leaves to 1½″ long, lance-like, mostly entire, stem leaves oblong, clasping; flowers white, pinkish, or purplish, petals ¼″–½″ long; stamens 6; pods nearly straight, 1½″–3″ long; May-July. DISTR. Yellow Pine to Subalpine belts and among piñons and junipers on e. side in dry stony places.

WF-38. Western Wall Flower. *Erysimum asperum* (pl. 10, col. pl. 6). Stem 1–2½ ft., erect, usually unbranched; leaves 1½″–5″ x ⅛″–½″, narrow, rough and hairy, entire or toothed; flower clusters terminal; flower dia. ⅓″–½″, bright orange; pod 3″–4″ x ¹⁄₁₂″, straight, 4-sided; Mar.-July. DISTR. Common below 8000 ft. on rocky slopes; a smaller yellow-flowered form grows at 7000–12000 ft.

WF-39. Draba. *Draba lemmonii* (pl. 10). Stems 1–3¼", from a compact leafy cushion; leaves ⅛"–½" long, entire, thick, oblong, base narrow, densely clustered; raceme short, flowers yellow, ⅛" long; pod ovate, ¼"–⅓", twisted; July-Aug. DISTR. Subalpine and Alpine belts at 8500–13000 ft., often in rock clefts; other alpine species have white flowers.

STONECROP FAMILY (CRASSULACEAE). Leaves succulent; sepals, petals, and pistils 5; stamens 10.

WF-40. Stonecrop. *Sedum obtusatum* (pl. 10, col. pl. 6). A mat-like succulent; stems 3"–6", erect; leaves to 1" x ¼", thick, in basal rosettes; flowers clustered, petals ¼"–⅜" long, yellow or white, joined at base into a tube; June-July. DISTR. Yellow Pine to Alpine belt, Tulare to Nevada Co. at 5000–13000 ft. on rocky slopes.

S. spathulifolium, living on shaded moss-covered rocks, has petals separate to the base.

SAXIFRAGE FAMILY (SAXIFRAGACEAE). Leaves mostly basal; sepals and petals 5; ovary superior or inferior.

WF-41. Alpine Saxifrage. *Saxifraga oregana* (pl. 10). Stems 1–3 ft., bare; leaves 2"–7" long, oblong-oval, narrowed at base, mostly in cluster at base of stem; flowers in terminal clusters, white, petals ⅛"–⅓" long; calyx 5-cleft; stamens 10; styles 2; May-Aug. DISTR. Yellow Pine to Subalpine belts at 3500–11000 ft. in wet meadows.

Dwarf species grow at high elevations and *S. californica,* 6 to 15 inches high, is common mostly below 2500 feet on shaded grassy banks.

WF-42. Alum-root. *Heuchera micrantha* (pl. 10). Stems 1–3 ft., hairy; leaves mostly basal, 1"–3½" long, rounded and shallowly lobed, hairy, petioles long; flowers in open loose panicle, to ⅛" long, white or reddish; calyx bell-shaped, greenish; stamens 5; styles 2; May-July. DISTR. Yellow Pine and Lodgepole–fir belts at 2500–7000 ft. on moist banks.

A smaller species (*H. rubescens*), 5 to 12 inches high with reddish calyx and longer flowers, inhabits dry rocky places mainly on the east slope at 6000 to 11900 feet, reaching Alpine fell-fields.

ROSE FAMILY (ROSACEAE). Sepals and petals 5; stamens 10 to many; pistils 1 to many.

WF-43. Wild Strawberry. *Fragaria californica* (pl. 10). Stems 4"–5", often as runners, rooting at joints; leaves basal, each with 3 leaflets 1"–1¼" long, roundly ovate, coarsely toothed, densely silky below; flowers clustered, white, dia. ½"–1"; calyx persistent, with 5 small bracts alternate with lobes; stamens about 20; pistils many; berry dia. ⅜", red; Mar.-June. DISTR. Foothill and Yellow Pine belts below 7000 ft. in shaded damp places.

The scarlet strawberry (*F. platypetala*), at 4000 to 10500 feet, blooms from May to July. Cultivated strawberries have escaped in places; some may be from roots brought by early settlers. Cultivated or wild, strawberries in the Sierra are of delicious flavor.

WF-44. Yellow Cinquefoil. *Potentilla glandulosa* (pl. 11, col. pl. 7). Stems 6"–4 ft., branching, erect, glandular; often reddish; leaves mainly basal, 4"–8" long, those at top smaller; 5–9 leaflets 1"–3" long, roundish ovate, edges notched; flowers terminal, pale yellow, dia. ⅓"–½"; stamens 20+; pistils 10–80, ripening to form dry achenes; May-Aug. DISTR. Widespread from foothills to 12400 ft. in many habitats.

There are many other species, the herbage being hairy and sticky in some. The Marsh Potentilla (*P. palustris*) has purplish flowers, and those of *P. lactea* are white or cream-colored.

PEA FAMILY (LEGUMINOSAE). Leaves usually compound; flowers irregular, butterfly-like; corolla of 5 petals (an upper banner, 2 wings at sides, and 2 below joined as a keel); stamens 10.

WF-45. Lupine. Genus *Lupinus* (pl. 11). Annual or perennial; stems short and single or many branches and bushy; leaves palmately compound, alternate, leaflets usually 5–17; flowers in terminal racemes, mostly blue or purple, a few yellow or white; calyx 2-lipped; fruit a 2-sided pod (legume), with row of 2–12 seeds. Many (60–80) species in California; a few Sierran species are mentioned here.

a. Brewer Lupine. *L. breweri* (pl. 11). To 9" high in gray, leafy mats; flower clusters dense, to 2" long; flowers ¼" long, blue, banner with white center; June-Aug. DISTR. Yellow Pine to Subalpine belts at 4000–11000 ft. on dry stony slopes.

b. Bush Lupine. *L. albifrons* (col. pl. 7). Ht. 2–5 ft., bushy, leaves silvery-silky; flower clusters 3"–12" long, open; flowers to ⅓" long; petals blue to red-purple, banner white- or yellow-centered; Mar.-June. DISTR. Foothills to 5000 ft.

c. *L. stiversii*. Ht. 6"–18"; flowers with yellow banner and rose-pink wings; Apr.-July. DISTR. Foothill and Yellow Pine belts at 1600–4600 ft. in sandy places.

WF-46. Clover. Genus *Trifolium*. Stems erect or spreading; leaves palmate, leaflets generally 3; flowers in heads, white, yellow, pink, red, or purple; calyx 5-toothed, lobes usually equal; pods spherical to elongate, 1–3-seeded.

There are many species in the Sierra. Carpet Clover and Tomcat Clover and their relatives have bracts just below the flower heads, whereas the introduced species and some others lack these. The Red Clover (*T. pratense*) and White Clover (*T. repens*), both introduced, are around settlements.

a. Carpet Clover. *T. monanthum* (pl. 11). Stems many, 1"–4", spreading; leaflets 1/12"–⅓" long, ovate to lance-shaped; flowers 1–2 (or 4) in a cluster,

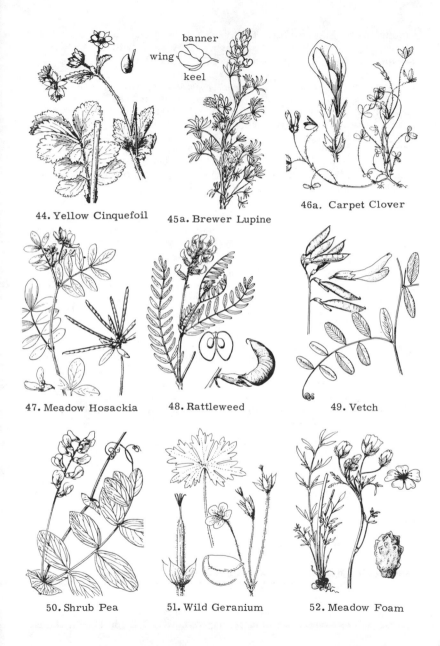

banner

wing

keel

44. Yellow Cinquefoil

45a. Brewer Lupine

46a. Carpet Clover

47. Meadow Hosackia

48. Rattleweed

49. Vetch

50. Shrub Pea

51. Wild Geranium

52. Meadow Foam

Plate 11. Wildflowers

½″ long, white (often pink-veined) with purple centers; June-Aug. DISTR. Yellow Pine to Subalpine belts, 5000–11500 ft. in wet places.

b. Tomcat Clover. *T. tridentatum*. Stems 4″–20″; leaflets ½″–⅜″ long, linear to oblong; toothed at edges; corolla ½″ long, red-purple; Mar.-June. DISTR. Foothill to lower Yellow Pine belts below 5000 ft. in grassy places.

WF-47. Meadow Hosackia. *Lotus torreyi* (pl. 11). Stems 8″–20″, slender, erect; herbage with short hairs; leaves pinnately compound, 7–11 leaflets ½″–¾″ long, lance-like to elliptic, tapered at both ends; flowers solitary or in small clusters, ⅖″–⅗″ long, yellow with white keel and wings; calyx teeth 5, nearly equal; pods straight, 1″–1½″ x 1⁄12″, slightly bent, tips short; May-Sept. DISTR. Foothill to Lodgepole–fir belts below 8500 ft. in wet places.

WF-48. Rattleweed. *Astragalus bolanderi* (pl. 11). Stems 9″–12″, many, erect; herbage hairy; leaves 3″–6″ long, pinnately compound, leaflets 9–23, linear-oblong, ¼″–1″ long; flowers 6–12 in terminal raceme; calyx 5-toothed; corolla ½″ long, white or tinged with purple; pod to ⅚″ long, curved, on stalk longer than calyx; seeds 12–14; June-Aug. DISTR. Mostly in Lodgepole–fir belt at 5200–10000 ft. on dry stony places and sand flats.

There are many species, some (*A. congdoni*) in the Foothill belt and others on the east side amid piñons and junipers. The plants are called rattleweed from the rattling of dried seeds in the inflated pod. The name, "locoweed" refers to the effects of some poisonous species on livestock.

WF-49. Vetch. *Vicia americana* (pl. 11). Stems 2–3 ft. trailing or climbing by 4-sided tendrils; leaves pinnately compound, of 4–11 leaflets ½″–1¼″ long, ovate; flowers ¾″ long, 4–8 in a raceme, purplish aging to bluish; calyx 5-toothed, 3 lower teeth longer; banner oblong, wings united to middle of keel; style with tuft of hairs around tip; pod 1¼″–2″ long, flat; Apr.-June. DISTR. Foothills below 5000 ft. in open places.

The smaller *V. californica* with hairy pods and smaller flowers grows at 2000–8000 ft. Several introduced weed vetches are found in lowland cultivated areas.

WF-50. Shrub Pea. *Lathyrus sulphureus* (pl. 11, col. pl. 7). Stems 1–2 ft., stout; leaves pinnately compound, ending in branched tendrils; leaflets 6–12, not paired, ¾″–2″ long; flowers 6–25, in crowded raceme; upper calyx teeth short; corolla ½″ long, dull white or banner pinkish, turning yellowish-brown; pods 1⅗″–3″ x ⅕″; Apr.-July. DISTR. Foothill to Lodgepole–fir belts below 8000 ft. on dry slopes.

Other species grow at middle elevations, and introduced forms, including the Sweet Pea, are in cultivated areas.

GERANIUM FAMILY (GERANIACEAE). Sepals and petals 5; stamens 10.

WF-51. Wild Geranium. *Geranium californicum* (pl. 11). Stems 1–3, 8″–24″ high, forking; herbage hairy, glandular; leaves 1″–4″ wide, palmately 3–5 parted, the divisions cleft; lower petioles 2"–10" long; petals ½"–⅓" long, rose-pink to white, dark-veined; June-July. DISTR. Yellow Pine and Lodgepole–fir belts at 4000–8000 ft. in damp woods and meadows.

MEADOW FOAM FAMILY (LIMNANTHACEAE). Sepals and petals 5; stamens 10; stigmas 5.

WF-52. Meadow Foam. *Limnanthes alba* (pl. 11). Stems 4"–12", simple or branched from base; leaves 1"–4" long including petioles; flowers solitary; calyx white-woolly; corolla bowl-shaped; petals ½" long, white, often rose-tinted at tips; nutlets reddish brown; Apr.-June. DISTR. Foothill and Yellow Pine belts, Merced Co. n. at 50–4000 ft. near spring pools or in moist places.

MALLOW FAMILY (MALVACEAE). Sepals and petals 5; stamens united into a tube.

WF-53. Wild Hollyhock. *Sidalcea reptans* (pl. 12). Stems 1–4 ft., rough with short hairs, reclining at base and often rooted at lower joints; leaves 1"–1½" broad, roundish in outline, lower ones lobed, upper leaves deeply parted; flowers in open raceme; petals ½"–¾" long, notched at tip, deep rose-purple; stamens many; pistil 1; July-Aug. DISTR. Yellow Pine and Lodgepole–fir belts, Amador to Tulare Co., 4000–7600 ft. in wet meadows.
Other Sierran species have the stems smooth or with very short hairs.

ST. JOHN'S WORT FAMILY (HYPERICACEAE). Leaves opposite, black-dotted; sepals and petals 5.

WF-54. St. John's Wort. *Hypericum formosum* (pl. 12). Stems 1–3 ft., erect, slender; leaves ½"–1¼" long, ovate or oblong, black-dotted on edges; flowers ½"–¾" dia., in branching clusters; sepals ⅛" long, ovate, black-dotted; petals ⅓" long, yellow; stamens many, in 3 groups; capsules ¼" long, 3-lobed; seeds brownish; June-Aug. DISTR. Mostly in Yellow Pine belt at 4000–7500 ft. in wet meadows; occasional in chaparral.
The introduced Klamath Weed (*H. perforatum*) has narrow sepals, the capsule is unlobed, and the seeds are shiny black. It occurs in pastures and partially cleared areas below 4500 ft. from Tuolumne County north. Poisonous to livestock, it has been eradicated over large areas by leaf beetles (I-128; *Chrysolina*) that help to control the plant in its native Europe.

VIOLET FAMILY (VIOLACEAE). Flowers slightly irregular; sepals 5; petals 5, unequal; 2 upper, 2 lateral, 1 lower spurred at base; stamens 5; stigma 1.

WF-55. Violet. *Viola adunca* (pl. 12). Stems leafy, to 8" long; leaves ⅓"–1" long, round-ovate to heart-shaped, edges toothed; petals ⅓"–½" long,

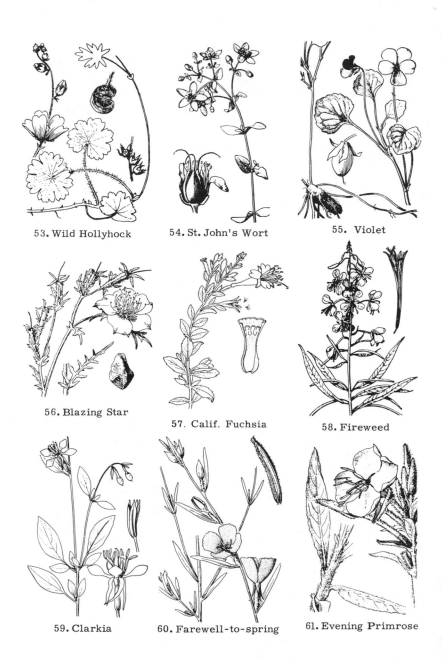

53. Wild Hollyhock

54. St. John's Wort

55. Violet

56. Blazing Star

57. Calif. Fuchsia

58. Fireweed

59. Clarkia

60. Farewell-to-spring

61. Evening Primrose

Plate 12. Wildflowers   91

violet turning purple, the side petals white-bearded; Mar.-July. DISTR. Yellow Pine and Lodgepole–fir belts, 3300–8500 ft. on damp banks and in meadows.

A dwarf variety with stems less than 2″ long grows in the Subalpine and Alpine belts at 9000 to 11500 ft. The Golden Violet (*V. pedunculata*), with yellow petals, blooms from February to April on grassy hillsides in the foothills below 2500 feet.

LOASA FAMILY (LOASACEAE). Stinging hairs on leaves; calyx 5-lobed; petals 5; style 1; ovary inferior.

WF-56. Blazing Star. *Mentzelia lindleyi* (pl. 12, col. pl. 7). Stems 6″–24″, simple or branching; leaves 2″–3″ long, pinnately lobed, the lobes mostly toothed, with barbed hairs that stick to clothing; flowers in leaf axils or terminal; petals 1″–1½″ long, ovate, tips narrow, golden yellow with red bases; stamens many, shorter than petals, about 15 enlarged at base of filament; seeds angled, covered with small tubercles; Apr.-June. DISTR. Foothill belt below 2500 ft., Tulare to Tuolumne Co. on rocky canyon slopes.

M. laevicaulis which blooms from June to October, is widespread and up to 8500 feet, including the east slope. It has narrower petals and 5 filaments enlarged at the base.

EVENING PRIMROSE FAMILY (ONAGRACEAE). Flowers usually regular; sepals and petals 4; stamens 8, pollen cobwebby; ovary inferior.

WF-57. California Fuchsia. *Zauschneria latifolia* (pl. 12, col. pl. 7). Stems 4″–20″, hairy; leaves ¾″–1¾″ x ½″, ovate to elliptic; flowers 1″–1½″ long, tubular; petals ⅛″–⅗″ long, 2-cleft; stamens project beyond corolla; sepals and petals red; capsule linear, 4-angled; seeds with tuft of hairs at one end; Aug.-Sept. DISTR. Yellow Pine to Subalpine belts, 5000–10000 ft. on dry slopes and ridges.

WF-58. Fireweed. *Epilobium angustifolium* (pl. 12, col. pl. 7). Stem 2–6 ft., erect; leaves 4″–6″ long, narrow, lance-like; flowers in long racemes; calyx cleft nearly to ovary; corolla slightly irregular, lilac-purple; petals ½″–⅔″ long, slightly notched at tips; stamens purple, filaments expanded at base, style longer than stamens; ovary 4-celled; seeds with long tuft of hairs at tip; July-Sept. DISTR. Yellow Pine and Lodgepole–fir belts below 9000 ft. on moist ground, especially in fire-swept areas.

Related forms occur from the foothills to 13000 feet and amidst piñons and junipers on the east slope. In some species the petals are deeply lobed and white or pinkish.

WF-59. Clarkia. *Clarkia rhomboidea* (pl. 12). Stem 1–3 ft., erect; leaves ½″–2″ x ¼″–¾″, oblong to ovate, petioles short; flowers in terminal racemes, rose-purple; petals ¼″–½″ long, with short broad lobe at base; stamens 8, those opposite petals short; stigma 4-lobed; ovary 4-celled; capsule 1″

long, straight or slightly curved; May-July. DISTR. Foothills to Lodgepole–fir belt below 8000 ft. on dry slopes.

Other species throughout the Sierra have flowers that are lavender, pink, purple or white.

WF-60. Farewell-to-spring. *Clarkia* (or *Godetia*) *viminea* (pl. 12, col. pl. 7). Stems 1–3 ft., erect, simple or few-branched; leaves ½"–2" long, linear or lance-shaped, usually narrowed basally to a short petiole; buds erect; flowers in leafy spike; calyx funnel-shaped, ¼"–½" long, lobes narrow, sharp-tipped; petals ½"–1" long, purplish or crimson, with large purple splotch in center or at tip and yellow at base; stamens 8, about half the length of petals; style as long or longer than stamens; ovary 4-celled; capsule straight; May-July. DISTR. Foothill and Yellow Pine belts, 1300–5000 ft. in dry open places.

WF-61. Evening Primrose. *Oenothera hookeri* (pl. 12, col. pl. 7). Stems 2–4 ft., stout, erect; herbage minutely hairy; leaves 4"–9" long, ovate to lance-shaped; calyx tube with lobes bent down; petals 1"–2" long and equally broad, yellow aging to orange-red; stamens 8; anthers attached near middle; stigma 1, with 4 slender lobes; ovary 4-celled; seeds angled; June-Sept. DISTR. Yellow Pine and Lodgepole–fir belts, 3000–9000 ft. in moist places.

The Evening Primrose is a favorite browse for deer. It blooms in the early evening. A foothill species (*O. venusta*) grows to 8 feet high and has green flower tube and sepals.

WF-62. Gayophytum. *Gayophytum diffusum* (pl. 13). Stems 6"–24", widely branched; bark papery; leaves ½"–2" long, linear or lance-shaped; flowers in leafy racemes, widely spaced along branchlets; calyx lobes bent at tips; petals to ¼" long, white turning pink with age, 2 small yellow dots at base; stamens 8; capsule 4-valved, up to ¼" long; seeds naked; June-Aug. DISTR. Yellow Pine to Subalpine belts, 3000–11000 ft. on dry slopes.

Other forms occur over the same range, and one species grows among piñons and junipers on the east side.

PARSLEY FAMILY (UMBELLIFERAE). Leaves compound; stems hollow; flowers in umbels; calyx usually 5-lobed; petals and stamens 5, stamens alternating with petals; ovary inferior, 2-celled; styles 2; fruit of 2 carpels, each with 5 ribs or ridges and small oil tubes in the fruit wall.

WF-63. Queen Anne's Lace. *Eulophus bolanderi* (pl. 13). Stems 1–2 ft., nearly naked; leaves 2"–6" long, triangular, pinnately divided in 3's, terminal lobes linear; flowers small, white, many, lacy in appearance, in compound umbels, peduncles long; fruit oblong, ribbed; June-Aug. DISTR. Yellow Pine to Subalpine belts, 3000–10500 ft. in meadows.

A foothill species (*E. californicus*) with leaves 6 to 10 inches long grows in meadows and along streams below 3000 feet from Stanislaus to Mariposa County.

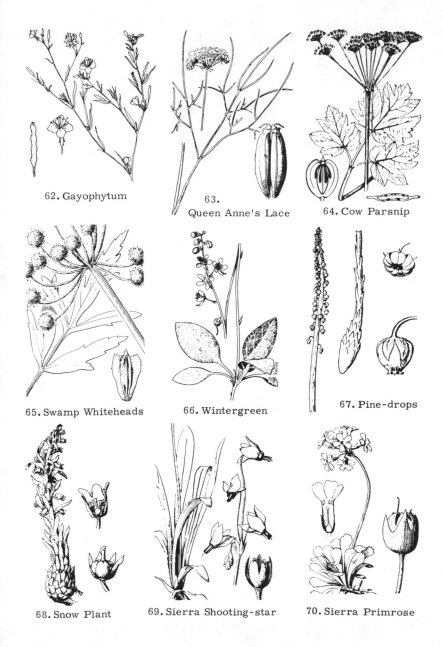

62. Gayophytum

63.
Queen Anne's Lace

64. Cow Parsnip

65. Swamp Whiteheads

66. Wintergreen

67. Pine-drops

68. Snow Plant

69. Sierra Shooting-star

70. Sierra Primrose

Plate 13. Wildflowers

WF-64. Cow Parsnip. *Heracleum lanatum* (pl. 13, col. pl. 7). Stems stout, 4–5 ft.; leaves palmately compound, petioles 4"–16" long, 3 leaflets 3"–6" across, broadly heart-shaped, lobed and toothed; flowers small, white, in compound umbel 6"–10" in dia.; fruit ⅓"–½" long, flat, rounded, with thin lateral ribs; Apr.-July. DISTR. Yellow Pine and Lodgepole–fir belts below 9000 ft. in moist or shady places.

WF-65. Swamp Whiteheads. *Sphenosciadium capitellatum* (pl. 13). Stems stout, 3–5 ft.; leaves 4"–16" long, pinnately compound, leaflets ½"–5" x ⅕"–2", narrowly ovate to lance-shaped, toothed; flowers white (rarely purplish), in compact balls on "stems" 1"–4" long; fruit tapering to tip, flattened, ribbed, and winged; July-Aug. DISTR. Yellow Pine to Subalpine belts at 3000–10400 ft. in swampy places.

HEATH FAMILY (ERICACEAE). Leaves basal or reduced to scales; sepals and petals 5; stamens 10; style 1.

WF-66. Wintergreen. *Pirola picta* (pl. 13). Stem 6"–15"; leaves 1"–2¼" long, basal, ovate or elliptic, evergreen, mottled or white-veined; flowers in terminal raceme, nodding, green-white; corolla nearly ½" dia., petals separate, concave; June-Aug. DISTR. Yellow Pine and Lodgepole–fir belts, 3000–9500 ft. growing in humus of dry forests.

WF-67. Pine-drops. *Pterospora andromedea* (pl. 13, col. pl. 8). Stem 1–4 ft., erect, stout, fleshy, sticky; leaves reduced to reddish-brown scales; flowers many in dense raceme, white; calyx deeply 5-parted; corolla ¼" long, urn-shaped, petals united, with 5 short bent lobes; June-Aug. DISTR. Yellow Pine and Lodgepole–fir belts, 2600–8500 ft. in forest humus.

This plant, a reddish-brown saprophyte, dies after flowering.

WF-68. Snow Plant. *Sarcodes sanguinea* (pl. 13, col. pl. 8). Stem 9"–18" high and 1" or more thick, erect, stout, fleshy; leaves reduced to reddish scales; flowers ½"–¾" long, crowded along stem in a raceme; corolla ¼"–⅓" long, red, fleshy, bell-shaped, with 5 outwardly bent rounded lobes; May-July. DISTR. Yellow Pine and Lodgepole–fir belts, 4000–8000 ft. growing in forest humus, often at edges of melting snow banks.

This unusual plant, with its bright red color against a carpet of pine needles, never fails to attract attention. Like Pine-drops it is a saprophyte, living on decayed organic matter.

PRIMROSE FAMILY (PRIMULACEAE). Leaves basal; flowers regular, the parts in 4's or 5's; stamens on tube at base of corolla opposite lobes.

WF-69. Sierra Shooting-star. *Dodecatheon jeffreyi* (pl. 13, col. pl. 8). Stems 12"–21", with an umbel of 5–15 nodding flowers; leaves basal, 2"–15" long, oblong to lance-shaped, tapering basally to winged petioles; corolla ⅔"–1" long with short tube and widened throat; petals long, bent backwards, pink-crimson, yellow at base, edged with purple; stamens on throat of corolla; filaments united below; June-Aug. DISTR. Yellow Pine to Subalpine belts, 2300–10000 ft. in wet places.

Other species of Shooting-star range from the foothills to Alpine fellfields.

WF-70. Sierra Primrose. *Primula suffrutescens* (pl. 13, col. pl. 8). Stem 2″–4″, creeping, with leaves basal and an umbel of several flowers; leaves ¾″–1½″ long, narrowly wedge-shaped, toothed at tip; calyx 5-lobed; corolla ½″–¾″ long, dia. to 1″, tubular, with 5 notched lobes bent outward, redpurple with yellow throat; July-Aug. DISTR. Subalpine and Alpine belts, 8000–13500 ft., Nevada to Tulare Co., often under overhanging rocks and cliffs.

Only hikers in the High Sierra will see the deep-colored display of this attractive flower in late summer.

GENTIAN FAMILY (GENTIANACEAE). Leaves opposite; lobes of calyx and corolla 4, stamens 4.

WF-71. Sierra Gentian. *Gentiana holopetala* (pl. 14). Stems 4″–14″, several from base, leafy below, each ending with 1 flower; leaves ½″–1½″ long, those on stems linear and acute, those at base broader; flowers ½″–2″ long; corolla funnel-form, its 4 or 5 lobes broad, blue; July-Sept. DISTR. Yellow Pine to Subalpine belts at 6000–11000 ft. in wet meadows.

Other gentians occur down to 4000 feet and as high as 12200 feet. In some the corolla is dotted with greenish white or yellow and the corolla lobes are notched or finely toothed.

DOGBANE FAMILY (APOCYNACEAE). Leaves opposite; sepals, petals, and stamens 5; pistils 2; juice milky.

WF-72. Mountain Hemp. *Apocynum androsaemifolium.* Stems 5″–15″, many-branched; leaves ¾″–1½″ long, ovate with round to heart-shaped base, dark green above, pale below, petioles short; flowers mostly in short clusters; calyx short, deeply 5-cleft; corolla nearly ¼″ long, tubular, with 5 broadly oblong lobes, red-purple to pinkish white; June-Aug. DISTR. Yellow Pine to Subalpine belts at 5000–9500 ft. on dry flats and slopes.

The Indian Hemp (*A. cannabinum;* pl. 14) is taller (2–4 feet) with a greenish white corolla. It grows along streams below 5000 feet, blooming from May to July, and is poisonous to cattle. The fiber prepared from the stems is fine, long, and strong. The Indians used it to make twine, fish lines, and small baskets.

MILKWEED FAMILY (ASCLEPIADACEAE). Leaves opposite or whorled; calyx and corolla 5-lobed; stamens 5, united as tube on base of corolla; juice milky.

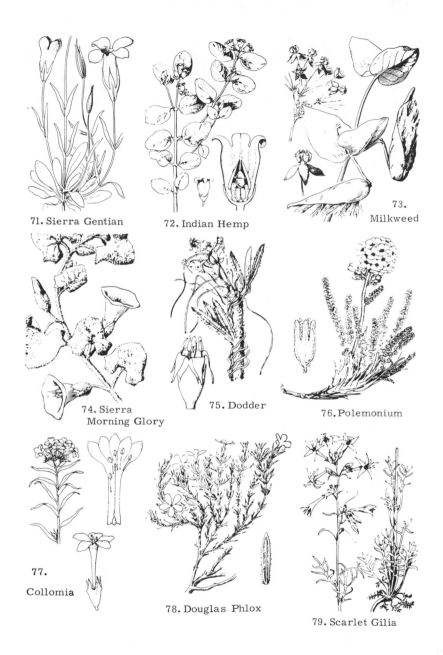

71. Sierra Gentian

72. Indian Hemp

73. Milkweed

74. Sierra Morning Glory

75. Dodder

76. Polemonium

77. Collomia

78. Douglas Phlox

79. Scarlet Gilia

Plate 14. Wildflowers   97

WF-73. Milkweed. *Asclepias cordifolia* (pl. 14). Stems 1½–2½ ft., erect, branching only at base; leaves 2½"–6" x 1½"–4", mostly opposite, ovate to lance-shaped, with heart-shaped clasping base; flowers many in loose umbels; corolla with 5 lobes bent backward, lobes ¼"–⅓" long, dark reddish purple; filaments united in a circle of 5 hoods; pods 2"–5" long, tapering; seeds each with tuft of silky hairs; May-July. DISTR. Foothill and Yellow Pine belts, 500–6300 ft. on open or wooded slopes.

Other species grow at middle elevations. All have a milky juice and most are poisonous to livestock, like the Narrow-leaf Milkweed (*A. fascicularis*). Stem of the Showy Milkweed (*A. speciosa*) yield a strong white fiber called "hook-ken" by the Indians, who also boiled down the milky juice to make a chewing gum. Insects of the milkweed may share the poisonous properties of the plant, for they advertise their presence to birds and other enemies by red, orange, and blue colors; the conspicuous Monarch Butterfly (I-90) is "mimicked" in some regions by the presumably tasty Viceroy.

MORNING GLORY FAMILY (CONVOLVULACEAE). Leaves alternate or reduced; sepals 5, often unequal; corolla 5-lobed; stamens 5; pistil 1.

WF-74. Sierra Morning Glory. *Convolvulus villosus* (pl. 14). Stems trailing, 3"–12" long, leafy; herbage velvety; leaves ½"–1" long, triangular or heart-shaped, petioled; flowers from leaf axils; calyx enclosed by 2 bracts; corolla 1"–1½" long, funnel-form, 5-angled, cream-colored; June-Aug. DISTR. Mostly in Yellow Pine belt but extending into Foothill belt and up to Lodgepole–fir belt at 1000–7500 ft. on steep dry slopes.

WF-75. Dodder. *Cuscuta californica* (pl. 14). Stems slender, twining, yellow to orange, fastened by suckers and parasitic on other plants; leaves reduced to minute scales; flowers ½"–⅓" long, in loose cymes, waxy-white; calyx colored like corolla, deeply 5–cleft; corolla nearly globose, with 5 slender narrow lobes; May-Aug. DISTR. Foothill to Lodgepole–fir belts, below 8200 ft. on many herbs and shrubs.

This apparently leafless plant lacks green coloring (chlorophyll). It germinates in the soil but later becomes completely parasitic on other plants, covering them as an orange or yellow mat.

GILIA FAMILY . (POLEMONIACEAE). Leaves alternate or opposite; calyx and corolla 5-lobed; stamens 5, inserted on corolla, alternate with its lobes.

WF-76. Polemonium. *Polemonium eximium* (pl. 14). Stems several, 2"–9", simple, erect; leaves in dense basal tuft, 1"–5" long, sticky and musky, pinnately compound; leaflets 1/25"–⅕" long, many, palmately divided into 2–5 elliptic lobes; flowers showy, clustered in a head; corolla ½"–⅗" long, basal tube white, roundish lobes blue and about twice as long as tube; July-Aug. DISTR. Alpine belt from Tuolumne to Tulare Co. on dry rocky ridges; other species at 2000–10000 ft.

WF-77. Collomia. *Collomia grandiflora* (pl. 14). Stem 8″–36″, erect; leaves 1″–3″ long, linear or lance-shaped; flowers crowded in head-like clusters at ends of stems with leafy bracts below; corolla 1″ long, trumpet-shaped, pale salmon color, creamy yellow or white, tube 3 times length of calyx and lobes broadly oblong; Apr.-July. DISTR. Foothill to Lodgepole–fir belts below 8000 ft. on dry slopes.

WF-78. Douglas Phlox. *Phlox douglasii* (pl. 14, col. pl. 8). Stems leafy, creeping, forming dense green mats 1″–3″ high by 3″–10″ dia.; leaves ¼″–½″ long, linear, rigid, sharp-pointed; flowers solitary in upper leaf axils; calyx ⅓″–½″ long, lobes about as long as tube (which later is ruptured by seed capsule); corolla about ⅚″ long, white, lavender, or pink, its base tubular, throat narrow, outer parts of petals bent at right angles forming a disc; Apr.-May. DISTR. Yellow Pine to Subalpine belts, 4700–10300 ft. on rocky ledges or sandy slopes.

Other species range from 1500 to 13000 feet, growing in the Alpine fell-fields and on the dry east side amid piñon pine and juniper.

WF-79. Scarlet Gilia. *Gilia* (or *Ipomopsis*) *aggregata* (pl. 14, col. pl. 8). Stems 1–2½ ft., erect, usually simple, minutely hairy; leaves 1″–2″ long, mostly alternate, pinnately divided into narrow linear lobes ⅖″–⅘″ long; flowers in long panicle; calyx ⅛″–¼″ long, lobes lance-shaped, twice as long as tube; corolla ¾″–1¼″ long, tubular, spreading, throat open, lobes ⅓″–½″ long, tapering to sharp tips; reddish to pink or white, rarely yellow; June-Aug. DISTR. Yellow Pine to Subalpine belts at 3500–10300 ft. on open sandy flats and rocky ridges.

WF-80. Mustang Clover. *Linanthus montanus* (pl. 15). Stem 4″–22″, erect, usually simple, hairy; leaves opposite, palmately 5–7 parted into lance-like or linear lobes ¼″–1¼″ long; flowers crowded in heads, with bristly bracts below; calyx ⅖″ long, about ⅓ as long as corolla tube, lobes awl-shaped; corolla 1″–1⅕″ long, funnel-form, red, pink, or white with purple spot on each lobe and yellow throat, lobes ¼″ long; May-Aug. DISTR. Foothill and Yellow Pine belts at 1000–5000 ft. Nevada Co. to Kern Co. in dry, gravelly places.

PHACELIA FAMILY (HYDROPHYLLACEAE). Leaves opposite or alternate; calyx and corolla 5-lobed; stamens 5, alternate with corolla lobes.

WF-81. Baby Blue Eyes. *Nemophila menziesii* (pl. 15, col. pl. 8). Stems 3″–18″, branching from base; leaves opposite, ⅘″–2″ long, oval to oblong in outline, pinnately divided into 5–11 divisions, the latter mostly 2- or 3-lobed, upper leaves less divided; flowers on slender pedicels, solitary, in upper axils or opposite leaves; calyx lobes ⅙″–½″ long, with bent appendage between lobes; corolla ½″–1″ dia., blue, center paler and often dotted; Feb.-June. DISTR. Foothills and lower Yellow Pine belt to 5000 ft. on moist flats and slopes.

Among other foothill species the "Five-spot" (*N. maculata*) has whit-

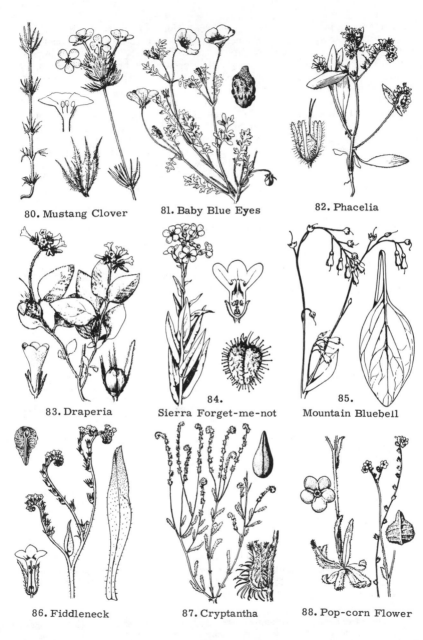

80. Mustang Clover

81. Baby Blue Eyes

82. Phacelia

83. Draperia

84.
Sierra Forget-me-not

85.
Mountain Bluebell

86. Fiddleneck

87. Cryptantha

88. Pop-corn Flower

Plate 15. Wildflowers

ish flowers with a large purple spot at the tip of each corolla lobe. The dwarfed *N. spatulata* has stems 1″–2½″ long, mostly 3-lobed leaves, and a small purple spot at the tip of each lobe. It ranges from 5000 to 9000 feet in the Yellow Pine and Lodgepole–fir belts from Nevada to Tulare counties.

WF-82. Phacelia. *Phacelia humilis* (pl. 15, col. pl. 8). Stems 2″–8″, one or several from base, usually branched; leaves 1″–1½″ long, mostly alternate, lance-shaped, minutely hairy and glandular; flowers in dense curved racemes; calyx lobes ⅛″–⅕″ long, linear to narrowly oblong; corolla ⅙″–¼″ long, bell-shaped, bluish with white center; stamens slightly longer than corolla tube; capsule 4–6 seeded, the seeds pitted; May-July. DISTR. Yellow Pine and Lodgepole–fir belts, 4000–8300 ft. on sandy or rocky slopes.

Other species range from the foothills to above timberline, some with flowers in open racemes but usually in coiled clusters.

WF-83. Draperia. *Draperia systyla* (pl. 15). Stems several, 4″–16″; leaves 1″–2″ long, silky-hairy, opposite, ovate; flowers crowded in terminal cyme; calyx deeply divided, lobes ⅙″–¼″ long, linear; corolla about ½″ long, funnel-form, pale violet, lobes 1⁄12″–⅛″ long, rounded; stamens short, unequal; May-Aug. DISTR. Yellow Pine and Lodgepole–fir belts at 2400–8000 ft. on dry slopes in woods.

BORAGE FAMILY (BORAGINACEAE). Flowers regular, in 1-sided coiled spikes; calyx and corolla 5-lobed; stamens alternating with corolla lobes; fruit of 4 nutlets.

WF-84. Sierra Forget-me-not. *Lappula velutina* (pl. 15, col. pl. 8). Stems 1–2 ft., erect; herbage velvety; leaves 1″–3″ long, oblong, tapering to tip, petioles short or none; flowers ⅛″–⅓″ dia. in loose raceme, blue or pink; calyx lobes oblong, ¼″ long; corolla tube ⅐″–⅕″ long, much exceeding calyx, its lobes rounded; nutlets ¼″ long, evenly armed with prickles on upper side; June-Aug. DISTR. Mostly in Lodgepole–fir belt at 5000–10000 ft., from Tulare to Mariposa Co. on dry wooded slopes.

Of several other species, *L. setosa* has the corolla about ½ inch in diameter and the nutlets with few short prickles. It grows mostly in the Yellow Pine belt from 1000–6000 feet from Sierra County northward. The alpine *L. sharsmithii,* less than one foot high, occurs near Mt. Whitney at 10750 to 12000 feet, blooming from July to September.

WF-85. Mountain Bluebell. *Mertensia ciliata* (pl. 15). Stems 2–5 ft., several, erect; leaves 2″–7″ x ¾″–1½″, oblong or ovate, narrowed to broad petiole or without petiole; flowers in racemes, drooping; calyx lobes shorter than corolla; oblong to linear; corolla tubular, about ½″ long, light blue with small yellow-tipped crests in opening of tube; style extends beyond corolla; nutlets not barbed; May-Aug. DISTR. Yellow Pine to Subalpine belts at 5000–10200 ft. in moist shady places.

WF-86. Fiddleneck. *Amsinckia intermedia* (pl. 15, col. pl. 9). Stem 1–2 ft., branching, erect or bent downward; herbage pale yellowish green, hairy; leaves 1″–6″ long, oblong, tapering; flowers in long curved spikes, yellow; peduncles short or none; calyx lobes 3–5, slender; corolla ⅓″–⅖″ long, 1/12″–¼″ broad at tip; nutlets ridged and granular; Mar.-June. DISTR. Mostly in Foothill belt below 5000 ft. in grassy open spaces.

Fiddleneck may grow among other plants or grasses but also in nearly pure stands when its blossoms color whole hillsides.

WF-87. Cryptantha. *Cryptantha flaccida* (pl. 15). Stems 5″–18″ rigidly erect, branched at top; leaves 1″–2″ long, linear; flower spikes 2″–4″ long; calyx parted to base, as long as corolla tube, lobes narrowly linear; corolla to ⅙″ dia., white; nutlets not barbed, grooved on inner side; Apr.-June. DISTR. Foothill and Yellow Pine belts below 6000 ft. on dry slopes and flats.

There are many other species including the montane *C. glomeriflora*, which is only 2 to 4 inches high. It grows from Nevada County south to Tulare and Inyo counties at 6000 to 11000 feet, blooming from June to September.

WF-88. Pop-corn Flower. *Plagiobothrys nothofulvus* (pl. 15). Stems 1–2½ ft., erect, 1 or several from base; herbage silky-haired with purple dye; leaves 1″–4″ long, mostly in basal rosette, narrow, lance-shaped; flowers in loose racemes, pedicels short; calyx ⅛″ long, cleft to middle; corolla ⅙″–⅓″ dia., white, with crests at throat; nutlets with rectangular ridges; Mar.-May. DISTR. Foothill belt mostly below 2500 ft. in grassy fields and on hillsides.

Other species grow in the foothills, and *P. torreyi* ranges from Sierra to Kern County at 4000 to 11000 feet. It is up to 6″ tall, blooming in June and July.

MINT FAMILY (LABIATAE). Leaves opposite; stems square; aromatic; flowers irregular; calyx 5-lobed; corolla tubular, 2-lipped, often 2 lobes in upper lip and 3 in lower; stamens in tube of corolla, 4 (or 2 with and 2 without anthers); ovary 4-lobed.

WF-89. Blue-curls. *Trichostema lanceolatum* (pl. 16). Stem 6″–16″, simple or branching from base, leafy; leaves ¾″–1¼″ long, oblong, tapering to tips, with 3–5 parallel ribs, petioles short or absent; flowers in cymes from leaf axils, light blue; calyx 1/10″–⅙″ long, of 5 narrow lobes; corolla tube ¼″–½″ long, longer than calyx and bent, lower lip ⅙″–⅓″ long; stamens 4, ½″–⅘″ long, arching far beyond corolla; Aug.-Oct. DISTR. Foothills and lower Yellow Pine belt, mostly below 3500 ft. in dry fields; *T. oblongum* reaches 10000 feet.

WF-90. Skull-cap. *Scutellaria angustifolia* (pl. 16). Stems 7″–13″, erect; leaves ¾″–1½″ long, linear to oblong, basal leaves smaller and ovate to heart-shaped, petioles short or none; flowers ¾″–1⅙″ long, solitary or in pairs in upper leaf axils, bluish violet; calyx with 2 short lips, upper lip a

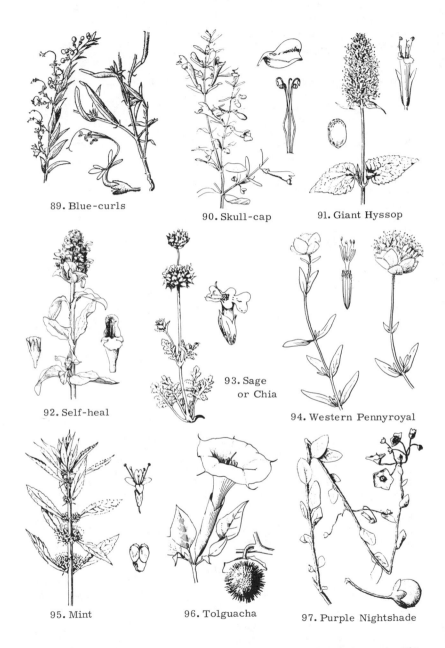

89. Blue-curls

90. Skull-cap

91. Giant Hyssop

92. Self-heal

93. Sage or Chia

94. Western Pennyroyal

95. Mint

96. Tolguacha

97. Purple Nightshade

Plate 16. Wildflowers

projecting hood; corolla 1″–1⅕″ long, upper lip beak-like; stamens 4, all fertile; ovary deeply 4-parted; May-July. DISTR. Foothill and Yellow Pine belts below 5000 ft. in dry places; other species in Lodgepole–fir belt.

WF-91. Giant Hyssop. *Agastache urticifolia* (pl. 16, col. pl. 9). Stems 2½–5 ft., erect, simple, widely spreading; leaves 1⅖″–3″ long, ovate, toothed, petioles ⅖″–1″ long; flowers crowded in terminal spike 1⅗″–6″ long; calyx equally 5-toothed, lobes tapering, pinkish or white; corolla ⅖″–⅗″ long, rose or violet, upper lip 2-lobed, lower lip spreading; stamens 4, extending beyond corolla; June-Aug. DISTR. Yellow Pine and Lodgepole–fir belts at 2500–9000 ft. in moist places.

WF-92. Self-Heal. *Brunella vulgaris* (pl. 16). Stem 4″–12″, erect; leaves 1″–3″ long, oblong-ovate, rounded at base, petioles short; flowers in dense terminal heads; calyx 2-lipped, purplish; corolla ⅖″–⅘″ long, pinkish or lavender, upper lip erect, lower lip 3-lobed, middle lobe hanging downward; stamens 4, in pairs beneath upper lip; May-Sept. DISTR. Introduced; Yellow Pine and Lodgepole–fir belts at 2500–7500 ft. in moist woods.

WF-93. Sage or Chia. *Salvia columbariae* (pl. 16). Stems 3″–15″, 1 or several from base, usually simple, with 1 or 2 pairs of leaves and 1 or 2 whorls of flowers; herbage minutely hairy, dark green; leaves 1″–4″ long, mostly near base, pinnately divided, petioles equaling or longer than lobes; flower heads with sharp purplish bracts beneath; calyx ⅓″–⅖″ long, purplish, 2-lipped, lower lip 2-cleft; corolla ½″–⅔″ long, blue, upper lip small and notched, lower lip with small lateral lobes and larger middle lobe; stamens in throat of corolla, lower pair fertile, upper pair as sterile filaments or none; Mar.-June. DISTR. Foothill and Yellow Pine belts, mostly below 4000 ft. in dry open disturbed places.

The seeds of Chia were used in Spanish days for medicinal purposes, and the Pomo Indians roasted and ground them into a meal called "pinole." This was baked as small cakes or loaves having a nutty flavor.

WF-94. Western Pennyroyal. *Monardella odoratissima* (pl. 16, col. pl. 9). Stems 6″–14″, erect, several in dense cluster; perennial; herbage gray-green; leaves ½″–1½″ long, narrowly oblong, tapered to tip, petioles short or none; flowers in terminal heads ⅗″–1″ dia., surrounded by thin purplish bracts; calyx ¼″–⅓″ long, tubular, with 5 short lobes; corolla ⅗″ long, pale purple, tubular, extending well beyond calyx, upper lip erect, cleft for about half its length, lower lip 3-parted; stamens 4, all fertile, the longer pair extending beyond corolla; style 2-cleft at tip; June-Sept. DISTR. Yellow Pine to Subalpine belts at 3000–11000 ft. on dry slopes. There are several subspecies, one with whitish flowers.

The aromatic leaves from old plants make a fragrant tea. Blossoms of pennyroyal are visited at dark by hummingbird moths (I-56). Of other Sierran species, the Mustang Mint (*M. lanceolata*), an annual, has few narrow leaves, and blooms from May to August. It grows mostly in the foothills at 1500 to 4000 feet.

WF-95. Mint. *Mentha arvensis* (pl. 16). Stems 1½–4 ft., simple or branched; leaves 1″–2¾″ long, ovate, edges toothed, tapering to tip and to base as a short petiole; flower clusters short, in leaf axils; calyx ⅛″ long, minutely hairy, lobes 5, acute, ¼–⅓ as long as tube; corolla ⅕″–¼″ long, pink to purplish, upper lip usually notched, about the size of lobes of lower lip; stamens 4, nearly equal, extending beyond corolla; July-Oct. DISTR. Foothill to Lodgepole–fir belts below 7500 ft. in marshes and meadows.

NIGHTSHADE FAMILY (SOLANACEAE). Calyx 5-cleft; corolla 5-lobed, tubular or saucer-shaped; stamens 5, inserted on corolla, alternate with its lobes.

WF-96. Tolguacha. *Datura meteloides* (pl. 16, col. pl. 9). Stems 2–3 ft., erect, many-branched; herbage grayish, bad-odored; leaves 1⅗″–5″ long, ovate, toothed, petioles short; flowers solitary, on short peduncles in forks of branching stems; calyx 3″–4″ long, tubular, with lance-shaped lobes; corolla 6″–7″ long and 4″–8″ broad, funnel-form, white tinged with violet; stamens 5, ½″–¾″ long; capsule 1″ long, nodding, densely covered with ⅛″ prickles; Apr.-Oct. DISTR. Foothill and lower Yellow Pine belts below 4000 ft. in sandy or gravelly open places.

WF-97. Purple Nightshade. *Solanum xantii* (pl. 16). Stems 1½–2 ft., several, spreading; herbage minutely hairy, stem hairs sticky; leaves ⅘″–1⅗″ long, ovate, petioles ⅙″–½″ long; flowers 6–10 in umbrella-like cyme; corolla ½″–⅚″ dia., saucer-shaped, angularly lobed, blue; anthers closely surrounding the style; fruit a light green berry with several seeds; Feb.-June. DISTR. Foothill and lower Yellow Pine belts to 4000 ft. in dry places near chaparral or woods.

The Black Nightshade (*S. nodiflorum*) grows as a weed in the foothills, blooming from March to October. It has small white flowers and black berries. The herbage and green berries of both species are poisonous.

FIGWORT FAMILY (SCROPHULARIACEAE). Leaves opposite or alternate; flowers tubular or saucer-shaped; calyx 5-cleft; corolla usually 2-lipped, upper lip 2-lobed or as a single hood or beak, lower lip 3-lobed or of 3 sacs (nearly regular in WF-98); stamens usually 4 fertile and 1 sterile.

WF-98. Common Mullein. *Verbascum thapsus* (pl. 17). Stems 3–6 ft., stout, erect, woolly; leaves mostly alternate, those at base in rosettes, 6″–12″ long, oblong-ovate, clasping stem; flowers in dense spike 1–3 ft. long and 1¼″ thick; calyx ⅓″ long; corolla ⅘″–1″ dia., wheel-shaped, with 5 nearly equal lobes, yellow; stamens 5, all with anthers; June-Sept. DISTR. Yellow Pine belt mostly above 4000 ft. in waste places and along roads; an introduced weed.

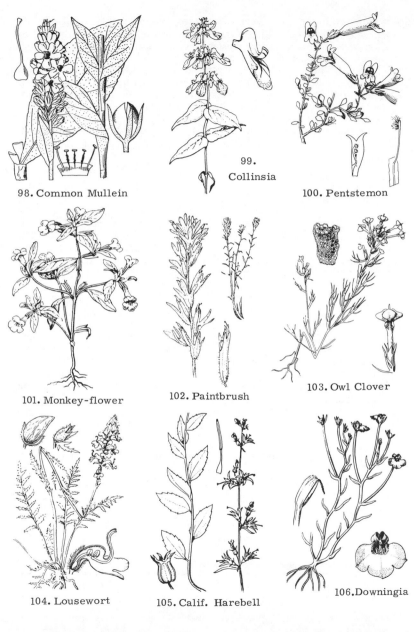

98. Common Mullein

99. Collinsia

100. Pentstemon

101. Monkey-flower

102. Paintbrush

103. Owl Clover

104. Lousewort

105. Calif. Harebell

106. Downingia

Plate 17. Wildflowers

WF-99. Collinsia. *Collinsia tinctoria* (pl. 17, col. pl. 9). Stems 6″–24″, erect, simple or branching; herbage sticky, staining brownish; leaves 1″–3″ (or 4″) long, opposite, simple, ovate to lance-shaped, petioles short or none; flowers in successive whorls along stem; calyx ⅕″–⅓″ long, bell-shaped, deeply 5-cleft, the lobes linear or oblong; corolla ½″–¾″ long with short tube, deeply 2-lobed, upper lip 2-cleft, lower 3-cleft, middle lobe enclosing 4 stamens and style, lilac or nearly white with pale yellow throat and purple markings; capsule about ⅛″ long; May-Aug. Distr. Mostly in Yellow Pine belt at 2000–6000 ft. in stony places.

Other species grow in the foothills, and *C. torreyi* of damp sandy places in the coniferous forest at 3000 to 10000 feet has flowers less than ½″ long on longer pedicels.

WF-100. Pentstemon. *Pentstemon menziesii* (or *davidsonii*) (pl. 17). Stems many, prostrate, woody below, forming a creeping mat 1 ft. or less high; leaves ⅛″–½″ long, opposite, ovate, petioles short; flowers several, near ends of stems; calyx ⅓″ long, 5-parted, lobes lance-shaped; corolla 1¼″–1½″ long, blue-purple, tubular, lobes short, upper lip deeply 2-lobed, lower 3-lobed; stamens 4, anthers long and woolly, 5th stamen short, sterile, bearded at tip; capsule with many angled seeds; July-Aug. Distr. Subalpine and Alpine belts, 9000–12000 ft. in rocky places.

Other species of Penstemon grow at all elevations. *P. heterophyllus* of the foothills (200–5500 ft.), has erect stems to 2 feet high, the flowers are blue or purple, and the sterile filament is unbearded; it blooms from April to July. The Mountain Pride (*P. newberryi;* col. pl. 9) has bright red flowers and a bearded sterile filament; it ranges from 5000 to 11000 feet, blooming from June to August. At middle elevations are tall bushy species (to 4 or 6 ft. high), including the white-flowered *P. breviflorus* and the yellow-flowered *P. lemmonii*. The sterile filament is naked in *breviflorus* but densely bearded in *lemmonii*.

WF-101. Monkey-flower. *Mimulus torreyi* (pl. 17, col. pl. 9). Stem 1″–10″, at first low and simple, later branched with many flowers; herbage sticky; leaves ½″–1″ long, opposite, elliptic, tapered at both ends; calyx about ⅓″ long, angular, lobes 5, unequal; corolla ½″–⅔″ long, funnel-form, widened into 2-lobed upper lip and 3-lobed lower lip, pink-purple with purple-dotted cream-colored area between throat folds; stamens 4, not enclosed in lower lip; capsule ⅓″ long, leathery; May-Aug. Distr. Foothill to Lodgepole-fir belts, 1500–8000 ft. in dry disturbed places.

There are many other species from the foothills up to 11000 feet. The Scarlet Monkey-flower (*M. cardinalis*) and Yellow Monkey-flower (*M. guttatus*) are common along streams and in moist places up to 8000 and 10000 feet, respectively.

WF-102. Paintbrush. *Castilleia pinetorum* (pl. 17, col. pl. 9). Stems 6″–12″, erect, often branching; herbage minutely hairy and glandular; leaves ½″–1″ long, oblong, wavy-margined, some 3-lobed; flowers clustered in spikes, bracts and calyx tips scarlet (sometimes orange or yellowish), upper bracts with 1 or 2 pairs of narrow lobes; calyx ½″–1″ long, cleft at middle for about half its length and shallowly at sides to form 4 lobes; corolla ⅘″–1⅕″ long, greenish, 2-lipped, upper lip ½″ long with wide red margins, lower lip 1/12″ long, minutely 3-lobed, green; stamens 4, unequal; style enclosed in upper lip of corolla; capsule ⅖″ long; seeds about 1/25″ long; May-Aug. DISTR. Foothill to Subalpine belts, 2000–11000 ft. in dry places; other species at all elevations; some parasitic on roots of other plants.

WF-103. Owl Clover or Johnny-tuck. *Orthocarpus erianthus* (pl. 17, col. pl. 9). Stem 4″–10″, branching; herbage purplish; leaves ⅖″–2″ long, mostly alternate, pinnately divided into several thread-like parts; flowers in terminal spikes; calyx ⅕″–⅓″ long, tubular, 4-cleft; corolla ⅖″–1″ long, tubular, yellow except for purple awl-shaped upper lip, lower lip of 3 inflated sacs ⅙″ deep, each sac usually with 2 greenish yellow spots; capsule ⅙″–⅓″ long, with many small brown seeds; Mar.-May. DISTR. Foothills, mostly below 2000 ft. in open places.

The related *O. purpurascens,* also of the foothills, has crimson or purplish flowers in a dense spike.

WF-104. Lousewort. *Pedicularis attollens* (pl. 17). Stems 6″–13″, 1 or more; leaves alternate or mostly at base, pinnately divided and feather-like, blades 1″–4″ long; flowers in dense spike; calyx about ⅕″ long, 5-cleft; corolla ⅓″ long, tubular, white or pink marked with purple, upper lip sac-like, with ¼″ upturned beak; lower lip with small middle lobe; stamens 4, below upper lip; capsule about ⅓″ long; June-Sept. DISTR. Mostly in coniferous forest above Yellow Pine belt at 5000–12000 ft. in wet meadows.

Other species include *P. semibarbata,* with a yellow corolla that grows at 5000 to 11000 feet, and *P. densiflora* found up to 6000 feet with purple-red corolla. Both lack the upturned beak of the upper lip.

BELLFLOWER FAMILY (CAMPANULACEAE). Calyx and corolla 5-lobed; stamens 5; juice milky.

WF-105. California Harebell. *Campanula prenanthoides* (pl. 17). Stem 1½–2 ft., slender, erect, angled, often branched; leaves ½″–1½″ long, oblong to lance-shaped, edges toothed; flowers clustered on short pedicels, mostly in leaf axils; calyx lobes short, awl-shaped; corolla ⅓″–½″ long, bright blue, bell-shaped, lobes long, narrow, and tapered; style 3-lobed, extending well beyond corolla; capsule hemispherical or top-shaped; June-Sept. DISTR. Foothill and Yellow Pine belts, 800–6000 ft. in dry wooded places.

LOBELIA FAMILY (LOBELIACEAE). Flowers irregular; calyx tube 5-lobed; corolla 2-lipped, 2 lobes in upper lip and 3 in lower; stamens 5, alternate with corolla lobes; anthers and filaments united as tube around style.

WF-106. Downingia. *Downingia bicornuta* (pl. 17). Stems 2″–10″, erect; leaves ¼″–⅔″ long, linear, no petioles; flowers in axils of slender bracts that are 1/5″–4/5″ long; calyx 1/8″–1/3″ long, lobes narrow, unequal; corolla 1/3″–3/4″ long, 1/2″ broad, a short tube expanding into a broad, 3-lobed lower lip with 4 small nipples at base and a small upper lip with 2 short, acute lobes; corolla blue with white center, 2 yellow spots in lower lip, and deep violet-purple lobes on upper lip; capsule 1 3/5″–2 3/5″ long, linear; Apr.-July. DISTR. Foothill and Yellow Pine belts below 6000 ft. in moist places.

SUNFLOWER FAMILY (COMPOSITAE). Leaves mostly alternate; flowers grouped in heads, on enlarged receptacle, surrounded by bracts; corolla tubular and 5-lobed (disc flowers), or strap-shaped and toothed at tips (ray flowers), rays appearing like petals of other flowers; calyx united, highly modified (pappus), the segments awn-like, hair-like, scale-like, or none; stamens 5, filaments free; ovary inferior, 1-celled, 1-ovuled, maturing into an achene crowned by the pappus.

WF-107. Sow Thistle. *Sonchus asper* (pl. 18). Stem 1–4 ft., erect; leaves 3″–12″ long, pinnately divided, clasping stem, lobes of clasping base rounded, edges prickly; flower heads 1″–2″ dia., swollen at base or jug-shaped; flowers many, all strap-shaped like ray flowers, yellow; achenes 1/10″ long, flat, oblong-ovate, margined with narrow wing, 3-ribbed on each face, with cottony-white fine hairs (pappi) at one end; blooms in most months. DISTR. Introduced from Europe, a common weed in wet places.

S. oleraceus also occurs in the Sierra. It has acute leaf-lobes clasping the stem and achenes that are wrinkled at right angles to the ribs. Naturalized from Europe, it grows as a weed in valleys and hills at low elevations.

WF-108. Hawkweed. *Hieracium albiflorum* (pl. 18). Stems 3/4–3 ft., several, erect; leaves 2″–6″ (or 12″) long, with pale bristly hairs, basal leaves oblong, tapering, narrowed basally to winged petiole, upper leaves few, small, linear; flower heads in a panicle, all flowers small, white, ray-like; achenes 1/8″ long, reddish-brown, 10-ribbed; pappus longer, dull white; June-Aug. DISTR. Foothill to Lodgepole–fir belts below 9700 ft. on dry wooded slopes; other yellow flowered species ranging to 11000 feet.

WF-109. Meadow Goldenrod. *Solidago elongata* (pl. 18, col. pl. 10). Stem 1–3 ft., simple, erect, leafy; leaves 2″–4″ long, oblong to lance-shaped, often toothed at edges; flower heads yellow, in dense panicle forming a mass 3″–7″ long; heads small, scarcely 1/4″ high; bracts thin, linear; rays 10–13, narrow; disc flowers usually fewer; achenes cylindrical, 5- to 10-nerved; pappus of many white bristles; May-Sept. DISTR. Yellow Pine to Lodgepole–fir belts below 8500 ft. in meadows.

Of other species the lowland *S. occidentalis* has 15–25 ray flowers, and the high mountain (8000–12500 ft.) *S. multiradiata* is less than a foot high.

WF-110. Sierra Lessingia. *Lessingia leptoclada* (pl. 18). Stem 6″–24″, erect, simple below, branching above; leaves 1/3″–2″ long, woolly, ovate to

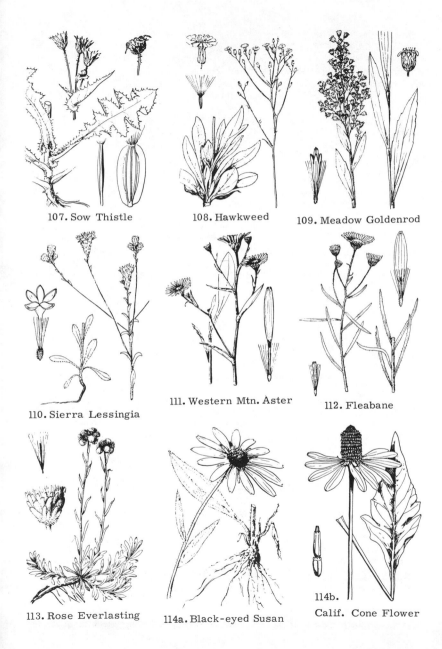

107. Sow Thistle

108. Hawkweed

109. Meadow Goldenrod

110. Sierra Lessingia

111. Western Mtn. Aster

112. Fleabane

113. Rose Everlasting

114a. Black-eyed Susan

114b.
Calif. Cone Flower

Plate 18. Wildflowers

lance-shaped, acute, some toothed at edges; flower heads few or 1 on slender stalks; heads scarcely ½″ long, lavender to blue-purple; marginal disc flowers enlarged; no ray flowers; pappus bristles brownish, 18–40; July-Oct. DISTR. Foothill and Yellow Pine belts, at 1000–6200 ft., Eldorado to Kern Co. on open dry ground.

WF-111. Western Mountain Aster. *Aster occidentalis* (pl. 18). Stem 1–2 ft., leafy; leaves 2″–4″ x ⅛″–⅖″, scattered, oblong-linear; flower heads ⅕″–¼″ high, dia. about ½″–¾″, 1 to several in a panicle; rays about 30, violet or purple; disc flowers yellow; achenes flat; pappus of many hair-like bristles; July-Sept. DISTR. Yellow Pine to Subalpine belts at 4000–10500 ft. in moist places.

Among other species are the Broad-leafed Aster (*A. radulinus*) of the foothills up to 5000 feet, and *A. peirsonii* of Alpine slopes and meadows at 11000 to 12250 feet.

WF-112. Fleabane. *Erigeron foliosus* (pl. 18). Stems 1–2 ft., many from base, erect, branching above; leaves ¾″–2″ x 1⁄12″–⅙″, narrowly linear or lance-shaped; flower heads few in flat-topped cluster, ⅚″ dia.; rays ⅙″–½″ long, about 30–40, blue; disc flowers yellow; achenes 2-nerved; pappus of 20–30 tawny bristles; May-Aug. DISTR. Foothill and Yellow Pine belts at 200–5000 ft., Amador to Mariposa Co.

There are other species ranging from 5000 to 10500 feet (*E. breweri*) and from 11000 to 14100 feet (*E. vagus*). The variety *covillei* grows on the east side up to 6000 feet among piñons and junipers.

WF-113. Rose Everlasting. *Antennaria rosea* (pl. 18). Stems 2″–12″, erect, from branching stolons with leaf tufts that form mats; herbage woolly; leaves ½″–1⅛″ long, to ⅛″ wide, basal ones ovate, upper leaves linear to broadly lance-shaped; flower cluster dense, flat-topped, heads several, small, ⅕″ high, no rays, bracts papery, overlapping, rose-colored or white; achenes smooth; ♂ flowers with thread-like corolla and scanty pappus; ♀ flowers with tubular 5-toothed corolla and much pappus; June-Aug. DISTR. Yellow Pine to Alpine belts at 4500–12000 ft. in wooded places.

WF-114a. Black-eyed Susan. *Rudbeckia hirta* (pl. 18, col. pl. 10). Stems 1–2¼ ft., 1 to several, erect, branched above; herbage rough-hairy; leaves 2″–4″ long, to 1″ wide, oblong to lance-shaped, a few teeth on edges; flower heads ¾″ high, large, sunflower-like, disc ovoid, brown or purplish; rays ¾″–1⅛″ long, 8–21, orange-yellow; pappus none; June-Aug. DISTR. At middle elevations, Amador to Mariposa Co. in meadows; introduced from eastern United States.

WF-114b. California Cone Flower. *Rudbeckia californica* (pl. 18, col. pl. 10). Stems 2–5½ ft., simple, erect, leafy, with one flower head on long peduncle; herbage minutely hairy; leaves 6″–13½″ x 1″–5″, ovate to broadly lance-shaped, lower leaves irregularly toothed; flower heads 1″–1½″ high; rays 1″–2″ long, yellow, 8–21; disc conical to cylindrical, brown or purplish;

achenes angled, flat; pappus an irregularly 4-toothed cup; July-Aug. DISTR. Yellow Pine and Lodgepole–fir belts, at 5500–7800 ft., Kern to Eldorado Co. in moist ground.

WF-115. Mule Ears. *Wyethia mollis* (pl. 19, col. pl. 10). Stems 1½–3 ft., simple, with one or few flower heads; young herbage white-woolly; basal leaves 7″–10″ x 2″–9″, oblong-ovate, petioles long; upper leaves few, small, short-petioled; flower heads large, bell-shaped, ½″ high; rays 1″–1½″ long, 6–8 (or 14), yellow; disc flowers many; achenes 4-sided or flattened, slate-colored; pappus an irregular crown of scales; May-Aug. DISTR. Yellow Pine to Subalpine belts at 5000–10600 ft. in dry, wooded areas.

Other species occur locally in the foothills, and *W. angustifolia* ranges into the Yellow Pine belt to 5000 ft. It has narrower leaves and 10 to 17 rays.

WF-116. Tarweed. *Madia elegans* (pl. 19). Stems 9″–24″, erect, simple below, branching above; herbage sticky and hairy; lower leaves 3″–5″ long, linear, edges scarcely toothed or entire; upper leaves reduced; flower heads ⅓″–⅔″ long, in flat-topped panicle, few to many on long peduncles; rays 9–15, 3-lobed, yellow or with red spot at base; achenes flat; no pappus; June-Aug. DISTR. Yellow Pine and Lodgepole–fir belts at 3000–8000 ft. on dry slopes.

Most of the flower heads close at midday. The foothill species (*M. vernalis*) blooms from March into June, and its all-yellow flowers remain open until later in the day.

WF-117. Tidy Tips. *Layia platyglossa* (pl. 19, col. pl. 10). Stem 4″–16″, simple or branching, erect or spreading; herbage hairy; leaves linear or lower leaves pinnate with short linear lobes; flower heads 1″–1¾″ dia.; rays 13, ½″ long, yellow, tips 3-lobed, white; disc achenes ⅛″ long, somewhat flattened; pappus bristles 15–20; May-June. DISTR. Foothill and lower Yellow Pine belts, 100–4600 ft. on grassy slopes.

An all-white form grows in the southern foothills, and another extends along the entire east side.

WF-118. Woolly Sunflower. *Eriophyllum lanatum* (pl. 19). Stems 5″–11″, many; herbage white-woolly; leaves ¾″–1¼″ long, ovate to linear, sometimes toothed or lobed, narrowed at base; flower heads ½″–⅚″ dia., single, on long, naked peduncles; ray flowers 8–13, yellow; achenes ⅒″–⅙″ long, 4-angled; May-July. DISTR. Foothill to Subalpine belts below 10000 ft. in brushy places.

WF-119. Bigelow Sneezeweed. *Helenium bigelovii* (pl. 19, col. pl. 10). Stem 2–4 ft., erect, branching above; leaves 4″–10″ long, ½″ or less wide, lance-shaped or linear; flower heads ⅗″–⅘″ dia.; rays 13–30, ½″–¾″ long, drooping, 3-lobed at tips, yellow; disc brown or brownish yellow; achenes 1/12″ long, hairy on ribs; pappus chaff-like, each scale tapering to a slender awn; June-Aug. DISTR. Yellow Pine to Subalpine belts at 3000–10000 ft. in moist meadows.

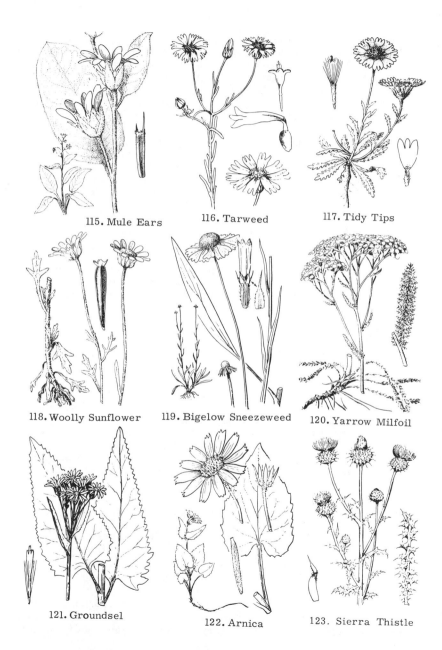

115. Mule Ears

116. Tarweed

117. Tidy Tips

118. Woolly Sunflower

119. Bigelow Sneezeweed

120. Yarrow Milfoil

121. Groundsel

122. Arnica

123. Sierra Thistle

Plate 19. Wildflowers

WF-120. Yarrow Milfoil. *Achillea millefolium* (pl. 19, col. pl. 10). Stem 1¼–3 ft., simple, erect; herbage hairy; leaves 2″–4″ x ⅜″ or less; flower heads in flat-topped or convex terminal cluster; rays 4–5, white; disc flowers white or yellow; achenes linear, no pappus; June-Aug. DISTR. Yellow Pine to Lodgepole–fir belts, 2500–9000 ft. in meadows.

An alpine species with narrower leaves grows from 9000 to 11300 feet, and another occurs in grassy places below 2500 feet.

WF-121. Groundsel. *Senecio triangularis* (pl. 19, col. pl. 10). Stems 2–6 ft., several, erect; leaves 1¼″–5½″ long, oblong to lance-shaped or triangular, edges minutely toothed, petioles ¼″–2″ long; flower heads ⅓″ high, in flat-topped terminal cluster, yellow; rays 6–12, ⅕″–⅓″ long; achenes cylindrical; pappus of many soft white hairs; July-Sept. DISTR. Yellow Pine to Alpine belts at 4000–11150 ft. in wet meadows and along stream banks.

Many other species of Groundsel grow at various elevations. The Creek Senecio (*S. douglasii*) in the foothills at 200 to 5000 feet blooms from June to October.

WF-122. Arnica. *Arnica cordifolia* (pl. 19). Stem ½–2 ft., erect; herbage hairy; leaves 1″–3″ long, opposite, heart-shaped or ovate, edges toothed, petioles 1″–2″ long; upper leaves smaller, broadly lance-shaped, mostly without petioles; flower heads few, in loose cyme with long peduncles, or single and ¾″ high; rays 7–13, ¾″–1″ long, yellow, 3-toothed at tips; achenes slender, spindle-shaped; pappus in 1 row of white bristles; May-Aug. DISTR. Yellow Pine to Subalpine belts at 3500–10000 ft.

WF-123. Sierra Thistle. *Cirsium californicum* (pl. 19, col. pl. 10). Stem 2–6 ft., slender, leafy near base, branched above; herbage white-woolly; leaves 1″–8″ long, narrowly oblong or lance-shaped, deeply and angularly pinnate, prickly; flower heads 1″–1¾″ high on long peduncles; outer bracts prickly; flowers many, alike, linear, cream-colored, white, or purplish; achenes oblong, flat, smooth; pappus in 1 series of bristles; Apr.-July. DISTR. Foothill to lower Lodgepole–fir belts below 7000 ft. on dry slopes.

Other species of thistles, some having red flowers, are found from the lowlands up to 11500 feet.

14. SHRUBS

A shrub is a perennial plant with several woody stems branching from the base. Some woody species may be either trees or shrubs according to local conditions. The growth requirements of different species vary —wet to dry, cool to hot, or sunlit to shady—in the foothills, middle altitudes, or subalpine areas.

California's most unique shrub association is the chaparral, a dense assemblage of plants low to medium in height, with multiple stiff branches, large deep root systems, and leaves that are mostly small, hard, flat, and evergreen. Foothill chaparral includes bush poppy (S-8), chamise (19), toyon (25), chaparral pea (28), poison oak (31), coffeeberry (32), redberry (33), fremontia (36), yerba santa (48), several species of ceanothus (34) and manzanita (45), and others. It grows where soil moisture is limited, the winters are cool, and the summers warm to hot and dry. Chaparral covers hundreds of square miles on interior hills and ridges, usually deficient in humus. The species are adapted by structure and function to live where peaks of moisture and temperature occur at different seasons. Their growth, blossoming, and fruiting are chiefly in a short period combining warmth with some topsoil moisture. Chaparral is subject to frequent fires, to which many of the species are adjusted—some stump sprout vigorously after a burn, and seeds of others germinate readily only after a fire.

Mountain chaparral grows in the conifer forest at higher altitudes under different climatic conditions. Common members are huckleberry oak (4; see pl. 30), bush chinquapin (5), bitter cherry (21), service berry (26), and other kinds of ceanothus (34) and manzanita (45).

A third shrub assemblage, with plants spaced more widely, is the Sagebrush belt over much of the Great Basin. The major element is sagebrush (*Artemesia tridentata;* 60) in company with rabbit brush (58), bitterbrush (20), and others adapted to scant moisture, cold winters, and hot, dry summers. Sagebrush "spills upward" into the high eastern Sierra and southerly on the west slope. Each of these shrubby environments includes distinctive species of herbaceous plants, insects, reptiles, birds, and mammals.

For aid in identifying shrubs see tables 1 and 2, figures 8 and 9.

LILY FAMILY (LILIACEAE). Leaves parallel-veined.

S-1. Spanish Bayonet. *Yucca whipplei* (pl. 20). Stem short with dense rosette of leaves at base; leaves gray-green, 12″–21″ x ¾″, dagger-like, rigid, narrow, sharp-tipped, margins toothed; flower stalk 8–14 ft. high; blossom panicle dense, 3–6 ft. long; flowers 1″–2″ long, hanging, creamy-white, fragrant; sepals + petals 6, fleshy; stamens 6; seed capsule to 2″ long, cylindrical; Apr.-May. DISTR. Walker Pass and w. slope Foothill belt n. to Kings River.

Spikes of this yucca stand conspicuously in the drab southern brushlands. The self-sterile flowers are visited at night and pollinated by a small moth (*Pronuba*) that carries pollen from flower to flower; the moth's eggs are laid in the blossoms. After producing flowers and seeds the yucca dies. New plants result from rooted basal shoots or seeds. Birds eat the fleshy fruit covering, and rodents take the seeds.

BIRCH FAMILY (BETULACEAE). Male flowers in catkins; female in groups of 3.

TABLE 3. Shrub Color Chart
(petals 5 except as noted in parentheses)

FLOWERS REGULAR, PETALS SEPARATE TO BASE

White, Cream, or Green		Yellow to Orange	Red, Pink, or Rose
1. Spanish Bayonet (6)	23. Sierra Plum	8. Bush Poppy (4)	2. Hazelnut
6. Clematis (4 sepals)	24. Mtn. Ash	20. Bitterbrush	7. Spice Bush (many petals)
9. Mock Orange (4–5)	25. Toyon		
12. Creamberry	26. Service Berry		
13. Thimbleberry	31. Poison Oak	37. Silk Tassel (catkins)	11. Spiraea
14. Raspberry	32. Coffeeberry		
15. Blackberry	33. Redberry		12. Creamberry
17. Kit-kit-dizze	34. Ceanothus		16. Wild Rose
19. Chamise	35. Wild Grape	Blue to Purple	(5, 6–8)
21. Bitter Cherry	38. Creek Dogwood (4)		23. Sierra Plum
22. Choke-cherry	39. Labrador Tea	34. Ceanothus	

FLOWERS BELL- OR FUNNEL-SHAPED, PETALS MORE OR LESS UNITED

White, Cream, or Green		Red, Pink, or Rose	Blue to Purple
18. Mtn. Mahogany (no petals)	47. Storax (6)	10. Currant, gooseberry (petals free)	48. Yerba Santa
	51. Button Bush (4)		
	52. Blue Elderberry (corolla saucer-shaped)		Yellow
40. Azalea		40. Azalea	
43. White Heather		41. Alpine Laurel	36. Fremontia (5 sepals)
	53. Red Elderberry (corolla saucer-shaped)	42. Red Mtn. Heather	
44. Sierra Laurel		45. Manzanita	49. Tree Tobacco (corolla flared)
45. Manzanita (4, 5)			
46. Blueberry (4)	54. Snowberry (4, 5)	54. Snowberry (4, 5)	

FLOWERS IRREGULAR

Cream	Yellow to Orange	Red, Pink, or Rose
50. Bush Monkey-flower	27. Redbud	27. Redbud
	29. Scotch Broom	28. Chaparral Pea
	30. Deerweed	
	50. Bush Monkey-flower	
	55. Twinberry	
	56. Chaparral Honeysuckle (4)	

FLOWERS IN COMPOSITE HEADS

White	Yellow
60. Sagebrush	57. Golden Fleece 58. Rabbit Brush 59. Golden Yarrow

S-2. California Hazelnut. *Corylus rostrata* (pl. 20). Ht. 5–12 ft.; many spreading loose stems; bark smooth, finely haired; leaves 1¼″–3″ x ¾″–2½″, roundish, tip rounded or bluntly pointed, thin, glandular-hairy, margin double-toothed; male catkins worm-like, hanging; female flowers solitary, small, pink, appearing before leaves; stigmas 2, long, bright red; nut ½″ long, hard, in 1″ hairy tube; Jan.-Apr. DISTR. Mainly in Yellow Pine belt at 2500–6000 ft.; in cool canyons along streams.

OAK FAMILY (FAGACEAE). Male flowers in catkins; female in groups of 1 to 3; nut in scaly cup or spiny bur.

S-3. Scrub Oak. *Quercus dumosa* (pl. 30). Ht. 2–8 ft., branches rigid, tough; leaves ¾″–1″ long, stiff, shape various, oblong to elliptical, usually with spiny-tipped teeth, sometimes entire; acorn ¾″–1⅛″ long, oval or cylindric, rounded or pointed, cup ⅔″ x ⁷⁄₁₆″ or smaller, shallow or deep, scales rounded. DISTR. Foothill belt of w. slope, less common to n., often in chaparral.

This small oak has the sturdy characteristics of its tree relatives expressed in shrub form so that it blends in with other members of the foothill chaparral. Usually it stump sprouts after a fire.

S-4. Huckleberry Oak. *Quercus vaccinifolia* (pl. 30). Ht. 2–4 ft., spreading or prostrate; bark smooth, grayish; branches slender, flexible, ending in broom-like tufts; leaves ½″–1¼″ x ⅜″–⅝″, elliptical and blunt-tipped or narrower and pointed, sometimes spiny-edged; gray-green above, paler below; catkins May-July; acorn ½″ x ¼″, cup thin, shallow, maturing 2nd autumn. DISTR. In Lodgepole–fir belt at 5000–10000 ft., mainly on w. slope, but on e. side of some passes and about Lake Tahoe; on dry ridges and rocky slopes.

The bushy Huckleberry Oak is the only oak in the higher altitudes, where it is part of the mountain chaparral. The little acorns are relished by chipmunks, squirrels, and other rodents.

S-5. Bush Chinquapin. *Castanopsis sempervirens* (pl. 20). Ht. to 8 ft., round-topped, spreading; bark smooth, brown or gray; evergreen; leaves 1½″–3″ x ½″–1″, elliptical, flat, yellow- or gray-green above, golden or rusty below; catkins 1″–1½″ long, in clusters, July-Aug.; fruit a spiny chestnut-like bur enclosing 1–3 bitter-tasting nuts, maturing 2nd year. DISTR. Chiefly in Lodgepole–fir belt above 6000 ft. in mountain chaparral under open forest or on dry, rocky slopes and ridges.

BUTTERCUP FAMILY (RANUNCULACEAE). Leaves opposite, compound; achenes many, feathery.

S-6. Western Clematis. *Clematis ligusticifolia* (pl. 20). A woody vine climbing bushes or trees to 40 ft.; bark of old stems smooth, stringy, gray; leaves compound, leaflets 5–7, 1″–3″ long, rounded at base, tapered at tip, bluntly toothed; petioles long, twining around twigs like tendrils; blossoms

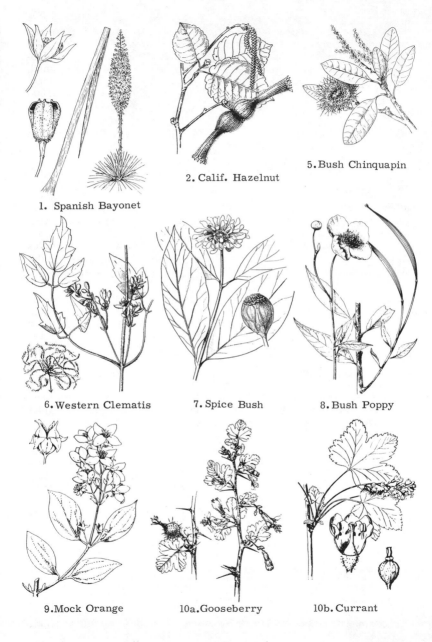

1. Spanish Bayonet

2. Calif. Hazelnut

5. Bush Chinquapin

6. Western Clematis

7. Spice Bush

8. Bush Poppy

9. Mock Orange

10a. Gooseberry

10b. Currant

Plate 20. Shrubs

many, in panicles, long-stalked; flowers ½″–¾″ dia., sepals 4, greenish white; no petals; stamens many, in clusters; achenes in groups, each with 1″–2″ feathery tail; Mar.-Apr. DISTR. Foothill and Yellow Pine belts at 100–3500 ft.

The Clematis, climbing on shrubs and trees, has showy white flower masses in spring and displays of the hairy fruits from May to August. Spanish Californians made an infusion of the herbage to treat cuts on horses.

SWEET SHRUB FAMILY (CALYCANTHACEAE). Leaves opposite, entire, no stipules; sepals and petals alike.

S-7. Spice Bush. *Calycanthus occidentalis* (pl. 20, col. pl. 11). Ht. 4–12 ft., erect, bushy; bark smooth, brown; leaves 2″–6″ x 1″–2″, narrowly ovate, tapered at end, 1 main vein, above rough, below smooth, aromatic when crushed; flowers bright brownish red, dia. 1½″–2½″, solitary at ends of branches; sepals and petals many, in several rows, 1″ long, oblong; fruit 1″ long, urn-like; May-July. DISTR. Foothill belt at 600–3500 ft. along streams or moist canyon slopes.

The distinctive flowers, fruits, and aroma have resulted in various common names including wine-flower, strawberry-bush, and sweet-scented shrub.

POPPY FAMILY (PAPAVERACEAE). Sepals 2; stamens many; pistil 1.

S-8. Bush Poppy. *Dendromecon rigida* (pl. 20, col. pl. 11). Ht. 2–8 ft., freely branched; bark shreddy, yellow-gray to white; leaves 1″–4″ x ¼″–1″, evergreen, broadly lance-like, leathery, gray- or yellow-green; flowers single on 1″–3″ peduncle, petals ¾″–1¼″ long, rounded, golden yellow; capsule slender, 2″–4″ long; Apr.-July. DISTR. Foothill belt of w. slope, in chaparral.

SAXIFRAGE FAMILY (SAXIFRAGACEAE). Calyx 5-parted; petals 4 or 5.

S-9. Mock Orange. *Philadelphus lewisii* (pl. 20, col. pl. 11). Ht. 4–10 ft., loosely branched; bark smooth, reddish on young shoots, gray on older stems; leaves 1¼″–3¼″ x ¾″–1½″, ovate, 3- to 5-veined, smooth to hairy above and below; flowers ¾″–1″ dia., white, in panicles; stamens 20–40; capsule ⅜″ long; May-July. DISTR. Sparse in Foothill and Yellow Pine belts of w. slope at 800–4500 ft. s. to Tulare Co.

Indians used the slender shoots to make shafts for arrows.

S-10. Currants and Gooseberries. Genus *Ribes* (pl. 20). Ht. 1–6 ft., stems often sparingly branched, prickly or smooth; leaves alternate, palmately lobed; flowers red and white in racemes or single, the parts in 5's; petals inserted on throat of calyx alternating with stamens; styles 2; fruit a berry, red or yellow. DISTR. Foothill to Subalpine belts at 3000–12000 ft. in canyons or on mountain slopes.

Gooseberry (10a, col. pl. 11) stems bear spines, the flowers are one or few in a group, and the berries spiny or smooth. Currants (10b, col. pl. 11) have unarmed stems, few or many flowers in a raceme, and smooth berries. The Sierra has 6 species of gooseberries and 3 of currants. Many of the plants have been destroyed by forest employees because they are intermediate hosts for white pine blister rust, a disease which affects 5-needled pines such as sugar pine. Scattered plants remain and at higher altitudes clumps sometimes have heavy fruit crops in late summer which attract squirrels, birds, and people.

ROSE FAMILY (ROSACEAE). Stamens 10 to many, inserted with petals on calyx or on edge of disc lining calyx tube.

S-11. Mountain Spiraea. *Spiraea densiflora* (pl. 21). Ht. to 3 ft.; stems slender, in dense clumps, bark gray, or reddish; leaves ½"–1½" x ¼"–¾", ovate to elliptic, base rounded, outer part unequally toothed, smooth green above, woolly white below; blossoms at top of stem in corymb, dia. ½"–1½", pink or rose, flower dia. ⅛"; calyx 5-lobed, sepals erect; petals 5, rounded; pods 5, several-seeded; July-Aug. DISTR. From Yellow Pine to Subalpine belts at 5000–10000 ft. in rocky moist soil, often in rock clefts.

S-12. Creamberry. *Holodiscus discolor* (pl. 21, col. pl. 11). Ht. 1–3 ft., erect or spreading, intricately branched; bark brown to ashy, shreddy on older shoots; leaves to ⅝" long, simple, alternate, deciduous, ovate, ends coarsely toothed, woolly below; blossom panicle oblong, 1"–2½", flowers many, ⅛" wide, creamy white to pinkish; petals 5, rounded; pistils 5, distinct; pod 1-seeded, to ⅛" long; June-Aug. DISTR. Higher mountains at 6000–11000 ft. on cliffs, rock ledges, and summits.

Creamberry plants may be short or tall, with few or many flowers, depending on soil conditions and altitude. Botanists recognize other species and varieties in the Sierra.

S-13. Thimbleberry. *Rubus parviflorus* (pl. 21). Ht. 3–6 ft., erect, stems not spiny, bark gray, peeling in long strips; leaves 2"–7" long and wide, simple, deciduous, rounded, 3- or 5-lobed, irregularly toothed on outer part, above sparingly haired, below woolly, petioles 1"–2", usually bristly and glandular; flowers 4–7 in terminal cluster, dia. 1"–2", white, sepals 5 (6–7), slender-tipped; petals 5, elliptic, white, ¾" long; berry ½"–¾" wide, hemispheric, red to scarlet, Apr.–June. Distr. Foothill to Lodgepole-Fir belts at 3000–8000 ft. along streams in partial shade.

The large thin-pulped berries are edible and often eaten by birds.

S-14. Western Raspberry. *Rubus leucodermis.* Ht. 3–6 ft.; stems and petioles with recurved spines; 1st-year stems erect, leaves of 5–7 leaflets; 2nd-year stems bending, straggling, leaves 3-parted or 3-lobed; leaflets 1"–3" long, ovate, tip long-pointed, base rounded, double-toothed, above green, slightly hairy, below white, woolly; flowers few, at ends of short branches of previous year, in clusters, dia. ½", white; calyx 5-parted, sepals ¼", hairy; petals 5, shorter; berry ½" dia., red to black; May-June. DISTR. Foot-

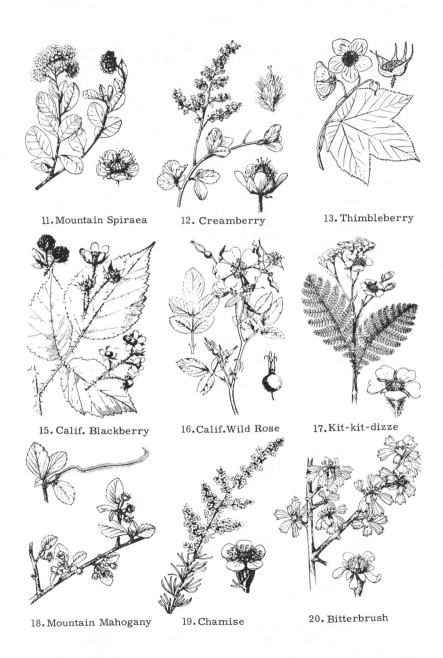

11. Mountain Spiraea   12. Creamberry   13. Thimbleberry

15. Calif. Blackberry   16. Calif. Wild Rose   17. Kit-kit-dizze

18. Mountain Mahogany   19. Chamise   20. Bitterbrush

Plate 21. Shrubs

hill and Yellow Pine belts at 2500–7000 ft. in canyon bottoms or on slopes. Wild raspberry thickets are local in occurrence. The tasty berries often are eaten by birds as soon as ripe.

S-15. California Blackberry. *Rubus ursinus* (or *vitifolius*) (pl. 21). Usually trailing or climbing, some stems to 20 ft. long; stems, branches, and foliage with slender or stout spines; leaves 3″–6″ long, evergreen, lobed or pinnately 3- or 5-lobed, leaflets to 3″ long, oblong to triangular, doubly toothed, midribs and veins prickly; flowers ¾″–1¼″ broad, usually in clusters; petals 5, white; fruit a black, sweet, many-lobed berry to ½″ long; Jan.-May. DISTR. From Great Valley into Yellow Pine belt along streams and on moist ground.

A century and more of settlement in the foothills of the Sierra has resulted in abandoned cultivated berry vines as well as those of the native blackberry. Fencerows and hedges sometimes are overrun by thickets that afford both berry food and spiny "briar patch" protection for various birds and mammals.

S-16. California Wild Rose. Genus *Rosa* (pl. 21, col. pl. 11). Ht. 3–6+ ft.; erect, stout, diffusely branched; stems pale brown to yellowish with firm curved prickles, young shoots bristly; leaves pinnate, of 5–7 leaflets ½″–1½″ long, oval, finely toothed, hairy below; flowers to 30 in panicle, rose to light pink; sepals with slender tips, persisting on fruit; petals 5 (6–8), ¾″–1″ broad, spreading; stamens and pistils many; receptacle globular, ripening into hard fruit enclosing several achenes; May-Nov. DISTR. Common on both slopes from foothills and e. base into Lodgepole–fir belt, up to 10900 ft.; on moist slopes or stream banks.

Wild roses of several species occur scatteringly or in thickets in many damp situations, such as open meadows or along shaded watercourses. The flowers are abundant and fragrant. The small, hard fruits or "hips" are food for some birds and mammals.

S-17. Kit-kit-dizze. *Chamaebatia foliolosa* (pl. 21, col. pl. 11). Ht. 12″–24″; low, much-branched, bark smooth, brown; foliage evergreen, heavily resin-scented; leaves pinnately divided 3 or more times, leaflets minute, elliptical, crowded, sticky, hairy; flowers to ½″ wide in loose clusters; sepals 5, slender; petals 5, broad, white; stamens many, in rows; fruit an achene in persistent calyx; May-July. DISTR. Common on w. slope, Kern to Sierra Co., in Yellow Pine belt and edge of Lodgepole–fir belt; often in extensive carpets under pine forest.

Old-timers walking through the dense, low fern-like growths of this sticky plant called it "mountain misery" or "tarweed." On warm days the resinous leaves and stems are fragrant. The name, kit-kit-dizze, is that given it by the Miwok Indians, who steeped the leaves in hot water and drank the infusion as a cure for various diseases.

S-18. Mountain Mahogany. *Cercocarpus betuloides* (pl. 21). Ht. 5–12 ft. as shrub or 20 ft. as tree; branches spreading, bark smooth, gray or brown;

branchlets short, spur-like, leaves clustered near tip; leaves ½″–1″ x ⅜″–1″, elliptic, tapered toward base, finely toothed toward tip, above dark, below pale to whitish, woolly; flowers 2 or 3 in cluster; calyx base a slender tube, outer ends spread, 5-toothed, triangular, whitish, ¼″ wide; no petals; stamens 15+ in rows on calyx; pistil 1; fruit a hard achene with feathery twisted plume 2½–3″ long in reddish calyx tube; Mar.-Apr. Distr. Foothill belt of w. slope in chaparral.

Birch-leaf Mountain Mahogany or Hard-tack is a browse plant for deer and livestock. The name Mountain Ironwood refers to the beautiful hard wood. Dense stands appear gray when the bushes are clothed with the feathery-plumed achenes. The Desert Mahogany (*C. ledifolius*) on the east slope has slender leaves with curled edges and a prominent midrib. It grows as a shrub or tree with spreading crown, contorted branches, and sometimes a large rough-barked trunk.

S-19. Chamise. *Adenostoma fasciculatum* (pl. 21, col. pl. 11). Ht. 2–12 ft., diffusely branched, stems straight, clothed with evergreen leaf bundles; old bark shreddy, reddish or grayish brown; leaves in bundles, linear, ¼″ long, tip sharp, often resinous; flower panicle dense, 1½″–4″ long; flowers minute; sepals 5, united around receptacle; petals 5, white; stamens 10–15; pistil 1; fruit an achene in hardened receptacle; Feb.-July. Distr. Foothill belt of w. slope, 500–5000 ft., in chaparral.

Often in nearly pure stand, this "greasewood" is the commonest of chaparral plants from the lower foothills up to the yellow pines. The thickets sometimes are almost impenetrable for man and pack animals but afford favorable shelter for many small native creatures. It stump sprouts abundantly after a fire.

S-20. Bitterbrush. *Purshia tridentata* (pl. 21, col. pl. 12). Ht. 1½–6 ft., diffusely branched, bark brown or gray, young twigs woolly, glandular; leaves deciduous, in bundles, ¼″–½″+ long, wedge-shaped, tip 3-lobed, margins with fine glands, woolly green above, white below; flowers ⅔″ wide, usually single; calyx tube with resin granules; petals 5, to ⅓″ long, spoon-shaped, cream yellow; stamens 18–30; pistil 1; fruit a leathery, hairy achene joined to persistent style; Apr.-July. Distr. Common on e. slope at 4000–7000 ft. on arid flats and slopes (some high on w. slope).

Bitterbrush or Antelope Brush is a silvery-barked shrub bright with small yellow flowers when blooming. On the dry eastern side of the Sierra it is useful as browse for deer and livestock in a region dominated by the unpalatable sagebrush.

S-21. Bitter or Red Cherry. *Prunus emarginata* (pl. 22). Ht. 4–12 ft. (rarely, a tree to 20+ ft.); branches slender, very long, bark gray or reddish; deciduous; leaves ¾″–2″ x ⅜″–1″, ovate to oblong, rounded at tip, edge finely toothed, 1 or 2 small glands near base; smooth and dark green above; blossoms 3–10 in short corymb; flower ½″ wide, white; sepals 5, united at base; petals 5, white, roundish; stamens 15–30; pistil 1; fruit ⅓″ long, bright

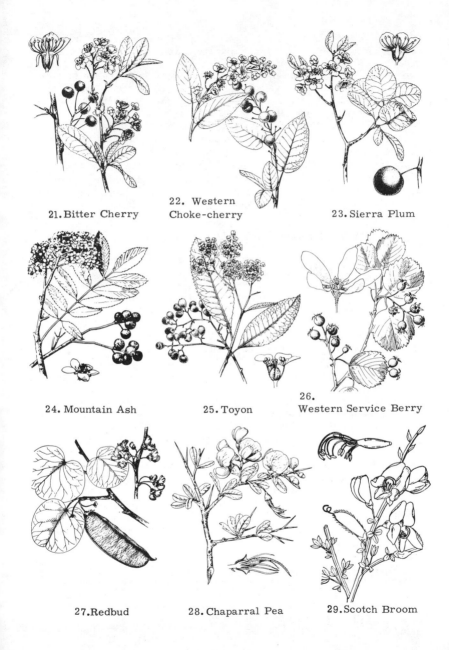

21. Bitter Cherry

22. Western Choke-cherry

23. Sierra Plum

24. Mountain Ash

25. Toyon

26. Western Service Berry

27. Redbud

28. Chaparral Pea

29. Scotch Broom

Plate 22. Shrubs

red, with stony pit, pulp very bitter; June-July. DISTR. Upper Yellow Pine and Lodgepole–fir belts at 4000–8000 ft. often in large thickets.

In summer many stream banks, moist slopes, and roadsides at middle altitudes have an almond-like fragrance from the open thickets of this cherry. Later the little fruits, too bitter for man, are eaten by several kinds of birds.

S-22. Western Choke-cherry. *Prunus demissa* (pl. 22, col. pl. 12). Ht. 2–12 ft. as shrub (or tree to 20 ft.), erect, slender; bark smooth or scaly, dark red or brown, young twigs hairy; deciduous; leaves 1½″–3½″ x ¾″–2″, broadly lance-shaped, tip tapered, edge finely toothed, 1 or 2 glands at base; blossoms many in cylindrical raceme 2″–5″ long; flower to ½″ dia., white; fruit globular, dia. to ¼″, red to dark purple, with stony pit, bitter but edible; Apr.-May. DISTR. W. slope in Foothill and Yellow Pine belts at 1500–6700 ft. in moist places.

Choke-cherry is a graceful shrub with showy white flower spikes followed by fruits too puckery in taste for most people.

S-23. Sierra Plum. *Prunus subcordata* (pl. 22). Ht. 4–8 ft. (or tree to 20 ft.) branches stiff, crooked, rough, gray-brown; branchlets thorny; deciduous; leaves ¾″–2″ x ½″–1½″, elliptic to round, finely toothed, usually 2 glands at base; blossoms in cluster of 2–5, flower ½″ wide, white, later pink, petals 5; fruit oblong, ¾″–1″ long, bright red or yellow, with stony pit; Mar.-Apr. DISTR. Mainly at 2500–4500 ft. in Yellow Pine belt, more common and fruitful on northeast slope of Sierra; on moist or dry rocky slopes.

Sierra Plum, the only edible stone fruit of the Sierra, is rather sparse on the west slope. It is commoner and yields larger fruits in some quantity on the east side from Plumas County northward. It was used by Indians and by early settlers for a delicious jam.

S-24. Mountain Ash. *Sorbus sitchensis* (pl. 22, col. pl. 12). Ht. 2–9 ft., erect, many-branched, bark smooth, dull red; deciduous; leaves pinnate, of 7–15 leaflets, each 1″–2½″ x ½″–1″, elliptic, finely toothed; blossom clusters flat-topped, dia. 2″–3″; flower dia. ½″, white; sepals 5; petals 5; stamens about 20; styles 2–5; fruit to ⅛″ dia., berry-like, coral red, pulp bitter; June-Aug. DISTR. Lodgepole–fir and Subalpine belts at 7000 ft. and higher, along streams and on moist slopes or flats.

The Mountain Ash is uncommon but showy when seen. In late summer or autumn the large clusters of coral red berries contrast strikingly with the greenery of other plants.

S-25. Toyon. *Heteromeles arbutifolia* (pl. 22, col. pl. 12). Ht. 5–15 ft., erect, bushy, young branches woolly; evergreen; leaves 2″–4″ x ¾″–1½″, elliptical, narrowed at ends, leathery, toothed, dark green above, paler below; flowers in dense terminal panicle 2″–3″ high; sepals 5, joined at base, persistent; petals 5, distinct, spreading, white; stamens 10; pistils 2–3; fruit dia. to ⅛″, ovoid, berry-like, bright red; June-July. DISTR. Mainly in Foothill belt of w. slope up to 3500 ft. on rocky slopes or in canyon bottoms.

From November to January the clusters of bright red "Christmas berries" contrast with the dark green foliage to make Toyon a most handsome shrub. It is planted commonly in home gardens and city parks. The berries are eaten by robins, waxwings, and other birds using such food in winter.

S-26. Western Service Berry. *Amelanchier alnifolia* (pl. 22, col. pl. 12). Ht. 3–12 ft., erect; older bark gray, younger reddish brown; deciduous; leaves simple, alternate, ¾"–1¾" x ½"–1", oval or roundish, 1-veined from base, margin entire or outer part serrate; flower racemes 1"–2" long; sepals 5, joined at base, free ends persisting on fruit; petals 5, slender, ½"–¾" long, white, falling early; stamens many; pistil 1; fruit berry-like, ¼" dia., spherical, purplish, pulpy, edible; May-June. DISTR. Yellow Pine and Lodgepole-fir belts at 2500–9000 ft. in moist places.

Service Berry often grows in large thickets that become white with blossoms. The leaves vary in shape, toothing of margins, and amount of woolly covering. Indians and early settlers ate the berries, which are sweetish but not very tasty.

PEA FAMILY (LEGUMINOSAE). Corolla irregular, butterfly-like (top petal or banner shorter than 2 side or wing petals, 2 lower or keel petals longer); fruit a 2-sided pod.

S-27. Redbud. *Cercis occidentalis* (pl. 22, col. pl. 12). Ht. 8–20 ft.; many long stems clustered at base; deciduous; leaves alternate, simple, dia. 2"–3½", round, heart-shaped at base, smooth; flowers in clusters, appearing before leaves; calyx to ⅜" wide, bell-shaped, 5-lobed; petals 5, red-purple, ½" long, irregular; stamens 10; fruit pod 1½"–3" x ½"–⅝", flat, maturing dull red; Feb.-Apr. DISTR. Foothill belt at 1000–5000 ft.

Redbud flowers appear in masses from late winter through spring, followed by leaves that are bronzy green and later glossy green. The clusters of reddish brown pods persist into the next winter.

S-28. Chaparral Pea. *Pickeringia montana* (pl. 22). Ht. 2–8 ft.; branches rigid, branchlets spiny; evergreen; leaves few, to ½" long, simple or palmately 3-parted, elliptical, wider beyond middle, no petiole; flowers usually single, near ends of branchlets; calyx bell-shaped, 5-lobed; corolla rose-purple, ¾" long, irregular, banner with yellowish spot near base, petals 5; stamens 10; fruit a flat pod to 2" long; May-June. DISTR. Sparingly in Foothill belt, Butte to Mariposa Co., in chaparral.

S-29. Scotch Broom. *Cytisus scoparius* (pl. 22, col. pl. 12). Ht. 3–10 ft.; branches green, angular, broom-like; evergreen; leaves few, 3-parted, leaflets to ⅛" long; flowers in terminal racemes from leaf axils; sepals 5, forming 2-lipped tube; corolla ¾" long, bright yellow, butterfly-like, petals 5, broad; stamens 10; pod 2" x ½", flat, hairy, black; Jan.-June. DISTR. Naturalized in Foothill belt, Amador to Nevada Co.

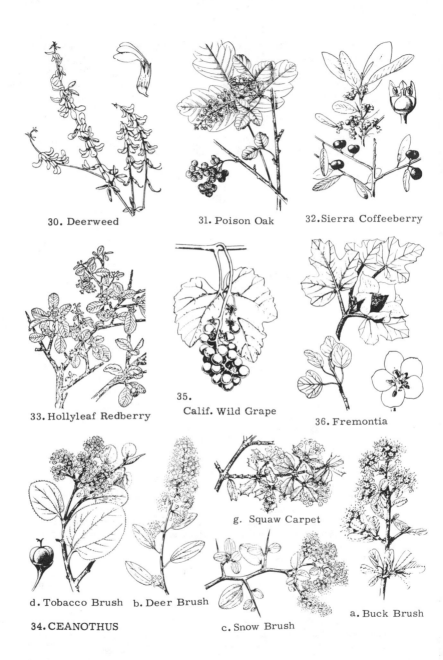

30. Deerweed

31. Poison Oak

32. Sierra Coffeeberry

33. Hollyleaf Redberry

35. Calif. Wild Grape

36. Fremontia

d. Tobacco Brush b. Deer Brush

34. CEANOTHUS

g. Squaw Carpet

c. Snow Brush

a. Buck Brush

Plate 23. Shrubs

127

Scotch Broom occupies 100,000 acres in the Coast Range and Sierran foothills. Its blossoms are a showy addition to roadsides near the Yellow Pine belt, but the plant is a pest on forest and range lands. Spanish or French Broom (*C. monspessulanus*), present in small numbers, has slightly-angled hairy branchlets, many leaves, and ½" fragrant flowers from April to June.

S-30. Deerweed. *Lotus scoparius* (pl. 23, col. pl. 12). Ht. 1½–5 ft.; bushy, branches long, slender, greenish; leaves alternate, usually 3-parted, leaflets to ⅜" long, oblong, pointed; umbels terminal, several-flowered; corolla ⅓" long, irregular, yellow to whitish with red or purple marks; pod thin, curved; Feb.-Oct. DISTR. Foothill belt n. to Amador Co. up to 2500 ft.

SUMAC FAMILY (ANACARDIACEAE). Juice oily.

S-31. Poison Oak. *Rhus diversiloba* (pl. 23). Ht. 2–8 ft.; erect or spreading, sometimes vine-like on tree trunks; deciduous; leaves alternate, usually 3-parted, leaflets 1"–4" long, variable, roundish or ovate, lobed or toothed; flower panicles appearing with leaves; flowers ⅛" long, regular, greenish white, petals 5, spreading; fruit to ¼" dia., berry-like, whitish or brown, stony-seeded; Apr.-May. DISTR. Common from borders of Great Valley streams through Foothill belt to lower mountain slopes and valleys, at 50–5000 ft.

Poison Oak (not an oak but related to the eastern poison ivy), is the most widespread California shrub. In fall its brilliant red foliage colors many slopes and roadsides. The plant's (non-volatile) juice produces an irritating rash, sometimes severe, on the skin of many persons. Contact with the leaves or with clothing that has touched the foliage or smoke from burning plants serves to carry the oily substance. Washing thoroughly with soap or applying special skin preparations reduces the trouble.

BUCKTHORN FAMILY (RHAMNACEAE). Flowers small; calyx tube lined with a disc.

S-32. Sierra Coffeeberry. *Rhamnus rubra* (pl. 23). Ht. 2–6 ft., erect; branchlets slender, deep reddish; semi-deciduous; leaves alternate, scattered, 1½"–2½", narrowly oblong, minutely toothed, tip usually pointed, yellowish green; flowers in short umbels, petals small, inconspicuous, greenish; flower parts in 5's; berry globular, dia. ¼", green, becoming reddish then black, with 2 seeds; May-Aug. DISTR. Common mainly in Yellow Pine belt, at 4000–7000 ft.; also on e. slope in Mono Co. at about 6500 ft.

Coffeeberry, related to Cascara Sagrada (T-39), has puckery-tasting bark with purgative qualities.

S-33. Redberry. *Rhamnus crocea* (pl. 23). Ht. 4–12 ft., stout shrub or tree-like; branchlets many, rigid, short; evergreen; leaves ¾"–1⅗" x ½"–1", ovate to roundish, 1-veined from base, edge finely or sharply toothed, smooth and dark green above, paler, slightly woolly below; flowers minute, greenish, rarely with petals; fruit to ⅓″ long, oval, bright red, in clusters; Feb.-Apr. DISTR. Foothill belt of w. slope s. to Tulare Co. below 5000 ft. on dry slopes.

The variety in the Sierra, *ilicifolia,* is called Hollyleaf Redberry.

S-34. Ceanothus. Genus *Ceanothus* (pl. 23). Leaves simple, petioled, opposite (*a, g, h*) or alternate (others), deciduous (*b, f*) or evergreen, usually 3-veined from base; flowers small, in clusters, showy, white (*a–d*) or blue (*e–h*); sepals 5, united at base to ovary; petals 5, stalked, scoop-shaped; stamens 5, opposite petals; fruit a 3-lobed capsule.

From the foothills into Subalpine areas there are species of ceanothus; 11 of 40 in California occur in the Sierra. Mostly they are shrubs (*a–f*), but two make spreading ground mats (*g–h*). Some are common and widespread, often in chaparral; others are local or scarce. The group has no common name; "buck brush" and "deer brush" refer to frequent browsing on leaves and stems by deer. The bushes give shelter and nest sites for birds, and the seeds are eaten by rodents and birds. In spring and early summer the masses of white or blue flowers add much to the local floral display.

a. Buck Brush. *C. cuneatus* (pl. 23, col. pl. 13). Ht. 3–8+ ft.; bark gray; branches dense, rigid, diverging, irregular; leaves *wedge-shaped,* wider at tip, ¼″–1″ x ¼″, 1-veined, *opposite;* flower clusters small, white (rarely blue), sweet-odored; Mar.-May. DISTR. Foothill belt at 300–4000 ft. on dry slopes.

b. Deer Brush. *C. integerrimus* (pl. 23, col. pl. 13). Ht. 3–12 ft.; bark green to yellow; branches loose, some drooping; *deciduous;* leaves large, ¾″–2″ x ⅜″–1½″, thin, elliptic, light green; flower panicles compound, large, 2½″–6″ x 1″–4″, white (occ. blue), fragrant; May-July. DISTR. Abundant in Yellow Pine belt at 2000–5000 ft. (north) and 3500–6000 ft. (south), often in forest.

c. Snow Brush or Mountain Whitethorn. *C. cordulatus* (pl. 23). Ht. 2–5 ft., dia. 3–9 ft., round-topped, flattish (depressed by snow); branchlets many, *spiny, whitish;* leaves small, ¼″–1″ x ¼″–½″, ovate, above light green, below whitish, margin usually entire; flower clusters to 1½″ long, white, strongly scented; May-July. DISTR. Abundant in pine forests at 3500–9000 ft. on both slopes.

d. Tobacco Brush. *C. velutinus* (pl. 23, col. pl. 13). Ht. 2–5+ ft., spreading, round-topped; branchlets brownish; leaves large, 1½″–2½″ x ¾″–1¼″, rounded to elliptical, edge finely toothed, *varnished dark green* above, woolly below, with strong cinnamon odor; flower clusters 2″–4″ long, white; May-Aug. DISTR. Lodgepole–fir belt and edges of adjacent areas at 3500–10000 ft. on both slopes. (See I-101, Calif. Tortoise-shell Butterfly.)

e. Chaparral Whitethorn. *C. leucodermis.* Ht. 5–12 ft.; branches rigid, *spiny, gray* to white; leaves ½″–1½″ x ¼″–½″, ovate, smooth, with white "bloom"; flower clusters 1″–3″, pale blue (to white); Apr.-June. DISTR. Foothill belt n. to Mariposa Co.

f. Littleleaf Ceanothus. *C. parvifolius.* Ht. to 3 ft., spreading, flat-topped;

branches flexible, olive green; *deciduous;* leaves ¼"–1" x ¼"–½", elliptic, margins entire, above light green; flower cluster simple, 1"–3", pale to deep blue; June-July. DISTR. Upper Yellow Pine belt and lower Lodgepole–fir belt, Tulare to Eldorado Co.

g. Squaw Carpet or Mahala Mat. *C. prostratus* (pl. 23). Prostrate, 2"–6" high, mats 2–8 ft. wide; branches many, often rooting at nodes; leaves ¼"–1" x ⅛"–⅝", *opposite,* wedge-shaped, thick, firm, dark green, often 3-toothed at end; flower clusters small, blue (pinkish with age); Apr.-May. DISTR. Yellow Pine belt at 2100–7800 ft. on forest floor, road edges, etc.

h. Fresno Mat. *C. fresnensis.* Nearly prostrate, mats 6–10 ft. wide, few branches erect to 12"; leaves to ½" long, *opposite,* elliptical, fine-toothed at end, leathery, dark green; blossoms in small umbels, blue; May-June. DISTR. Yellow Pine belt at 3000–7000 ft. Plumas to Fresno Co.

VINE FAMILY (VITACEAE). Climbing by tendrils.

S-35. California Wild Grape. *Vitis californica* (pl. 23). A woody vine, stems 5–50 ft. long, climbing by tendrils; deciduous; leaves 1½"–5" wide, alternate, roundish, base heart-shaped, 3- or 5-veined, edge toothed, surfaces woolly; tendrils opposite leaves, branched, twisted; flowers 5-parted, many, small, in branched clusters, greenish, fragrant; fruit a juicy berry, dia. ¼"–½", purplish, covered with white bloom; May-July. DISTR. Great Valley and Foothill belt, on trees near streams.

Wild Grape climbs most often on oaks and cottonwoods. Sometimes its foliage blankets and kills the tree by exclusion of sunlight. The sweet-smelling blossoms attract many bees. The berries are edible but have large seeds.

STERCULIA FAMILY (STERCULIACEAE). Stamens 5, united in to a tube at base.

S-36. Fremontia. *Fremontia californica* (pl. 23, col. pl. 12). Ht. 6–15 ft., a loosely branched shrub or small tree; branchlets long, flexible, tough, with many short hairy spurs bearing leaves or flowers; evergreen; leaves ovate, entire or 3-lobed, ¼"–1½" long, thick, roughish and dark green above, with dense gray or whitish felt below; flowers single, showy; calyx lemon yellow, dia. 1½"–2", of 5 rounded petal-like sepals united at base; no petals; style 1, slender; fruit capsule ovoid, densely hairy, ¾"–1⅛" long, persistent; May-June. DISTR. Foothill belt of w. slope, at 1500–5300 ft., abundant s. of Mariposa Co.; on slopes with some seepage.

Fremontia, called Flannel Bush because of its hairy covering, is a showy shrub with many conspicuous large yellow blossoms. It has been brought into cultivation for gardens.

SILK TASSEL FAMILY (GARRYACEAE). Branchlets 4-sided.

S-37. Silk Tassel. *Garrya fremontii* (pl. 24). Ht. 4–10 ft., branches erect, usually yellowish green; evergreen; leaves opposite, elliptical, tapered at

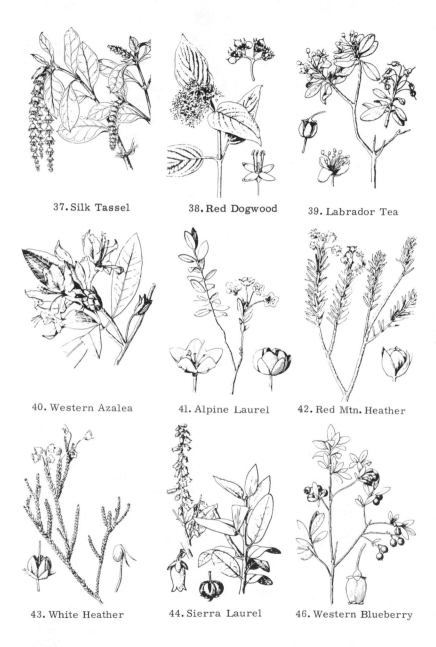

37. Silk Tassel   38. Red Dogwood   39. Labrador Tea

40. Western Azalea   41. Alpine Laurel   42. Red Mtn. Heather

43. White Heather   44. Sierra Laurel   46. Western Blueberry

Plate 24. Shrubs

ends, 1-veined from base, $1\frac{1}{4}''$–$2\frac{1}{2}''$ long, usually thick and leathery, smooth and shiny above, grayish and woolly below; ♂ and ♀ flowers on separate plants, small, on hanging, tassel-like catkins; no petals; ♂ catkins 3''–8'' long, in clusters of 2–5, flowers yellowish, sepals 4, stamens 4; ♀ catkins $1\frac{1}{2}''$–2'' long (to $3\frac{1}{2}''$ with fruit), sepals 2 or none; fruit berry-like, later dry on outside, dia. $\frac{1}{4}''$, buff to black; Jan.-Apr. DISTR. Foothill and Yellow Pine belts at 2000–7000 ft. in chaparral or under forest.

Known also as Bear Brush, this Silk Tassel is a hard-leaved member of the chaparral in the foothills or lower forest. The bark, leaves, and fruit contain a bitter substance sometimes used as a tonic, so that some related species are called "quinine bush."

DOGWOOD FAMILY (CORNACEAE). Sepals 4, minute; petals 4; stamens 4; ovary inferior.

S-38. Red or Creek Dogwood. *Cornus californica* (or *stolonifera*) (pl. 24). Ht. 5–15 ft., branches smooth, red or purplish; deciduous; leaves 2''–4'' long, ovate, rounded at base; tip pointed, veins furrowed, lower surface with many 2-branched hairs; blossoms many in round-topped clusters, dia. $1\frac{1}{2}''$–2''; flowers small, petals $\frac{1}{8}''$ long, white, sometimes finely haired; fruit spherical, flattened, dia. $\frac{1}{4}''$, white to blue; May-July. DISTR. Mainly in Yellow Pine belt of w. slope at about 5000–7000 ft. in moist places.

Stream sides and damp slopes at middle altitudes often support small thickets of this reddish-stemmed dogwood. The Blackfruit Dogwood (*C. sessilis*), with few yellowish flowers and larger oval and shiny fruits, occurs at 500 to 5000 ft. in the foothills from Calaveras County north, blooming in March and April.

HEATH FAMILY (ERICACEAE). Petals joined and corolla bell- or urn-shaped (except no. 39).

S-39. Labrador Tea. *Ledum glandulosum* (pl. 24). Ht. 2–5 ft., erect, rather rigid; evergreen; leaves crowded toward ends of branches, alternate $\frac{3}{4}''$–$2\frac{1}{2}''$ x $\frac{1}{2}''$–$\frac{3}{4}''$, oblong, edges often curved, dark green and smooth above, paler with gland-dotted felt below; blossoms small, white, in crowded terminal clusters; flower dia. to $\frac{1}{2}''$; sepals 5; petals 5, oval, spreading; stamens 10, separate, longer than petals; fruit a 5-celled oval capsule, $\frac{1}{8}''$ long; June-Aug. DISTR. W. slope at 4000–10000 ft. in damp places.

The leaves, elsewhere known as "trapper's tea," give a turpentine-like odor when bruised. The plant is somewhat poisonous for livestock.

S-40. Western Azalea. *Rhododendron occidentale* (pl. 24, col. pl. 13). Ht. 2–10 ft., loosely branched; deciduous; leaves clustered at ends of twigs, elliptical, 1''–4'' x $\frac{1}{2}''$–1'', thin, smooth or scatteringly haired; blossoms clustered, large, showy; sepals 5, small; petals 5, joined as bell-shaped corolla $1\frac{1}{4}''$–$1\frac{3}{4}''$ long, white or pinkish, upper lobe with yellow splotch; stamens 5, style 1, all protruding from corolla; fruit capsule oblong, $\frac{3}{8}''$–$\frac{3}{4}''$, hairy;

May-July. DISTR. Mainly in Yellow Pine belt at 3500–7500 ft. along streams and on moist slopes.

The handsome fragrant Azalea is a showy shrub of late spring and early summer, on damp sites in the forest. Often the blossoms lean out over a stream. The foliage is poisonous to livestock.

S-41. Alpine Laurel. *Kalmia polifolia* (pl. 24). Ht. 2–6 ft., spreading; evergreen; leaves oblong, narrow, ¼″–¾″ long, edges rolled backward, shiny green above, whitish below; blossoms in umbels at ends of branches; calyx deeply 5-parted; corolla 5-lobed, bowl-shaped, dia. ½″–¾″, bright pink to rose-purple; stamens 10, short, in pouches on petals; fruit a valved capsule; June-Aug. DISTR. W. slope in Lodgepole–fir belt and above at 6500–12000 ft. in wet places.

Borders of lakes or meadows and swampy places up to timberline are the home of the pale Alpine Laurel, a plant deadly for sheep and cattle. The stamens are held outward by the petals; when stamens or corolla are touched, the elastic filaments spring inward and pollen is shaken from the anthers.

S-42. Red Mountain Heather. *Phyllodoce breweri* (pl. 24, col. pl. 13). Stems 4″–12″ high, erect from branching base on ground; evergreen; leaves alternate, crowded on stems, ¼″–½″ long, linear, blunt-tipped, margins thickened; blossoms in crowded terminal clusters; sepals 5; corolla bell-shaped, 5-lobed, dia. to ½″, rose-purple, petals joined at base, tips spreading; stamens 7–10 and style 1, all protruding from bell; fruit a spherical capsule; June-Aug. DISTR. Subalpine and Alpine belts at 6500–12000 ft. from Tulare Co. n. in swampy places.

Wet acid soils of the High Sierra are the home of our "red heather," where it grows in irregular patches that may be small or large. Soon after the snow departs the small upright leaf-clothed stems bear clusters of little rose-purple flowers making carpets of bright color.

S-43. White Heather. *Cassiope mertensiana* (pl. 24). Stems to 12″ high, erect, rigid; evergreen; leaves ⅛″ long, thick, boat-shaped, narrow, in 4 rows against stem; each flower drooping at top of erect flower stem, bell-shaped, white, ¼″ long, 5-lobed; stamens 10 (or 8); fruit a globular capsule; July-Aug. DISTR. Subalpine and Alpine belts at 8000–10000 ft. on rocky ridges.

Only mountain climbers in high country will find the cassiope or White Heather. Amid granite ledges the perennial wiry stems and basal branches often form dense mats that are brightened by the small bell-like flowers in late summer.

S-44. Sierra Laurel. *Leucothoe davisiae* (pl. 24). Ht. 2–5 ft., erect, branches mostly smooth; evergreen; leaves alternate, ¾″–2¾″ x ⅜″–⅝″, oblong or oval, thick, somewhat leathery, minutely toothed, shiny deep green above, duller and paler below; blossoms in erect racemes 2″–4″ long; flowers white, hanging; calyx star-shaped; corolla bell-shaped, ¼″–⅜″ long,

5-lobed; stamens 10; fruit capsule spherical, ¼″ long, smooth; June-July. DISTR. Sparse at 5000–8000 ft. on moist ground; poisonous to livestock.

S-45. Manzanita. Genus *Arctostaphylos* (pl. 25). Ht. 3 ft. or more (except *f*); branches crooked; bark red, smooth; evergreen; leaves thickish, firm; flowers in terminal clusters; calyx 4- or 5-parted, broad-lobed; corolla urn-shaped with 4 or 5 recurved lobes at small opening; stamens 10; fruit usually a flattened sphere with nutlets enclosed in soft pulp.

Manzanita, with its irregular reddish branch system, is a common element of foothill chaparral and parts of the Yellow Pine forest; one ground-sprawling species grows at 6000 to 10000 ft. The many clusters of small urn-shaped flowers are followed by large crops of reddish or brownish "berries" that are eaten by some birds and by foxes and bears; the seeds are relished by chipmunks. Of 38 species in California, about 6 are in the Sierra. Hybrids sometimes occur where two species are present.

a. White-leaf Manzanita. *A. viscida* (pl. 25). Ht. 4–12 ft., stems and branches crooked with smooth red bark, branchlets slender, whitish, and smooth; leaves ovate, 1″–2″ x ¾″–1½″, whitish, smooth on both surfaces; flowers in open panicles or racemes, rosy to white, ⅜″ long; fruit globular, dia. ¼″–⅜″, light brown to deep red, often sticky-surfaced; Feb.-Apr. DISTR. Common in Foothill belt s. to Amador Co. in chaparral.

b. Mariposa Manzanita. *A. mariposa* (pl. 25, col. pl. 13). Ht. 4–8 ft., compactly branched; bark smooth, reddish brown, branchlets glandular, hairy; leaves 1″–2″ x ¾″–1″, oval, thick, rough, grayish green to whitish; flowers ¼″ long, white to pinkish, in compact panicle; fruit ⅜″ dia., red, sticky-surfaced; Feb.-Apr. DISTR. Narrow area in Foothill belt, Amador to Kern Co.

c. Indian Manzanita. *A. mewukka.* Ht. 3–8 ft., erect, branches crooked; bark deep red to purple; branchlets smooth or finely downy; leaves 1″–1½″ x ½″–⅞″, elliptical, smooth, pale gray-green; flowers ¼″ long, white, in loose panicles; fruit ⅜″–⅝″, flattish, dark red, smooth; Mar.-Apr. DISTR. Upper Foothill belt, Butte to Tulare Co.

d. Common Manzanita. *A. manzanita.* Ht. 6–12 (rarely 22) ft.; erect, tall, sometimes widely branched from base; branches long, crooked; bark dark reddish brown; leaves elliptic to ovate, 1″–1¾″ x ¾″–1½″, thick, firm, pale or dark green; flower panicles rather open, drooping; flowers ¼″ long, white or pale pink; fruit globular, sometimes flattish, dia. ⁵⁄₁₆″–⁷⁄₁₆″, white, maturing deep reddish brown; Feb.-Apr. DISTR. Mainly in Foothill belt s. to Mariposa Co. on low hills and valley flats.

e. Green Manzanita. *A. patula* (pl. 25). Ht. 3–7 ft.; stems several, usually from swollen base; old bark smooth, reddish brown; branchlets sometimes greenish yellow; leaves 1″–1¾″ x ¾″–1½″, broadly ovate to roundish, smooth, bright or yellow-green; flowers pinkish, ¼″ long, in dense panicles; fruit dia. ¼″–½″, chestnut brown to blackish; May-June. DISTR. Mainly in Yellow Pine belt at 2500–5000 ft. (north) or 5000–9000 ft. (south); in open forest.

f. Pinemat Manzanita. *A. nevadensis* (pl. 25). Ht. 6″–18″; main stems on ground or rocks, rooting freely; bark smooth, reddish brown, peeling in thin

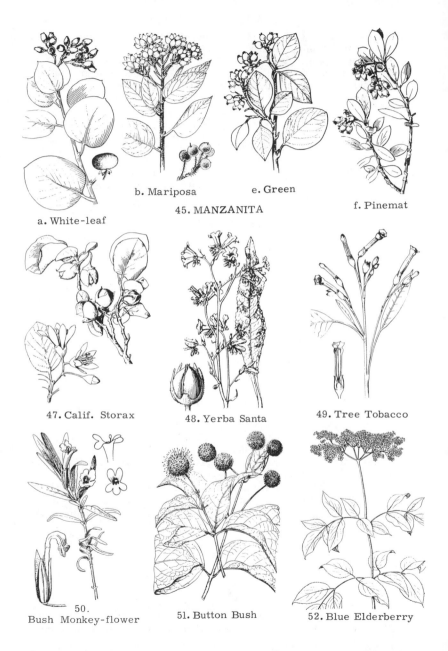

b. Mariposa

e. Green

45. MANZANITA

f. Pinemat

a. White-leaf

47. Calif. Storax

48. Yerba Santa

49. Tree Tobacco

50.
Bush Monkey-flower

51. Button Bush

52. Blue Elderberry

Plate 25. Shrubs   135

pieces; leaves ¾"–1½" x ¼"–¾", elliptic, thick, leathery, patterned with dark veins, mostly shiny green above and below; flowers usually white, ¼" long, in short racemes; fruit globose, dia. ¼", smooth, dark brown; May-June. DISTR. Upper Yellow Pine and Lodgepole–fir belts at 6000–10000 ft. from Tulare Co. n.; often in dense carpet-like mats on forest floor or sprawling over granite.

S-46. Western Blueberry. *Vaccinium occidentale* (pl. 24). Ht. 1–2½ ft.; compact, stems smooth and stoutish, branchlets many, clustered, erect; deciduous; leaves ⅜"–¾" x ⅛"–⅜", elliptic to oval, tapered to base, light green and smooth above, whitened below; flowers solitary or 2–4 in cluster; calyx 4- or 5-lobed; corolla white, cylindric, 4-lobed; berry elliptic, ¼" long, blue-black with white bloom; June-July. DISTR. Lodgepole–fir and Subalpine belts at 5000–8000 ft. in wet meadows or near streams.

STORAX FAMILY (STYRACEAE). Calyx tubular at base.

S-47. California Storax. *Styrax officinalis* (pl. 25). Ht. 3–8 ft.; erect, twigs grayish; deciduous; leaves alternate, 1"–3½" x ¾"–3", oval, 1-veined from base, finely woolly when young, later smooth; flowers somewhat like orange blossoms, 2–5 in terminal cluster; calyx bell-like; irregularly 5-toothed; petals white, usually 6 (4–8), oblong, ½"–1" long, united at base; stamens 10–16, united into a tube at base; fruit globular, dia. ½", 3-valved with 1 nut-like seed; Apr.-June. DISTR. Scattered in Foothill belt at 500–2300 ft.

PHACELIA FAMILY (HYDROPHYLLACEAE). Stamens 5, inserted near base of corolla, alternate with its lobes.

S-48. Yerba Santa. *Eriodictyon californicum* (pl. 25, col. pl. 13). Ht. 2–8 ft., erect, open, branchlets and leaves usually sticky; leaves 2"–4+" x ⅜"–2", lance-shaped, pinnately veined, edge toothed, leathery, brownish green, smooth, and sticky above; lower surface with fine felt between veins; blossoms in 1-sided compound clusters; sepals 5, nearly separate; corolla funnel-like, petals 5, ⅜"–⅝" long, lavender or pale blue (rarely whitish); stamens 5, on corolla tube; fruit capsule 4-valved; May-July. DISTR. Foothill belt up to 5000 ft. and n. to Plumas Co. in dry areas.

Leaves of Yerba Santa give a pleasant aromatic odor when crushed. They have been brewed into a syrupy remedy for colds, and also dried and used as a "miner's tobacco"; the plants occur in chaparral and often on cleared roadsides.

NIGHTSHADE FAMILY (SOLANACEAE). Calyx and corolla tubular, end flared into 5 lobes.

S-49. Tree Tobacco. *Nicotiana glauca* (pl. 25). Ht. 6–15 ft., erect, branched; evergreen; leaves 2½"–5" x 1"–2"; ovate, smooth with white "bloom," petioles 1"–2"; blossoms yellow in terminal panicles; calyx united, 5-toothed; corolla to 1½" long, tubular, 5 short lobes; stamens 5 on corolla;

fruit capsule ½″ long, seeds many, small; Apr.-Aug. or longer. DISTR. Common in Great Valley and Foothill belt to 3000 ft. often in stream beds.

Native to South America, this plant was introduced from Mexico during Spanish days and has spread widely in lowland places.

FIGWORT FAMILY (SCROPHULARIACEAE). Calyx 5-cleft; stamens 4, inserted on 2-lipped corolla.

S-50. Bush Monkey-flower. Genus *Diplacus* (pl. 25). Ht. 9″–4 ft.; erect or spreading, branchlets often sticky and downy-haired; evergreen; leaves 1″–3″ x ³⁄₁₆″–⅝″ wide, narrowly oval or linear, edge curved, often toothed, yellowish to dark green and sticky above, paler and woolly below; flowers many, yellow, cream, or salmon-colored; calyx tubular, 5-angled, ¾″–1¼″ long; corolla 1½″ or longer, lower part funnel-shaped, outer portion spread as 2 upper and 3 lower lobes; stamens 4, inserted on corolla; fruit capsule ½″–¾″ long; Apr.-Aug. DISTR. Common, mainly in Foothill belt, n. to Plumas Co., on dry sites.

Three slightly different species of sticky-surfaced shrubby monkey-flowers are common in different parts of the western foothills and up into the lower forest: *D. leptanthus,* Plumas to Placer Co.; *D. auranticus,* Eldorado to Tuolumne Co.; and *D. longiflorus,* from Fresno Co. south. Often the plants are grouped on roadside cuts, providing colorful displays for passers-by.

MADDER FAMILY (RUBIACEAE). Leaves opposite; blossom heads spherical; corolla 4-cleft.

S-51. Button Bush. *Cephalanthus occidentalis* (pl. 25). Ht. 3–12+ ft.; young branches commonly in 3's, smooth and green, yellow, or reddish, older bark gray or brown and furrowed; deciduous; leaves simple, opposite, or in whorls of 3 (to 5), 3″–6″ x ¾″–1½″, ovate or elliptic, often wavy-edged, glossy pale green; blossom heads spherical, dia. ½″–1½″, each of many small flowers; sepals 4, making ⅛″ green tube; corolla white, funnel-shaped, ¼″–⅛″ long; stamens 4; fruit hard, ¼″ long; July-Sept. DISTR. Great Valley and into Foothill belt, up to 1000 ft. along flowing streams.

HONEYSUCKLE FAMILY (CAPRIFOLIACEAE). Leaves opposite; corolla 5-lobed.

S-52. Blue Elderberry. *Sambucus caerulea* (or *glauca*) (pl. 25, col. pl. 13). Ht. 4–10 ft. as shrub, occasionally a tree 25–30 ft.; branches slender, pithy, brownish; deciduous; leaves pinnately compound, 5″–8″ long; leaflets 5–9, usually narrowly oblong, 1″–6″ x ½″–2″, edges finely toothed, smooth to sparsely hairy; blossom clusters compound, flat-topped, 2″–8″ wide; flowers small, white or cream; calyx minute or none, 5-lobed; corolla saucer-like, 5-lobed; stamens 5; berry dia. ¼″, blue to black with whitish bloom; Apr.-Aug. DISTR. Edge of Great Valley into Yellow Pine belt at 5400 ft., commonly on stream slopes.

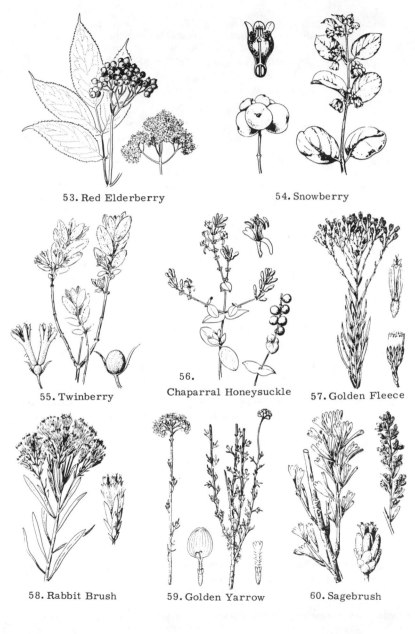

53. Red Elderberry

54. Snowberry

55. Twinberry

56. Chaparral Honeysuckle

57. Golden Fleece

58. Rabbit Brush

59. Golden Yarrow

60. Sagebrush

Plate 26. Shrubs

Bushes of Blue Elderberry become covered with masses of large white flower clusters as warm weather arrives. Later they bear quantities of small bluish berries that are relished by many kinds of birds. With some labor they yield excellent material to make pies or tarts. A slightly differing form (*S. velutina*) with smaller berries occurs on dry, open Sierran slopes at 300 to 8000 feet.

S-53. Red Elderberry. *Sambucus racemosa* (or *melanocarpa*) (pl. 26). Ht. 2–6 ft.; spreading, young branches green, pith brownish; deciduous; leaves pinnately compound, 3″–6″ long, leaflets 5–7, ovate or elliptic, 1½″–5″ x ¾″–1½″, sharply toothed; blossom clusters dome-shaped, dia. 1½″–2½″; flowers creamy to white (structure as in S-52); berry bright red, dia. ³⁄₁₆″; May-July. Distr. Lodgepole–fir and Subalpine belts at 6000–11800 ft. on moist slopes and stream margins.

S-54. Snowberry. *Symphoricarpos albus* (pl. 26). Ht. 2–6 ft.; erect or spreading, branches slender; young bark thin, light brown, later shreddy, gray or dark brown; deciduous; leaves ovate to nearly round, ¾″–2″ x ½″–1½″, edge smooth or slightly wavy, dull green, usually smooth; flowers in short clusters, pink, ⅛″–¼″ long; calyx minute; corolla bell-shaped, 4- or 5-lobed; stamens 4–5, on corolla; berry globular, dia. ⅜″–½″, white; May-June. Distr. Foothill belt to 2000 ft.

Other species of Snowberry (*S. mollis, S. rotundifolius*) are low or sprawling shrubs with smaller leaves and whitish to pinkish flowers. They grow up to 10000 feet in altitude and on the east slope from Mono County to Lake Tahoe.

S-55. Twinberry. *Lonicera involucrata* (pl. 26). Ht. 2–3 ft., upright; deciduous; leaves 2″–5″ x ¾″–2½″, opposite, oval, smooth dark green above, paler and faintly hairy below; flowers with reddish bracts at base, in pairs on ½″–1″ stalk in leaf axils; corolla cylindrical, 5-lobed at end, yellow, to ½″ long, sticky-hairy; berries in pairs, dia. ⅓″, black, bad-tasting; Mar.-July. Distr. Higher forest belts at 6000–10000 ft. in moist shady sites and along streams.

S-56. Chaparral Honeysuckle. *Lonicera interrupta* (pl. 26). Rigid woody trunk 1–2 ft. high, branches climbing on other shrubs; young branches often smooth purplish; evergreen; leaves ¾″–1″ long, opposite, elliptic to roundish, green above, whitish below; blossom spikes 2″–5″ long; corolla ⅜″–½″ long, yellow, tubular at base, upper lip 4-lobed, lower lip 1-lobed; berry globular, dia. ¼″, red; May-July. Distr. Foothill and Yellow Pine belts at 1500–4000 ft. on dry slopes.

Sunflower Family (Compositae). Blossoms in dense heads on enlarged receptacle surrounded by many bracts; individual flowers of 2 kinds: strap-shaped ray flowers and small tubular disc flowers.

S-57. Golden Fleece. *Haplopappus arborescens* (pl. 26). Ht. 3–12 ft.; branches erect, clustered; evergreen; leaves narrowly linear, 1″–2½″ long, crowded, resinous with minute pits; blossom heads (cymes) 2½″–3½″ high with 20–25 narrow bracts; no ray flowers; disc flowers 20–25, yellow; achenes 5-angled, pappus white; July-Oct. DISTR. Foothill belt at 1000–2000 ft., in chaparral.

S-58. Rabbit Brush. *Chrysothamnus nauseosus* (pl. 26, col. pl. 13). Ht. 1–7 ft.; main stems fibrous-barked; stems erect, much-branched, flexible, leafy, woolly, gray-green to white, ill-smelling; evergreen; leaves linear, ¾″–2½″ long to ⅛″ wide, linear, more or less woolly; blossom cymes terminal, round-topped, heads small; no ray flowers; 5–6 disc flowers, yellow; achenes 5-angled, smooth to hairy; Aug.-Nov. DISTR. E. slope and northern Sierra up to 9000 ft. on dry slopes.

Roadsides, flats, and slopes of the dry east slope and Great Basin support rabbit brush (of several species and varieties) in abundance. The colorful yellow blossom masses are seen from late summer until snow arrives.

S-59. Golden Yarrow. *Eriophyllum confertiflorum* (pl. 26). Ht. 12″–30″; stems erect, few to many from root crown, leafy, densely woolly; leaves 1⁄12″–⅛″ long, parted in 3–7 narrow lobes; blossoms many, in compact terminal clusters, deep yellow; composite flower 1⁄12″ high, bracts 5; rigid, ray flowers 4 or 5 (or none); achenes 4-angled, slender; May-July. DISTR. Foothills and mountains to 7500 ft. on dry slopes or ridges.

S-60. Sagebrush. *Artemisia tridentata* (pl. 26, col. pl. 3d). Ht. 3–6+ ft.; distinct trunk with gray shreddy bark; much branched; herbage aromatic, all grayish white or silvery, finely woolly; evergreen; leaves narrowly wedge-shaped, ¾″–1¾″ long, usually 3- (or 4-) toothed at tip; blossom panicles many, dense, narrow, 6″–18″ long; flowers narrow, to 1⁄12″ long, no ray flowers, disc flowers 4–6; achenes oblong, top disc-like; late July-Nov. DISTR. Along e. slope s. to Inyo Co. and on w. slope from Mariposa to Kern Co. at 1500–10600 ft. on high flats and mountain slopes.

The gray Sagebrush is the most widespread and best known shrub of the Great Basin, being the dominant plant over thousands of square miles. It shelters a distinctive fauna of insects, reptiles, birds, and mammals. This and other varieties or species of sagebrush are spread among forests of the east slope, and some are also present on dry areas well to the west of the Sierran summits.

15. TREES

A tree is a perennial plant usually with one woody trunk. Most mature trees are 15 feet or higher, although the Utah Juniper varies from a 20-foot tree to a 2-foot many-stemmed shrub according to local conditions.

Trees are the dominant plants over most of the Sierra. They literally make their own habitat, adding organic matter to the soil by leaf decay

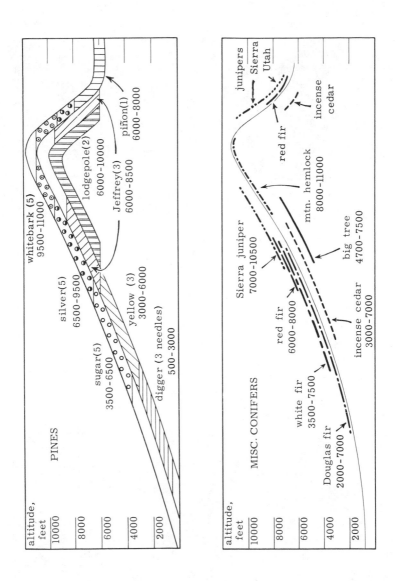

Figure 10. Distribution of coniferous trees across the Sierra Nevada by altitude.

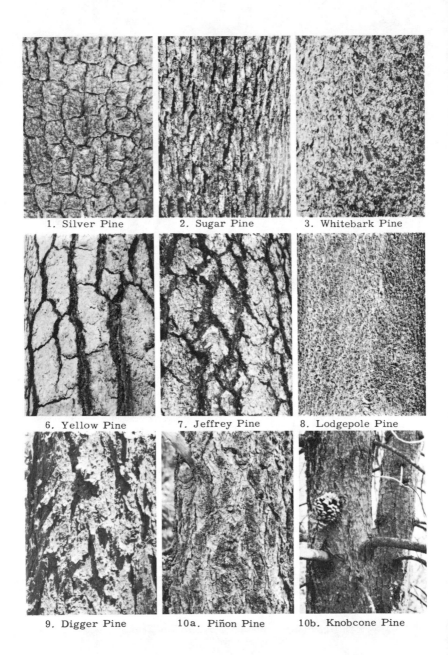

1. Silver Pine   2. Sugar Pine   3. Whitebark Pine

6. Yellow Pine   7. Jeffrey Pine   8. Lodgepole Pine

9. Digger Pine   10a. Piñon Pine   10b. Knobcone Pine

Figure 11. Bark texture of Sierran pines.

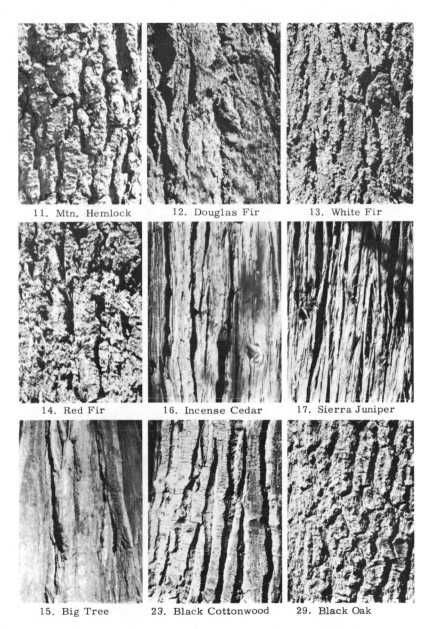

11. Mtn. Hemlock   12. Douglas Fir   13. White Fir

14. Red Fir   16. Incense Cedar   17. Sierra Juniper

15. Big Tree   23. Black Cottonwood   29. Black Oak

Figure 12. Bark texture of miscellaneous conifers, cottonwood, and oak of the Sierra Nevada.

and creating shade and moisture conditions that favor particular associations of plants and animals. A mature forest is stable and may persist indefinitely unless destroyed by fire or disease. Unlike the eastern states with their broad-leaf deciduous forests, the Sierra is covered largely by evergreen conifers (20 of 42 trees in this handbook but only 25 of 239 trees in southeastern United States).

Ornamental trees have been planted around Sierran settlements, but only one, the "Tree of Heaven" (*Ailanthus altissima*), introduced by Chinese in the Mother Lode, has become naturalized. The tree is deciduous, often shrub-like, with light green compound leaves having a disagreeable odor.

Only native trees are included in this handbook. Broad-leaved trees may be identified by reference to the illustrations and descriptions, aided by the "Guide to Families of Flowering Plants" (p. 62).

The cone-bearing trees (conifers or Gymnosperms) have leaves that are either needle-shaped or scale-like and naked seeds borne in cones. Most conifers can be identified easily by these characters and by their growth form (see figs. 5 and 6). Pine trees are conspicuous and reliable guides to the plant belts (map 2; fig. 10). In many parts of the world pines are variable and difficult to identify, but in the Sierra the species are easily recognized; when learned they will aid in understanding other aspects of local natural history.

Across the central Sierra from the foothills over the crest to the east side at most elevations there is one 3-needled and one 5-needled pine, and at 6000 to 10000 feet also the 2-needled lodgepole pine. On the east side, below the Jeffrey and lodgepole pines, there is only the 1-needled piñon and its occurrence is spotty. The pattern of distribution of the other conifers is also related to altitude but does not show such regular replacement.

Bark texture and pattern are characteristic for each Sierran tree, and in the Jeffrey and yellow pine aid in identification. Figures 11 and 12 show the bark of mature trees. Young firs are generally smooth and white and young yellow pines have rough brown bark rather than the broad yellowish plates of mature trees.

The age of a tree can be learned by counting growth rings in wood near the base—on the stump of a felled tree or by boring out a small cylinder from a living tree. Huge yellow or sugar pines may be 500 to 600 years old, and giant sequoias 900 to 2100 years old. Only bristlecone pines (*Pinus aristata*) on ranges east of Owens Valley are older. The largest (oldest) trees are mostly in national or state parks.

A *forest* is a rather dense stand of trees, with or without shrubs below. In some forests the crowns make a dense canopy that largely excludes sunlight from the ground underneath. Many Sierran forests are more open than those of humid regions, although some stands of red fir or lodgepole pine are dense. By contrast, the lower flanks of the

Sierra support more open woodlands—trees in moderate numbers interspersed with shrubs and grass as in the pine-oak woodland of the western foothills and the piñon or juniper woodlands on the east side.

There has been a major lumber industry in Sierran conifer forests since the 1850's. The trees used are mostly yellow (ponderosa) and Jeffrey pines, Douglas fir, incense cedar, some white fir, and locally giant sequoia. Young lodgepole pine trunks serve for walls in some mountain cabins. Oak is cut mainly for firewood.

T-1. Silver Pine. *Pinus monticola* (pl. 27, fig. 11). Ht. 50–125 ft., dia. to 6 ft., bark smooth or checked into small square plates, whitish or reddish; needles in 5's or 4's, slender, 1"–3¾", bluish green with whitish tinge, persisting 1–3 yrs.; cones on long stalks, in clusters of 1–7, at ends of high branches, 6"–8" long, slender, tapered, and blackish-purple when young, later tawny, dia. 3"–3½" when open, scales thin. DISTR. Lodgepole–fir and Subalpine belts at 5500 ft. (north) and 8000–11000 ft. (south), n. to B.C. and Mont.

Known also as Western White Pine and Mountain (Sugar) Pine, this species is scattered through the upper part of the main timber belt and higher but is not abundant except in small patches. The wood is soft, light, smooth, and close-grained.

T-2. Sugar Pine. *Pinus lambertiana* (pl. 27, fig. 11). Ht. 100–180 ft., dia. 3–7 ft.; bark 2"–4" thick, vertically ridged with surface of loose purple or cinnamon scales; upper branches nearly horizontal, large, and long; needles in 5's, 2"–3½" long, rigid, sharp-pointed; cones hang from stalks at ends of higher branches, 13"–18" long and 4"–6" dia. when open, scales thin. DISTR. Mainly in Yellow Pine belt on w. slope at 3500–6500 ft. (north) and 4500–9000 ft. (south).

A big mature Sugar Pine on a mountain crest, with long cones hanging at the ends of its spreading branches, conveys the feeling of a beneficent patron. This magnificent tree is a striking element in the main forest belt, although it is usually outnumbered by other conifers. The cones ripen and shed their seed in the second summer of growth but commonly remain in place until the following winter or spring. Because of their size and bright tawny coloring, they are much sought for decorative use. The soft wood resembles that of the Silver Pine and has high commercial value; in consequence Sugar Pine has become scarce in many forests. Fire or axe wounds into the wood of a living tree result in a fluid exudation that hardens into white nodules. Indians and early settlers learned to chew this gum, which is sweet with a pine sugar; it has little resin but is a cathartic.

T-3. Whitebark Pine. *Pinus albicaulis* (pl. 27, fig. 11). Of varied form from tree of 40 ft. to dwarfs of 6 ft. with 2 or more trunks and crown mats 6–8 ft. wide; bark thin, whitish, smooth or in scaly plates on trunk; needles in 5 s, 1"–2½" long, rigid, blunt-tipped, clustered at ends of flexible branches,

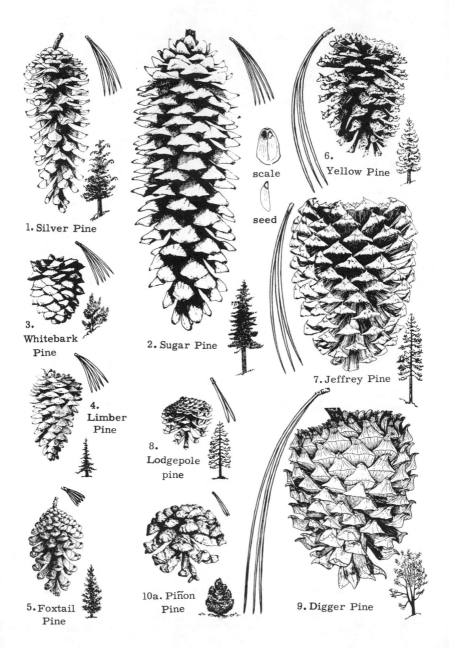

1. Silver Pine

2. Sugar Pine

scale

seed

3. Whitebark Pine

4. Limber Pine

5. Foxtail Pine

6. Yellow Pine

7. Jeffrey Pine

8. Lodgepole pine

9. Digger Pine

10a. Piñon Pine

146

Plate 27. Trees

persisting 4–8 yrs.; cones 1″–3″ long, dark purple when young, yellow brown by end of 2nd yr., closed until disintegrated. DISTR. Subalpine belt, mainly on rocky summits at 7500–9500 ft. (north) and 9500–11000 ft. (south), Mt. Whitney and upper Kings Canyon to Mt. Shasta and B.C.

The sturdy Whitebark lives near timberline, where it is buffeted by winter storms and summer winds. It grows slowly; a 5-inch branchlet may be 12 to 17 years old. Occasional trees in protected sites are upright, with unusually heavy trunk, but most individuals are distorted. Some have prostrate trunks 12 to 18 inches in diameter and broad mats of densely placed twigs and needles over which a person may scramble. White-tailed jackrabbits often find shelter under the mats, as indicated by accumulations of their droppings. The trees produce few ripe cones, and seeds that mature are usually eaten by nutcrackers (B-78) and squirrels.

T-4. Limber Pine. *Pinus flexilis* (pl. 27). Ht. 15–60 ft., trunk dia. to 3 or 4 ft., bark on trunk to 2″ thick in dark brown plates with thin scales; branches tough, flexible light gray or silvery; needles in 5's, 1″–2¼″, dark yellow green, in dense brush-like tufts on ends of branches; cones 3½″–10″, oval, pale brown, scales inturned at end. DISTR. On e. slope scattered from Mono Pass to Monache Peak at 9300–10000 ft.; and w. slope on S. Fork of Kings River at 10500–12000 ft. Also s. to San Jacinto Mts. and e. across Great Basin to Rocky Mts.

Few people see the Limber Pine in the Sierra because of its small and rather inaccessible range. Its growth habits are unlike those of most pines. On young trees the branches are in separate whorls extending horizontally, then dipping toward the ground. Older trees have branches 16 to 18 feet long, those at the top angling gracefully downward. The branch system seems to develop at the expense of the trunk, which remains stunted.

T-5. Foxtail Pine. *Pinus balfouriana* (pl. 27). Ht. 20–45 ft., dia. to 3 ft. at base; bark reddish brown, checked into square plates; branches short, irregular; needles in 5's, ¾″–1″, bright green above, whitish beneath, persisting 10–15 yrs.; cones 2½″–5″ x 1¾″–2″, thick, deep purple. DISTR. In s. Sierra on both slopes from head of San Joaquin River to Monache Peak, near timberline, at 9000–12000 ft. Also in Scott Mts. and Yolla Bolly Mts. in n. Calif. at 6000–8000 ft.

To find this hardy alpine tree one must climb to high altitude in either of its separate and limited areas of occurrence. In the Sierra it grows in scattered stands, usually apart from other plants, on bare rocky elevated slopes or cirques. There it is exposed to extremes of daily and seasonal temperature, unlimited sunlight, severe winds and snowstorms, and long summer droughts. The trunk is tapered and in older trees the dead tip (possibly killed by lightning) projects through the dense green crown foliage as a bleached spire. The common name derives from the way in which the short needles densely clothe the terminal 10 to 20 inches of a branch, nearly parallel to the stem and all around it—like a foxtail.

T-6. Yellow Pine. *Pinus ponderosa* (pl. 27, fig. 11). Ht. 60–225 ft., dia. to 8 ft.; bark of older trees 2″–4″ thick, yellowish tan, divided by shallow furrows into large scaly-surfaced plates 1–4 ft. long x 3″–18″ wide; bark of younger trees narrowly furrowed, red-brown to blackish; branches short, usually upturned at ends, forming spire-like or flat-topped crown; branchlets orange, darkening with age; needles in 3's, 5″–10″ long, dark yellowish green, in tufts on ends of branchlets, persisting about 3 yrs.; cones near ends of branches, 2″–5″ x 2¾″–3½″, reddish brown, each scale tip with *outturned prickle;* seed shed in 2nd year, cone later falling, leaving some scales on tree. DISTR. On w. slope at 1500–5000 ft. (north), 3000–6000 ft. (center), and 5000–7000 ft. (south); also on e. slope from Lake Tahoe northward; n. to B.C., s. to San Diego, e. to Rocky Mtns.

The common name, Yellow Pine, refers to the pale color of bark on mature trees, unlike that of any other local conifer. The lumber industry uses the term "ponderosa pine" to designate its wood. This pine is the commonest and most widely distributed of western conifers, and it defines the main forest on the west flank of the Sierra Nevada. Its vertical range seemingly depends on two different factors—at least 25 inches of annual precipitation (save near water) at the lower limit, and prolonged winter freezing at the upper. Between these limits it grows in various environments—fertile moist slopes and plateaus, rocky ridges, and rather arid sites. Common forest associates are the Black Oak, Incense Cedar, Sugar Pine, and White Fir. The largest Yellow Pines are usually along ridges where the traveler may walk over needle-carpeted ground with little underbrush among the great trunks of this impressive tree. The wood is fine and straight-grained, usually with abundant resin, and supplies much of the lumber produced in California.

T-7. Jeffrey Pine. *Pinus jeffreyi* (pl. 27, fig. 11). Ht. 60–170 ft., dia. to 4 (or 7) ft.; bark on young or old trees reddish brown, divided into rough plates by deep, rather closely spaced furrows; needles in 3's, 5″–10″ long, dull, grayish blue-green (with white bloom); cones heavy, 4¾″–8″ x 4″– 5½″, purple, then russet brown, each scale with *inturned prickle.* DISTR. In Lodgepole–fir belt on w. slope at 5200–8000 ft. (north), 5800–8500 ft. (center), and 6000–9000 ft. (south); and on e. slope often in pure stands, ranging downward to piñons and sagebrush.

The Jeffrey Pine resembles the Yellow Pine but is a distinct species. Compared with the latter, its bark is darker and more narrowly furrowed, with a vanilla odor. The needles average thicker in diameter and duller in color; when crushed they often have a distinctive odor (heptane), like that in a firm winter apple. The cones are larger and heavier with smooth exterior; the prickle on each scale turns inward, not outward as on Yellow Pine cones. On the west slope Jeffrey Pine occurs in the belt immediately above the Yellow Pine, sometimes mingled with that tree. From the latitude of Lake Tahoe northward the two species occur together in many places, especially in the eastern part of the Sierra. To the south, at its lower limits, the Jeffrey Pine is on meadow margins in company with Lodgepole Pine, but at higher levels it is often on rather barren rocky sites. In pure stands it forms a somewhat open forest where the trunks are conspicuous. When subjected to severe weather it may be stunted or distorted, and upright trees often are flat-topped or broken in the crown.

T-8. Lodgepole Pine. *Pinus murrayana* (pl. 27, fig. 11). Ht. 50–80 (125) ft., dia. 6″–20″ or more; bark thin (to ¼″), smooth, flaking off in thin scales, pale reddish to gray; needles in 2's, 1″–2¾″ long, densely clothing branchlets, persisting 2–3 yrs.; cones 1″–1¾″ long, nearly globular when open, pale brown, scales thin with sharp points. DISTR. Throughout higher Sierra from upper edge of Yellow Pine belt nearly to timberline at 5000–7000 ft. (north), 6000–10000 ft. (center), and 7000–11000 ft. (south); on meadows, moist slopes, and broad ridges; occasionally down to 4000 feet, as in Yosemite Valley.

This pine ranges from Lower California to Alaska and South Dakota. In the north it is often in dense pure stands producing slender pole-like trunks, but in California its form is varied. Some trees here are symmetrical, and others have short trunks with heavy branches. In regions of heavy snow some young lodgepoles are bent and held down throughout the winter, whereby their trunks become distorted near the base. The cones ripen at the end of summer but some remain closed, even for several years. This reserve seed stock helps to regenerate a stand destroyed by fire. In such circumstances young trees may shoot up in profusion, shading one another so that lower branches are soon lost and an immature "pole forest" results. "Ghost forests" result from stands killed by needleminer moths (I-47). Lodgepole cones, green or ripe, are cut by chickarees (M-17) to obtain the seeds. Chipmunks, crossbills, nutcrackers, and others also levy on the ripe seed crop. This tree is mistakenly called Tamarac(k) Pine, but the true Tamarack (*Larix*) does not grow in California. The wood is very pitchy.

T-9. Digger Pine. *Pinus sabiniana* (pl. 27, fig. 11). Ht. 40–90 ft., dia. 1–4 ft.; trunk often slanting and frequently divided at 10–15 ft. above the ground into several slender upright branches, forming an open broom-like top; bark on older trees to 2″ thick, gray-brown, vertically furrowed; needles in 3's. 7″–12″ long, sparse, gray-green to blue; cones stalked, 6″–10″ x 5″–7″, nearly globular, tips of each scale with 1″ triangular hook. DISTR. Along w. foothills at about 500–3000 ft. and on s. end of Sierra at 2500–5000 ft. None from Kings River to vicinity of Tule River.

The foothill Digger Pine bears little resemblance to its stately relatives in the deep green forests above. It is grayish green, with several upper "trunks" and a spreading crown. The foliage is so open that it affords scant shelter in the heat of summer. The wood is coarse-grained and pitchy and warps badly. Small wonder that early settlers, who gave the name "Digger" to local aborigines as a term of contempt, applied it also to the tree. The abundant seed crops (pine nuts) were relished by the Indians, who also ate the soft central core of green cones in early summer. The nuts are staple food for squirrels, woodpeckers, jays, and other foothill birds. To the traveler of today the Digger Pine is a picturesque element of the landscape because of its varied growth pattern.

T-10a. Piñon Pine. *Pinus monophylla* (pl. 27, fig. 11). Ht. 8–25 ft., trunk dia. 12"–15"; bark on young trees smooth, dull gray, on old trees to 1" thick, rough and furrowed, with thin scales, dark brown; needles 1 (rarely 2), 1¼"–2" long, stiff, curved, sharp-pointed, pale yellow-green, persisting 5 yrs.; cones nearly spherical, 1"–2¼" x 2½"–3½", scales 4-sided, thick at end. DISTR. E. slope from Loyalton, Sierra Co., s. at 6000–8000 ft., and on desert ranges; also in lower Kings and Kern River drainages and in Walker Pass; on dry, rocky slopes.

Young piñons are covered by needles from base to tip, making a roundedly conical exterior that masks the branches and bark. Older trees become irregular with more exposed framework. These "nut" pines occupy dry, exposed slopes below the Jeffrey Pines of the east side, sometimes accompanying Sierra Junipers. More often they are in the upper part of the Sagebrush Belt along with the Utah Juniper and Mountain Mahogany. Indians gathered piñon nuts for food, and they are staple diet for some birds and mammals.

T-10b. Knobcone Pine. *Pinus attenuata* or *tuberculata* (fig. 11). Small groups on a few rocky sites at 2500–4000 ft., on w. slope foothills from Mariposa Co. north. Usually is less than 30 ft. high, with sparse yellow-green needles 3 to 5" long in 3's; small cones (3"–6" long) grow in tight clusters around trunk, remaining unopened for years until heated by a fire.

T-11. Mountain Hemlock. *Tsuga mertensiana* (pl. 28, figs. 6, 12). Alpine tree, narrowly conical, ht. 15–90 ft.; trunk tapered, base dia. 6"–30", old bark red-brown, 1"–1½" thick, in broad flat ridges deeply furrowed, leading shoot nodding; branches from ground upward, slender, curved, mostly drooping; leaves to 1" long, narrow, blunt-pointed, flattish above, ridged below, curved, growing from all sides of branchlet, blue-green; cones 1½"–3" x ½"–¾", narrowed at both ends, purple when young, later red-brown, scales thin, rounded at tip. DISTR. Upper edge of forest at 6000–11000 ft.

This graceful tree lives at high elevations where snow lingers well into summer. It forms small open groves commonly in sheltered north- or east-facing canyons. When winter snowfall is heavy, the tips of saplings are bent over to touch the ground, but they recover when summer returns. In protected sites at lower altitudes this hemlock becomes a large forest tree, in pure stands or with Silver Pine, Lodgepole Pine, or Red Fir. Wherever present, its tapered form and nodding top add pleasantly to many a rocky vista.

T-12. Douglas Fir. *Pseudotsuga menziesii* (formerly *taxifolia*) (pl. 28, figs. 5, 12). Magnificent forest tree, ht. 70–110 ft. or more, trunk to 30″ dia., bark on young trees thin, smooth, ashy brown, on old trees thick, soft, dark brown, with broad ridges and deep furrows; lower branches drooping (and shed early if heavily shaded), upper branches flat or upturned at ends; leaves ½″–1½″, narrow, blunt at tip, upper surface with center groove, ridged below, yellow- to blue-green with 2 pale lines along under side; cones mature 1st autumn, 1¾″–3″ x 1¼″–1¾″ when open, red-brown, scales broad, thin at edge; a narrow 3-pointed bract extends over and beyond each scale. DISTR. Yellow Pine belt of w. slope s. to San Joaquin River; at 900–7000 ft. (north), 2000–7000 ft. (center), and 900–6000 ft. (south); n. to B.C., e. to Rocky Mts., mainly on shaded slopes.

In the lower main forest belt this "fir" or "spruce" grows mainly on fertile, moist, shaded slopes alone or mixed with Yellow and Sugar pines, Incense Cedar, White Fir, and Black Oak. In the Pacific Northwest as "Oregon pine" it is prized for the logs yielding large, long, and straight-grained timber. The needles often show a flat 2-ranked arrangement resembling those of White Fir. Both trees are prized for Christmas use.

T-13. White Fir. *Abies concolor* (pl. 28, figs. 5, 12). Ht. 60–200 ft., crown usually pointed, narrow; trunk to 4 ft. dia.; bark on young trees smooth, whitish, on old trees 2″–4″ thick, broken into rounded vertical ridges, gray or drab brown; branches in whorls around trunk, branchlets extending laterally as flat sprays; needles ½″–2½″, flat, often grooved on upper surface and keeled on lower; twisted at base; leaf scar round, smooth; cones nearly cylindric, 2″–5″ x 1″–1¾″, erect on upper branches, cone scales fan-shaped, wider (to 1¼″) than long, bracts ½ length of scales. DISTR. Yellow Pine belt and into Lodgepole–fir belt across Sierra in n. at 2500–7500 ft. and on both sides toward s. at 5000–8000 ft.; e. to Rocky Mts.

The White Fir is common in the main timber portion of the Sierra, usually on better soil with more moisture than is needed by Yellow Pine. Its needles are in flat 2-ranked arrangement on lower branches but curving upward on the higher ones, where they differ also in being 4-sided. The pale green pitchy upright cones grow mainly near the tree summits, where they remain until mature; then the scales and seeds are shed, leaving the central axis. Green cones may be dislodged and fall in storms, and many are cut by tree squirrels. Once in October on an area 50 feet square 484 of these were counted. They had been cut by a chickaree for its winter food. In refrigeration, under winter snow, the seeds would keep until used. White fir makes a soft, second-grade lumber.

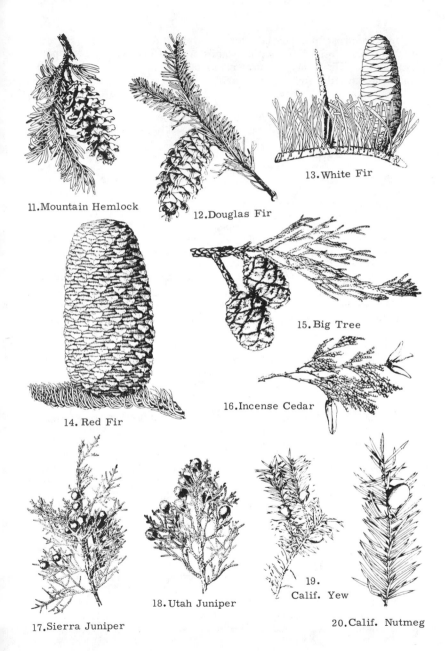

11.Mountain Hemlock

12.Douglas Fir

13.White Fir

14. Red Fir

15. Big Tree

16.Incense Cedar

17.Sierra Juniper

18.Utah Juniper

19. Calif. Yew

20.Calif. Nutmeg

152

Plate 28. Trees

T-14. Red Fir. *Abies magnifica* (pl. 28, figs. 6, 12). Ht. 60–175 ft., trunk to 50″, crown at maturity in forest short, narrow, round-topped; bark on young trees and tops of old ones smooth and whitish, on old trees dark red, 2″–3″ thick, hard and rough narrow ridges between deep, rough diagonal furrows; branches (except topmost) downcurved, then upcurved at ends; foliage dense, dark blue-green; needles ¾″–1½″, 4-sided, whitish in 1st year, bent outward all around branchlet; cones oval, 4″–8″ x 2½″–3½″, brown, scales with upturned edges. DISTR. Upper main forest belt mainly on w. slope at 5000–7000 ft. (north) and 6000–9000 ft. (south), n. to southern Ore.; on moist slopes or around wet meadows, also on rocky ridges or plateaus.

In the upper Sierra this fir is a stately element. On many north-facing slopes it forms a dark forest with scant ground cover. Shafts of sunlight between the densely foliaged crowns make a striking contrast with the big, somber, dark red fluted columns of the mature trees. At the higher altitudes, where winter storms are severe, there are many casualties every year among the red firs, which have wood that is easily broken. The crowns of some are snapped off; others break at midlength, and many are felled completely. Because of the scarcity of other food-producing plants, a Red Fir forest has mainly birds that find their forage on the big conifers—woodpeckers, nuthatches, and creepers on the trunk, chickadees, kinglets, and occasional warblers in the dense needle foliage, and various seed-eaters harvesting from the maturing cone crops in autumn. Cavities in damaged firs provide nest retreats for chickarees, chipmunks, and other mammals—even martens on occasion.

T-15. Big Tree. *Sequoia gigantea* (pl. 28, fig. 12). Ht. 150–331 ft., dia. 5–30 ft., bark 4″–24″ thick, in broad rounded ridges and deep furrows, fibrous, cinnamon-brown; branches form in compact cone-like head; leaves awl-shaped to ½″ long, blue-green, lying flat on branchlets; cones oblong, 1¾″–2¾″ long, of 34–40 thick scales, maturing in 2d autumn. DISTR. Yellow Pine belt on w. slope at 4700–7500 ft. in 32 scattered groves from Placer to Tulare Co.

Greatest of all Sierran plants is the giant sequoia, which lives in 7 isolated groves from Placer County to Kings River and in greater numbers in the Kings Canyon and Sequoia National Parks. Some of the named trees are 13 to 27½ feet in diameter at 10-12 feet above the base. Counts of growth rings on downed trees show ages up to 2100 years, and the General Sherman Tree (272 ft. high x 27½ ft. dia.) is estimated at 3500 years. In aged mature trees the base is broadly buttressed, the trunk a huge clear column with slight taper and free of branches for 100–150 feet, and the foliage crown is somewhat cone-shaped. The fibrous non-resinous bark is highly resistant to fire. Freshly cut wood is pink, aging to dark red, fairly strong, and highly resistant to decay. The small cones are produced in abundance, each having 200 to 300 seeds. Young trees are few or none in the northern groves but numerous in the larger southern ones. Big Tree is a "living fossil" of far wider distribution in past geologic time. Seeds have been shipped widely, and there are many examples of this tree now growing in distant cities and countries.

T-16. Incense Cedar. *Libocedrus decurrens* (pl. 28, figs. 5, 12). Aromatic tree with flat branchlets; ht. 50–125 ft., dia. 2–7 ft.; trunk tapered from broad base, bark bright cinnamon, fibrous, thin and scaly on young trees, 1″–3″ thick on older trees; needles minute (⅛″–⅖″), flat, pointed, adhering to branchlets in alternate pairs; "cone" ¾″–1″ long of 2 broad, flat seed-bearing scales. DISTR. Throughout Yellow Pine belt at 2000–7000 ft., commoner on w. slope.

The frond-like sprays of foliage, tapered trunk, and fragrant wood are features of the Incense Cedar. It never grows in pure stands but is mixed with other conifers of the Yellow Pine belt. Young trees are clothed with branches from pointed top to base, whereas older ones have open irregular crowns with branches only on the upper third of the trunk, heavy shreddy bark, and buttressed bases. The durable wood is used for posts and shingles (also lead pencils). A dry-rot fungus (see Fu-9, *Polyporus amarus*) produces parallel-sided cavities in the wood, but lumber so marked is sought for decorative interior finish!

T-17. Sierra Juniper. *Juniperus occidentalis* (pl. 28, figs. 6, 12). Ht. 10–25 (even 65) ft., trunk dia. 1–5 ft., bark to ⅔″ thick, shreddy, dull red; leaves to ⅛″ long in 3's, gray-green, scale-like, overlapping, closely pressed on branchlets; berries rounded, to ⅓″ long, blue-black with whitish bloom. DISTR. Lodgepole–fir and Subalpine belts at 7000–10500 ft. mainly on granite ridges.

Sheltered Sierra Junipers on granite flats have rounded dome crowns, a good clothing of branches, and a short conical trunk often 4 to 5 feet in diameter. More often, however, the tree is found on rocky summits exposed to fierce winter storms, where it becomes spectacularly deformed. Long, heavy roots cling to the granite, the trunk is short and often deformed, scored by lightning and bleached by wintry blasts, and the foliage masses are broken and irregular. Such junipers attract pictorial photographers because of the irregular form and weathered exposed wood patterns. For several Sierran birds the abundant crops of berries are welcome food in autumn and early winter.

T-18. Utah Juniper. *Juniperus utahensis* (pl. 28, fig. 6). Often shrubby, ht. 2–15 ft., occasionally a 40-ft. tree; trunk crooked, to 3″ dia.; bark thin, shredded; leaves in 2's (rarely 3's), to ⅙″ long, light green, pointed, flat on branchlets; berry rounded, ⅓″ long, reddish brown with some white bloom and dry, fibrous sweet flesh. DISTR. Along lower e. slope and base of Sierra and across Great Basin on gravelly or sandy soil.

The shrubby inland juniper grows scatteringly in the arid region east of the Sierran crest. In many places it offers the only elevated perches for birds living in these dry interior areas. The wood is hard, fine-grained, and durable; it served for fence posts and as fuel for early settlers.

T-19. California Yew. *Taxus brevifolia* (pl. 28). Ht. 10–30 ft., trunk straight, conical, ridged on surface; bark thin, shreddy, red-brown; needles ⅔″ long, deep green, straight, pointed, with raised midribs, in flat 2-ranked sprays on branchlets; fruit berry-like, scarlet. DISTR. Rare and scattered on w. slope at 2500–4000 ft., s. to Calaveras Co. in moist well-shaded sites.

Only chance or persistent search will reveal the occasional tree of this species in the Sierra or elsewhere in California. It is more common in the Pacific Northwest.

T-20. California Nutmeg. *Torreya californica* (pl. 28). Ht. to 50 ft., trunk 6″–36″ dia., straight; bark to ⅝″ thick, pale brown, finely checked with scaly ridges; leaves 1¼″–2½″, narrow, flat, rigid, bristle-tipped, dark green above, yellowish green below with 2 white grooves, arranged in flat 2-ranked spray; fruit elliptical, 1⅛″–1¾″ long, yellow-green streaked with purple, exterior wrinkled, pulp thin and resinous. DISTR. Uncommon on w. slope near upper edge of Foothill belt at 2000–4500 ft. in moist canyons.

California Nutmeg is handsome with dark green foliage, sometimes of shrubby form. Merced River Canyon above Arch Rock is a typical growth site. The fruit resembles the true nutmeg (of the Molucca Islands) but has no value for flavoring. The needles, branchlets, or green bark, when crushed, emit a sharp odor, so woodsmen call the tree "stinking" yew or cedar.

T-21. Aspen. *Populus tremuloides* (pl. 29, fig. 6). Ht. 10–60 ft., trunk straight, dia. to 10″ or more; form slender, branchlets drooping at end; bark smooth, greenish white, blackened and ribbed at base with age; leaves ¾″–2″ long, round ovate, tip sharp, edge toothed or entire; ♂ catkins 1½″–2½″ long, ♀ 2″–4″; seeds minute, brownish, white-haired. DISTR. Throughout Sierra on both slopes at 5000–8000 ft. (north), 6000–10000 ft. (south); in swampy meadows or gravelly slopes and bases of lava jumbles.

In high altitudes aspen is the most conspicuous deciduous tree. Often it is in groves with straight vertical trunks branched only near the crown, but where exposed to severe storms and heavy snows the trunks are distorted, some nearly prostrate. The leaves, having vertically flat petioles, quiver in any breeze. In autumn the foliage turns golden yellow, providing bright color masses on many slopes. The wood is soft but tough and fine-grained, and will burn when green without sparking. Beavers planted in the Sierra rely largely on aspen bark for food.

T-22. Fremont Cottonwood. *Populus fremontii* (pl. 29, fig. 5). Ht. 40–90 ft., trunk dia. 1–5 ft.; round-topped, crown often spreading; bark whitish, 1″–5″ thick, roughly fissured; leaves 2″–4″ wide, broader than long, triangular or roundish, edges round-toothed, yellow-green; ♂ catkins dense, 2″–4″ long, ♀ catkins loosely flowered; seeds with many long white hairs,

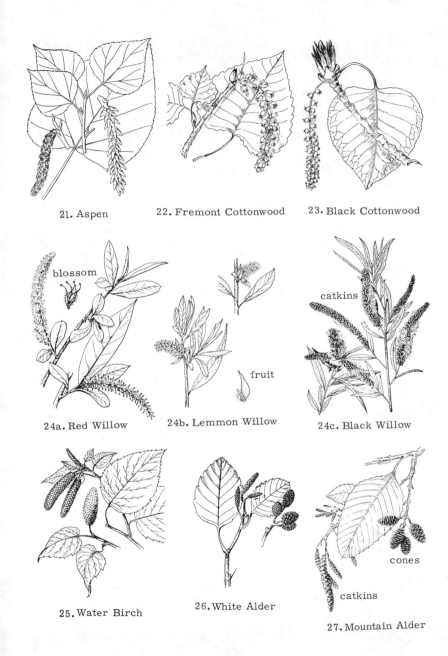

21. Aspen

22. Fremont Cottonwood

23. Black Cottonwood

blossom

24a. Red Willow

fruit

24b. Lemmon Willow

catkins

24c. Black Willow

25. Water Birch

26. White Alder

cones

catkins

27. Mountain Alder

Plate 29. Trees

making catkins soft cottony masses. DISTR. On w. side from Great Valley into Foothill belt, up to 2500 ft.; on moist soil along stream courses.

This is the cottonwood of the lowlands west of the Sierra. Along with willows it helps to make up the streamside or riparian growths so richly populated by birds in nesting time. Rotted cavities in the trunks are used by raccoons, wood ducks, and other hole-inhabiting animals. Clusters of mistletoe on cottonwoods produce berries attractive in winter to robins, waxwings, and bluebirds.

T-23. Black Cottonwood. *Populus trichocarpa* (pl. 29, figs. 5, 12). Ht. 40–125 ft., trunk dia. 1–3 ft.; bark smooth, yellowish white, with age divided into long, narrow dark plates; leaves 2½"–10" long, ovate, heart-shaped at base, tapered at tip, finely toothed, dark green above, rusty brown and later whitish below; ♂ catkins to 5" long, ♀ to 3", when mature 4"–10". DISTR. On w. slope mainly in Yellow Pine belt at 3000–6000 ft.; on e. slope in Truckee R. Valley (to 7000 ft.); and on Hockett trail in s. Sierra; mainly along stream banks or moist bottom lands.

River canyons in the lower forest belt are lined by this tree, which has dark tapered leaves. It is intolerant of shade but by rapid growth sends its small crown up into full light, where it competes with the conifers. Many insects live on the foliage and twigs in summer, and the tree provides forage and nesting places for various species of birds in that season.

T-24. Willows. Genus *Salix* (pl. 29). Trees or shrubs of rapid growth and light wood; bark bitter-flavored; young shoots smooth, yellow or red, trunk bark of older trees fissured and dark; leaves simple, narrow, short-petioled; flowers in catkins (♂ and ♀ separate), usually erect, appearing before or with leaves.

The slender pointed leaves, flowering catkins or "pussy willows," and close adherence to water—stream banks, lake borders, wet meadows, and seepage slopes—make willows as a group easy to recognize. More than 14 species occur in the Sierra, but precise identification usually requires blossoms, seed-capsules, and a botanical key. Waters below 5000 feet are bordered by willow trees 6 to 25 feet high, such as Red and Black Willows (T-24a, c). These are a major element of the lowland riparian habitat, and they accompany the larger streams where margined by soil up into the Yellow Pine belt. In the lower elevations they and associated wetland plants often form dense thickets, sometimes all but impenetrable by man. Here from late April into June are the largest nesting bird populations. (One census at Snelling in late May, 6–9 A.M., totaled 41 species and 425+ birds.) Other animals also abound in these places. At 5000–10000 ft. in swampy meadows the Lemmon Willow (*S. lemmonii,* T-24b) grows in dense clumps that are the summer domain of White-crowned Sparrows, Lincoln Sparrows, blackbirds, some flycatchers and warblers, and other small birds. The Alpine Willow (*S. petrophila*) is the dwarf of this group. Its erect branches, 2 to 4 inches high, rise from creeping stems that make carpet-like growths bordering streams of snow melt at 8500 to 12000 feet.

T-25. Water Birch. *Betula occidentalis* (pl. 29). Ht. 10–25 ft.; bark smooth, red-brown, twigs warty; leaves 1"–2" long, round-ovate, sharply toothed (serrate); ♂ catkins 2"–2½" long, ♀ 1½" long in fruit. DISTR. From Fresno and Inyo Co. n. on both slopes at 2500–8000 ft. in cool stream canyons.

The birch grows as a slender tree or tall shrub. It is sparse on the west slope but more common on the southerly part of the east side near Owens Valley.

T-26. White Alder. *Alnus rhombifolia* (pl. 29, fig. 5). Ht. 30–115 ft., trunk dia. to 24", tall, slender; bark smooth, thin, scaly, whitish or grayish brown with dark ∧ -shaped marks where branches start; leaves 2"–4" long, oblong, tapered to base and tip, wavy-bordered, light yellowish green; ♂ catkins 4½"–5½" long, slender, hanging; ♀ short, erect, ripening into brown woody cone ½"–⅞" long. DISTR. From Great Valley up into Yellow Pine belt on w. slope to 2500 ft. (north) and 6000–8000 ft. (south); along rivers and smaller streams.

More tolerant of shade than cottonwoods, the White Alder lines many canyon bottoms and gorges having permanent water. The tall trunks and open crowns are attractive, as are the small upright cones.

T-27. Mountain Alder. *Alnus tenuifolia* (pl. 29). Shrub or tree, ht. 8–14 ft., trunk often bent; bark smooth, thin, dark gray-brown, on larger trunks lightly seamed, scaly, red-tinged; young twigs red; leaves 1"–3" long, round-ish, edge double-toothed, deep grass green; ♂ catkins to 3", ♀ maturing as cones to ⅝" long. DISTR. From Tulare Co. n. at 5000–8000 ft. on wet slopes.

Mountain Alder grows in dense pure thickets with leaning, some-times almost horizontal, stems on mucky slopes, lake borders, and gulches saturated with water. Seedlings abound in shady or open sites, but later the alders need top light. The thickets often are almost im-penetrable by people but good harbor for small animals and birds.

T-28. Tan-bark Oak. *Lithocarpus densiflora* (pl. 30). Small tree or shrub; bark smooth on young trees, later in squarish plates and pale reddish brown; young twigs woolly; leaves 2½"–4½" x 1"–1¾", evergreen, oblong, veins strong and ending in teeth at margin, above smooth, shiny, below woolly, red-brown; catkins single, erect, 2"–4" long; acorn short, thick, woolly, 1"–1½" long, maturing 2nd autumn. DISTR. Sparse on w. slope, Butte to Mariposa Co. at 2000–5000 ft. mostly in Yellow Pine belt.

The Tan-bark Oak, intermediate between oaks and chestnuts, is com-moner in the northern Coast Ranges than in the Sierra. Here it occurs scatteringly in dense forest. A shrubby form, 2 to 10 feet high, with thick small leaves (1"–2" long) and small acorns is found from Placer to Mariposa County.

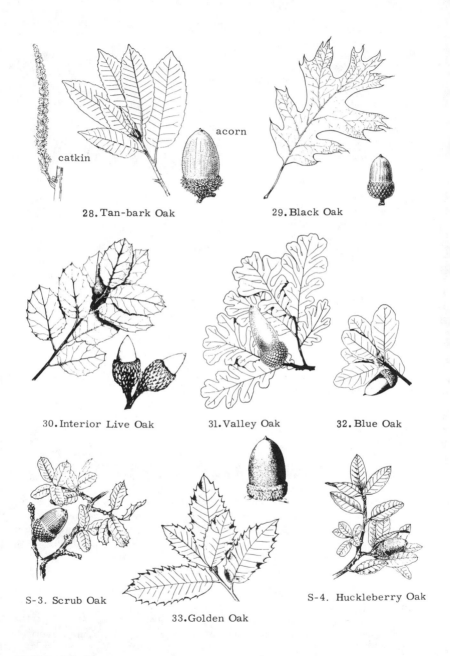

catkin

acorn

28. Tan-bark Oak

29. Black Oak

30. Interior Live Oak

31. Valley Oak

32. Blue Oak

S-3. Scrub Oak

33. Golden Oak

S-4. Huckleberry Oak

Plate 30. Trees

159

T-29. Black Oak. *Quercus kelloggii* (pl. 30, figs. 5, 12). Ht. 30–80 ft., trunk dia. 1–4½ ft.; crown broad, rounded; bark smooth, dark, on trunk in small plates; leaves 4″–10″ x 2½″–6″, deeply lobed, about 3 lobes per side, each ending in 1–3+ coarse teeth, above lustrous green, below paler; acorn 1″–1½″ x ¾″, deep in large thin-scaled cup, maturing 2nd season. DISTR. Common on w. slope in Yellow Pine belt at 3000–5000 ft. (north), 4500–7000 ft. (south); on slopes and in valleys on good to rocky soil.

Black Oak is a member of the Yellow Pine forest belt along the western flank of the Sierra, scattered among conifers on slopes and forming oak woodlands in some flat valleys. In spring its reddish leaf buds produce the pale green leaves that contrast then with the dark greens of the conifers. In autumn the ground becomes carpeted with the crisp golden-brown leaves. Tree squirrels and some owls nest in rotted cavities of the trunks and limbs, woodpeckers and deer relish the acorns, and the summer foliage is host to many birds for foraging and nesting.

T-30. Interior Live Oak. *Quercus wislizenii* (pl. 30, fig. 5). Ht. 30–75 ft., trunk dia. 1–3 ft., round-headed; bark thick, smooth or roughly fissured; leaves 1″–2½″ long, evergreen, oblong, tip tapered or rounded, margin entire or toothed, above smooth green, below yellowish green; acorn 1¼″–1⅝″ long, slender, tapered, deeply set in cup with thin brown scales. DISTR. Common on w. slope from border of Great Valley through Foothill belt at 2000–5000 ft. on slopes or stream bottoms, good or poor soils.

At all seasons the roundish evergreen or "live" oak is easily recognized. It grows variously on hills, in ravines, or near chaparral. The dense, dark foliage gives protected roosting places for valley quail and other birds. Insects on the leaves are sought by viroes, some warblers, titmice, and their associates.

T-31. Valley Oak. *Quercus lobata* (pl. 30). Ht. 40–125+ ft., trunk dia. 2–10 ft., round-topped, often broader than high; bark thick, with cube-like checks; main branches huge, branchlets cord-like, drooping; leaves 3″–4″ x 2″–3″, with 3–5 pairs of broad rounded lobes, above green, paler below, yellow-veined; acorn long, conical, 1½″–2¼″ x ½″–¾″, maturing reddish brown, cup warty. DISTR. Great Valley and broad level foothill valleys of w. slope to 2000 ft. (north), 4000 ft. (south); on loamy well-watered soil.

Most majestic of California oaks is the great Valley Oak that grows on the broad, flat fertile lowlands. The crown is wide and rounded, the trunk huge, and the long drooping branchlets sometimes reach the ground. In summer the leaf crown provides welcome shade from the sun's heat, and in autumn jays, woodpeckers, and other birds harvest its acorns—as Indians and grizzlies did formerly.

T-32. Blue Oak. *Quercus douglasii* (pl. 30, fig. 5). Ht. 20–60 ft., trunk dia. 1–2 ft.; bark whitish, in small thin scales on trunk and even small branches; leaves variable in size and outline, 1″–3″ x ½″–3″, oblong, shallowly lobed, or with few teeth, above bluish green, below paler; acorn

$\frac{3}{4}''-1\frac{1}{2}''$ x $\frac{1}{2}''-\frac{3}{4}''$, oval or tapering, cup small, $\frac{1}{3}''-\frac{1}{2}''$ long, smaller than nut. DISTR. Common in w. slope Foothill belt at 300–1500 ft. (north), 500–3000 ft. (south); on dry or rocky places.

When going from the west toward the mountains one meets scattered Blue Oaks well before other plants of the Foothill belt. As one continues, they become common, in pure stands or among Digger Pines and Live Oaks. The Blue Oak affords perches and nesting places for the Nuttall Woodpecker, Western Kingbird, Ash-throated Flycatcher, California Jay, Plain Titmouse, and associated birds.

T-33. Golden Oak. *Quercus chrysolepis* (pl. 30, fig. 5). Ht. 20–60+ ft., trunk dia. 1–5 ft., crown rounded, spreading; bark rather smooth, whitish; leaves 1″–2″ long, evergreen, leathery, ovate, tip pointed, margin entire or toothed (even on same branch), thick, above green, below yellow with fine fuzz or powder; acorn 1″–1¼″ x ¾″–1″, ovate to cylindric, tip usually pointed, cup thick, rounded, felted with yellow fuzz, suggesting a yellow turban. DISTR. Locally common from upper part of Foothill belt through Yellow Pine belt of w. slope at 1500–5000 ft. (north), 3000–8000 ft. (south); on valley walls and floors and on ridges.

Golden Oaks densely clothe many sunlit cayon walls in the Yosemite, Kings, Kern, and other drainages. The wood is dense and straight-grained and seasons well, hence was used by early settlers and mountain packers, who gave it many names, including Golden-cup, Canyon, White, and Maul Oak. Acorns and leaf insects of these trees are food for many birds and tree-climbing mammals; Band-tailed Pigeons can swallow the acorns entire! More than 50 kinds of gall-forming insects work on this oak.

T-34. California Laurel. *Umbellularia californica* (pl. 31). Ht. 40–60 ft., trunk dia. 1–2 ft., crown dense, of erect slender branches; bark thin, scaly, dark brown; leaves 3½″–4½″ x ⅔″–1¼″, evergreen, oblong, short-petioled, emit strong pungent odor when bruised; flowers 4–10 in group, sepals ⅓″ long, cream-colored; fruit (drupe) to 1″ long, long ovate, greenish, ripening to dark purple. DISTR. In upper Foothill and Yellow Pine belts of w. slope at 1200–4000 ft. (north), 2500–6500 ft. (center), and higher (south), s. to Tule R. basin; in moist canyons.

In the northern Coast Ranges this Laurel is common and often large. In the Sierra the trees are smaller and some grow as shrubs. The wood (called pepperwood because of its odor) is heavy, hard, and strong. Under the name Oregon Myrtle it is often made into trays and bowls.

T-35. California Sycamore. *Platanus racemosa* (pl. 31). Ht. 40–90 ft., trunk dia. 1–5 ft.; branches long, irregular, crown open; bark smooth, sheds thin reddish brown surface sheets yearly, exposing green or white areas beneath, giving mottled appearance; leaves 4″–12″+, broader than long, in 3–5 palmate lobes, light yellowish green; flowers in ball-like clusters scattered on slender axis (♂ and ♀ separate); balls fall apart in winter, releas-

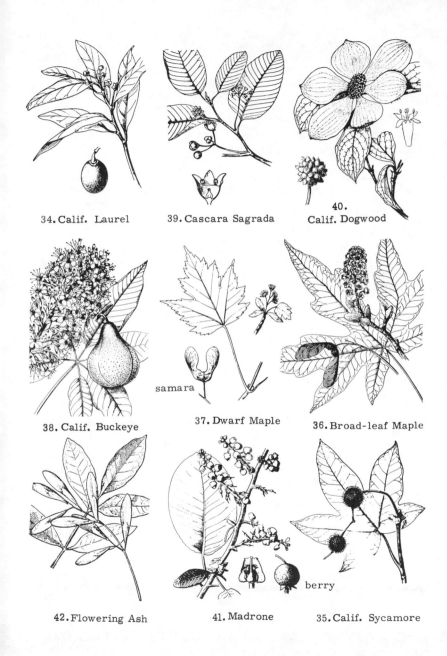

34. Calif. Laurel

39. Cascara Sagrada

40.
Calif. Dogwood

38. Calif. Buckeye

samara

37. Dwarf Maple

36. Broad-leaf Maple

42. Flowering Ash

41. Madrone

berry

35. Calif. Sycamore

ing seed-like nutlets. DISTR. Great Valley and Foothill belt up to about 2500 ft.; along stream bottoms.

Solitary sycamores growing along lowland rivers or creeks are broad and open-framed, but those living in deep canyons are taller and narrower in form. The seed heads are fed on by goldfinches in autumn or winter.

T-36. Broad-leaf Maple. *Acer macrophyllum* (pl. 31, fig. 5). Ht. 30–65+ ft., trunk dia. 1–2+ ft.; broad-crowned; bark brownish gray with narrow interwoven ridges or checked in small squarish plates; leaves 4″–10″ broad, roundish in outline, in 5 broad palmate divisions, above dark shiny green, below paler; flowers small, in drooping clusters, yellow, fragrant; fruit a bristly samara, wings 1″–1½″ long. DISTR. On w. slope from upper Foothill belt through Yellow Pine belt at 2000–4500 ft. (north), to 5600 ft. (central), higher in s. to Kaweah region; along stream borders.

This is the only large maple in the West. The trees are scattered in shaded canyons, in company with other stream-margin species, and often have tall straight trunks. The wood is hard, close-grained, and reddish brown; the sap contains sugar.

T-37. Dwarf Maple. *Acer glabrum* (pl. 31). Ht. 5–15+ ft., trunk dia. 2″–3″; branches slender, upright; bark smooth, reddish brown; leaves 1″–3″ broad, palmately 3- or 5-lobed, margin unequally serrated, above shiny green, below pale green, veins yellowish, leaf stems red; flowers few in corymb; samaras in clusters, smooth, wings to 1″ long. DISTR. Lodgepole–fir belt on w. slope at 5000–9000 ft. along stream margins or on slopes.

Often the Dwarf Maple is shrubby rather than tree-like and grows in thickets on stream borders or damp hillsides, sometimes in company with other shrubs.

T-38. California Buckeye. *Aesculus californica* (pl. 31). Ht. 10–15+ ft., trunk dia. 8″–20″, or several stems 3″–6″ dia.; crown open, spreading, flattish; bark smooth, gray to whitish; leaf stems 4″–5″, leaves palmate, of 5–7 lobes, each 3″–5″ long, pointed, edge toothed; flower clusters 4″–6″ long, blossoms many, white, petals ½″ long; fruit a pear-shaped pod; seeds 1″–2″ dia. DISTR. Foothill belt of w. slope at 500–2000 ft. (north), 1000–3000 ft. (south); on hillsides or stream borders.

The Buckeye or "horse chestnut" puts forth a showy display of white flower clusters in May or June, then sheds its leaves in late summer to leave the pear-like seed pods hanging from the tips of bare branches. No other local deciduous tree has the same habit of "closing shop" during the heat of summer.

T-39. Cascara Sagrada. *Rhamnus purshiana* (pl. 31). Ht. 8–20 ft., as tree or shrub 3–6 ft. high; bark smooth, gray or brownish; leaves 4″–7″ x 1½″–2¼″, oblong, tapered at base, blunt-pointed, leathery; flowers greenish, 5-lobed, lower part remains as collar under fruit; berry black, with 3 nutlets. DISTR. On w. slope from Bear Valley, Nevada Co., north.

T-40. California Dogwood. *Cornus nuttallii* (pl. 31). Ht. 10–30+ ft., slender; bark thin, smooth, ashy brown or reddish with small, thin scales on old trees; leaves 3″–5″, narrow or oval, tip pointed, minutely haired, veins conspicuous, pale green; flowers small, greenish yellow, in button-like cluster surrounded by 4–6 showy petal-like broad white bracts 1½″ or longer; fruit clumps scarlet, of 25–40 in group. DISTR. Yellow Pine belt on w. slope at 2500–5100 ft. or higher; in woods on moist soil.

May or June brings the showy "blossoms" of this dogwood, scattered through the lower coniferous forest, in canyons or other moist slopes. With autumn the leaves turn pink to rosy red, making bright color patches among the dark greens of pines and firs. The fruit clumps are sought by birds for the seeds.

T-41. Madrone. *Arbutus menziesii* (pl. 31). Ht. 20–80 ft., trunk dia. to 2 ft., often widely branched; bark thin, smooth, red or tan and peeling on twigs and branches, scaly and reddish brown on old trunks; leaves 3″–6″ long, narrowly elliptical, above shiny dark green, below whitish; flowers in panicle of dense racemes, white, corolla ¼″ long; fruit berry-like, dia. to ½″, red or orange. DISTR. Yellow Pine belt of w. slope s. to Tuolumne Co. in forest on various soils.

Against the somber coniferous forest the Madrone stands in contrast. As summer growth begins the bark peels off in thin layers, leaving a pale green satiny surface that ages to terra cotta or light red. The dense blossom clusters are followed by clumps of reddish berry-like fruits in autumn.

T-42. Flowering Ash. *Fraxinus dipetala* (pl. 31). Occasionally of tree form, usually shrubby, ht. 5–15 ft.; new twigs smooth, 4-angled; leaves 2″–6″ long, pinnate, leaflets ¾″–1½″ long, elliptical, toothed above middle, tip narrow; flowers appearing before leaves, in small panicles, petals 2, white, ¼″ long; samara 1″–1¼″ long, wing often notched at tip. DISTR. Foothill belt of w. slope at 1500–4000 ft. in canyons near streams or in gulches.

The little Flowering Ash is rather uncommon, living in clumps, sometimes mixed with chaparral in dryish or slightly moist soils, either rocky or gravelly.

THE ANIMALS

16. MISCELLANEOUS ANIMALS

BESIDES the insects and the vertebrates (fishes to mammals), there are various smaller animals of the waters and land in the Sierra. Some are found often, but others will require special search; the smallest can be seen only under a microscope. Representative common forms are included here. There is much to learn about all of them—the species present, their distribution and habits, and their ecology.

Abbreviations: L., length; ht., height. On snail shell: whorl, one complete coil; spire, central point or tip on upper side.

PLANKTON. Fresh waters contain varying numbers of microscopic floating plants (algae, diatoms) and animals (protozoans, rotifers, etc.). Collectively these are called the plankton. In sunlight the algae and diatoms, both containing chlorophyll, multiply and become the plant food that is eaten by many aquatic insect larvae, water snails, freshwater clams, and other small creatures. Plankton thus is the start of the aquatic "food chain" that leads up to the fishes. Plankton abounds in quiet lowland waters but is scarce in swift mountain streams and scant or absent in alpine lakes. In consequence, fishes and other aquatic animals are numerous in lakes and streams at lower elevations but fewer in waters of the High Sierra.

MA-1. Freshwater Sponge. Genus *Spongilla* (or Family Spongillidae; pl. 32). In tufts or irregular or flat masses growing on stones, sticks, or plants; firm-textured, surface bristly, with many large and small pores; color green, yellow, or brown. DISTR. In quiet lake and stream margins up to 6500 ft., on objects in water.

MA-2. Freshwater Hydra. Genus *Hydra* (pl. 32). L. 1″ or less; body a slender cylinder, flexible, highly contractile, with 6–10 delicate tentacles around mouth at upper free end of body; side of body sometimes with 1 or more "buds." DISTR. On vegetation or debris in quiet cooler waters.

MA-3. Freshwater Jellyfish. *Craspedacusta sowerbyi* (pl. 32). Transparent, gelatinous, shape of inverted bowl, dia. to ⅘″; margin with many slender, delicate tentacles in 3 rows; young stage smaller, only 8 tentacles. DISTR. Occasional in foothill lakes (Folsom, Avocado, etc.).

Careful search or towing a small-meshed net in permanent lowland lakes during the warmer months may reveal this only freshwater relative of the marine jellyfishes. Its small alternate stage is somewhat like hydra (MA-2) but with branched tubular body and no tentacles.

MA-4. Planaria. Genus *Euplanaria* (pl. 32). L. ⅔"–1"; thin, slender, soft; front end bluntly triangular with 2 black eyespots; body tapered, flexible, contractile, often brownish, sometimes with black markings; mouth midway on under surface with a tubular proboscis extended to capture food. DISTR. On leaves and plant debris in cool, quiet waters.

Planarians avoid strong light, hiding by day under objects in the water. After dark they come out to feed on small live or dead animals. Often they can be attracted to small pieces of meat placed on the bottom.

MA-5. Rotifers. Class Rotifera (pl. 32). Mostly microscopic, transparent, shape and size various in different species; head region with 1 or 2 discs rimmed with microscopic hair-like structures (cilia) that beat with whirling motion; end of body ("tail") with cement gland for attaching to objects in water. DISTR. Common in many quiet waters at low and middle altitudes.

Under a microscope a drop of water from any pond or puddle may show one or several kinds of these little animals. They can be recognized by the wheel-like movements on the head region.

MA-6. Freshwater Bryozoan. *Pectinatella magnifica* (pl. 32). Mature form an oval or rounded gelatinous mass, watery to firm, dia. to 4" or more; surface with many small star-like colonies; each colony includes several microscopic individuals (zooids) with short retractile tentacles, firm body enclosure, complete digestive tract, etc. DISTR. Occasional in quieter waters of lower Foothill belt (Phoenix Reservoir, Tuolumne Co.; Dry Creek, Fresno Co., etc.).

If one examines rocks or twigs in lowland lakes or slow streams during spring or summer, he may find the jelly-like colonies of this animal. Late in the season individuals produce small dark-colored bodies (statoblasts, dia. to 1 mm.) that overwinter after the colony dies. When the water again becomes warm, each begins to produce a colony of the form described above.

MA-7. "Horsehair Worm." Class Nematomorpha (pl. 32). L. ½"–12", dia. to ⅒"; body thin, cylindrical, firm, opaque; front end blunt; color yellow, gray, brown, or black. DISTR. In shallow ponds, puddles, stream borders, or water troughs at lower altitudes.

The long, slim adults wriggle slowly in quiet water where the females deposit strings of swollen gelatinous eggs. From these the microscopic larvae hatch and soon attach to damp leaves. If such vegetation

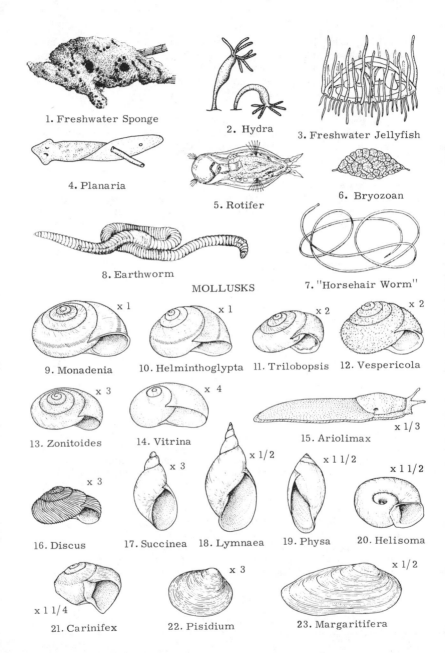

1. Freshwater Sponge

2. Hydra

3. Freshwater Jellyfish

4. Planaria

5. Rotifer

6. Bryozoan

8. Earthworm

7. "Horsehair Worm"

MOLLUSKS

x 1
9. Monadenia

x 1
10. Helminthoglypta

x 2
11. Trilobopsis

x 2
12. Vespericola

x 3
13. Zonitoides

x 4
14. Vitrina

x 1/3
15. Ariolimax

x 3
16. Discus

x 3
17. Succinea

x 1/2
18. Lymnaea

x 1 1/2
19. Physa

x 1 1/2
20. Helisoma

x 1 1/4
21. Carinifex

x 3
22. Pisidium

x 1/2
23. Margaritifera

Plate 32. Miscellaneous animals   167

is eaten by crickets, grasshoppers, or some kinds of beetles, the larva burrows into soft parts of the insect's body to grow and become adult in a few weeks. If an infested insect falls into water the worm soon emerges. People formerly believed that these worms, seen in water, were horsehairs that had "come to life."

MA-8. Earthworms. Class Oligochaeta (pl. 32). L. to 6″ (or more); body soft, cylindrical, blunt at both ends, divided into many similar ring-like segments separated by slight grooves; able to extend, contract, and twist in any direction. DISTR. In damp soils up to middle altitudes.

Probably there were some native species of earthworms in good soil of meadows and near streams of the west slope. Others doubtless have been introduced with potted plants brought into the mountains and by anglers who have "planted" worms from elsewhere in meadows with the hope of establishing convenient supplies for fish bait. Earthworms feed on decaying plant materials that they draw into their burrows in the soil. They respond to changes in temperature and soil moisture, living near the surface when the ground is damp and moderately warm but burrowing deeper in the drought of summer or chill of winter.

MOLLUSKS. About 50 species of snails, a slug or two, and two clams live in the Sierra. Most of them measure ⅛″ to ¾″, and fully half are rare; few have common names. The majority are land snails (nos. 9–17) that eat leafy vegetation on the ground at night or on damp days; they remain hidden during summer dryness or winter cold. Each lays a number of small gelatinous eggs, usually in a crevice or under a stone or log. Of the aquatic forms (nos. 18–23) the water snails feed on microscopic algae (green scum on rocks or twigs) and the clams on plankton.

MA-9. Genus *Monadenia* (pl. 32). Dia. to 1″, ht. to ½″, whorls 5½–6; shell and spire low; opening U-shaped, edge rolled outward and whitish; surface slightly shiny with faint diagonal lines; pale cinnamon brown, outer whorl with 2 buffy bands enclosing 1 dark band. DISTR. W. slope of central Sierra at 3500–5000 ft. in broken granite bordered by moss.

MA-10. Genus *Helminthoglypta* (pl. 32). Dia. ¾″–1¼″, ht. ⅜″–¾″, whorls 5–5½; shell height moderate, spire low; opening U-shaped, upper edge thin, lower edge rolled outward and pinkish; surface faintly roughened with fine diagonal lines; color olive buff with 1 narrow brownish band. DISTR. Central and s. Sierra (few in n.), Mariposa to Kern Co., from lower foothills up to 7000 ft. under boulders or debris, usually near moisture (16 species).

MA-11. Genus *Trilobopsis* (pl. 32). Dia. ¼″–⅓″, ht. to ⅕″, whorls 5; shell low, thin; opening relatively large, with 3 "teeth," edge thin, flared, its inner end over cavity (umbilicus) in center of shell below; surface matte or finely hairy; color pale yellowish brown, no band. DISTR. From Mariposa Co. n. in Foothill belt and up to Mariposa Big Trees (4 species).

MA-12. Genus *Vespericola* (pl. 32). Dia. to ⅝″, ht. to ⅜″, whorls 5¼–6; shell slightly higher than MA-11; opening moderate, with 1 or no "teeth," edge flared, its inner end partly over umbilicus; color pale yellowish brown. DISTR. Foothill belt from Eldorado Co. north (2 species).

MA-13. *Zonitoides arboreus* (pl. 32). Dia. ⅙″, ht. ⅒″, whorls 4½; shell low, thin, translucent, glossy, color olive buff; opening nearly circular, edge thin, not rolled. DISTR. Common above 2000 ft. on w. slope in rotting logs; also widespread over N. Amer., especially in cultivated areas.

MA-14. Glass Snail. *Vitrina alascana* (pl. 32). Dia. ⅕″, ht. 1⁄12″, whorls 3, the last composing most of shell which is delicate, shiny, transparent, and faintly greenish; opening large, circular, edge not rolled. DISTR. Common from Tulare Co. n. at 6000 ft. or higher among aspens.

MA-15. Slug. *Ariolimax columbianus* (pl. 32). L. to 6″; body soft, flexible, and contractile, slimy-surfaced, olive green to brown, sometimes brown spotted; a saddle-like mantle on forepart; "head" with 2 pairs of soft retractile tentacles; "foot" occupying most of under surface, edges with alternating dark and light vertical lines; shell internal. DISTR. Mostly in foothills to 5000 ft. south to Tuolumne Co. on damp leafy ground. The smaller grayish *Agriolimax laevis* occurs in wet meadows above 5000 feet.

MA-16. *Discus cronkhitei* (pl. 32). Dia. ¼″, ht. ⅛″, whorls 3½–4½, all visible on both upper and lower surfaces of shell; shell thin, outer whorl circular in section, surface with fine diagonal ribbing, light brown; opening large, thin-edged. DISTR. Above 5000 ft. on w. slope.

MA-17. Genus *Succinea* (pl. 32). Dia. ⅕″, ht. ¼″–⅓″; shell high, thin, translucent, pale brown; opening oval, higher than wide. DISTR. Throughout Sierra above 4000–5000 ft. on muddy shores (2 species).

MA-18. Large Water Snail. *Lymnaea stagnalis* (pl. 32). Dia. to ¾″, ht. to 2″; shell high, with tall pointed spire on top, outer surface with faint curving striations, thin, translucent, and yellowish (when cleaned); opening on right side, higher than wide, edge rolled only at lower left part. DISTR. Common in slower streams at all altitudes.

In life the exterior usually has a greenish brown covering (periostracum) that protects the limy shell from being dissolved by any acids present in the water. This and other freshwater snails (MA-19 to -21) have lungs and come to the surface to breathe at intervals.

MA-19. Small Water Snail. *Physa heterostropha* (pl. 32). Dia. ¼″, ht. ½″; shell vertically oval in outline, spire low; shell thin, shiny, transparent (when cleaned), faintly brownish; opening on left side, higher than wide, edge slightly rolled out at bottom. DISTR. Common in waters at low altitudes.

MA-20. Ram's-horn Snail. *Helisoma subcrenatum* (pl. 32). Dia. ¾"–1", ht. ⅜", whorls 3¾; shell a flat coil with smaller whorls sunken on both upper and lower surfaces; exterior with fine irregular ribs; color yellowish brown; opening on right side, irregularly circular, edge flared, white inside. DISTR. From Great Valley into middle altitudes, in quiet waters.

MA-21. Keel Shell. *Carinifex newberryi* (pl. 32). Dia. ½", ht. ⅜", whorls 3; shell somewhat angular with slight keel around outer whorl, surface ribs fine, irregularly curved, color yellowish brown; opening on right side, irregular, somewhat ear-shaped, flared on lower part, edge thin. DISTR. In mountain streams s. to Lake Tahoe; under stones.

MA-22. Fingernail Clam. *Pisidium casertanum* (pl. 32). L. to ¼"; shell oval, swollen at middle, brown. DISTR. In quiet streams, springs, and ponds up to 8600 ft.

MA-23. Freshwater Clam. *Margaritifera margaritifera* (pl. 32). L. to 3½"; shell thick, elliptical, somewhat angular, ridged with concentric growth lines and with horny brown or blackish covering (periostracum); interior of shell pearly, in life often pale blue or orange. DISTR. Streams up to middle altitudes, on bottom in sand or mud.

These clams burrow and crawl slowly on stream bottoms, leaving narrow grooves in the surface mud. Their eggs are fertilized and begin developing in a pouch within the female parent; then millions of the microscopic young (glochidia) are discharged into the water. For growth to continue, each must attach to the gills or skin of a fish and live as a parasite for several weeks, ultimately escaping as a minute clam. These "larval" stages sometimes heavily infest trout in Sierran hatcheries, resulting in loss of many of the fish. Flesh of this clam is tough and rather unpalatable but is eaten by some persons. Shells of Midwestern relatives (*Unio*) of this mollusk are cut to make the "pearl" buttons used on clothing.

JOINT-FOOTED ANIMALS. ARTHROPODA. Members of this group have pairs of jointed movable appendages (legs and feet, antennae, mouthparts, etc.; see grasshopper, fig. 13). The body is subdivided into few or many segments, alike or differing, and the body wall is firm or rigid. In number of species this is by far the largest group of animals. It includes the insects (see section 17), crustaceans, spiders and their allies, centipedes, millipedes, and others. Some kinds are microscopic, many are an inch or less long, and a few grow to 6 inches or more. Described here are the common Sierran forms.

CRUSTACEANS. CLASS CRUSTACEA. All have 2 pairs of antennae (insects have 1 pr.), and varying numbers of paired appendages for locomotion, feeding, respiration, etc. Sowbugs live in moist places on land, but other crustaceans are aquatic. The smaller kinds feed on microscopic material in the plankton and in turn are eaten by small fishes and insect larvae.

MA-24. Fairy Shrimp. *Branchinecta shantzi* (pl. 33). L. about 1″; thorax of 11 segments, each with pair of leafy appendages bearing gills; abdomen of 9 segments; translucent, greenish or reddish; swims upside down. DISTR. High Sierra at 7000–12800 ft. in small pools, often of snow melt water.

These delicate creatures swim inverted, often near the surface, by wavelike action of their slender appendages. The related *Eubranchipus vernalis,* of wide occurrence in springtime pools, has an additional small structure between the antennae. The little brine shrimp (*Artemia salina*), $\frac{2}{5}$″ long, with 8 abdominal segments, lives in salty ponds and desert lakes, including Mono Lake.

MA-25. Water Flea. *Daphnia pulex* (pl. 33). L. $\frac{1}{10}$″; head free, 1 (fused) eye, 2nd antenna long, 2-branched and bristly, used for swimming; body thin, in folded oval shell (seemingly of 2 parts) with 1 spine at rear; transparent. DISTR. Common in ponds and lakes.

MA-26. Ostracod or Mussel Shrimp. *Eucypris* (pl. 33). L. $\frac{1}{25}$″; body thin, completely enclosed in 2-part smooth, oval hinged shell; antennae finely hairy, project from shell, used for swimming; 7 pairs of appendages; whitish or greenish. DISTR. Throughout Sierra in ponds and lakes.

MA-27. Copepod. *Cyclops* (pl. 33). L. to $\frac{1}{12}$″; body egg-shaped, shell large at front; abdomen of 5 segments, tapered, with hair-like projections at end, in female with 2 external oval egg cases; 9 trunk segments, last 4 without appendages. DISTR. Common in ponds and lakes.

MA-28. Sowbug. *Porcellio* (pl. 33). L. to $\frac{1}{2}$″; oval, convex above, shell of separate segments extended as plates at sides; appendages beneath on most segments; gray or brown. DISTR. On land in moist places under logs or stones.

Sowbugs are scavengers on humus. The related pill bugs roll up when disturbed.

MA-29. Amphipod or Scud. *Hyalella* (pl. 33). L. to $\frac{1}{2}$″; body thin, humped, segments separate (thorax 6, abdomen 7), appendages slender; brown. DISTR. In or near water, in springs, or under wet stones or logs.

MA-30. Crayfish. *Pacifastacus leniusculus* (pl. 33). L. to 6″; a firm rounded shell over top and sides of head and thorax; abdomen of 6 separate, jointed segments; 1st pair of legs large, with stout pincers for grasping prey; 4 pairs of walking legs; reddish brown. DISTR. In quiet stream pools or lakes (down to 30 ft. in Lake Tahoe); hides in vegetation or under stones, but conspicuous on white sandy bottoms.

SPIDERS AND RELATIVES. CLASS ARACHNIDA. No antennae; 2 pairs of mouth parts (chelicerae, pedipalps) and 4 pairs of walking legs; mostly on land. All prey on insects except a few mites.

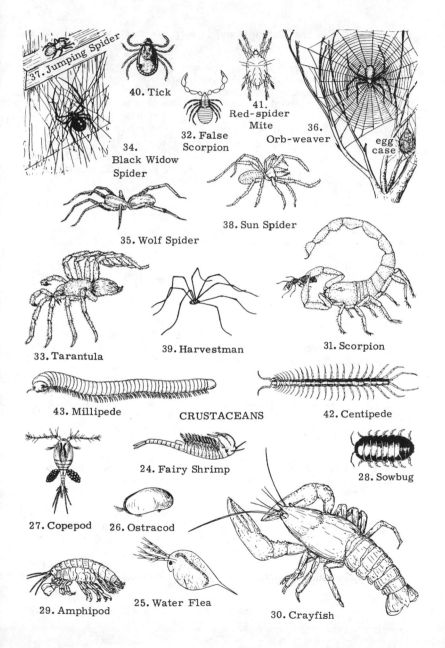

37. Jumping Spider

40. Tick

41. Red-spider Mite

36. Orb-weaver

egg case

32. False Scorpion

34. Black Widow Spider

38. Sun Spider

35. Wolf Spider

33. Tarantula

39. Harvestman

31. Scorpion

43. Millipede

CRUSTACEANS

42. Centipede

24. Fairy Shrimp

28. Sowbug

27. Copepod

26. Ostracod

29. Amphipod

25. Water Flea

30. Crayfish

Plate 33. Miscellaneous animals

MA-31. Scorpion. *Vejovis* (pl. 33). L. to 2″; flattened; head region with 1 pair of small "jaws" (chelicerae) and 1 pair of stout pincers on long jointed arms (pedipalps); thorax with 4 pairs of slender jointed legs; abdomen narrowed into jointed flexible tail with sharp "poison claw" at end; yellow or brown. DISTR. Mostly at lower elevations on ground under logs or stones.

Scorpions hide by day and come out at night to feed on insects and small ground-dwelling animals. Prey is caught by the pincers, killed with the sting, and torn apart to eat. In Sierran species the sting is painful but not dangerous to man. Young are born alive and ride on the female's back until their first molt.

MA-32. False Scorpion. *Apocheiridium* (pl. 33). L. to ¼″; resembles scorpion but smaller, no tail or sting; brown. DISTR. On or under loose bark of dead trees.

MA-33. Tarantula. *Aphonopelma* (pl. 33). Body L. about 1½″, legs spread 3″–4″; hairy, brownish; tarsal claws 2; jaws move horizontally (vertically in other spiders). DISTR. To middle elevations in the Sierra.

Tarantulas are mostly ground dwellers, active at night. They do not bite unless provoked; the bite is painful but not dangerous.

MA-34. Black Widow Spider. *Latrodectus mactans* (pl. 33). L. ¼″–⅖″; female globose, shiny black, usually with red hourglass mark on under side of abdomen, sometimes with red spots on back; male smaller, narrower, with white lines on sides; young orange and white; tarsal claws 3, legs without spines; web irregular, tough, sticky, retreat funnel-shaped. DISTR. Common at lower elevations under rocks, in hollow logs, in old outbuildings, or under houses.

The bite is much feared and rightly so because the venom is a nerve poison producing severe symptoms and even death in man. Fortunately the spider is not aggressive, usually trying to escape rather than attack a person. If accidentally disturbed it can bite only through soft skin. Treatment (unlike that for rattlesnake bite) must be by a physician.

After mating the female sometimes kills and eats the male. Her eggs are laid in white or tan sacs about ½ inch in diameter, suspended in the web.

MA-35. Wolf Spider. *Lycosa* (pl. 33). L. to 1″; brown with pale and dark marks above; tarsal claws 3; legs with spines; eyes unequal in size; female carries pale spherical egg cocoon, later the young; hunts on ground, no web. DISTR. On ground or under stones.

MA-36. Orb-weaver. *Argiope* (pl. 33). L. to 1″; bright black and yellow with silvery hairs; tarsal claws 3; web large, flat, of geometrical pattern, with heavy zigzag band; female lives at center of web; egg sac brown, tough, dia. about 1″, one end tapered. DISTR. In bushes or grass in open sunny places.

MA-37. Jumping Spider. *Salticus* (pl. 33). L. ⅛″–¼″; gray with white markings and a few reddish scales; tarsal claws 3; front pair of eyes much larger than others; hunts in daylight by sudden, quick jumps at prey; no web for snaring prey but closely woven retreat made for night or hibernation. DISTR. Common on fences, logs, stones, etc.

MA-38. Sun Spider. *Eremobates* (pl. 33). L. to ¾″; hairy; "head" with 2 swollen tapering pincers (chelicerae); pedipalps leg-like, giving appearance of 5 pairs of legs; no "waist"; abdomen of 10 segments; no spinning organs or "tail." DISTR. At low elevations on ground in open sandy places.

MA-39. Harvestman or "Daddy longlegs." *Phalangium* (pl. 33). Body L. to ⅜″; round; chelicerae 3-jointed; pedipalps 6-jointed, not pincer-like; legs long, delicate, 7-jointed; tarsi many-jointed; pale brown. DISTR. In fields, woods, sometimes in buildings.

MA-40. Tick. *Dermacentor* (pl. 33). L. ¼″; body oval, flat, with shield behind head on back; chelicerae and pedipalps formed into small beak; legs 8 in adults, 6 in young; brown or gray. DISTR. Widespread at low and middle elevations in the Sierra.

Female ticks suck blood of deer and other large mammals, swelling to ¾ inch long, then drop to ground, where each lays thousands of eggs. The larvae hatch and climb bushes to the tips of branches, waiting to attach to a host mammal walking by. Larvae, nymphs, and adults feed on different hosts, usually of increasing size. In the northern Sierra and beyond (to Montana) this tick may transmit the disease spotted fever to man. Other ticks (*Ornithodorus*) lack the shield. They are common on squirrels, chipmunks, and other rodents and may leave nests under mountain cabins to bite people. They transmit relapsing fever and hence should be avoided—by not permitting rodents to nest in or around residences. There is no immediate sensation when a tick bites. After walking through woods or chaparral where host animals are common, a person should search his skin and clothing and remove any ticks present. When removing a tick, take care that the mouthparts are not broken off and left in the skin to cause a secondary infection.

MA-41. Red-spider Mite. *Tetranychus* (pl. 33). Almost microscopic, L. to ¹⁄₅₀″; oval, compact, 8 legs; mouthparts minute, piercing; red or yellow, sometimes with black spots. DISTR. On leaves of many broad-leaved trees and shrubs, causing pale spotting.

Other species of mites attack nearly all kinds of Sierran plants. Some give rise to gall-like swellings on leaves of willows. Still others feed on native birds and mammals, producing scabs and itching. Another group lives in streams and ponds; their larvae appear as small red sacs attached to dragon-flies and other insects. There are no chiggers in the Sierra that bite man.

CENTIPEDES AND MILLIPEDES. CLASS MYRIAPODA. Head with 1 pair each of antennae and jaws; trunk slender, of few or many like segments, each with 1 or 2 pairs of legs.

MA-42. Centipede. *Scolopendra* (pl. 33). L. to 4"; slender, flat; segments 21, each with 1 pair of legs; 1st pair of body appendages 4-jointed, hook-like, with poison ducts; pale reddish brown. DISTR. Common under loose bark and on ground beneath stones, etc.

Different species of centipedes have various numbers of segments and legs; some are small and almost white. None in the Sierra is dangerous to man—but some large tropical species are. Centipedes prey on insects and other small animals.

MA-43. Millipede. *Spirobolus* (pl. 33). L. to 4"; cylindrical; body wall hard, limy; segments about 100, each with 2 pairs of legs. DISTR. In moist places on ground or in rotten logs.

The "thousand-legged worms" glide smoothly along with wave-like movements of the many legs. When disturbed they coil up and may secrete an offensive odor from stink glands. Their food is dead plant and animal material and roots.

17. INSECTS

Of land animals, insects are by far the commonest. More than 10000 kinds probably inhabit the Sierra, and new species are being found yearly. Larvae or adults live variously in the soil, in all kinds and parts of plants (roots, stems, wood, leaves, and flowers), and in fresh or brackish waters. Some damage forests and crop plants (figs. 15 and 16), and some carry diseases to plants, animals, and man. Bees and other flower-visiting insects are essential to pollinate flowers of many wild and cultivated plants. Termites and some beetles reduce fallen trees to humus by their feeding, aided by the bacteria and molds they spread. Ants serve as scavengers, as do flies and beetles whose larvae consume carrion and dung. Every kind of insect is preyed upon by one or more other species of insect. Spiders, scorpions, and similar creatures feed on insects, as do many vertebrates from fishes to mammals.

Characteristics (fig. 13). Insects are small, typically with 3 pairs of legs, 2 pairs of wings, and 1 pair of sensory *antennae* or "feelers." The body covering is usually hard, and is shed or molted at intervals during the young stages of growth to allow for increase in size. The body consists of a series of segments grouped in 3 major parts, a movable head, rigid thorax, and flexible abdomen. The end of the abdomen often has a pair of short appendages (*cerci*), and in females has an egg-laying apparatus (*ovipositor*). The legs and antennae are jointed to permit

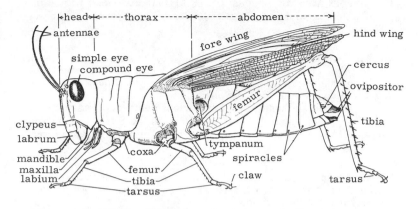

Figure 13. Insect structure: the grasshopper.

movement. Each leg is of several parts: hip or shoulder joint (*coxa*), thigh or *femur, tibia,* and foot or *tarsus;* the last is of 1 to 5 joints (or none), usually with 2 claws. Eyes are of 2 kinds, simple (*ocelli,* with single lenses) and compound (masses of hundreds of individual eyes) that see by "mosaic" vision. Nearly all adult insects have 2 compound eyes, and some have 2 or 3 simple eyes as well. Respiration is by many microscopic tubes (*tracheae*) that carry air from openings (*spiracles*) in the body wall to all interior parts. Insects are "cold-blooded" (lacking temperature regulation) and must adjust their daily and yearly cycles to avoid extremes of heat and cold.

Grasshoppers and some other insects have chewing mouthparts (fig. 13). These comprise a flap-like upper lip (*labrum*), a pair of strong upper jaws (*mandibles*), a pair of lower jaws (*maxillae*) usually with sensory feelers (*palps*), and a fused lower lip (*labium*) with central plates and lateral lobes and palps. In the center is a fleshy tongue (*hypopharynx*). From this general type the true bugs have evolved tube-like sucking mouthparts, the mandibles and maxillae modified as slender, piercing stylets. Butterflies and moths have a coiled tube (*proboscis*) for sucking plant nectar. Two-winged flies have mouthparts adapted for sucking (mosquitoes) or soft lapping (house flies). Bees combine mandibles for chewing with a labium and palps for sucking nectar from flowers.

Life Cycles (fig. 14). Among primitive insects such as silverfish the egg at hatching yields a small individual of adult form. At each of several molts the animal increases in size, finally becoming a sexually mature adult. This group (I-1, I-2) undergoes no metamorphosis or transformation in form during growth. Next, in the grasshoppers, true bugs, and related forms (I-3 to I-42), the young, called *nymphs,* at hatching resemble adults but lack wings. At successive molts, wing pads on the middle (meso-) and hind (meta-) thorax increase in size. At the last molt the nymph becomes an adult with membranous wings. This type of growth is called "incomplete metamorphosis." Finally, in the butterflies, beetles, flies, and wasps (I-43 to I-173), the young hatch as worm-like *larvae* (caterpillars, grubs, or wrigglers). This is the stage of feeding and growth, totally unlike the adult in form and habits. Wing pads develop internally. The full-grown larva transforms into a *pupa (chrysalis, cocoon)* within which larval structures are remade into those of the adult. The legs and wings are folded in the mummy-like case. From this the adult emerges and its wings unfold—a "complete metamorphosis."

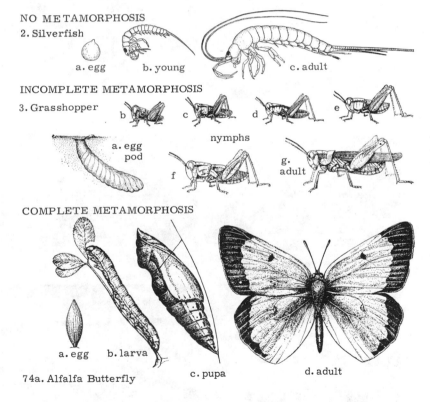

NO METAMORPHOSIS
2. Silverfish
a. egg   b. young   c. adult

INCOMPLETE METAMORPHOSIS
3. Grasshopper   b   c   d   e
a. egg pod   nymphs   f   g. adult

COMPLETE METAMORPHOSIS
a. egg   b. larva   c. pupa   d. adult
74a. Alfalfa Butterfly

Figure 14. Insect life histories.

161. Galls of 2 cynipid wasps on oaks

46. Work of Blotch Leafminer
on oak

54. Tent Caterpillars
on snowbrush

145. Craters of "worm lion"
(Vermileo) in sand

164. Nest entrance of Formica Ant
in sand

9. Galleries and pellets of
Damp-wood Termite

164. Carpenter Ant tunnels
in incense cedar

Figure 15. Work of insects

a. Newly killed
yellow pine

b. Winding burrows
on yellow pine

c. Pitch tube and hole
in lodgepole pine

d. "Engraved" tunnels in Douglas fir
119. Work of Bark Beetles

 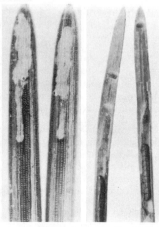

a. Ghost forest of lodgepole pine; Lake Tenaya
47. Lodgepole Pine Needleminer

b. Mines in
needles

c. Pupa and
larva

Figure 16. Work of insects

179

Collecting. Insects are ideal subjects for nature study because they are easy to find and collect (with a net or the hands) and easy to preserve. Specimens may be killed in a bottle containing plaster of Paris or wadded paper saturated with cleaning fluid (carbon tetrachloride). Hard-shelled adults dry quickly and require no "skinning" or preservative. They may be laid on cotton under glass or mounted by inserting a fine pin through the thorax (for beetles, through the right wing cover). Butterflies should be spread while soft so that the hind margins of the front wings form a line at right angles to the body and the hind wings are brought up to touch the front wings (see fig. 14, lower right). Corrugated cardboard is useful for a spreading board if a trough is cut to hold the thick body. Then the wings can be held in place with strips of paper pinned to the cardboard. The specimen will dry in a few days and remain in the spread position. It may then be pinned in a box with corrugated cardboard or cork bottom. If the specimen is to have scientific value, exact information as to place and date of capture and name of collector is written on a small label put on the pin under the insect. A permit is required to collect insects in national or state parks, but elsewhere in the Sierra there are no restrictions and this hobby may be pursued with no harmful effects and great benefit to the collector.

In this handbook the commonest species of butterflies are described (as with the plants and vertebrates). Other insects are described mostly at the family level (as are the grasshoppers [Acrididae] and crickets [Gryllidae]), with mention of Sierran examples. Species mentioned in text that are also shown in the figures are marked with an asterisk (*). Abbreviations: L., length of insect, head to end of abdomen, not including wings; WS., wing spread; ♂, male; ♀, female. Number of segments in antennae or tarsi are stated as "11-jointed," etc. Scientific names of insect orders are shown thus: COLLEMBOLA; of suborders, CRYPTOCERATA.

I-1. Springtails. COLLEMBOLA (pl. 34). L. minute to ¼"; no wings; chewing mouthparts (retracted in head); antennae 4- to 8-jointed; abdomen of 6 segments, usually a springing organ below. Young like adults. In logs, wet leaf mold, or soil; some on snow; eat decaying plants. *Entomobrya**, common on ground; *Podura aquatica,* may blacken surface of ponds.

I-2. Silverfish. THYSANURA (fig. 14). L. ½"–1"; no wings; chewing mouthparts (sometimes retracted into mouth); antennae long; body slender with gray scales; abdomen of 10–11 segments with short appendages below and 3 slender "tails" at end. Young like adults. On ground, eat decayed plants. *Pedetontus californicus**, in foothills; *Mesomachilis,* under fallen needles or loose bark in Yellow Pine forest.

I-3 to I-8. GRASSHOPPERS, KATYDIDS, CRICKETS. ORTHOPTERA. L. to 2½"; wings usually present, forewings tough, colored like body, hind wings membranous, large, folded fan-like at rest; chewing mouthparts;

TABLE 4. Guide to Orders of Insects (Adults)

	Mouth-parts[a]	Cerci[b]	Tarsal joints[c]
WINGS NONE			
Springtails, I-1; abdomen of 6 segments, with jumping organ	c	−	1
Silverfish, I-2; abdomen with 2 or 3 "tails"	c	+	2–3
Jerusalem Crickets, etc.; I-4, -7, -8; eat plants or animals	c	+	3–5
Termites, I-9; mostly pale-colored; eat wood; 3 castes	c	+	4
Psocids, I-13; minute, white, under bark	c	−	2–3
Ants, I-164, -165; narrow-waisted	c	−	5
Chewing Lice, I-11; flat, head wide; mostly parasites on birds	c	−	1–2
Sucking Lice, I-12; flat, head narrow; parasites on mammals	s	−	1
Aphids, Scales, etc., I-37 to I-39; beak at base of head	s	−	1–3
Water Striders, I-20; beak at front of head	s	−	1–3
Fleas, I-157; minute, narrow, hind legs for jumping	s	−	5
WINGS 2			
Flies, I-138 to I-156; knob-like balancers replace hind wings	s	−	5
WINGS 4, ALL CLEAR			
Termites (sexual forms), I-9; fore and hind wings equal	c	+	4
Stone-flies, I-10; hind wings large, folded at rest	c	+	3
Psocids, I-13; wings held roof-like at rest	c	−	2–3
Dragon-flies, etc., I-40, -41; wings at rest horizontal or vertical	c	+	3
May-flies, I-42; wings held vertical at rest; 2 or 3 "tails"	c	+	1–5
Lacewings, etc., I-110 to I-113; wings held roof-like at rest	c	−	5
Bees, Wasps, Ants, I-158 to I-173; abdomen usually narrow-waisted	c	−	5
Cicadas, Aphids, etc., I-31, I-36 to I-38; beak at base of head	s	−	1–3
WINGS 4, FORE PAIR AT LEAST PARTLY OPAQUE OR LEATHERY			
Grasshoppers, etc., I-3, -5, -6; hind legs large for jumping	c	+	3–5
Beetles, I-114 to I-137; fore wings hard, shell-like	c	−	1–5
Leafhoppers, etc., I-32 to I-35; beak at base of head	s	−	1–3
True Bugs, I-15 to I-30; beak at front of head	s	−	1–3
WINGS 4, BROAD, COVERED WITH HAIRS OR SCALES			
Caddis-flies, I-44; wings with short hairs	c	−	5
Butterflies, Moths, I-45 to I-109; wings minutely scaled	s	−	5
WINGS 4, NARROW, NAKED OR WITH LONG HAIRS			
Scorpion-flies, I-43; head lengthened as a beak	c	−	5
Thrips, I-14; tarsi inflated, bladder-like	s	−	1–2

[a] Mouthparts: c = chewing jaws; s = sucking.
[b] Cerci (at end of abdomen), + = present; − = none.
[c] Tarsal joints = number of segments.

antennae many-jointed; hind legs large for jumping (except certain wingless forms). Some adults "sing" (stridulate) by rubbing together rough edges of legs, wings, etc. Young like adults but with short wing pads. Eat green plants; a few predaceous.

I-3. Grasshoppers. Acrididae (figs. 13, 14). L. to 1½"; antennae short; tarsi 3-jointed. On meadows or rocky slopes; egg pods laid in ground. *Cratypedes neglectus,* wings yellow-marked, in mountains; flies with clicking noise.

I-4. Jerusalem Crickets. Stenopelmatidae (pl. 34). L. to 1¼"; robust, wingless, head large; antennae long; tarsi 4-jointed; abdomen cross-barred. On ground; carnivorous; eggs laid singly in ground. *Stenopelmatus fuscus*.

I-5. Katydids. Tettigoniidae (pl. 34). L. to 2½"; antennae very long; tarsi 4-jointed; ovipositor on abdomen long, blade-like. Live in green foliage which they resemble. Males "sing" day or night. Eggs laid in rows on leaves or twigs. *Microcentrum rhombifolium,* the Angular-winged Katydid, up to middle elevations.

I-6. Crickets. Gryllidae (pl. 34). L. to 1½"; antennae long; tarsi 3-jointed; abdomen with 2 long tails, also long ovipositor in ♀; ♂ chirps. Ground Cricket (*Acheta assimilis;* 6b), stout-bodied, brown to black, under stones, eggs laid in ground; Snowy Tree Cricket (*Oecanthus fasciatus;* 6a), delicate pale green, young white, on foliage where eggs are laid.

I-7. Timemas. Timemidae (pl. 34). L. to 1"; form of short stout "walking stick"; no wings; legs short, tarsi 3-jointed. Usually green or pink, resembling foliage which they eat. *Timema californica*, ranges through the foothills to middle elevations.

I-8. Grylloblattas. Grylloblattidae (pl. 34). L. to 1"; slender; no wings; legs short, tarsi 5-jointed. Live deep in crevices under snow or glaciers and in ground above 7000 ft. *Grylloblatta bifratrilecta* occurs at Sonora Pass, and other species are known at elevations to 12000 ft.

I-9. Termites. Isoptera (pl. 34, fig. 15). L. ¼"–1"; chewing mouthparts; antennae short, 9+ jointed; young or workers and soldiers (with big heads and jaws) wingless, blind, soft-bodied, whitish—hence called "white ants"; sexual forms ♂ and ♀ (queen) flat-bodied, wings 4, long, equal, filmy, broken off after mating flight (usually after a rain). Colony lives in tunnels in soil or wood, feeds on wood (cellulose) and fungi digested by bacteria and protozoans in termite gut. *Reticulitermes,* small, in wood and soil; *Zootermopsis*, large, in pine logs up to 9000 ft.

I-10. Stone-flies. Plecoptera (pl. 34). L. to 1½"; chewing mouthparts often reduced; antennae long, slender; wings 4, membranous, hind wings larger, pleated over back at rest; body pale green to brown. Eggs dropped on water or glued to rocks. Nymphs long and slender (*Alloperla*) or stout,

a. Streamside. Willows, cottonwoods, and oaks

b. Foothill belt. Digger Pine-Blue Oak woodland

c. Foothill belt. Chaparral

d. Yellow Pine belt. Yellow Pine and Black Oak

Color Plate 1. Plant associations

b. Mountain chaparral on logged and burned area

a. Yellow Pine belt. Coniferous forest and chaparral

d. Lodgepole Pine with Aspen: autumn color

c. Lodgepole Pine and Red Fir forest

Color Plate 2. Plant associations

a. Subalpine belt. Whitebark Pine. Mountain Hemlock

b. Subalpine belt. Meadow with Lodgepole Pine

c. Alpine fell field

d. Sagebrush and Bitterbrush

Color Plate 3. Plant associations

1. Death Camas   2. Corn Lily   3. Camas

5. Swamp Onion   6e. Twining Brodiaea   7b. White Mariposa

9. Fritillaria   10b. Small Tiger Lily   12. Sierra Iris

Color Plate 4. Wildflowers

13. Blue-eyed Grass   14. Rein-orchis   **16. Striped Coral Root**

19. Knotweed   21. Buckwheat   22. Pussy Paws

24. Indian Pink   25. Indian Pond Lily   27. Red Columbine

Color Plate 5. Wildflowers

28. Small Larkspur 30. Anemone 31. Buttercup

32. Cream Cups 33. California Poppy 34. Bleeding Heart

35. Streptanthus 38. West. Wall Flower 40. Stonecrop

Color Plate 6. Wildflowers

44. Yellow Cinquefoil   45b. Bush Lupine   50. Shrub Pea

56. Blazing Star   57. Calif. Fuchsia   58. Fireweed

60. Farewell-to-spring   61. Evening Primrose   64. Cow Parsnip

Color Plate 7. Wildflowers

67. Pine-drops 68. Snow Plant 69. Shooting-star

70. Sierra Primrose 78. Douglas Phlox 79. Scarlet Gilia

81. Baby Blue-eyes 82. Phacelia 84. Sierra Forget-me-not

Color Plate 8. Wildflowers

86. Fiddleneck   91. Giant Hyssop   94. Western Pennyroyal

96. Tolguacha   99. Collinsia   100. Red Pentstemon

101. Monkey-flower   102. Paintbrush   103. Owl Clover

Color Plate 9. Wildflowers

109. Meadow Goldenrod   114a. Black-eyed Susan   114b. Calif. Cone Flower

115. Mule Ears   117. Tidy Tips   119. Bigelow Sneezeweed

120. Yarrow Milfoil   121. Groundsel   123. Sierra Thistle

Color Plate 10. Wildflowers

7. Spice Bush 8. Bush Poppy 9. Mock Orange

10a. Gooseberry 10b. Currant 12. Creamberry

16. Calif. Wild Rose 17. Kit-kit-dizze 19. Chamise

Color Plate 11. Shrubs

20. Bitterbrush   22. West. Choke-cherry   24. Mountain Ash

25 Toyon   26. West. Service Berry   27. Redbud

29. Scotch Broom   30. Deerweed   36. Fremontia

Color Plate 12. Shrubs

34d. Tobacco Brush   34b. Deer Brush   34a. Buck Brush

40. Western Azalea   42. Red Mountain Heather   45b. Mariposa Manzanita

48. Yerba Santa   52. Blue Elderberry   58. Rabbit Brush

Color Plate 13. Shrubs

49. Budworm Moth 46. Blotch Leaf-miner Moth 45. Fairy Moth 47. Needleminer Moth

48. Clear-winged Moth

51. Snout Moth

52. Plume Moth

50. Carpenter Moth

54. Tent caterpillar & Moth

58. Owlet Moth

55. Measuring-worm & Moth

59. Tiger Moth, larva & adult

56. Sphinx Moth hornworm & adult

57. Tussock Moth larva, ♀ (wingless), & ♂

53a. Sheep Moth

53b. Polyphemus Moth silky cocoon & ♂

Color Plate 14. Insects: moths

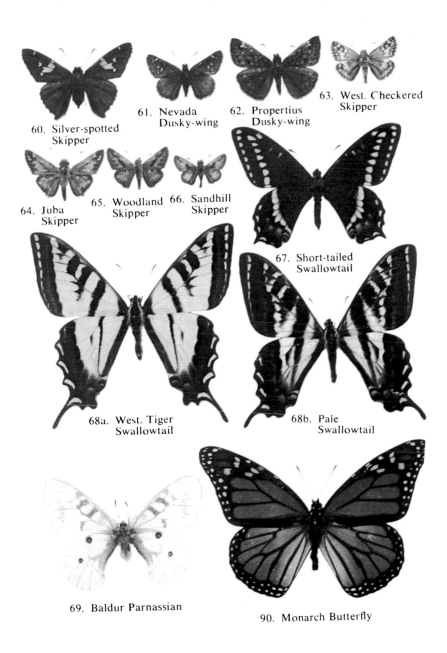

60. Silver-spotted Skipper

61. Nevada Dusky-wing

62. Propertius Dusky-wing

63. West. Checkered Skipper

64. Juba Skipper

65. Woodland Skipper

66. Sandhill Skipper

67. Short-tailed Swallowtail

68a. West. Tiger Swallowtail

68b. Pale Swallowtail

69. Baldur Parnassian

90. Monarch Butterfly

Color Plate 15. Insects: butterflies

70. Pine White

71. Common White

72. Colorado Marble

73. Sara Orange-tip

74a. Alfalfa Butterfly

74b. Behr's Sulfur

75. Boisduval's Hairstreak

76. Great Purple Hairstreak

77. Common Hairstreak

78. Behr's Hairstreak

79. Nelson's Hairstreak

80. Western Banded Elfin

81. Lustrous Copper

82. Acmon Blue

83. Gray Blue

84. Behr's Blue

85. Square-spotted Blue

86. Tailed Blue

87. Echo Blue

88. Arrowhead Blue

89. Mormon Metal-mark

91. Calif. Ringlet

92. Riding's Satyr

93. Sylvan Satyr

94. Ivallda Arctic

Color Plate 16. Insects: butterflies

95. Mountain Fritillary 97. Chalcedon Checker-spot

98. Northern Checker-spot

96. West. Meadow Fritillary

102. Mourning-cloak

99. Mylitta Crescent

101. Calif. Tortoise-shell

100. Satyr Anglewing

103. Red Admiral

104. Painted Lady

105. Virginia Lady

106. West Coast Lady

108. Lorquin's Admiral

107. Buckeye

109. Calif. Sister

Color Plate 17. Insects: butterflies

3. Brown.   4. Cut-throat.   5. Golden.   6. Rainbow.   7. Eastern Brook.

Color Plate 18. Fishes: trouts

49. Red-shafted Flicker. 51. California Woodpecker. 52. Lewis Woodpecker. 53. Yellow-bellied Sapsucker. 55. Hairy Woodpecker. 56. Downy Woodpecker. 58. White-headed Woodpecker. 59. Black-backed Three-toed Woodpecker.

Color Plate 19. Birds: woodpeckers

79. Mountain Chickadee. 82. White-breasted Nuthatch. 83. Red-breasted Nuthatch. 84. Pygmy Nuthatch. 85. Creeper. 102. Golden-crowned Kinglet. 103. Ruby-crowned Kinglet.

Color Plate 20. Small forest birds

110. Orange-crowned Warbler. 111. Calaveras Warbler. 112. Yellow Warbler. 113. Audubon Warbler. 114. Black-throated Gray Warbler. 115. Hermit Warbler. 116. Tolmie Warbler. 117. Yellowthroat. 119. Wilson Warbler.

Color Plate 21. Wood warblers: adult males

132. Purple Finch.   133. Cassin Finch.   134. California Linnet.   136. Gray-crowned Rosy Finch.

Color Plate 22. Red finches: males (above) and females

143a. Savannah Sparrow. 143b. Grasshopper Sparrow. 146. Rufous-crowned Sparrow. 147a. Bell Sparrow. 147b. Sage Sparrow. 149. Chipping Sparrow (summer). 149*. Chipping Sparrow (winter). 150. Brewer Sparrow. 151. Mountain White-crowned Sparrow (adult). 151. Mountain White-crowned Sparrow (immature). 151b. Gambel Sparrow. 152. Golden-crowned Sparrow (adult).

Color Plate 23. Miscellaneous sparrows

15a. Alpine. b. Sagebrush. c. Mono. e. Lodgepole. f. Allen. g. Long-eared. h. Merriam.

Color Plate 24. Mammals: chipmunks

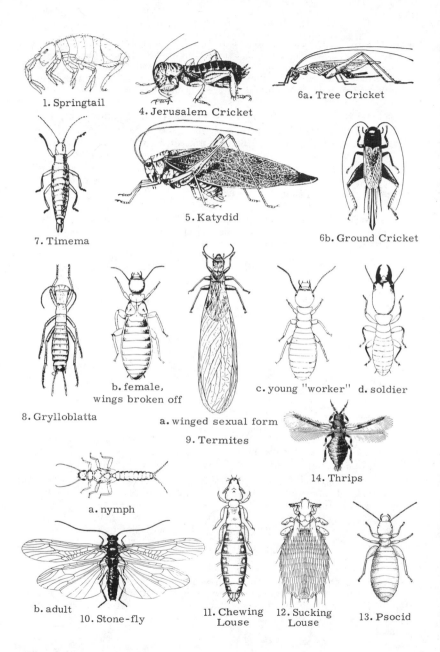

1. Springtail

4. Jerusalem Cricket

6a. Tree Cricket

7. Timema

5. Katydid

6b. Ground Cricket

8. Grylloblatta

b. female, wings broken off

a. winged sexual form

c. young "worker"   d. soldier

9. Termites

14. Thrips

a. nymph

b. adult
10. Stone-fly

11. Chewing Louse

12. Sucking Louse

13. Psocid

Plate 34. Insects

183

with 2 "tails"; crawl out on streamside rocks or plants for molting to adult form, leaving dried skins. Nymphs eat plant tissues or aquatic insects. Important as fish food and as bait for anglers. Adults appear in any month. *Brachyptera pacifica** ranges up to 7000 ft. *Capnia lacustra,* adults wingless, live nymphs at depths of 100 to 400 ft. in Lake Tahoe.

I-11, I-12. LICE. MALLOPHAGA, ANOPLURA. L. to ¼"; body flat, pale; wingless; eyes reduced or none; antennae short, 3- to 5-jointed; legs short, stout, with large claws. External parasites on birds and mammals.

I-11. Chewing Lice. MALLOPHAGA (pl. 34). Head broad, chewing mouthparts. Feed on feathers of birds (e.g., Duck Louse, *Philopterus squalidus**) or on hair of some mammals.

I-12. Sucking Lice. ANOPLURA (pl. 34). Head narrow, mouthparts piercing-sucking, retractable; suck blood of deer, ground squirrels (*Neohaematopinus laeviusculus**), rabbits, and other mammals.

I-13. Psocids. CORRODENTIA (pl. 34). L. to ¼"; body flat, wingless, and pale, or convex, winged, and pigmented; wings 4, clear, held roof-like over body at rest; chewing mouthparts; antennae slender. Young (Bark Lice) and adults on bark or foliage of coniferous and other trees; Book Louse (*Troctes divinatorius**) in houses.

I-14. Thrips. THYSANOPTERA (pl. 34). L. to ⅓"; body slender, wings 4, narrow, fringed with long hairs; mouthparts for rasping and sucking; tarsi end in protrusible "bladder"; antennae 6- to 9-jointed. Young with external wing pads. Young and adults suck fluids of flowers and leaves, producing pale spots. A few large black species prey on mites under bark of conifers and other trees. The Bean Thrips (*Hercothrips fasciatus**), live on grasses up to middle elevations.

I-15 to I-30. TRUE BUGS. HEMIPTERA. Wings 4 (rarely absent), front pair leathery at forward end (*base*), membranous at hind part (*apex*), tips overlap at rest, leaving triangular area (*scutellum*) between bases; mouthparts form slender sucking tube attached forward on head; scent glands produce "buggy" odor. Young (nymphs) like adults but with wing pads.

A. WATER BUGS. CRYPTOCERATA. Antennae short, hidden under head.

I-15. Water Boatmen. Corixidae (pl. 35). L. to ½"; oval; black or brown; swim with back up, using fringed oar-like hind legs. Air for breathing in silvery film on abdomen (obtained by touching thorax to surface of water). Eat minute plants and animals gathered with comb-like front tarsi. *Sigara,* small, to ¼"; *Cenocorixa** to ½". In ponds and stream pools at all elevations.

I-16. Backswimmers. Notonectidae (pl. 35). L. to ½″; body narrow, convex above, concave below; swim upside down with long oar-like hind legs. Obtain air by touching tip of abdomen to water surface. Prey on other insects and may bite people. *Buenoa,* slender, to ⅓″ long; *Notonecta unifasciata*,* stout, to ½″ long.

I-17. Giant Water Bugs. Belostomatidae (pl. 35). L. to 3″; body long, oval, flat above; 2 short strap-like posterior tubes under wings used to obtain air at surface of water; beak short, stout. Prey on young fish and insects; bite man severely if handled. *Lethocerus americanus*,* L. 2″–3″, attracted to lights at night, lays eggs on plant stalks at water surface; *Abedus,* L. to 1½″, and *Belostoma,* L. to ¾″, glue eggs on back of ♂.

I-18. Water Scorpions. Nepidae (pl. 35). L. to 2″; slender, stick-like; front legs long, grasping, abdomen with 2 slender breathing tubes. *Ranatra fusca*,* usually hidden among sticks and plants in shallow water; predaceous.

I-19. Toad Bugs. Gelastocoridae (pl. 35). L. to ½″; rough-surfaced; oval, eyes big; color matches shores of sandy or muddy ponds and streams. *Gelastocoris oculatus*,* preys on small insects.

    B. LAND AND SURFACE-WATER BUGS. GYMNOCERATA. Antennae well developed, not concealed.

I-20. Water Striders. Gerridae (pl. 35). L. to 1″; body narrow; legs long, tarsi with claws attached above tip (to avoid breaking surface film on which strider walks); some have wings reduced or absent. *Gerris remigis*,* on ponds and stream pools at all elevations; eggs laid on floating objects.

I-21. Plant Bugs. Miridae (pl. 35). L. to ½″; oval or slender; no simple eyes; beak 4-jointed; forewings with small area bent down on outer edge beyond middle. One or more species on each kind of Sierran plant; *Lygus hesperus*,* on lupines; *Platylygus,* stout, tawny, on pines; *Orthotylus,* slender, green, on willows; *Dacerla,* ant mimic, on pines and lupines; *Deraeocoris,* preys on aphids.

I-22. Damsel Bugs. Nabidae (pl. 35). L. to ⅓″; slender, gray; beak long, 4-jointed; with simple eyes. *Nabis ferus*,* agile, on plants or ground, preys on insects.

I-23. Bat, Swallow, and Bed Bugs. Cimicidae (pl. 35). L. to ¼″; oval, light brown; no simple eyes; beak 3-jointed; wing pads short in adults. *Oeciacus vicarius,* in swallow nests under bridges, etc.; *Cimex pilosellus,* on bats in tunnels or caves; *Cimex lectularius*,* in beds of men.

I-24. Pirate Bugs. Anthocoridae (pl. 35). L. to ⅛″; oval, brown or black and white; with simple eyes; beak 3-jointed; forewings like Plant Bugs (I-21). On flowers (*Orius tristicolor**), foliage of trees, and bark of conifers; prey on mites and minute insects.

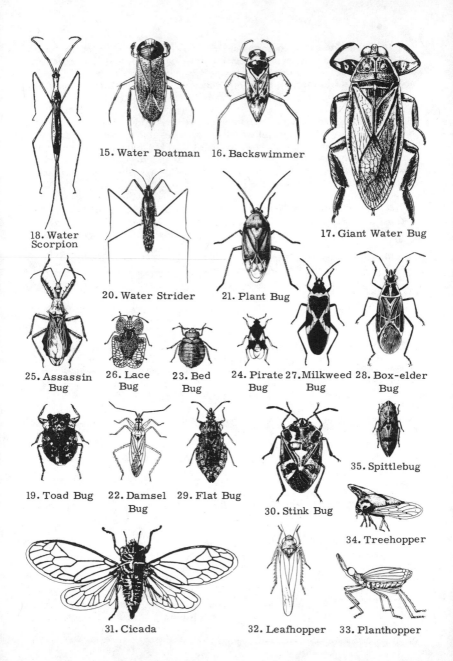

15. Water Boatman 16. Backswimmer

18. Water
Scorpion

20. Water Strider 21. Plant Bug

17. Giant Water Bug

25. Assassin
Bug

26. Lace
Bug

23. Bed
Bug

24. Pirate
Bug

27. Milkweed
Bug

28. Box-elder
Bug

19. Toad Bug 22. Damsel
Bug

29. Flat Bug

30. Stink Bug

35. Spittlebug

34. Treehopper

31. Cicada

32. Leafhopper 33. Planthopper

Plate 35. Insects

I-25. Kissing Bugs, Assassin Bugs, etc. Reduviidae (pl. 35). L. to 1"; with simple eyes; beak 3-jointed, touching groove between front legs by which insect can chirp. *Apiomerus,* preys on bees in flowers; *Sinea diadema*,* takes other insects on foliage; ambush bug (*Phymata*), edges of body jagged, coloration banded (camouflage), waits in flowers to attack bees; kissing bug (*Triatoma protracta*), L. ¾"–1", dark brown, sucks blood of wood rats (*Neotoma*), may attack man when these rats nest in foothill houses. Kissing bug bites are not painful but may cause serious illness in persons who have become sensitized by repeated attacks.

I-26. Lace Bugs. Tingidae (pl. 35). L. to ¼"; wings lacy, whitish or clear, many-celled; no simple eyes; beak 4-jointed. *Corythucha* feeds on under surface of leaves of ash, alder, lupine, etc., producing white areas and black fecal spots; cast skins of young often adhere to leaves; eggs inserted into leaf tissue.

I-27. Chinch Bugs, Milkweed Bugs, etc. Lygaeidae (pl. 35). L. to ¾"; with simple eyes; beak 4-jointed; wing membrane with only 5 veins. Small false chinch bugs (*Nysius*) on composites and other plants; cone bugs (*Gastrodes*) eat seeds of digger pine; milkweed bugs (*Oncopeltus, Lygaeus kalmii**) on milkweed.

I-28. Squash Bugs, Box-elder Bugs, etc. Coreidae (pl. 35). Like I-27 but many veins in wing membrane. Feed on squashes (*Anasa*), box elder (*Leptocoris rubrolineatus**), legumes (*Alydus*), etc.

I-29. Flat Bugs. Aradidae (pl. 35). L. to ½"; oval, flat, brown; no simple eyes; beak 4-jointed, with long tube (setae) that uncoils to suck juices from fungi. Live under bark or in termite galleries (*Mezira*), on bracket and other fungi (*Aradus debilis**). One under bark scales of growing tips of pines (*A. cinnamomeus*).

I-30. Stink Bugs. Pentatomidae (pl. 35). L. to ¾"; oval; with simple eyes; beak 4-jointed; antennae 5-jointed; usually with triangular "scutellum." Feed on many plants; harlequin cabbage bug (*Murgantia histrionica**) on plants of cabbage family; a few (*Podisus*) prey on caterpillars.

I-31 to I-39. CICADAS, LEAFHOPPERS, APHIDS, SCALE INSECTS. HOMOPTERA. Wings 4, 2, or none, front pair of uniform texture throughout. Mouthparts form slender sucking tube, attached below at back of head. Young (nymphs) usually like adults but with wing pads.

A. AUCHENORRHYNCHA. Antennae short, bristle-like; tarsi 3-jointed; full-winged, active.

I-31. Cicadas. Cicadidae (pl. 35). L. to 1½"; stout; 3 simple eyes. Males "sing" or click to attract females. Eggs inserted in plant tissue. Nymphs mole-like, forelegs huge, burrow in ground and feed on roots for 1 to 17 years. Singing cicadas (*Okanagana*) vibrate plate-like membranes at base of abdomen; smaller, narrower black springtime cicadas (*Platypedia minor**) make clicking noise with wings. All wary, some ventriloquists.

I-32. Leafhoppers. Cicadellidae (pl. 35). L. to ⅛"; slender; 2 simple eyes. Eggs inserted in plants. Nymphs resemble adults, feed on vegetation, jump readily. Many species in mountain meadows and on willow, alder, etc. *Empoasca abrupta**, in foothills.

I-33. Planthoppers. Fulgoridae (pl. 35). Like leafhoppers but head projects forward. *Scolops pallidus,* in meadows.

I-34. Treehoppers. Membracidae (pl. 35). Like leafhoppers but prothorax projecting as spine or hump. In meadows and on oak trees (*Platycotis vittata**).

I-35. Spittlebugs. Cercopidae (pl. 35). Like leafhoppers but plant-sucking nymphs surrounded by a white froth or "spittle." *Aphrophora permutata**, on conifers, chapparal, and other plants.

B. STERNORRHYNCHA. Antennae usually well developed; tarsi 1- or 2-jointed; females usually slow-moving or fixed.

I-36. Jumping Plant Lice, Psyllids. Psyllidae (pl. 36). L. to ¼"; pale-colored; antennae 9- or 10-jointed; legs enlarged for jumping; tarsi 2-jointed. Common on alders along stream margins; also on willows and chapparal plants. The potato psyllid (*Paratrioza cockerelli**) breeds on plants of the nightshade family and also occurs on piñon pine and manzanita on the east side.

I-37. Plant Lice or Aphids. Aphidae (pl. 36). L. to ¼". Legs not developed for jumping; antennae 3- to 7-jointed; tarsi 2-jointed; some with 4 wings, many wingless (or successive winged and wingless generations, often on alternate host plants). Some produce waxy covering, and many secrete honeydew. Most Sierran plants attacked by one or more aphids; aphids on manzanita produce a reddish rolled gall on the edges of leaves. The green bug (*Toxoptera graminum**) lives on wild and introduced grasses.

I-38. White-flies. Aleyrodidae (pl. 36). L. to ⅛"; body and wings covered with white powder; tarsi 2-jointed; nymphs scale-like, attached to manzanita and other plants. *Dialeurodes citri** is a valley and foothill species.

I-39. Scale Insects, Mealybugs. Coccidae (pl. 36). L. to ¼"; tarsi 1-jointed; males usually minute, with 1 pair of wings and a pair of white "tails"; females wingless, stationary (scales) or slow-moving (mealybugs); body covered with powdery or scaly wax; mouthparts threadlike, often longer than body, inserted through tough woody bark to suck juices of pines, oaks, etc. On bark and needles of pines (*Matsucoccus*), on roots and foliage of many Sierran plants (mealybugs), on bark of aspen and other deciduous trees (San José scale, *Aspidiotus perniciosus**).

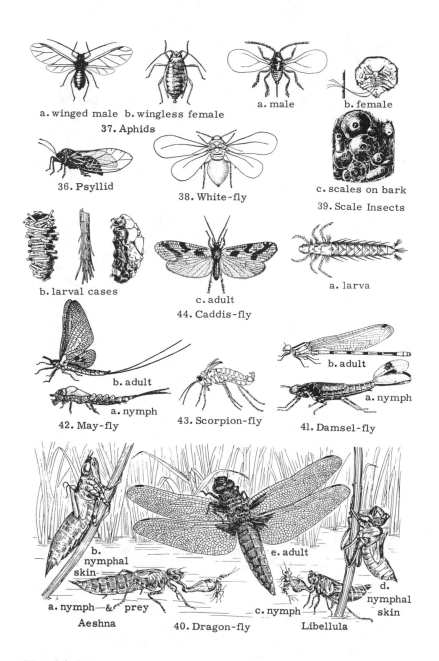

a. winged male b. wingless female
37. Aphids

a. male

b. female

36. Psyllid

38. White-fly

c. scales on bark
39. Scale Insects

b. larval cases

c. adult
44. Caddis-fly

a. larva

b. adult

a. nymph

42. May-fly

43. Scorpion-fly

b. adult

a. nymph

41. Damsel-fly

b. nymphal skin

e. adult

a. nymph—& prey
Aeshna

c. nymph

d. nymphal skin

40. Dragon-fly

Libellula

Plate 36. Insects

189

I-40, I-41. DRAGON-FLIES, DAMSEL-FLIES. ODONATA (pl. 36). L. to 4″, WS. to 5″; wings 4, membranous, with strong veins and many cross veins; chewing mouthparts; eyes very large; antennae short, bristle-like; abdomen long, slender; color brown or black with red, green, or blue and yellow patterns. Mating flights in tandem, male holding head or thorax of female by tip of his abdomen; female obtains sperm by touching end of her abdomen to receptacle on 2nd abdominal segment of male. Eggs dropped in water or inserted on or in stems of aquatic plants. Young (nymphs) in ponds or streams, stout, with short wing pads, lower jaws on long, hinged part (labium) to catch aquatic insects, small fish, and tadpoles. Adults prey on flying insects.

I-40. Dragon-flies. ANISOPTERA (pl. 36). Large, strong fliers; hind wings wider at base than fore wings; all wings held horizontally at rest. Nymphs breathe by gills in rectum where oxygenated water circulates, often ejected forcibly, producing jet-propelled forward movement. Large green "darner" (*Anax junius*), up to 6000 ft.; blue "darner" (*Aeshna multicolor*), to 4500 ft.; *A. interrupta,* 4500–7000 ft. Of smaller species, *Libellula saturata,* reddish, only into foothills; ten-spot (*L. pulchella*), up to 6000 ft.; four-spot (*L. 4-maculata*), to 7000 ft.; small-spotted (*L. nodisticta*), 500–3000 ft. on w. slope only; many others.

I-41. Damsel-flies. ZYGOPTERA (pl. 36). Smaller than Dragon-flies; weak fliers; wings held vertically over back at rest. Nymphs with 3 external leaf-like gills at tip of abdomen. Ruby-spot (*Hetaerina americana*), in foothill streams; *Argia vivida**, blue and gray, at all elevations.

I-42. May-flies. EPHEMEROPTERA (pl. 36). L. to 1″; body soft, delicate; wings 4, membranous, hind pair often reduced, all held vertically at rest; chewing mouthparts poorly developed; antennae short. Tip of abdomen with 2 or 3 long, slender "tails." Mating flights usually over water, in swarms; eggs dropped in streams or lakes. Aquatic nymphs flattened (*Epeorus*) or streamlined (*Callibaetis**), with gills at sides and 3 "tails" on abdomen; feed on algae and other plant materials. Important food for fish; emerge as soft, pale "subimagoes" which molt after a few hours, to sexually mature adults. Adults live only a few hours or days ("ephemeral").

I-43. Scorpion-flies. MECOPTERA (pl. 36). L. to ½″; body slender, with 4 narrow wings or wing vestiges; head extended as a beak; chewing mouthparts; end of abdomen upturned. Larvae caterpillar-like, 6 legs on thorax and 8 on abdomen. On soil and moss in damp places; predaceous. A small black form (*Boreus**) emerges and mates on surface of snow in February.

I-44. Caddis-flies. TRICHOPTERA (pl. 36). L. to 1″; body and wings moth-like, but covered by hairs, not scales; wings 4, roofed over body at rest; chewing mouthparts; antennae slender, many-jointed. Adults fly over streams at dusk and drop eggs on water or crawl into water and glue eggs to stones (*Phryganea**). Larvae grub-like, in silken cases camouflaged with sticks or pine needles (*Limnephilus*), or sand grains (*Lepidostoma*), or free in nets (*Hydropsyche*) in swift-flowing waters to catch floating plant or animal food; larvae are "caddis worms," a main source of trout food, often used as bait.

I-45 to I-109. MOTHS AND BUTTERFLIES. LEPIDOPTERA. Adult mouthparts joined as long spiraled tube (proboscis) uncoiled to suck nectar from flowers; wings 4, covered with microscopic overlapping scales; compound eyes large; antennae many-jointed. Larvae (caterpillars) worm-like, 3 pairs of jointed legs and 2–5 pairs of stumpy abdominal "pro-legs"; glands on labium used to spin silk for cocoon of pupa, sometimes to cover larva.

A. MOTHS. HETEROCERA. Antennae often plume-like or thread-like, not swollen at tip; mostly nocturnal.

I-45. Fairy Moths. Adelidae (col. pl. 14). WS. to ¾"; hind tibiae bristled; wings fringed with long hairs. *Adela trigrapha**, black with oblique white bars across fore wings; antennae of ♀ longer than wings, of ♂ 3 times as long. Day-flying. Eggs and larvae on seed capsules of flowers.

I-46. Blotch Leafminers. Gracilariidae (col. pl. 14, fig. 15). WS. to ⅝"; hind tibiae smooth-scaled. Many species on forest trees and shrubs. Oak leafminer (*Lithocolletis agrifoliella**), fore wings orange, white-barred, hairy-fringed at tip, hind wings narrow, broadly margined with fine hairs. Larvae flat, tapered behind, black-spotted; mine oak leaves, widening galleries into broad blotches with translucent covering; pupate in leaf blotch.

I-47. Needleminer Moths. Gelechiidae (col. pl. 14, fig. 16). WS. to ⅔"; hind tibiae hairy. Lodgepole Needleminer (*Evagora milleri**), wings white, black-speckled. Eggs laid at needle bases, hatch in 2 weeks; young larvae mine into needles and spend 1st winter there; usually 2 more needles mined in following summer; grown larva ⅓", head dark, body yellow to orange, a red line along back; pupate in last needle mined, in June.

In Yosemite National Park adults fly in July and August of odd-numbered years. Attacks result in large "ghost forests" of lodgepole pine. Chemical spraying reduces damage locally, but moths reinvade from other areas.

I-48. Clear-winged Moths. Aegeriidae (col. pl. 14). WS. to 1½"; form and flight wasp-like; wings mostly scaleless, transparent; abdomen banded black, yellow, red; fly in daytime. The Locust Clear-wing (*Paranthrene robiniae**), yellow and black; larvae bore into locust and poplar trees.

I-49. Budworm Moths. Tortricidae (col. pl. 14). WS. to 1¼"; fore wings abruptly widened at base. Sugarpine Tortrix (*Choristoneura lambertiana**), speckled tan to golden. Eggs laid in July or August, young larvae hibernate in cocoons and resume feeding in spring, binding needles, new buds, and staminate cones with webs in which they pupate.

I-50. Carpenter Moths. Cossidae (col. pl. 14). WS. to 2¾"; body stout, tapered behind; hind wings small; mottled gray above with hind wings partly reddish orange. Goat Moth (*Prionoxystus robiniae**) larvae bore in wood of oaks and cottonwoods at lower altitudes; life cycle 2 to 3 years.

I-51. Snout Moths. Pyralidae (col. pl. 14). WS. to 1¾"; slender, wings fold close over body; palpi on head form a "snout." Larvae of many species feed in stems and fruits. Metal Mark (*Parargyractis truckeealis**), WS. ½"– ¾", grayish red with white and brown marks and a row of black spots on hind wings. The light-bodied delicate moth swims or crawls under water of streams or ponds to lay eggs on stones. The larvae, with many gill filaments on sides, spin webs on rocks and feed on algae. There are 3 generations per year, at up to 6000 ft. in the Sierra.

I-52. Plume Moths. Pterophoridae (col. pl. 14). WS. to 1"; all wings cleft, the hind ones deeply to form 3 lobes or "plumes"; mottled brown, 3 dark spots near tip of fore wing. At rest wings held at right angles to body. Larvae of *Platyptilia sierrae** feed on and web flowers and leaves of Paintbrush.

I-53. Giant Silkworm Moths. Saturniidae. WS. to 5"; antennae of ♂ feathery; wings usually with eyespots (53c). Polyphemus Moth (*Antheraea polyphemus**; col. pl. 14), ♂ tan to reddish brown; wing spots translucent, ringed with yellow, those on hind wings also with blue and black. Larvae to 3" long, on deciduous trees and shrubs, pupate in oval brownish cocoons (53b) to 2" long. The Sheep Moth (*Pseudohazis eglanterina*, 53a; col. pl. 14), WS. to 3", purplish orange with black markings, flies in the daytime; larva spiny, feeds on many chaparral plants; life cycle 2 years.

I-54. Tent Caterpillars. Lasiocampidae (col. pl. 14, fig. 15). WS. to 3¾"; proboscis reduced. *Malacosoma pluviale**, rusty red to pale brown, fore wings with 2 oblique pale lines. Larvae spin tent-like community webs among branches and leaves of ceanothus, bitterbrush, etc., in spring; over-wintering eggs cemented in rings around twigs; common at high elevations, mainly on east side. Other species occur on w. side up to 4000 feet.

I-55. Measuring-worms or "Loopers." Geometridae (col. pl. 14). WS. to 2¼"; some females wingless. Larvae walk by "looping" because prolegs are reduced except at end of body. Pine Looper (*Phengommataea edwardsata**), wings fawn-colored, the fore wings broad, crossed by irregular brown band.

I-56. Sphinx Moths. Sphingidae (col. pl. 14). WS. to 5"; wings narrow, fly at dusk, wings beat rapidly (like hummingbirds), hover at flowers when feeding. Larvae usually with "horn" (spine) at hind end. Pupa naked, brown, in ground. White-lined Sphinx (*Celerio lineata**), brown with reddish bars, fore wings with broad pale stripe from base to tip, veins white, hind wings with broad pinkish area. Larvae green or black, on many plants.

I-57. Tussock Moths. Lymantriidae (col. pl. 14). WS. of ♂ to 1", ♀ of some wingless. Tussock Moth (*Hemerocampa vetusta**), brownish gray, fore wings mottled, ♀ stout, wingless. Larvae gray with red, blue, and yellow spots, hair tufts black and white, on oak, poplar, willow, etc. One brood per year.

I-58. Owlet Moths, Cutworm, and Armyworm Moths. Noctuidae (col. pl. 14). WS. to 2″ (6″ in one species). Mostly brown or variegated; rest by day against concealing backgrounds such as bark of trees, and fly at night. Larvae naked, feed on foliage or fruits; cutworms live in ground, where they feed on roots or cut stems of young plants; armyworms "march" in search of food plants at night. Pupae in soil. Semi-looper (*Autographa celsa**), fore wings variegated, gray with black and white. Larva with middle prolegs reduced, hence walk by "looping."

Noctuids are the commonest moths in the Sierra. Many species are attracted to lights on calm, warm nights.

I-59. Tiger Moths. Arctiidae (col. pl. 14). WS. to 2½″; wings usually contrastingly marked. Caterpillars are "woolly bears" that roll up into a ball when disturbed; often seen in autumn in open spaces, seeking places to hibernate. *Halisidota maculata**, fore wings tan with wavy brown splotches, hind wings pale buff-colored. Larvae with long black and white hairs and a wide band of yellow hairs at middle; on willow and other deciduous trees.

B. BUTTERFLIES. RHOPALOCERA. Tips of antennae enlarged as small "clubs"; diurnal.

I-60 to I-66. Skippers. Hesperiidae. WS. to 2″; head wide; antennae usually curved at tips. Fly with skipping motion. Hind wings (also front wings in some groups) spread horizontally when at rest. Larva naked, with large head and constricted neck.

I-60. Silver-spotted Skipper. *Epargyreus clarus* (col. pl. 15). WS. to 1¾″; dark brown, fore wings above with orange spots, hind wings below with irregular silver spot. Caterpillars on legumes; construct leafy daytime shelter, emerging at night to feed. Chrysalis brownish, on ground; 2 or 3 broods a year. Foothill belt.

I-61. Nevada Dusky-wing. *Thorybes nevada* (col. pl. 15). WS. to 1¼″; dark brown, fore wings above with oblique rows of small pale spots, below mottled gray. From Lodgepole–fir belt into Alpine belt.

I-62. Propertius Dusky-wing. *Erynnis propertius* (col. pl. 15). WS. to 1½″; dark mottled brown, fore wings with small white spots. Larvae feed on oak, ranging upward through Lodgepole–fir belt.

I-63. Western Checkered Skipper. *Pyrgus communis* (col. pl. 15). WS. to 1″; color mainly black with many white spots above, much paler below. Feeds on mallows at all elevations except Alpine belt.

I-64. Juba Skipper. *Hesperia juba* (col. pl. 15). WS. 1½"; above orange with large black areas and 2 orange spots near tips of fore wings; below pale orange, 2 white spots near tips of fore wings and V-shaped white band on hind wings. At middle elevations on w. slope. *Hesperia miriamae* in Alpine belt from Mono Pass, Tioga Pass, and the Dana Plateau; color paler orange, body and hind wings darker.

I-65. Woodland Skipper. *Ochlodes sylvanoides* (col. pl. 15). WS. to 1"; like *Hesperia* but lacks the two spots near tips of fore wings and is almost unspotted on hind wings below. Western foothills and about Mono Lake.

I-66. Sandhill Skipper. *Polites sabuleti* (col. pl. 15). WS. to ⅞"; like Woodland Skipper but darker and with hind wings speckled and barred below. In Foothill and arid Yellow Pine belts on grasses. The darker Tecumseh Skipper (*P. tecumseh*) lives on high barren slopes in the Lodgepole–fir and Subalpine belts.

I-67 to I-69. Swallowtails. Papilionidae. WS. 2½"–4"; front legs well developed; middle of tibia with short spur; hind wings usually with long or short "tail"; yellow with black borders, stripes and veins or primarily black, some with small blue or reddish spots on hind wings. Larvae with forked organ at front which projects when disturbed and gives off a pungent odor. Pupae rough-surfaced, attached at tip, suspended by thread-like silk girdle.

I-67. Short-tailed Swallowtail. *Papilio indra* (col. pl. 15). WS. to 2½"; inner half of each wing all black; tails about ⅛". Larvae feed on plants of parsley family (Umbelliferae). Lodgepole–fir and Subalpine belts.

I-68a. Western Tiger Swallowtail. *Papilio rutulus* (col. pl. 15). WS. to 2½"; tails ⅜" or more; inner parts of wings yellow with oblique black bars. Larvae on cottonwood and willow, in Foothill to Lodgepole–fir belts; adults often in higher altitudes.

I-68b. Pale Swallowtail. *Papilio eurymedon* (col. pl. 15). WS. to 2½"; like no. 68a but ground color whitish, not yellow. Larvae on many chaparral plants in Foothill and Yellow Pine belts; adults go higher in Sierra. Anise Swallowtail (*P. zelicaon*), WS. to 3"; fore wings broadly black along front near base and yellow areas not black-striped; tails ¼". Larvae feed on plants of parsley family from Foothill to Subalpine belt.

I-69. Baldur Parnassian. *Parnassius clodius* (col. pl. 15). WS. to 2½"; white with extensive dark markings on fore wings above and 2 small red spots ringed with black on hind wings of ♂ (3 in ♀); antennae black; no tails. Larvae covered with fine black down, each segment with orange or yellow raised areas; pupation in ground debris. Lodgepole–fir and Subalpine belts on stonecrop (*Sedum*).

I-70 to I-74. Whites, Sulfurs, and Orange Tips. Pieridae. WS. to 2¼″; color white or orange-yellow marked with black, sometimes red. Front legs fully developed; tarsal claws forked. Eggs long, tapered; larvae slender, no spines; pupae supported by a fine thread.

I-70. Pine White. *Neophasia menapia* (col. pl. 16). WS. to 1¾″; white, fore wings with black at tips and line along front margin curving in beyond middle; hind wings with black-ringed marginal cells and with black (♂) or orange (♀) veins below. Flies high among trees. Larvae dark green, with white stripe on each side and one on back; 2 short tails; on Yellow and Lodgepole pines.

I-71. Common White. *Pieris protodice* (col. pl. 16). WS. to 1½″; white, wings with black spots or streaks; hind wings below with veins outlined in blackish brown. On mustard and other plants of that family in Foothill and Yellow Pine belts; adults fly to 12000 ft. California White (*P. sisymbrii*) has veins of hind wings below outlined in gray or pale brown; in Yellow Pine and Lodgepole–fir belts. The common Cabbage Butterfly (*P. rapae*) is white with fore wings dark-tipped, a small black spot above on each wing and hind wings below unmarked. Larvae often on cabbage, but also feed on other plants of the mustard family; in Foothill and Yellow Pine belts.

I-72. Colorado Marble. *Euchloe coloradensis* (col. pl. 16). WS. to 1½″; white, fore wings with small black bar beyond middle and tips black, with white between veins; hind wings below marbled with green. On plants of mustard family, especially rock cress, in Lodgepole–fir and Subalpine belts. The smaller Edward's Marble (*E. hyantis*) in same zones has heavier green marbling on hind wings below, and light spots between marbling are pearly.

I-73. Sara Orange-tip. *Anthocharis sara* (col. pl. 16). WS. to 1½″; white above, tips of fore wings red edged with black, below orange tips paler and much greenish marbling, especially on hind wings. Feeds on plants of the mustard family; from Foothill belt to Lodgepole–fir belt. Boisduval's Marble (*A. lanceolata*), WS. to 1½″; lacks orange on fore wings, and hind wings below are marbled with brown; in Foothill and Yellow Pine belts.

I-74a. Alfalfa Butterfly. *Colias eurytheme* (fig. 14, col. pl. 16). WS. to 2″; sulfur yellow, outer edges of wings above black in ♂ , broken black in spring in ♀ ; fore wings with a small black dot near front, and hind wings with an orange dot; below paler, with small black spots near margin, hind wings with silvery spot ringed by pink or red. Summer form more intensely colored; also a whitish ♀ form. Larvae dark green with fine white hairs and 4 white stripes, each enclosing a crimson stripe. Chrysalis green with yellow and black markings. Central Valley into Lodgepole–fir belt, on plants of pea family: alfalfa in cultivated areas and rattleweed (*Astragalus*) in Sierra.

I-74b. Behr's Sulfur. *C. behrii* (col. p. 16). WS. to 1½″; color greenish with dark wing margins, fore wings with ill-defined dark spot near middle, hind wings with whitish spot. Confined to Subalpine belt; larvae on *Gentiana newberryi* and *Vaccinium caespitosum*.

I-75 to I-89. Hairstreaks, Coppers, Blues, and Metal-marks. Lycaenidae. Blue or coppery; fore legs fully developed; eyes notched near antennae; width of face between eyes less than length. Eggs flat; larvae slug-like, with small heads; some secrete a fluid attractive to ants. Pupae short, rounded, supported by a filament. When perched, the Metal-marks spread the wings, but other butterflies hold them upright.

I-75. Boisduval's Hairstreak. *Habrodais grunus* (col. pl. 16). WS. to 1¼″; dark brown above, yellowish brown below, faint spots and lines near margins; hind wing with a short tail. Larvae on golden oak. Foothill and Yellow Pine belts.

I-76. Great Purple Hairstreak. *Atlides halesus* (col. pl. 16). WS. to 1¾″; hind wings with 2 slender tails; above iridescent blue, broad wing margins and veins black; below black, ends of hind wings with white and blue spots; tip of abdomen orange. Larvae green with short, velvety orange hairs; feed on mistletoe of oaks. Chrysalis brown, mottled with black with short orange hairs. Foothill and Yellow Pine belts.

I-77. Common Hairstreak. *Strymon melinus* (col. pl. 16). WS. to 1¼″; above dark slate gray; corner of hind wing with one red spot and several blue and black spots; below light gray with black and red marks near margin of hind wing; each wing with white-edged black line, straight on fore wings, zigzag on hind wings; hind wings with slender tail. On mallow, legumes, etc., in Foothill and Yellow Pine belts.

I-78. Behr's Hairstreak. *Satyrium behrii* (col. pl. 16). WS. to 1⅛″; orange with dark brown wing margins above and spotted gray below; no tails. On lupine and other legumes on e. side through Jeffrey Pine belt; related species elsewhere in the Sierra.

I-79. Nelson's Hairstreak. *Mitoura nelsoni* (col. pl. 16). WS. to 1″; above coppery brown, below dark spotted near the short tails, a broken white line near margin of each wing. Yellow Pine and Lodgepole–fir belts. *M. siva* occurs on juniper in the Sierra.

I-80. Western Banded Elfin. *Callophrys eryphon* (pl. 16). WS. to 1″; above dark brown, below paler and mottled with angular dark lines edged by white, giving checkered appearance; no tails. Larvae on pines in Lodgepole–fir and Subalpine belts.

I-81. Lustrous Copper. *Lycaena cupreus* (pl. 16). WS. to 1″; above coppery orange with brown spots and wing margins; below coppery on fore wings and brownish gray on hind wings with brown spots. In Subalpine belt.

I-82. Acmon Blue. *Plebejus acmon* (col. pl. 16). WS. to 1″; above blue (♂) or mostly brown (♀), wing edges darker; hind wing with submarginal stripe of orange; below gray with black spots, hind wing orange near margin. Larvae on buckwheat and legumes. Foothill belt to Subalpine belt. Of other Sierran species, some have and others lack orange markings.

I-83. Gray Blue. *Agriades glandon* (col. pl. 16). WS. to 1″; ♂ blue above with gray or silver cast, darker toward wing margins; ♀ brown above, below brownish gray with dark spots circled with whitish, no orange. Lodgepole–fir and Subalpine belts in meadows.

I-84. Behr's Blue. *Glaucopsyche lygdamus* (col. pl. 16). WS. to 1¼″; above blue (♂) or mostly brown (♀); below brownish gray, many rounded black spots sharply ringed with white; no orange. Yellow Pine and Lodgepole–fir belts on legumes.

I-85. Square-spotted Blue. *Philotes battoides* (col. pl. 16). WS. to ⅞″; ♂ blue above, sparsely black spotted, below pale bluish with squarish black spots and blackish stripe near wing margin; ♀ brown above with orange stripes at rear of hind wing; hind wings below with orange spots near margin and black spots and stripes like male. On buckwheat in Subalpine belt.

I-86. Tailed Blue. *Everes comyntas* (col. pl. 16). WS. to 1″; above blue, wing edges dark; a little orange on hind wing margins; below gray with small black spots and a touch of orange; tails hair-like, distinct. On legumes, to middle elevations.

I-87. Echo Blue. *Celastrina argiolus* (col. pl. 16). WS. to 1″; above blue (♂) or blue with black wing margins (♀); below pale gray to whitish with faint, fine dark spots; no orange. Larvae on various shrubs: dogwood, ceanothus, *Hosackia,* blueberry, and *Spiraea,* extending up through Lodgepole–fir belt.

I-88. Arrow-head Blue. *Phaedrotes piasus* (col. pl. 16). WS. to 1¼″; above blue, darker toward wing margins; below pale gray with black spots, hind wings with broad pale areas, ends of wing dusky; no orange. Larvae on lupines in upper Yellow Pine and Lodgepole–fir belts.

I-89. Mormon Metal-mark. *Apodemia mormo* (col. pl. 16). WS. to 1″; brown with black and white spots, fore wings below with orange ground color on basal half; hind wings with orange at middle and narrowly white on outer margins. Larvae short, broad, dark violet, 4 rows of black and white spots with clumps of bristles. Chrysalis short, plump, corrugated, with wavy hairs, brown with 2 orange spots. On buckwheat in Yellow Pine and Lodgepole–fir belts.

I-90 to I-109. **Brush-footed Butterflies.** Nymphalidae. Front legs much reduced (hence called 4-footed butterflies); chrysalis suspended at tip of abdomen, no girdle of thread. No. 90, the Monarch, has unscaled antennae; its larva is hairless, with 4 fleshy filaments; the chrysalis is smooth and cylindrical. In nos. 91–94 veins on the fore wings are swollen at the base, and the wings have "eyespots"; the larvae are smooth, thickest at middle, with a double tail. Nos. 95–109 lack the above-mentioned characters. Their larvae have spines and tubercles, and the chrysalids are rough-surfaced.

I-90. Monarch. *Danaus plexippus* (col. pl. 15). WS. to 3¾"; orange, veins and wing margins black, 2 rows of white spots. Larva green, banded with black and yellow. Chrysalis green, gold-spotted. Larvae on milkweed. Foothill and Yellow Pine belts, occasional adults higher in the mountains. The Monarch migrates to coastal and southern areas for the winter.

I-91. California Ringlet. *Coenonympha tullia* (col. pl. 16). WS. to 1¼"; above pale yellowish brown; below darker with irregular pale bars; hind wings with many eyespots. Spring form nearly white; summer form more yellow. On grasses in Foothill belt.

I-92. Riding's Satyr. *Neominois ridingsii* (col. pl. 16). WS. to 1½"; grayish brown, all wings with transverse white bars near edges, fore wing with 2 white-centered black eyespots. On grasses at high elevations.

I-93. Sylvan Satyr. *Cercyonis silvestris* (col. pl. 16). WS. to 1½"; above light brown, below mottled gray, each fore wing with 2 bold black eyespots ringed with yellow and white at center. On grasses in Foothill belt.

I-94. Ivallda Arctic. *Oeneis ivallda* (col. pl. 16). WS. to 2"; ashy with some paler areas above and below; fore wing with 1 to 3 small eyespots, hind wing with 1 spot at back and mottled below. On grasses in Alpine and upper Subalpine belts.

I-95. Mountain Fritillary. *Speyeria egleis* (col. pl. 17). WS. to 2¼"; above dark orange (♂), veins and many spots black; below tan with black and silver spots. On violets in Lodgepole–fir and Subalpine belts. Other species differ in size of black and silver spots.

I-96. Western Meadow Fritillary. *Boloria epithore* (col. pl. 17). WS. to 1½"; like no. 95 but smaller; hind wings lack silver or white spots below. On violets in Yellow Pine and Lodgepole–fir belts.

I-97. Chalcedon Checker-spot. *Euphydryas chalcedona* (col. pl. 17). WS. to 2"; above dark brown to black with pale orange spots; below brick red with black veins and large yellow spots. Larva black with white stripe along back and broken stripe on each side; covered with small white hairy tubercles. Chrysalis gray, spotted with orange and black. On monkey-flowers, figworts, etc., in Foothill belt. Other species common in Sierra.

I-98. Northern Checker-spot. *Chlosyne palla* (col. pl. 17). WS. to 1¼"; like no. 97 but smaller and paler. On paintbrush in Yellow Pine and Lodgepole–fir belts.

I-99. Mylitta Crescent. *Phyciodes mylitta* (col. pl. 17). WS. to 1¼"; above orange with rows of black bars and dots paralleling wing margins (♀ darker than ♂); below irregularly checkered with brown, tan, and whitish. On thistle in Yellow Pine belt.

I-100. Satyr Anglewing. *Polygonia satyrus* (col. pl. 17). WS. to 2"; eyes hairy, wing margins irregularly concave, hind wing with tail; above and below orange-brown with large black spots; hind wing of ♀ below with white comma mark. Larva with 7 rows of long bristles on large black head, body black, a greenish stripe along back and a V-shaped black mark on each segment. Chrysalis brown, angular. On nettle in Foothill and Yellow Pine belts.

I-101. California Tortoise-shell. *Nymphalis californica* (col. pl. 17). WS. to 2"; eyes hairy; wing margins irregular but inner margin of front wing straight; hind wing with short tail; above dark brown, centers of wings orange; this color reaching front margin of fore wings; below mottled, gray-brown, with irregular, broad pale band on outer half of each wing. Larva velvety black with broken yellow line along back; each segment with 5 branching spines supported on blue tubercles and small white dots between spines. Chrysalis ashy gray, 2 black projections on head; thorax mottled brown, 2 spines near wing cases. Western North America and in Sierra through Lodgepole–fir belt mainly on ceanothus.

In favorable years this species increases enormously and disperses by the millions, adults then flying over the highest peaks. One entomologist took more than 50 butterflies in a single sweep of his net. Sometimes the flights continue for days. There is no regular pattern of outbreaks or of dispersal routes. During an outbreak ceanothus is defoliated over a wide area and the pupae, suspended from twigs, make a rustling sound when disturbed. Dead butterflies become scattered over snow fields at high elevations. Usually there are two or more broods per season, and adults hibernate in protected places.

I-102. Mourning-cloak. *Nymphalis antiopa* (col. pl. 17). WS. to 2½"; eyes hairy; wing structure as in no. 101; above dark brown to black, sides of wings broadly margined with yellow paralleled by row of bluish spots; below dusky, yellow-margined. Overwinters as adult. On willow and cottonwood up through Lodgepole–fir belt.

I-103. Red Admiral. *Vanessa atalanta* (col. pl. 17). WS. to 2"; eyes hairy; hind wings lack a tail; above dark brown; fore wing with contrasted oblique orange bar across middle and white dots near tip; hind wing with broad orange band along rear margin; below mottled, with oblique red stripe and white spots as above. On nettle, up through Yellow Pine belt.

I-104. Painted Lady. *Vanessa cardui* (col. pl. 17). WS to 2"; blotched orange, tan, and black; fore wing above with white bar beyond middle of front margin and white spots near tip; below ashy brown blotched with darker color, fore wing partly orange and black, hind wing with 3 or 4 eyespots near edge. Larva lilac color with scattered black spots and lines of yellow, black, and white; spines on 7 rows of tubercles. Chrysalis brown with rows of short spines. On nettles, mallow, etc., up through Lodgepole–fir belt; range nearly worldwide.

I-105. Virginia Lady. *Vanessa virginiensis* (col. pl. 17). Resembles Painted Lady but hind wings with only 2 large eyespots below. Over North America; in Sierra up through Lodgepole–fir belt.

I-106. West Coast Lady. *Vanessa carye* (col. pl. 17). WS. to 1¾"; resembles Painted Lady but fore wing above with bar beyond middle of front margin red, not white. On nettle and mallow, up through Lodgepole–fir belt.

I-107. Buckeye. *Precis coenia* (col. pl. 17). WS. to 1¾"; eyes hairless; above pale brown, each wing with large eyespot, a second smaller spot on hind wing; fore wing above with dull white around eyespot reaching to front margin and 2 reddish bars on inner half; below ashy, mottled, markings of fore wings as above. Two broods per year. Larvae on monkey-flower and stonecrop, mostly in Foothill belt but up through Lodgepole–fir belt.

I-108. Lorquin's Admiral. *Limenitis lorquini* (col. pl. 17). WS. to 2½"; enlarged end of antenna longer and more slender than in other butterflies; above black with broad white stripe across middle of both wings, fore wings orange-tipped; below more brown, with white stripe, also a pale stripe near edge of wings. Larva olive-brown, mottled, with white band on each side; head 2-lobed; 2 rough horns on 3rd segment, and pairs of tubercles behind. Chrysalis olive-green to purple, mottled with white, a large lobe at base of abdomen. Larvae on willow, cottonwood, etc., up through Lodgepole–fir belt.

I-109. California Sister. *Limenitis bredowii* (col. pl. 17). WS. to 2¼"; resembles no. 108; above brownish black, fore wing with large orange spot near tip; below variegated brown, blue, and whitish, with blue stripes on inner half and near margin of wings. On oaks in Foothill and Yellow Pine belts.

I-110 to I-113. LACEWINGS, ANT LIONS, AND SNAKE-FLIES. NEUROPTERA. Antennae long; chewing mouthparts; wings 4, net-veined, alike, transparent, held roof-like over body at rest; tarsi 5-jointed. Larvae stout, spiny, 3 pairs of legs, jaws long and grooved to suck juices of other insects used as prey. Pupae in cocoons on plants or in ground.

I-110. Green Lacewings. Chrysopidae (pl. 37). L. to ¾". *Chrysopa*, delicate, pale or bright green, eyes golden, wings lacy, green; on vegetation; each minute egg on end of thread-like filament; larva bristly, feeds on aphids, etc.

I-111. Ant Lions. Myrmeleontidae (pl. 37). L. to 2". *Myrmeleon*, slender, with short, knobbed antennae; larva or "doodle bug" short, stout, lives in

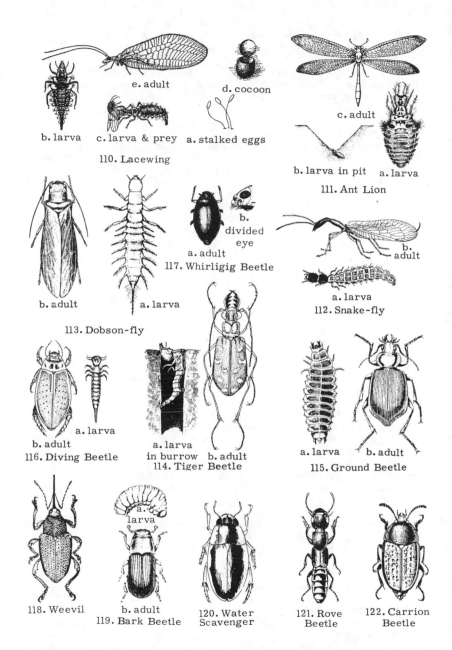

e. adult

d. cocoon

b. larva

c. larva & prey

a. stalked eggs

110. Lacewing

c. adult

b. larva in pit   a. larva

111. Ant Lion

b. divided eye

a. adult

117. Whirligig Beetle

b. adult

a. larva

112. Snake-fly

b. adult   a. larva

113. Dobson-fly

a. larva

b. adult

116. Diving Beetle

a. larva in burrow   b. adult

114. Tiger Beetle

a. larva   b. adult

115. Ground Beetle

118. Weevil

a. larva

b. adult

119. Bark Beetle

120. Water Scavenger

121. Rove Beetle

122. Carrion Beetle

Plate 37. Insects   201

small conical pit in sand or dust into which ants and other prey fall and are captured before they can escape.

I-112. Snake-flies. Raphidiidae (pl. 37). Like Lacewings but fore part of thorax and head long, cylindrical; female with long tail-like ovipositor. Larvae slender, can run both backward and forward. *Agulla,* on oaks and many conifers.

I-113. Dobson-flies, Alder-flies. Sialidae (pl. 37). L. to 2″; like Lacewings but wing veins unforked near wing margins. Aquatic larvae (hellgrammites) long, with 2 slender tapering gills on each abdominal segment; predaceous. Dobson larvae (*Corydalus, Chauliodes*) among stones in shallow water at sides of streams; no central filament at tip of abdomen. Alder-fly larvae (*Sialis**) have a terminal filament and live at bottom of deep pools in streams and lakes. Both serve as trout food and fish bait.

I-114 to I-137. BEETLES. COLEOPTERA. Antennae usually 11-jointed; mouthparts for chewing; fore wings thick, leathery, meet along midline; hind wings folded under fore wings at rest. Larvae worm- or grub-like, usually with 3 pairs of legs; pupae usually free, not in cocoons.

1. ADEPHAGA. First segment on abdomen completely divided by hind coxae into 2 or 3 parts. Larvae with legs of 5 segments and 2 claws.

I-114. Tiger Beetles. Cicindelidae (pl. 37). L. to 1″. *Cicindela** long-legged and bright-colored, head as wide as thorax; run and fly rapidly; in open sandy places; larvae live in deep holes, move up and down by use of hooks on 5th abdominal segment; prey on insects on ground surface. *Omus,* all black, flightless, nocturnal.

I-115. Ground Beetles. Carabidae (pl. 37). L. to 1″; mostly blackish, long-legged, head narrower than thorax. Common at all elevations, under stones and at edge of water; nocturnal; larvae active, long, flattish above, with 2 cerci at end of body; prey on caterpillars, other insects, and snails. Pupate in cell in ground. *Cychrus* large (to 1″), wing covers broadly rounded, preys on snails; up to Subalpine belt. *Bembidion,* L. to ⅛″, black, at edge of ponds and streams. *Calosoma**, L. to 1½″, stout, blue or black, on ground, preys on caterpillars.

I-116. Predaceous Diving Beetles. Dytiscidae (pl. 37). L. to 1½″; oval, smooth, shiny; eyes undivided; hind legs flat, fringed with hairs, used as oars for swimming; air taken at surface by tip of abdomen and stored under wing covers when diving. Eggs laid on water plants; larvae (water tigers) long, slender, with 2 long cerci; prey on many insects. Pupate in small earthen cells at edge of water. Many species at all elevations.

I-117. Whirligig Beetles. Gyrinidae (pl. 37). L. to ½″; oval, lustrous, eyes divided horizontally, upper pair for surface vision, lower for sight under water. Larvae long, slender, with 2 gills on each abdominal segment, 2 pairs on 9th segment. Pupate in mud cells on plants above water. Whirl and gyrate in "schools" on surfaces of ponds and streams; predaceous.

2. POLYPHAGA. First abdominal segment complete; legs of larvae with not more than 4 joints and 1 claw; some legless.

A. RHYNCHOPHORA. Front of head often a long beak; palpi jointed but rigid; sutures on under side of head fused into one or lacking; larvae legless.

I-118. Weevils. Curculionidae (pl. 37). L. to ½"; beak distinct, usually longer than broad; antennae elbowed. Larvae feed in seeds, fruits, stems, or roots, often pupate in a cocoon. Acorn Weevil (*Balaninus**) lays eggs in a hole in shell; when acorns begin to drop larvae mature and enter ground to overwinter. Pine Reproduction Weevil (*Cylindrocopturus*), small, attacks growing tips of young pines, especially new plantings in burned areas.

I-119. Bark Beetles. Scolytidae (pl. 37). L. to ⅓"; short, cylindrical, antennae clubbed; adults and larvae feed under bark, "engraving" branched channels (fig. 16). Western Pine Beetle (*Dendroctonus brevicomis**) most destructive insect on Yellow Pine. Adults emerge in spring and summer, attacking weak or even apparently vigorous trees and excavating winding egg galleries between bark and sapwood. Small white larvae feed on inner bark and then pupate in outer bark, with 2 to 4 generations a year. New attacks indicated by resin tubes at entrance holes and by reddish foliage. Control by clean management of forests so infested trees are not left to build up populations. Parasites and predators normally maintain a balance and prevent epidemic infestations. Infested trees in parks should be felled, peeled, and the bark burned, from late fall to early spring. Every Sierran conifer is attacked by one or more species of Bark Beetle.

B. PALPICORNIA. Antennae shorter than palps, with hairy club which breaks surface film of water to obtain air.

I-120. Water Scavengers. Hydrophilidae (pl. 37). L. to 1"; with hind legs adapted for swimming. Eggs laid in cases; larvae slender, some with lateral gills; cerci jointed; pupation in ground cell on shore. Some nonaquatic species live in dung.

C. BRACHELYTRA. Wing covers usually short; hind wings with simple straight veins.

I-121. Rove Beetles. Staphylinidae (pl. 37). L. to ¾"; wing covers short, exposing 3 to 6 abdominal segments; abdomen of 7 or 8 segments below. Scavengers in dung or predators. Larvae resemble those of carabids (I-115).

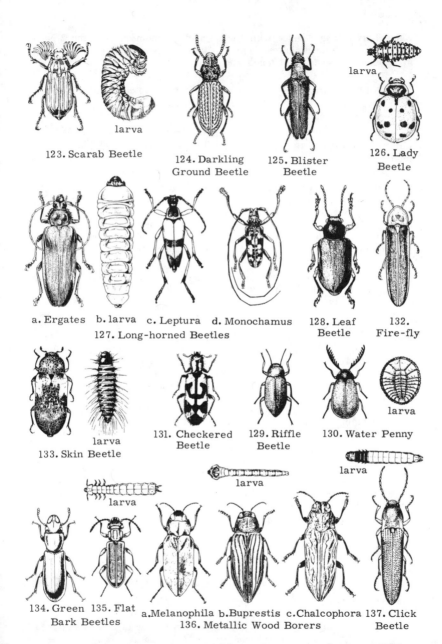

123. Scarab Beetle

larva

124. Darkling
Ground Beetle

125. Blister
Beetle

126. Lady
Beetle

larva

a. Ergates b. larva c. Leptura d. Monochamus
127. Long-horned Beetles

128. Leaf
Beetle

132.
Fire-fly

larva
133. Skin Beetle

131. Checkered
Beetle

129. Riffle
Beetle

130. Water Penny

larva

134. Green 135. Flat
Bark Beetles

a.Melanophila b.Buprestis c.Chalcophora 137. Click
136. Metallic Wood Borers   Beetle

Plate 38. Insects

I-122. Carrion Beetles. Silphidae (pl. 37). L. to 1½"; body broad, flat above (*Silpha**) or stout with short wing covers (*Necrophorus*); abdomen of 6 segments below. Eggs laid in carrion, fungi, or decaying plants where larvae feed. Larvae broad, black, with lateral plates. *Necrophorus* buries small animals as food for larvae.

D. LAMELLICORNIA. Antennae with last 3 to 7 segments extended as flattened plates.

I-123. Scarab Beetles. Scarabaeidae (pl. 38). L. to 1½"; body broad, deep, convex; legs spiny; antennal plates flattened, usually touching. Larvae stout, crescent-shaped "white grubs," commonly feed on roots in soil; some live in dung. The 10-lined June Beetle (*Polyphylla**) lives on roots and is attracted to lights in early summer. Other common scarabs are the metallic green Pine Chafers (*Dichelonyx*), small brown Dung Beetles (*Aphodius*), and stout brown *Pleocoma* beetles that emerge during first heavy rains of fall when males fly to wingless females remaining in emergence holes. A bluish Sierran species (*Canthon simplex*) like sacred scarabs of Egypt, rolls dung into a ball and lays an egg on ball before burying it to provide food for larva.

E. DIVERSICORNIA. Antennae diverse but neither plate-like nor palpi-like.

(1) Heteromera. Tarsi of front and middle legs 5-jointed; those of hind legs 4-jointed.

I-124. Darkling Ground Beetles. Tenebrionidae (pl. 38). L. to 1½"; black or brown, front coxal cavities closed behind; nocturnal. Larvae (false wireworms) long but thoracic legs short; labrum distinct. *Nyctoporis carinata**, rough-surfaced, under loose bark. Large black *Eleodes* leaves trails in sand or dust, its pointed rear end being raised when alarmed.

I-125. Blister Beetles. Meloidae (pl. 38). L. to ¾"; front part of thorax narrow, neck-like; claws toothed or cleft; soft-bodied, black, some marked with yellow or red; secrete an oily liquid that blisters human skin. Adults feed on rabbit brush and other plants, laying thousands of eggs. The minute first-stage larva wanders in search of a host—grasshopper egg pods in *Epicauta** and some related genera, and bee nests in others. The first larva of *Meloe* attaches to a bee (*Anthophora*) visiting a flower and rides to the bee's nest. There it molts to a grub-like larva with reduced legs but well-developed mouthparts and feeds on bee larvae and on honey and pollen. After two more molts the legs disappear and a prepupa stage ensues, followed by pupation and emergence as an adult. Such a life history is known as hypermetamorphosis.

(2) Trimera. All tarsi 3-jointed.

I-126. Lady or Ladybird Beetles. Coccinellidae (pl. 38). L. to ⅓"; body round, convex, usually brightly colored and spotted. Eggs laid on plants. Larvae soft, spiny, pupate in last larval skin. Larvae and adults prey on aphids and scale insects. *Hippodamia convergens** breeds during spring in lowlands, and swarms of adults fly in open air to heights of several thousand feet; some are carried by prevailing west winds into the Sierra. The black-spotted orange beetles hibernate at middle elevations under logs and needles covered with snow. In spring a reverse flight takes them back to feeding grounds. Collecting these beetles in the Sierra for release to prey on crop pests is useless because they do not feed during hibernation period.

(3) Tetramera. All tarsi with apparently 4 joints, sometimes with a minute fifth joint between 3rd and 4th.

I-127. Long-horned Beetles. Cerambycidae (pl. 38). L. to 2½"; antennae long, bases usually partly surrounded by eyes. Larvae are grub-like, cylindrical, and legless, the "round-headed" borers in dead or dying trunks and branches of forest trees. Adults of gray or brownish species live on bark, those of brightly colored yellow and black species (*Leptura**, 127c) on flowers. The brown *Prionus* with 3 lateral spines on prothorax and *Ergates** (127a, b) with many thoracic spines are the largest Sierran species; larvae of *Prionus* bore in roots of oaks, those of *Ergates* in dead pine trees. Another "pine sawyer" (*Monochamus**, 127d), has antennae much longer than the body.

I-128. Leaf Beetles. Chrysomelidae (pl. 38). L. to ½"; antennae shorter than body, bases not at all surrounded by eyes. Larvae grub-like, with 6 legs, feed on leaves or roots or mine leaf tissue. The Cottonwood Leaf Beetle (*Lina scripta*) ⅓" long, is yellowish with variable black markings above. Larvae eat all the leaf tissue except the network of veins, and pupate on the leaves. The Milkweed Beetle (*Chrysochus cobaltinus**) is ½" long, stout, and blue. The Klamath Weed Beetle (*Chrysolina quadrigemina*) is ¼" long, and bronze to metallic blue or green. Introduced from Europe, this beetle has eliminated the poisonous Klamath weed from all but a few shaded wet places in the foothills and in the lower Yellow Pine belt.

(4) Pentamera. All tarsi with 5 distinct joints.

I-129. Riffle Beetles. Elmidae (pl. 38). L. to ¹⁄₁₀"; brown or black, covered with fine hairs; abdomen of 5 segments below; claws large. Larvae cylindrical, with 6 legs. Adults live in fast-flowing well-aerated water, using oxygen from air film surrounding body, but cannot swim; they crawl over stream bottom or cling to roots of plants in water.

I-130. Water Pennies. Psephenidae (pl. 38). L. to ¼"; oval, brownish, covered with fine hairs; abdomen of 6 segments below; legs with large claws. Adults terrestrial but crawl under water to lay eggs. Larvae to ¾" long, oval, flat, with gills on 2nd to 6th abdominal segments, cling to rocks in swift-flowing streams. *Eubrianax** extends up to Lodgepole–fir belt.

I-131. Checkered Beetles. Cleridae (pl. 38). L. to ¾"; body hairy; 5 or 6 ventral abdominal segments; brightly colored. Larvae cylindrical, hairy, prey on bee larvae, grasshopper eggs, and larvae of wood-boring beetles. A yellow and black species (*Trichodes ornatus**) frequents flowers and has a life history similar to Meloidae (I-125). Some brown species of *Enoclerus* are important natural enemies of bark beetles.

I-132. Fire-flies and Glow-worms. Lampyridae (pl. 38). L. to ½"; head covered by large thorax, abdomen 7-segmented. Larvae slender, with 6 legs, prey on earthworms, snails, and insects in the ground. The pink glow-worm (*Microphotus angustus*) of the Foothill belt has winged males with the prothorax and wing covers grayish brown. Females lack wings, resemble larvae, and glow with cold light in late summer and autumn nights.

I-133. Skin Beetles. Dermestidae (pl. 38). L. to ½"; oval, covered with hairs or scales; abdomen of 5 visible segments below. The small black or pale marked adults of *Anthrenus* are common on flowers. Larvae 6-legged, covered with long hairs. Larvae and adults of the Larder Beetle (*Dermestes lardarius**) in bird nests and in animal carcasses, feeding on dried skin and feathers.

I-134. Green Bark Beetles. Ostomidae (pl. 38). L. to ½"; oval and brownish or long and metallic green or blue; tarsi slender. Larvae narrow, white with black head and a double-spine plate at end of body. *Temnochila virescens** preys effectively on bark beetles in Sierran conifers.

I-135. Flat Bark Beetles. Cucujidae (pl. 38). L. to ½"; flat, red with black antennae, eyes, tibiae, and tarsi; front coxal cavities open behind; hind tarsi of ♂ may be 4-jointed. Larvae flat, pale brown, with two short spines at hind end. *Cucujus clavipes** preys on wood-boring beetles under bark. Smaller brownish species occur in seeds, fruits, etc.

I-136. Metallic Wood Borers. Buprestidae (pl. 38). L. to 1½"; spine on under surface of thorax fits into groove; hind angles of thorax not spine-like. Larvae or "flat-headed" borers legless, with prothorax (not head) large and flat; bore in wood of living or dead trees, making tunnels that are flat (shape of prothorax), not round like those of "round-headed" cerambycid larvae (I-127).

Commonest of many Sierran species is the Golden Buprestid (*Buprestis aurulenta**, 136b); it is iridescent coppery-green with gold margins. Eggs are laid on fire scars or exposed pitchy wood of conifers. Larvae bore into heartwood, reducing value of tree for lumber. Pupation and transformation to adults takes place during summer and early fall in tunnels. Adults hibernate there, emerging the following summer. There are records of adults emerging from timbers in houses 26 years after the logs were milled. Other common buprestids are the large mottled brown *Chalcophora** (136c) on conifers; the small, smooth *Melanophila** (136a), which attacks conifers after a forest fire; and the black and white or yellowish *Acmaeodera* on chaparral plants. Adults of the last frequent flowers.

I-137. Click Beetles. Elateridae (pl. 38). L. to 1½″; spine on prosternum fits a groove in metasternum; the latter has a catch, so that the body can be arched when upside down and then suddenly bent forward, causing a "click" as the beetle leaps into the air. Hind angles of prothorax projecting, spine-like. Larvae (wireworms) long, slender, with 3 pairs of short legs. Feed on roots of plants in ground and pupate there.

I-138 to I-156. TRUE FLIES. DIPTERA. Fore wings transparent, few veins; hind wings lacking, represented by a pair of short, knobbed "halteres"; mouthparts piercing-sucking, or "sponging," often forming a proboscis. Larvae lack jointed thoracic legs.

A. NEMATOCERA. Antennae long, 6- to 39-jointed; joints similar and free (not fused).

I-138. Crane Flies. Tipulidae (pl. 39). L. to 1½″; WS. to 3″. Like enlarged mosquitoes; 2 slender wings, legs long, fragile; a V-shaped groove on middle of thorax above. Larvae ("leather worms") worm-like, head partly within thorax, 2 mandibles; live in moist soil of meadows or at edges of ponds or streams, some on bottom of swift streams. A wingless spider-like "snow gnat" (*Chionea*), ⅕″ long, occurs at high altitudes.

I-139. Mosquitoes, etc. Culicidae (pl. 39). L. to ½″; slender, delicate, 10 veins or their branches reach wing margins. Adults swarm for mating; larvae ("wigglers") with distinct head; aquatic.

This family includes 3 groups. (a) Phantom Midges (Chaoborinae) with scaly wings and plume-like antennae. They are nonbiting and attracted by lights at night. Larvae are predaceous and almost transparent, living in bottom mud of lakes and streams by day and rising to surface waters at night. (b) Dixa Midges (Dixiinae), without plume-like antennae or scaly wings, are nonbiting and inconspicuous. Their larvae are common at the water edge, having a U-shaped posture when resting or moving. (c) True Mosquitoes (Culicinae), with scaly wings, a biting proboscis in ♀, and plume-like antennae in ♂.

True mosquitoes are of 3 types: 1. *Anopheles* has eggs that float individually, and larvae that rest parallel to surface of water. Adult females have palpi about as long as proboscis, and they stand in a tilted position with head down when biting. *A. freeborni* occurs in the Central Valley and foothills; its larvae breed in sunlit pools containing algae or grasses and sedges. This was the carrier of malaria in early times and is still a hazard if persons with malarial parasites in their blood visit the region and infect local mosquitoes. 2. *Culex* has black eggs (139a) laid vertically in rafts that float on water. Larvae (139b)

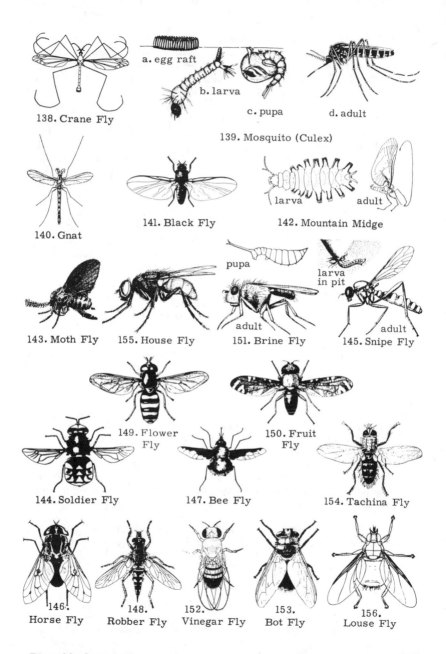

138. Crane Fly

a. egg raft

b. larva

c. pupa

d. adult

139. Mosquito (Culex)

140. Gnat

141. Black Fly

142. Mountain Midge

larva

adult

143. Moth Fly

155. House Fly

pupa

adult

151. Brine Fly

larva in pit

adult

145. Snipe Fly

149. Flower Fly

150. Fruit Fly

144. Soldier Fly

147. Bee Fly

154. Tachina Fly

146. Horse Fly

148. Robber Fly

152. Vinegar Fly

153. Bot Fly

156. Louse Fly

Plate 39. Insects

209

have a long breathing tube at end of body and hang downward from the surface. Pupae (139c) are stout "tumblers," with 2 short breathing "trumpets." Adults stand with the body nearly horizontal when biting. *C. tarsalis* (139d) breeds in sunlit pools up to 7200 feet. It is the most efficient carrier of encephalitis in California. 3. *Aedes* lays eggs on moist surfaces, where they remain dry for several months, hatching when they are wetted by rains or melting snow water. Larvae have a short breathing tube and hang downward from the water surface. Females stand horizontally to bite. *A. varipalpus,* mainly of the Foothill and Yellow Pine belts, breeds in water held in rotted-out holes in oaks and other woodland trees. *A. communis* and 8 other species are known as snow mosquitoes. They range in elevation from 3500 to over 10000 feet and emerge from April through July. Adults do not fly far from their breeding places and do little biting on cold windy days or during the cold nights at high elevations. The commonest breeding places are woodland pools or meadow pools resulting from melting snow. In the Sierra, where there are many breeding places, mosquito control is mainly by screening tents and houses and using repellents.

I-140. Gnats. Chironomidae (pl. 39). L. to ½"; mosquito-like, but mouthparts reduced; wings scale-less, usually 6 veins or branches reaching margin. Larvae with distinct head, mostly in water—the "blood worms," with hemoglobin, in bottom mud of lakes. They are important fish food organisms. Adults swarm near lakes and streams throughout the Sierra. Other "gnats" include those that make galls on sagebrush, pines, etc. (Cecidomyiidae) and those that breed in fungi (Mycetophilidae).

I-141. Black Flies. Simuliidae (pl. 39). L. to ¼"; short, chunky, wings broad, legs short and thick, first tarsal joint dilated; antennae short and bare; mouthparts short, in ♀ adapted for piercing. Larvae attach by anal end to rocks in running water and catch "drift" food in mouth brushes. Pupae are within silken cocoons, with breathing filaments; adults emerge from turbulent waters in protective air bubbles.

Simuliid larvae probably occur in every Sierran stream, but the adults are seldom seen because they usually bite wild mammals and birds. In the far north they are serious pests of livestock and man, and in the tropics they transmit several human diseases.

I-142. Mountain Midges. Deuterophlebiidae (pl. 39). L. to ½"; long-legged with large wings having a network of fine lines due to creasing when folded in pupa case; antennae of ♂ much longer than body. Larvae have 7 pairs of finger-like lateral lobes, each with concentric small hooks to cling on surface of smooth rocks in mountain streams and waterfalls; pupae attach to rocks. Adults emerge and fly briefly in early morning.

I-143. Moth Flies. Psychodidae (pl. 39). L. to ⅕"; wings held roof-like over densely hairy (scaled) body, thus resembling small moths. Larvae breed

in muck and swampy places in meadows or sewage drains (*Psychoda**).
Others (*Maruina*) have 8 suckers on lower surface and cling to rocks in
splash areas of mountain streams; pupae are small black discs.

B. BRACHYCERA (AND ASCHIZA). Antennae usually 3-jointed; if
many-jointed, fewer than 6 joints free. Face not separated by grooves
into a plate around bases of antennae.

I-144. Soldier Flies. Stratiomyiidae (pl. 39). L. to ¾″; brightly colored,
often metallic, somewhat flattened above, no bristles; 3rd antennal joint divided into several rings; tarsi with 3 nearly equal pads beneath claws. Larvae tapered at both ends, surface hardened by limy secretion, often bristly;
with mouth hooks; often aquatic, in mud, but some in decaying vegetation,
rotting fruit, or under bark; feed mostly on algae and other microörganisms,
but some species are carnivorous; pupate in last larval skin. Adults nonbiting
(*Stratiomys maculosa**) on streamside vegetation, especially flowers.

I-145. Snipe Flies. Rhagionidae (pl. 39). L. to ¾″; gray or brown, some
with yellow bands; body without bristles; 3rd antennal joint not divided into
rings; tarsi with 3 nearly equal pads beneath claws; tibiae with small spines
at tips. Larvae of aquatic forms (*Atherix*) to 1″ long, spiny at sides, 2 tapering gills behind, and 8 pairs of stumpy "prolegs"; prey on other insects in
streams. Adults lay eggs on branches over streams and die there, forming
large clusters of dead flies. Adults of *Symphoromyia* bite man at high elevations. Sierra Worm Lion (*Vermileo*, 145a, b, c; fig. 15), larva of Snipe
Fly, lays eggs in sand. Larvae tapered, with small heads, but hind ends thick
with 4 small lobes; burrow in sandy soil, making craters like Ant-Lion larvae (I-111); pupate in last larval skin in sand. Adults in Yosemite emerge
in June. Feed on small ants and other insects that fall into pits; hundreds of
pits often under mountain cabins, also at edge of granite boulders where
there is a little protection from rain and snow. Adult does not bite.

I-146. Horse Flies and Deer Flies. Tabanidae (pl. 39). L. to 1″; broad,
flattish, some (*Tabanus**) gray to brown, others (*Chrysops*) marked with
yellow and with patterned wings; antennae with 3rd joint ringed; tibiae
spurred; tarsal claws, with 3 equal pads; ♂ feeds on nectar and pollen;
mouthparts of ♀ dagger-like, bite painful to man. Eggs laid on plants over
water. Larvae in muck near water; body cylindrical, tapered at both ends,
with girdle of false feet on each segment; carnivorous; pupate in moist soil.

I-147. Bee Flies. Bombyliidae (pl. 39). L. to ¾″; stout, usually densely
hairy, often with patterned wings; 3rd joint of antennae not ringed; tarsi
with 2 pads under claws. Eggs often laid near entrance to ground nests of
wild bees; larvae feed on pollen and honey stores and on young bees; pupate
in sealed cells of bees; others parasitic on cutworms, sawflies, and grasshopper eggs. Adults on flowers or hovering in air.

I-148. Robber Flies. Asilidae (pl. 39). L. to 1″; body long, narrow or
tapering, with bristles and hairs, including hairy "beard" on face; 3rd joint

of antennae not ringed; tarsi with only 2 pads under claws; mouthparts horny, adapted for piercing and sucking fluids in other insects. Eggs usually laid in soil; larvae resemble those of Tabanidae (I-146) but feed on decomposing plants. Adults swift in flight, capture other insects on the wing.

I-149. Drone Flies and Flower Flies. Syrphidae (pl. 39). L. to ¾"; usually brightly colored with yellow stripes, no bristles; 3rd joint of antennae not ringed; tarsi with 2 pads under claws; on flowers and hovering. Eggs of Flower Flies* laid on plants; larvae stout or tapering to front end; prey on aphids and other insects. Eggs of Drone Flies in mud or decaying organic matter; larvae aquatic, "rat-tailed" with anal breathing tube much longer than body; adults resemble drone bees.

C. SCHIZOPHORA. Antennae 3-jointed, with a plain or hairy bristle on 3rd joint; face separated by grooves into a plate around bases of antennae.

I-150. Fruit Flies. Tephritidae (pl. 39). L. to ½"; stocky with dark-patterned wings and tapered abdomen in ♀; 2nd antennal segment not cleft above. Larvae of *Epochra canadensis* develop in fruit of gooseberries; others mine leaves of various plants and some, like *Xanthaciura maculata**, feed in flower heads of composites, where galls may be formed.

I-151. Shore Flies and Brine Flies. Ephydridae (pl. 39). L. to ⅕"; brownish gray, mouth wide, face strongly arched; 2nd antennal segment not cleft above and bristle on 3rd joint usually plume-like only on upper side. Eggs of the brine flies, *Ephydra,* are laid in brackish or salty water. Larvae have 8 pairs of stubby false legs and a long breathing tube behind; feed on algae. The brown pupae (in last larval skin) retain breathing tube; they may be attached under water but often float on surface.

Millions of brine flies live near the shores of Mono Lake. In earlier years the Paiute Indians collected and dried larvae and pupae in the fall. The skins were removed by rubbing and winnowing in scoop-shaped baskets. The resulting "kernel," called koo-chah-bee, was described by Wm. H. Brewer (1863) as "oily, very nutritious, and not unpleasant to the taste." Brine flies were also used to salt acorn meal cakes by west slope Indians.

I-152. Small Fruit Flies. Drosophilidae (pl. 39). L. to ⅕"; yellowish brown, 2nd antennal joint lacks cleft above, bristle plume-like on both sides; wings clear. Life cycle of *Drosophila melanogaster** 11 days at 77° F. Oblong eggs have 2 appendages; pale larvae are ¼" long; pupae shorter, with 2 horn-like breathing tubes. Larvae breed in decayed vegetable matter and in fermenting fruits and seepage from trees; in the Sierra they are not easy to find on wild food sources, but geneticists collect adults, using fermenting bananas as the bait. This insect is commonly called the Vinegar or Pomace Fly.

I-153. Bot Flies. Oestridae (pl. 39). L. to ½"; stout, 2nd antennal joint with a cleft above, mouthparts reduced or vestigial. Eggs or young larvae are laid on skin or in nostrils of mammals. Larvae bore through flesh to the skin and form pouches (tumors) with breathing holes; when grown they emerge and drop to the ground to pupate. In the Sierra the Deer Bot Fly (*Cephenomyia pratti**) is common, and species of *Cuterebra* attack rabbits, wood rats, and mice.

I-154. Tachina Flies. Tachinidae (pl. 39). L. to ½"; stout, usually bristly, 2nd antennal joint cleft above, antennal bristle bare or only slightly hairy, mouthparts usually well developed. Hundreds of species parasitize other insects. Eggs are laid on the host insect or scattered over its food plant to be eaten by caterpillars or other hosts. The fly larvae feed on the internal organs of the host, usually not killing it until the parasite is ready to pupate. Adults are sometimes found laying eggs but more commonly are seen resting on flowers.

I-155. House Flies. Muscidae (pl. 39). L. to ½"; black, green or blue, 2nd antennal segment cleft above, antennal bristle plume-like or with dense hairs, mouthparts well developed. The House Fly (*Musca domestica**) breeds in animal excrement and other refuse. The white eggs soon hatch, and the pale tapered maggots develop rapidly; pupae are oval- to barrel-shaped and reddish brown. Complete life cycle may take only 8 or 9 days. Mouthparts of adult are of the sponging or lapping type, so bacteria are readily spread from breeding places to the food of man. The Stable Fly (*Stomoxys*) has biting mouthparts. The Blue Bottle and Green Bottle Flies lay eggs on decaying flesh or on open wounds of animals, and larvae can feed on living tissue. They pupate on or in soil. Meat left exposed is commonly "blown" or covered with eggs of these flies.

D. PUPIPARA. Exterior leathery or horny-surfaced; claws usually toothed; wings often reduced or absent; larvae born when nearly ready to pupate (hence "Pupipara"); live as external parasites clinging to feathers or hairs of birds or mammals.

I-156. Louse Flies. Hippoboscidae (pl. 39). L. to ½"; brownish to black, body flat, legs widely separated at bases. Deer Tick Flies (*Lipoptena*) are common in the Sierra, and Bird Tick Flies (*Olfersia**) occur on towhees, jays, juncos, etc. Related families (Streblidae, Nycteribiidae) are found only on bats.

I-157. Fleas. SIPHONAPTERA (pl. 40). L. to ¼"; body compressed; no wings; mouthparts piercing-sucking; antennae short, in grooves; eyes simple or none; hind legs adapted for leaping. Eggs laid in habitat of host; larvae cylindrical, legless, to ¼" long, mandibles for feeding on organic debris; 3 larval stages. Pupae in cocoons. Life cycle from egg to adult usually about a month. Adults intermittent ectoparasites, sucking blood of birds and mammals. Two common species in the Sierra are the Ground Squirrel Flea (*Diamanus montanus*) to 6000 feet elevation and the Chipmunk Flea (*Monopsyllus eumolpi*) at high elevations. Both bite man and both are involved in transmission of plague from wild rodents to man. The Cat Flea (*Ctenocephalides felis**) is carried to the Sierra by man and his domesticated animals.

I-158 to I-173. ANTS, BEES, AND WASPS. HYMENOPTERA. Wings 4 (or none), membranous, few veins, interlocked in flight; mouthparts chewing, or chewing-lapping; ♀ with ovipositor for sawing, piercing, or stinging; pupae often in cocoons. Some species social, in colonies, others parasitic on insects; a few chew plant tissue or make galls on plants.

A. CHALASTROGASTRA. Abdomen broadly joined to thorax (thick-waisted); larvae caterpillar-like leaf feeders with legs or grub-like wood borers without legs.

I-158. Horntails and Wood Wasps. Siricidae (pl. 40). L. to 1½″ plus ½″ ovipositor in ♀; body straight-sided; front tibia with 1 spur at end; ♀ with long ovipositor and sheaths. Larvae long, cylindrical, grub-like, legs reduced, bore in wood of trees and shrubs. The Western Horntail (*Sirex areolatus*) is dark metallic blue with brownish wings. Female bores an inch or more into freshly felled or injured conifers to lay eggs. Larvae make round holes in heartwood and sapwood; after 1 or 2 years pupal cells are formed near surface of wood and adults cut emergence holes.

I-159. Sawflies. Tenthredinidae (pl. 40). L. to ⅓″; body robust; front tibia with 1 apical spur; ovipositor of ♀ saw-like, concealed. Larvae like caterpillar or slug, 3 pairs of thoracic legs and 6 to 8 pairs of prolegs. The Pine Sawfly (*Neodiprion*) is black or brown, ♂ with feathery antennae. Eggs laid in slits cut in needles; greenish larvae scatter over foliage, feeding on needles until September, then drop to the ground and pupate in cocoons. New adults emerge the following spring. Other species attack willow, cherry, and currant.

B. CLISTOGASTRA. Base of abdomen a narrow "waist" behind thorax; larvae legless.

I-160. Chalcid Wasps. Chalcididae (pl. 40). L. to ⅛″; body metallic, antennae elbowed; *trochanters* (joint between coxa and femur) 2-jointed; hind femur swollen; ovipositor of ♀ issuing from under surface of abdomen forward of tip. Seed Chalcids (*Megastigmus*) attack most Sierran conifers, drilling through young, green cones to lay eggs in seeds. Larvae reduce seeds to mere shells. Adults emerge in the second or third year. Other Chalcids are beneficial parasites on caterpillars or are parasites on other parasites.

I-161. Gall Wasps. Cynipidae (pl. 40, fig. 15). L. to ¼″; body compressed; antennae not elbowed; trochanters 2-jointed; front wings without pigmented spot at outer third of front margin. Eggs laid in plant tissues, mainly on oaks.

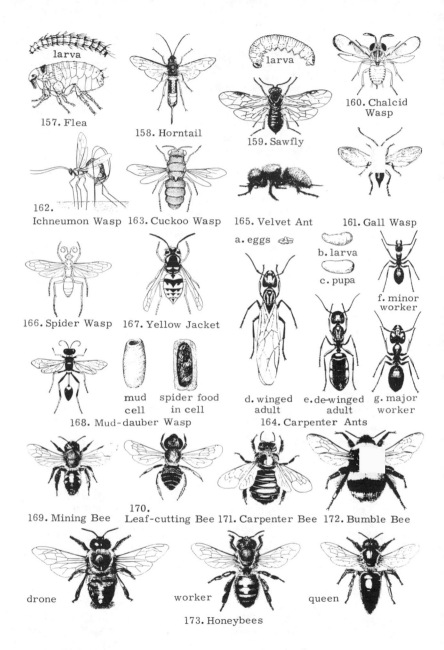

larva

157. Flea

158. Horntail

larva

159. Sawfly

160. Chalcid Wasp

162.
Ichneumon Wasp 163. Cuckoo Wasp

165. Velvet Ant

161. Gall Wasp

a. eggs

b. larva

c. pupa

166. Spider Wasp 167. Yellow Jacket

f. minor worker

mud cell

spider food in cell

168. Mud-dauber Wasp

d. winged adult

e. de-winged adult

g. major worker

164. Carpenter Ants

169. Mining Bee

170.
Leaf-cutting Bee 171. Carpenter Bee 172. Bumble Bee

drone

worker

queen

173. Honeybees

Plate 40. Insects

215

The California Gall-fly (*Andricus californicus*) produces the large "oak apples" 2″ to 4″ in diameter on valley and foothill oaks. Many small larvae inhabit a single gall, and a variety of other insects are associated as predators, parasites, etc. This and other Cynipids alternate between a bisexual generation and a generation with only females. Other galls are woody, fleshy, or thin-skinned, spotted, and spherical; the latter type is produced on huckleberry oak by *Cynips maculipennis*. On valley and foothill oaks seed-like galls ¹⁄₁₂″ in diameter are produced by *Neuroterus saltatorius*. Fully grown "seeds" drop to the ground, and thousands are sometimes seen "jumping" as the larvae jerk back and forth in their tiny capsules.

I-162. Ichneumon Wasps. Ichneumonidae (pl. 40). L. to 1½″; antennae not elbowed; trochanters 2-jointed; front wings with pigmented spot (see no. 161); abdomen long, several segments distinct on upper surface; ovipositor to 3″ long. Larvae are parasites of caterpillars and other insects, and pupate in host. The largest Sierran Ichneumonid is *Megarhyssa*, which loops its long ovipositor and bores through bark to lay eggs in tunnels of horntail wasps. Braconid wasps are like Ichneumonids but usually smaller and pupate outside of host.

I-163. Cuckoo Wasps. Chrysididae (pl. 40). L. to ½″; metallic green, bluish, or golden; antennae elbowed; trochanters 1-jointed; abdomen with only 3 segments visible above, flat below, curled under body for protection. Eggs are laid in provisioned cells in nests of solitary wasps and bees; larvae eat food and larvae of host, and pupate in a cocoon within host cell, to emerge in spring.

I-164. Ants. Formicidae (pl. 40, fig. 15). L. to ¾″; black or paler, sometimes reddish; trochanters 1-jointed; waist at front of abdomen of 1 or 2 knob-like segments. Social, in colonies, with sexual females (queens), males, and wingless workers; queen removes her wings after mating flight and starts colony by laying eggs and caring for first young. Later she is fed and the brood is tended by workers.

Most ants are scavengers and therefore useful in cleaning up organic material in field or forest. A few are predaceous or eat seeds, and some colonize aphids and "milk" the honeydew. In the Sierra myrmicine ants have been recorded up to 8600 feet; these have a 2-jointed pedicel, no simple eyes, a well-developed sting, and naked pupae. The other common group, Formicinae, has the waist 1-jointed, simple eyes, and the pupae in cocoons. Instead of a structure to inject formic acid, the stinger is reduced; the ants gain protection by squirting a spray as much as 2 inches from the tip of abdomen. The Brown Ant (*Formica fusca*) nests in the ground, some forming crater nests in sandy soil. The Red Ant (*F. rufa*) makes large mound nests of pine needles in open forests. The Amazon Ant (*Polyergus rufescens*), with narrow pointed mandibles, nests under logs and stones; it raids colonies of the Brown Ant, stealing pupae which are then raised and used as "slaves." Carpenter Ants (*Camponotus**) are the largest

Sierran ants, the body of a wingless queen reaching ⅗". These ants tunnel in stumps, logs, and even milled lumber. They do not eat the wood but are general scavengers; also they tend aphids and the caterpillars of Lycaenid butterflies (I-75 to I-89).

I-165. Velvet Ants. Mutillidae (pl. 40). L. to ½"; body black, densely covered with long hairs, usually reddish in Sierran species; trochanters 1-jointed; ♂ winged, ♀ wingless but with effective sting; unlike true ants, Mutillids have a thin, unknobbed "waist" or petiole. At dusk in the foothills they run about in sandy soil. Eggs are laid in burrows of solitary bees and wasps and the larvae feed on young of their hosts.

I-166. Spider Wasps. Pompilidae (pl. 40). L. to 1⅗"; body dark blue or black, wings often red or orange; legs long; trochanters 1-jointed. Adults at flowers or on ground. Females sting spiders, paralyzing but not killing them. Then the spider is buried with an egg which soon hatches, the larva feeding on the fresh spider. "Tarantula Hawks" (*Pepsis**) are common throughout the Sierra except at highest elevations. The battle between a large *Pepsis* and an even larger tarantula is usually won when the wasp stings the spider in a part of the nervous system near the head.

I-167. Yellow Jackets. Vespidae (pl. 40). L. to ¾"; yellow and black; trochanters 1-jointed; wings folded lengthwise; sting potent, painful. Young females overwinter and each starts a colony that lasts 1 season. Nests are made of paper (chewed wood) with "combs" of cells to house eggs and larvae, which are reared on fragments of insects, meat, sweets, etc. Many small females perform work of the social colony. Males are produced late in summer from unfertilized eggs. *Polistes* (abdominal petiole long, narrow) makes a flat, uncovered nest attached by a short stem, the cells opening downward; colonies number up to 200. *Vespula* (petiole short, abdomen appears broad at base) makes nests below ground or above ground (typical). *Dolichovespula* broadly fastens nests to tree limbs. Nests are large, with hundreds or thousands of cells and workers; those on trees sometimes larger than a football. The cells are protected by a paper covering. In the Sierra *Polistes fuscatus* occurs up to 8000 feet and the Vespulas are common everywhere.

The common Yellow Jacket (*Vespula pennsylvanica**) is a ground nester. In some years it is excessively abundant—1 per square yard in places. The cause of such outbreaks is not known. In these times the wasps are annoying to vacationers and picnickers. Yellow Jackets do not pursue people; they merely seek bits of food from table or lunch box. They sting only when molested. Protection is by screening homes and, when plagued by wasps out-of-doors, by being calm and avoiding direct contact. Wasps may be destroyed by spraying or dusting with household insecticides into the holes or nest openings at night. Stings can be treated with an ice pack and then a paste of water and bicarbonate of soda. If stung many times, or if the reaction is severe, it is well to see a doctor.

I-168. Thread-waisted or Mud-dauber Wasps. Sphecidae (pl. 40). L. to 1″; waist long, slender; wings not folded lengthwise; trochanters 1-jointed. Nests provisioned with caterpillars, grasshoppers, spiders, etc., which have been stung, remaining alive but unable to move. *Sphex* (*Ammophila*), black with reddish legs and base of abdomen, buries its prey in the ground with an egg, covers the hole, and taps the soil in place with a small pebble. The yellow and black Mud-dauber (*Sceliphron servillei**) builds mud cells to 1½″ in length side by side under rocks, or eaves and rafters of houses. The cells are provisioned with spiders on which the white, grub-like larvae feed.

I-169. Mining Bees. Andrenidae (pl. 40). L. to ½″; body clothed with branching hairs (as in all bees); trochanters 1-jointed; tongue short, hind tarsi with pollen baskets. Place pollen and eggs in cells in tunnels, dug in ground. Important pollinators of Sierran plants.

I-170. Leaf-cutting Bees. Megachilidae (pl. 40). L. to ½″; abdomen with a dense mat of hairs for collecting pollen. Nests of *Megachile* are in hollow stems or in holes in wood, etc., lined with discs cut from leaves of roses and other plants. Several cells are placed end to end, separated by discs and provisioned with a nectar-pollen paste. The 1-inch circular holes cut in leaves of wild rose are the work of these bees. Other species nest in the ground.

I-171. Carpenter Bees. Xylocopidae (pl. 40). L. to ¾″; stout, black or bluish, mandibles powerful, used to tunnel in solid wood of buildings, bridges, etc. The Mountain Carpenter Bee (*Xylocopa orpifex*) makes burrows 5 to 12″ long, provisioned with a honey-pollen mixture packed into a cell in which an egg is laid. The larvae feed for about a month, pupate 2 weeks later, and emerge after another 2 weeks. Since many bees may tunnel close together, timbers sometimes are weakened.

I-172. Bumble Bees. Bombidae (pl. 40). L. to ⅘″; densely hairy, black with yellow or reddish markings; tongue long for gathering nectar from clover and other plants. An overwintering young queen starts new colony (lasts 1 season) in an old rodent burrow; she lays eggs and collects pollen and nectar to feed brood. After the first generation small female workers take over the labor in the field and colony. Late in the season the colony is large with much brood and much stored food in honeypots. Then males and future queens are produced. After mating, the males and workers gradually die and the queens seek protected places under loose bark, etc., to hibernate. Bumble bees are dominant in northern latitudes including the Arctic; they occur from the Central Valley to the Alpine fell-fields. They are important pollinators of many flowering plants.

I-173. Honeybee. Apidae (pl. 40). L.: queen to ⅘″, worker about ½″; golden brown to dark brown; eyes hairy, female workers with pollen baskets on hind legs; queens with relatively short wings; drones (males) broad, eyes large. The honeybee, native to the Old World, has spread everywhere. These bees are scarcely domesticated and will sting anyone who interferes with their work. Those seen visiting flowers at all elevations derive mostly from Foothill colonies or others moved to high meadows by beekeepers during the short period when flowers are producing the most nectar. If wild colonies become established in trees they cannot survive High Sierra winters. Because of their catholic tastes, honeybees are probably more important than native bees in pollinating native Sierran plants.

18. FISHES

The crest of the Sierra divides the waters and fish fauna in two. To the east are those of the Lahontan Basin served by the Truckee, Carson, and Walker rivers and some lesser streams; a few drain into Mono Lake. The other waters flow westward, mostly into the Sacramento-San Joaquin river system. Since American occupation in the 1850's, there have been great changes. Various species of warmwater fishes have been introduced into lowland streams and two trout have been added to the colder waters, where there has been much transplanting and artificial replenishment. Many west-slope streams have been dammed, so that migrant fishes can no longer ascend them; and some reservoir lakes have been stocked with non-native fishes.

As with birds, certain fishes are resident and others migrate, especially for spawning. Trout need cool, well-oxygenated waters, but other fishes thrive in warm places. Some kinds live in groups or schools, and others are solitary; some occupy shallows near shores, and others

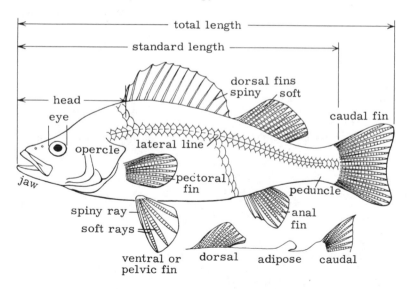

Figure 17. Structure of a fish.

frequent open or deeper waters. The several species thus have differing habits and environmental requirements, as do land animals.

Fishes grow throughout life, but more slowly with age, so that actual measurements of body parts are less useful than for birds and mammals, where each species reaches a certain adult size and then changes little. In consequence, fish descriptions, besides mentioning structural features and color, include proportional measurements, numbers of supporting rays in fins, and numbers of scales on certain regions of the body (fig. 17). Part of a description may read: "Head 4–5; depth $3\frac{1}{2}$–4; eye 6; D 11–14, A 11–13, scales 8–10, 80–89, 7–10." Anglers measure the total length of a fish but the fish student bases his work on the "standard length" (tip of snout to end of last body vertebra) to avoid error due to any damage of the tail fin, and "length of head" (snout to end of opercle covering gills). Then *head 4–5* means its length goes 4 to 5 times in the standard length; *depth $3\frac{1}{2}$–4* means greatest depth of body goes $3\frac{1}{2}$ to 4 times in standard length; *eye 6* is its diameter into length of head; *D 11–14*, dorsal fin has 11 to 14 rays; *A 11–13*, anal fin has 11 to 13 rays; *scales 8–10*, number of scales in diagonal line from middle of back to lateral line; *80–89*, along lateral line from edge of opercle to base of tail fin; and *7–10*, from lateral line diagonally to middle of belly. If the fin formula reads *D X + 12–13*, the dorsal fin has 10 hard (bony or spiny) rays and 12 or 13 soft rays.

Other abbreviations: L., length; wt., weight; ♂, male; ♀, female.

Fi-1. Pacific Lamprey. *Entosphenus tridentatus* (pl. 41). L. to 24″, dia. to $1\frac{1}{2}$″; body soft, cylindrical, compressed behind; skin smooth, slimy; mouth a circular funnel with horny teeth; top of head with 1 nostril and 3rd (pineal) eye; 2 small lateral eyes; gill openings 7 pairs, separate; fins on back and tail soft (no paired fins); plain brownish or bluish gray. Distr. Streams of w. slope, occasionally up to 3500 ft.

The lowly lamprey, not a true fish, has no jaws, paired fins, or scales. To feed, it attaches to a fish by the sucking mouth, rasps a hole with the horny teeth, and sucks out blood and flesh. Mature lampreys ascend freshwater streams and make nests by moving rocks in the pebbly bottom; each female lays thousands of eggs. The young hatch as small slender larvae (ammocoetes) without eyes or teeth. Each makes a U-shaped hole in sand or mud where it lives 3 or 4 years, drawing in water for respiration and feeding on bottom ooze. Gradually it becomes adult in form, migrates to salt water to feed and grow, and finally returns to a stream to spawn and die.

Fi-2. Mountain Whitefish. *Prosopium williamsoni* (pl. 41). L. to 16″; slender; 2 flaps between nostrils; mouth small, reaching only to front of large eye; tail deeply forked; scales large; back bluish, sides silvery, adipose and caudal fins steel blue, all fins black-tipped; breeding ♂ white below;

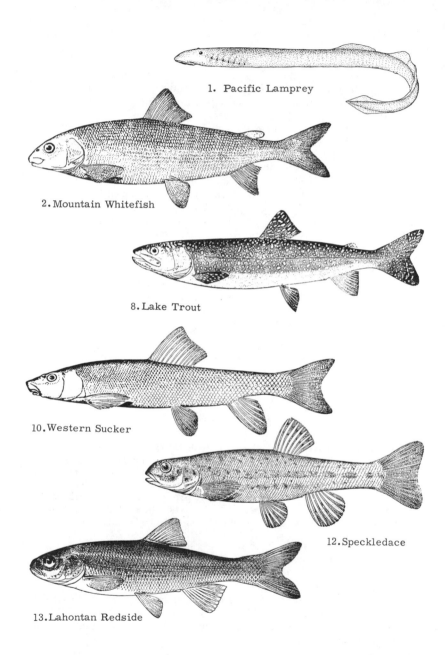

1. Pacific Lamprey

2. Mountain Whitefish

8. Lake Trout

10. Western Sucker

12. Speckledace

13. Lahontan Redside

Plate 41. Fishes

head 4–5, depth 4⅔–6, eye 3–4, D 11–12, A 11–12, scales 8–10, 80–89, 7–8. DISTR. Lake Tahoe, Donner Lake, and the Truckee, Carson, and Walker rivers.

This native Whitefish, related to the trouts, lives in waters of the Lahontan system. It spawns in October, ascending tributaries of Lake Tahoe. Males then have small tubercles on scales near the tail. Sometimes Whitefish will rise to a fly and then are as game as trout. Like the trouts, they will eat eggs of other fishes while they are spawning.

Six species of trouts inhabit Sierran streams. They differ from salmon in having 12 or fewer rays in the anal fin and usually have dark spots on the dorsal fin; the peduncle, at base of tail, is deep in a trout. True trouts (*Salmo,* nos. 3–6) have darkish spots on a lighter background, fewer than 190 scales in the lateral line, and a row of teeth in center of roof of mouth. Chars (*Salvelinus,* nos. 7, 8) have light spots on darker background and smaller scales (190+).

Fi-3. Brown Trout. *Salmo trutta* (col. pl. 18). Back dark or olive brown, sides golden or greenish brown, belly white or yellow (no bright side band or wavy marks); head, body, and dorsal fins with large, distinct dark spots, some orange-edged; lower sides with red or orange spots pale-bordered; head 3⅕, depth 3⅕, eye 5, D 10–11, A 9, scales 30–32, 115–150, 23. DISTR. In many Sierran waters.

The European Brown or Loch Leven Trout, planted in Sierran waters since 1895, is widely established. This is the only trout with both black and red spots. It is wary, often escaping hooks and enemies to become old, deep-bodied, heavy, and cannibalistic. Skilled anglers enjoy attempts to catch this elusive species. It spawns in autumn. Growing young have dark parr marks (vertical bands on sides) and pale-ringed dark spots.

Fi-4. Cut-throat Trout. *Salmo clarkii* (col. pl. 18). Head and body slender; usually dark yellow-olive from back to belly, with broad pinkish side stripe; body and fins with few or many scattered black spots; 2 red "cut-throat" stripes on membrane of lower jaw; minute (basibranchial) teeth on tip of tongue; head 3¾–4¼, depth 4, eye 6¼–9, D 9–12, A 10–12, scales 28–38, 150–170, 27–37; max. wt. 30 lbs. DISTR. On e. slope in Lahontan drainage: Lakes Webber, Donner, and Tahoe, and the Truckee, Carson, and Walker rivers.

Originally the Cut-throat or Black-spotted Trout abounded in Lake Tahoe and other east-side waters. Late in autumn there was a heavy upstream migration in the Truckee River, but the fish did not spawn until April. In early days it was caught commercially to supply mining camps. Over-fishing and later water diversions for irrigation reduced the population drastically. Stocks in various drainages differ slightly in shape and color. A local race, the Paiute Cut-throat, is isolated in Fish Valley, Alpine County.

Fi-5. Golden Trout. *Salmo aguabonita* (col. pl. 18). Back olive, sides golden yellow, belly whitish; cheeks and opercle bright red as also the pectoral, pelvic, and anal fins; side stripe rosy; parr marks on sides persist in streams (up to 1 yr. in lakes); dark spots few on back, more on dorsal and caudal fins; dorsal and anal fins white-tipped, sometimes edged with black; head 3¼–3¾, depth 3¾–4⅓, eye 4½–5½, D 11–12, A 10–11, scales 50, 200, 40. DISTR. Originally in few high streams of Kern River drainage; transplanted to many waters from Placer County to Tulare and Inyo counties.

This beautiful relative of the Rainbow Trout developed as a distinct species in the high southern Sierra, several streams having slightly unlike races. In those remote waters Golden Trout abounded and were easily caught. The first transplant was in 1876 and many have been made since, so the species is now in waters up into the central Sierra.

Fi-6. Rainbow Trout. *Salmo gairdnerii* (col. pl. 18). Back often bluish gray, belly silvery white; side stripe reddish to violet; black spots minute to ⅛" on upper half of head and body; lower side of head often reddish (no cut-throat red on lower jaw, no brown or red spots, no wavy bars); dark parr marks on sides usually disappear early in life; head 4, depth 3⅘, eye 4½–5, D 11–12 (10–13), A 9–12, scales 20–24, 115–180 (usually below 150), 20; max. wt. 21⅕ lbs.

Originally the Rainbow was *the* trout of all cool streams west of the Sierran crest. During nearly a century it has been transplanted or reared and planted in most suitable California waters. Also it has been established in some eastern states, Europe, and New Zealand. It is the gamiest of trout, sought every year by thousands of anglers.

Wild Rainbows spawn during the spring (Feb.-June) in small, clear, cool and swift streams. A pair will meet over clean gravel where the flow keeps the site clear of silt and well aerated. The female uses her tail to flip little rocks aside and form a nest or redd. The two move over the redd, the female expels some ripe eggs, and the male ejects white milt containing sperm. She promptly moves gravel over the eggs, which meanwhile are fertilized by the sperm and absorb water until they are spherical. At 40° F. the eggs hatch in about 80 days, but sooner in warmer water. Each young or fry at hatching has a yolk sac hanging on its lower surface—a food supply while it lives amid the gravel. When the yolk is consumed, the little trout or fingerling emerges to start feeding on minute insects in the stream. Growth depends on water temperature and food supply. In a cold brook after one year the fish may be only 3½ inches long and after 2 years only 5 inches, whereas a 2-inch fingerling planted in a rich, warm lake may reach 14 inches in a year.

The Steelhead Rainbow of coastal streams migrates into the ocean when a year or two old, remains in salt water for about two years, and then returns each year to spawn in its parent stream. When freshly returned it is gray above and silvery on the belly with little of the red or violet seen on resident Rainbows.

Fi-7. Eastern Brook Trout. *Salvelinus fontinalis* (col. pl. 18). Tail scarcely forked; scales very small; back and sides dark olive-green with light wavy lines on dorsal fin and back; sides with red or light gray spots, some red spots with blue borders; front edge of pelvic and anal fins usually white; head 4½, depth 3½, eye 5¼, D 9–10, A 8–9, scales 37, 180+ (154–254), 30; max. wt. 9 lbs. 12 oz. DISTR. Widely planted throughout California but established mainly in mountain lakes and meadow streams at 5000–9000 ft.

Brook Trout do best in high lakes lacking tributary streams, where they spawn in springs emerging from the lake bottoms. In Sierran waters they do not reach the size attained in some eastern states. Many persons consider this the best flavored of our trout. It spawns from September to December.

Fi-8. Lake or Mackinaw Trout. *Salvelinus namaycush* (pl. 41). Tail deeply forked; no bright color; body gray, pale to blackish, with large pale spots except on belly; dorsal and caudal fins with dark, wavy lines; head 3¾–4¼, depth 4, eye 7½, D 11, A 10–11, scales 32, 185–205, 32; max. wt. 15 lbs. DISTR. Introduced in lakes of Truckee River drainage: Tahoe, Donner, Fallen Leaf, and Stony Ridge.

Introduced in 1895 from Michigan, this trout lives deep in lakes and is caught usually on large heavily weighted spinners with minnow bait. It becomes large and feeds on other fish; therefore is not planted elsewhere. Unlike other trout, which make gravel nests, this species sheds its eggs loosely over rocks or shelves in lake bottoms.

Fi-9. Chinook Salmon. *Oncorhynchus tshawytscha.* L. 24″–60″, wt. 16–18 (to 70) lbs.; body robust, compressed, deepest near middle; head conic, mouth wide, teeth moderate (jaws of breeding ♂ curved, teeth large at front); an adipose fin; peduncle slender; caudal fin deeply forked; above dusky, sides with olive or bluish tinge, below silvery; back, dorsal fin, and tail with round black spots; breeding fish tinged with red; head 4, depth 4, eye 9–9⅓, D 10–13, A 11–16, scales 25–32, 130–155, 29. DISTR. Streams of Great Valley and foothills on w. slope; migratory.

Originally this common Pacific Coast salmon ascended the major west slope streams to spawn in tributaries well above the Foothill belt. Dams built on many streams now exclude them, and spawning is mainly in the upper Sacramento River. The salmon make nests in bottom gravel to receive the eggs, in the manner of Rainbow Trout (Fi-6). The young, when 4 to 12 months old, migrate to the ocean to live and grow for 3 to 5 years. When mature they cease feeding, return to the upper freshwater streams, spawn, and die. Other species of salmon have been recorded at times in Great Valley rivers. The Coho Salmon (*O. kisutch*) was planted in Truckee River before 1937, and the Kokanee (*O. nerka kennerlyi*) was introduced during the 1940's into Tahoe, Donner, and other lakes and reservoirs.

Fi-10. Western Suckers. Genus *Catostomus* (pl. 41). L. to 24″; body slender, somewhat cylindrical; eye small, high on tapered head; mouth below tip of snout, toothless; lips thick; upper lip covered with papillae and protractile, lower with broad free margin and divided into 2 lobes; scales small, crowded at front; pelvic fins under dorsal; anal fin short, high; tail forked; above dark, below pale, breeding ♂ with reddish side band; head 4, depth 5, eye 5–6, D 10–14, A 7–8, scales 13–21, 60–96, 10–16. Distr. Common in streams on both slopes, some to above 6000 ft.

Suckers graze over rocks and other objects in stream bottoms, using the thick soft lips to gather algae and other edible materials; thus they act as scavengers and seldom compete with game fishes. Their nonadhesive eggs are put out in water over gravel with no attempt at nest making.

Fi-11. Lahontan Mountain-sucker. *Pantosteus lahontan.* L. to 6"; resembles Western Sucker but with deep notches at junction of upper and lower lips; jaws with cartilaginous sheaths; above dark, scales with dark points; head 4⅓–4¾, depth 5–6¼, eye 5¼–5¾, D 10–11, A 7, scales 15–18, 77–83, 11–13. Distr. Streams and lakes of e. slope; introduced into North and Middle Forks of Feather R.

Fi-12. Speckledace. *Rhinichthys osculus* (pl. 41). L. 2"–3"; slender, snout pointed; upper lip joined to skin of snout; tail stout, forked; above brownish or yellowish green, with dark blotch on opercle, some with imperfect stripe on side; fins red-tinted in spawning season; head 4, depth 4–5, eye 4–5, D 7–9, A 7–8, scales 12–14, 65–76, 9–11. Distr. Streams and lakes on both slopes.

The Dace is a small minnow, secretive in habits, that is common on riffles in small streams and among the shelter of rocks and gravel along lake shores. It seldom lives over sand, in vegetation, or in quiet waters. The food is of small insects and scraps of bottom debris. In spring the few large eggs are deposited over rocks in riffles.

Fi-13. Lahontan Redside. *Richardsonius egregius* (pl. 41). L. 3½"; body compact, mouth large, terminal; base of pelvic fins ahead of dorsal; lateral line nearly straight; tail bluntly forked; back and upper sides green with blood-reddish streak along ⅓ of body (in breeding ♂) and another dusky streak on side; crescent on cheek and belly golden; belly white; head 3⅔–4¼, depth 3⅕–4¼, eye 3½–4¼, D 7–8, A 8–9, scales 12–13, 52–60, 6–7. Distr. Common in streams and lakes of Lahontan system on e. slope.

Fi-14. Sacramento Squawfish. *Ptychocheilus grandis* (pl. 42). L. 24"–48"; head and body long, slender; mouth large, extending to front of eye, toothless; throat (pharyngeal) teeth large and sharp; scales small; lateral line nearly straight; front of dorsal fin behind that of ventrals; lobes of caudal fin equal; above olive or brownish green, below silvery, scales dark-spotted; fins red or orange in spring; young with black caudal spot; head 3⅔, depth 5½, eye 6⅓, D 8–9, A 8–9, scales 13–14, 71–73 (65–78), 6–7. Distr. Common in rivers of Great Valley and Foothill belt and in larger streams of w. slope well into Yellow Pine belt.

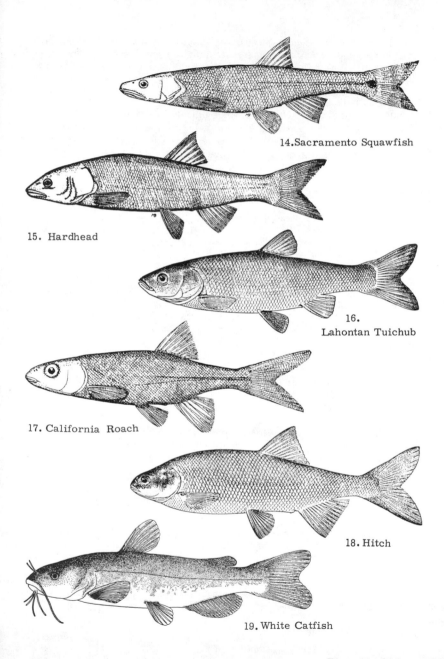

14. Sacramento Squawfish

15. Hardhead

16. Lahontan Tuichub

17. California Roach

18. Hitch

19. White Catfish

Plate 42. Fishes

This second largest of American minnows is common in the Sierra. When young it eats aquatic insects; later it preys on small frogs and other fishes. Although bony, it is occasionally used for food.

Fi-15. Hardhead. *Mylopharodon conocephalus* (pl. 42). L. to 36"; body long, compressed; head broad and short; mouth small, toothless; throat (pharyngeal) teeth large, blunt; scales small, loosely overlapped; lower lobe of caudal fin longer than upper, above bronze-green, below paler; head 3½–4, depth 4⅔, eye 4½, D 9, A 8–9, scales 18–19, 69–77, 8–9. DISTR. Common in streams of Great Valley and Foothill belt and in larger w. slope streams well into Yellow Pine belt.

The Hardhead is second in size only to the squawfish. Like that species it has been recorded from Alturas to Bakersfield in many of the west slope streams. It feeds on insects and plant materials and spawns in the spring.

Fi-16. Tuichub. *Siphateles bicolor* (pl. 42). L. to 13", head large, conical, flat on sides; eyes large; lateral line curved downward; scales large; dorsal fin over pelvic fins; tail sharp-forked; above olive-green, at times brassy or silvery, below white to yellow-white; head 4, depth 4½, eye 4½, D 8–9, A 7–8, scales 12–16, 43–63, 6–8. DISTR. Waters of e. slope; introduced into some w. slope streams and lakes.

Lakes and quiet parts of large streams are the habitat of the Tuichub, which often lives in large schools. The food includes plankton, some plant materials, insects, and fish larvae. Small Tuichubs are eaten by blackbass and trout, but if such predation is slight the chub becomes overnumerous. Then eradication is attempted as a measure of aid to trout. The adhesive eggs are spawned in spring when the water is about 60° F.

Fi-17. California Roach. *Hesperoleucus symmetricus* (pl. 42). L. to 5"; head slender, snout slightly convex, mouth small, slightly oblique, low in head; eye large; lateral line downcurved at front; dorsal fin well behind pelvic fins; above dusky, sides pale, below silvery, scales black-dotted; may have dark stripe from snout to tail; base of pectoral fins orange; cheek silvery; head 4, depth 4⅖, eye 3⅖, D 9–10, A 8–9, scales 10–14, 47–56, 5. DISTR. Tributary streams of Great Valley into Foothill belt.

The Roach lives in small, clear creeks, feeding on insects, crustaceans, and some algae. In spring it spawns several hundred adhesive eggs in shallow water over rocks or large gravel.

Fi-18. Hitch. *Lavinia exilicauda* (pl. 42). L. to 12"; body deep, compressed, tapering at ends; peduncle slender; head and mouth small, upper lip on level with lower part of pupil; eye large, well forward; dorsal fin small, pectoral short, anal long and high; caudal well forked; above dark, sides silvery; scales dark-spotted; head 4⅔, depth 3⅓, eye 4, D 12 (10–13), A 13 (11–14), scales 13, 54–62, 8. DISTR. Lowland streams, sloughs, and lakes up into Foothill belt.

The Hitch, a native minnow, usually avoids swift waters. The young feed on plankton and small insects near shore; adults take plankton in open water. Spawning occurs during early spring rains, in small creeks or gravelly lake shallows. A 10-inch female is recorded as having 112,000 eggs. The fish grow rapidly, averaging about $5\frac{1}{2}$ inches at one year of age. The Hitch has been much used as bait.

Fi-19. White Catfish. *Ictalurus catus* (pl. 42). L. to 24", usually smaller; body slender in young, heavier and head broader with age; mouth small with 4 pairs of "feelers" (barbels), those on top of snout shortest; tail fin forked, upper lobe longer; an adipose fin; skin scaleless, leathery; dorsal and pectoral fins each preceded by stout spine; dorsal fin midway between snout and adipose fin; base of anal fin shorter than head; front anal rays shortest; above bluish-olive, below silvery; head 3, depth 4, eye $9\frac{1}{2}$, D I + 7, A 18–22. DISTR. Introduced 1874, now common in lower warm waters of Great Valley and into Foothill belt.

Several catfishes of eastern states were introduced into California many years ago and the White is the one that has been abundant. Peeled of its tough skin and cooked, it is a favored food of many persons.

Fi-20. Brown Bullhead. *Ictalurus nebulosus* (pl. 43). L. 12"–18", wt. 1–2 (7) lbs.; upper jaw usually longer than lower; 4 pairs of "feelers" on snout; tail fin squarish, not forked; skin scaleless, leathery; dorsal and paired fins each with stout spine; dorsal nearer adipose than snout; anal fin with rays longest at front; dark yellowish brown, mottled; head $3\frac{1}{4}$–$3\frac{1}{5}$, depth $3\frac{1}{2}$–$4\frac{1}{2}$, eye $7\frac{1}{2}$–10, D I + 6–7, A 17–27. DISTR. Introduced 1874, now in lakes and streams on both sides of Sierra.

The Common Bullhead or Horned Pout is another successful transplant from eastern waters. A pole, line, hook, and doughball or scrap of meat is all that is required to catch this fish. Commonly the hook is swallowed and then the fisherman needs care to recover it while avoiding the fish's sharp spines.

Fi-21. Mosquitofish. *Gambusia affinis* (pl. 43). L. ♀ $1\frac{1}{2}$"–2", ♂ $\frac{1}{2}$"–1"; ♂ smaller and scarcer than ♀; head flat, body relatively deep, especially in ♀; dorsal fin far back in ♀, its base behind that of anal in both sexes; ♂ with mating organ (as long as head) projecting from back of anal fin; light olive, scales dark-edged; a triangular bar below eye; head $3\frac{1}{4}$–4, depth $3\frac{2}{3}$–4, eye 3–$3\frac{1}{2}$, D 7–9, A 8–10, scales in lateral line 30 (29–32). DISTR. Introduced 1922 from s.e. United States and common in clear sluggish streams and ponds.

The little topminnow swims near the surface, feeding on small insects and crustaceans. It has been widely planted in California to aid in control of mosquitoes, which it does by eating their larvae and pupae. The eggs are fertilized internally in the female and the young develop there. They are about $\frac{3}{8}$ inch long when hatched, in broods of 8 to 11; a female may produce several broods in a season.

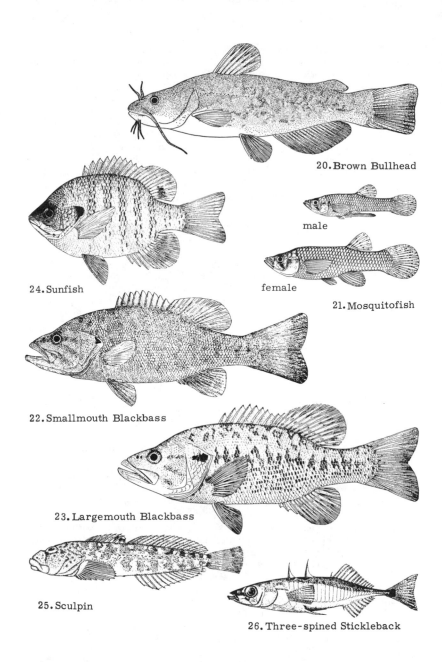

20. Brown Bullhead

24. Sunfish

male

female

21. Mosquitofish

22. Smallmouth Blackbass

23. Largemouth Blackbass

25. Sculpin

26. Three-spined Stickleback

Plate 43. Fishes

Fi-22. Smallmouth Blackbass. *Micropterus dolomieui* (pl. 43). L. to 28";
wt. to 14 lbs.; body long ovate, deeper with age; mouth large but ending
before eye; cheek scales minute, about 15–18 rows; scales on trunk moderately small; edges of spiny dorsal fin notched; above dark bronzy-green, dark
spots on sides in young, 3 bronzy cheek bands radiating from eye, a small
dusky spot at end of opercle, below white; dorsal fin bronze-spotted, edge
dusky; caudal fin yellow at base, then black, white-tipped; head 2½–3½,
depth 2¾–3½, eye 5–6½, D X + 13–15, A III + 10–12, scales 11–14, 67–
81, 19–25. DISTR. Introduced and now present in w. slope streams at least
into foothills.

The two blackbasses are rated among the gamiest of fishes in fresh
waters. They rise either to fly or minnow bait and by their rushes and
leaps test the angler's skill. The Smallmouth favors cleaner and cooler
waters, while the other species does well in shallow warm places. In
large waters having both gravel and mud bottoms the two may occur
together.

Fi-23. Largemouth Blackbass. *Micropterus salmoides* (pl. 43). L. to 37½",
wt. to 23⅛ lbs.; mouth reaching beyond eye in adult; cheek scales in 10–11
rows; above dark green, lower sides greenish silvery, belly white; 3 dark
oblique stripes on cheek and opercle; some dark spots above and below
lateral line; young with blackish line along entire side; caudal fin pale at
base, then blackish, white-tipped; head 3–3½, depth 3–3¼, eye 5–6, D
X + 12–13, A III + 10–12, scales 7–9, 58–69, 15–18. DISTR. Introduced
1891, now common in waters of w. slope.

Fi-24. Sunfishes. Genus *Lepomis* (pl. 43). L. to 8"; body short, high, thin,
back elevated; mouth small, terminal; opercle ending in black flap; form of
body and height of spines varies with age and condition; color brilliant,
yellow or greenish, sexes alike; head about 2½–3½, depth 2–2½, eye 3–5¼,
D X + 10–12, A III + 9–12, scales 6–7, 38–55, 13–16. DISTR. In many waters of both slopes.

Several species of small deep-bodied sunfishes have been brought
from eastern states to California and become common, especially in
lowland waters. These include the Green Sunfish (*L. cyanellus*), Blue-
gill (*L. macrochirus*), and Pumpkinseed (*L. gibbosus*). They serve as
food for larger fishes and are caught by many anglers.

Fi-25. Sculpins. Genus *Cottus* (pl. 43). L. 3"–5"; mouth large, lips thick;
eyes small, on top of broadly rounded head; body slender, scaleless, with
patches of prickles; fins relatively large, dorsal fin double, pectoral close
behind opercle; grayish olive with darker mottling; head 3, depth 4½, eye
5–6, D VI–VIII + 15–17, A 11–13. DISTR. W. slope streams and well into
Yellow Pine belt (*C. gulosus*); also on e. side in Truckee R. and other
streams of Lahontan system (*C. beldingii*); on gravelly bottom of flowing
streams.

These small fishes, often called Muddlers or Bullheads, live among
loose rocks in stream riffles, keeping position by use of the large pec-

toral fins. Their coloration matches bottom materials, providing effective camouflage. They eat eggs of other fishes, including trout; in turn they are preyed on by Largemouth Bass, White Catfish, and trout.

Fi-26. Three-spined Stickleback. *Gasterosteus aculeatus* (pl. 43). L. to 4"; body spindle-shaped, caudal peduncle slender; mouth small, lower jaw projecting; eye large; scaleless but sides often with row of vertical plates (5–25), smaller toward tail; 2 large and 1 small spines on back ahead of dorsal fin; small erectile spines at anal fin, and 1 large spine low on each side at midbody; above greenish olive, below silvery; spring breeding colors: ♂ throat and belly scarlet, fins greenish, eyes blue; ♀ throat and belly pinkish; head 3–3½, depth 3–3¾, eye 4, D III + 11, A I + 8. DISTR. Lower Foothill and Great Valley streams; introduced in waters of e. slope.

Sticklebacks occur in fresh or brackish waters over the Northern Hemisphere. They eat larvae and young of other fishes, insects, and algae and become prey of trout and largemouth bass. The male builds a nest of twigs held together by a secretion from his body. Several females may spawn in one nest, which then is guarded by the male until hatching.

19. AMPHIBIANS

Salamanders, toads, and frogs have moist glandular skins and are "cold-blooded." The Sierran species are small and must live in damp or wet places, avoiding both the dry heat of summer and the freezing of winter. They all hibernate in winter, and salamanders at the lower elevations are hidden below ground in midsummer. In consequence they are limited in occurrence and activity. The local lungless land salamanders (nos. 3–6, Family Plethodontidae) are never in water; their eggs are laid in moist chambers under rocks or logs or in burrows. All the other amphibians spawn in water. The frogs (*Rana*) live in or close to water, where they may be found in the daytime. Toads and the treefrog leave the water after egg laying and hide in damp retreats by day.

Abbreviations: H. & B., head and body length; T., tail length; T.L., total length; ♂, male; ♀, female.

A-1. Long-toed Salamander. *Ambystoma macrodactylum* (pl. 44). H. & B. to 5", T. 2"; eyes large; side of body with 12–13 grooves; toes 4, 5, slender; upper surface dark brown or black with yellow or greenish yellow spots and blotches along middle of back; under surface sooty or brown; sides and belly with minute white spots. DISTR. Yellow Pine and Lodgepole–fir belts to 7000–8000 ft. from Ebbetts Pass n. to B. C.

The only aquatic salamander in the upper Sierra is this species. Soon after the ice of ponds and lakes melts in spring, the adults enter the water and pair. The female lays 8–10 eggs, each in a gelatinous covering about ⅝″ in diameter. Eggs are deposited singly or in clumps, on the bottom or attached to plants along the margin. After some weeks the larvae hatch. They are gray, of olive or brownish cast, with 3 pairs of gills. They feed and grow to about 3″ long, then lose the gills and transform into small adults; at high altitudes this change is usually in the second year. In summer adults hide by day under rocks and in or under decaying logs.

A-2. California Newt. *Taricha torosa* (pl. 44). H. & B. to 3½″; head flattish, body and limbs stout, tail long, vertically oval in section; skin thick, rough, with fine dark-tipped warts; upper surface and sides uniform tan to reddish brown, under surface yellow to orange; no spots. Distr. Foothill and Yellow Pine belts of w. slope; spawns in quiet streams, ponds, or reservoirs.

The common "water dog" emerges from below-ground shelters toward the end of winter. Adults hide in damp spots under rocks or logs and may be abroad on cloudy days. Males enter the water in March or April, preparatory to mating. Their skin then becomes smooth and puffy and the tail develops a fin to aid in swimming. When females arrive the pairs join for mating. Then, crawling on the bottom, the male deposits a gelatinous mass capped with sperm (spermatophore). The female picks this up in her vent, and the sperm serve later to fertilize her eggs. Each roundish egg mass is of firm jelly, to 1¼″ long, contains 7–29 eggs, and is attached to vegetation or other objects in the water. The larvae hatch in 5 to 10 weeks, being yellow with 2 lengthwise blackish stripes, 3 pairs of gills, and a thin fin along back and tail. When about 2¼″ long they transform and leave the water. Larvae eat small animals and organic matter on objects in the water; adults feed on worms, insects, and small mollusks.

A-3. Ensatina. *Ensatina eschscholtzi* (pl. 44). T.L. to 6″; tail rounded above, compressed below, constricted at base; eyes large, protruding; 12 grooves on side of body; upper surface dark brown with reddish orange spots, under surface whitish or gray; upper arms and legs orange, terminal parts like back but paler. Distr. Yellow Pine belt of w. slope.

This salamander is above ground in the Sierra at least from late April into September. When its damp hiding place under or in a log is opened, the animal usually is quiet, then crawls away. If molested, it stands on extended legs, arching the tail or sweeping it sideways and occasionally producing a sticky astringent secretion. Its food includes earthworms, insects, spiders, centipedes, etc. A female lays 8–12 eggs about ¼″ in diameter, each in a jelly coat; she remains with them during development. One set, freshly laid, was found in late May, and several near hatching were seen in August and September.

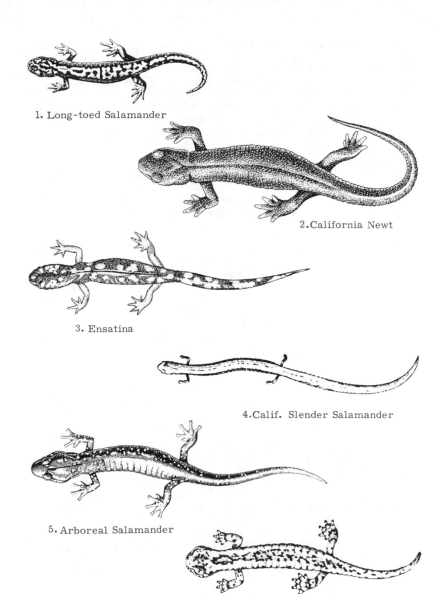

1. Long-toed Salamander

2. California Newt

3. Ensatina

4. Calif. Slender Salamander

5. Arboreal Salamander

6. Mt. Lyell Salamander

Plate 44. Amphibians

A-4. California Slender Salamander. *Batrachoseps attenuatus* (pl. 44). T.L. to 5", T. to 2¼"; head small, body wormlike, diameter under ⅜", 18–21 grooves on side; legs ¼" or less, 4 toes on each foot; coloration black, sometimes with straight reddish brown stripe along back. DISTR. Foothill belt of w. slope, at least from Butte Co. to Tulare Co.

During the wet season any log, board, or stone under or near a tree or loamy soil may hide one or several of these wormlike creatures, some coiled or looped like diminutive snakes. This salamander crawls slowly with its small legs, or makes lateral sweeps of its body and tail. If picked up it may lash from side to side and the tail may break off at any place beyond its base. Its food is of small ground-dwelling insects, earthworms, sowbugs, etc. Eggs, about 12 per female, are laid in or under logs, beneath rocks, and probably in small cavities in the earth during the winter months. The young at hatching are about ⅔" long.

A-5. Arboreal Salamander. *Aneides lugubris* (pl. 44). T.L. to 7½", T. to 3"; head large, bluntly triangular, deeper behind eyes, hind margin of mouth upcurved; 12 furrows on side of body; tips of toes blunt, enlarged; teeth at front of upper jaw exposed in male; body plain dark brown (no stripes), often with scattered dots of yellow. DISTR. Foothill belt of w. slope from Calaveras Co. to Madera Co., into edge of Yellow Pine belt.

This somewhat sturdy animal, with enlarged toes and a prehensile tail, can climb, and individuals or groups may be found to 30 ft. above ground in moist cavities in oaks. It also lives on or near the ground in damp logs or wood rat nests and beneath flat rocks or boards. Active adults have been taken at the first of May in the Sierran foothills. The food (in other localities) includes beetles, ants, moth larvae, and centipedes. There are no breeding records in the Sierra Nevada. In coastal counties eggs have been seen (in trees or at ground level) from July into September. The clutch is 12 to 18, guarded and kept moist by the female. The jelly coat of each egg has a short stalk by which it is attached. This salamander occasionally makes a mouse-like squeak and its large sharp teeth can wound a captor's hand, although it rarely bites.

A-6. Mt. Lyell Salamander. *Hydromantes platycephalus* (pl. 44). T.L. to 4", head often broader than body; head and body flattened; 13 grooves on side of body; tail short, blunt at tip; toes short, blunt, partly webbed. Above dark chocolate to blackish, mottled with pale gray or buff; under surface sooty, patched with pale gray. DISTR. Central High Sierra from Alpine Co. to n. Tulare Co. at 4500–10800 ft. in moist places under flat granite slabs.

In 1915 this exclusively Sierran salamander was discovered by accident when two were caught in a mousetrap. Since then, by much searching, it has been found in scattered localities. Altitudinally it is recorded from the top of talus slopes above Camp Curry in Yosemite Valley and the top of Half Dome to above timberline. The broad flat feet aid the salamander in walking over flat granite, and it can use its tail like a walking stick. Individuals were active in one place where the temperature was only 44°–49° F. Aboveground activity probably is limited to a short season—May to November or less. In summer both females containing eggs and small young have been found, suggesting that development occurs when the animals are underground. Insects and larvae, spiders, and centipedes serve as food.

A-7. Western Spadefoot. *Scaphiopus hammondi* (pl. 45). T.L. to 2½"; eye large, pupil vertically elliptical; sole of hind foot with black, sharp-edged, horny "spade" on inner edge; body smooth (no enlarged glands behind eyes, no folds along back); above dusky green, gray, or brown with 2 (or 4) broad pale stripes along back and sides; under surface white (♂ with black throat). DISTR. Only at w. and e. edges of Sierran region in open flat country.

By use of its spades this toad can dig backward in the soil, make a burrow, and soon disappear. It is mostly nocturnal, seldom being seen except when spawning. Breeding follows heavy rains that form transient ponds—February to April on the west and May or June on the east side. The sexes gather at night, called by notes of the males, a low rasping *a-a-a-ah* or *tirr-r-r-r*. While clasped, a female lays 300–500 eggs, which are immediately fertilized by the male. Larvae hatch in a few days, and tadpoles may transform into young 1 inch long within a month.

A-8. Western Toad. *Bufo boreas* (pl. 45). H. & B. 2½"–5"; eardrums small; large gland (parotoid) on shoulder oval, about size of upper eyelid; glands on leg large; upper surface dull gray, black, brown, or green; warts usually light brown; white stripe down middle of back; under surface whitish to buff, black-spotted. DISTR. Great Valley into Yellow Pine belt, higher in s. Sierra (to 10000 ft.); also on e. slope; in open valleys or meadows, near water, in woods, and around settlements.

The Western Toad is common over most of California. It is active at dusk and by night—sometimes also in daylight. It finds shelter under rocks, logs, or boards on the ground, and in rodent burrows. Small individuals hop, but the bigger ones walk, dragging the hind feet which leave imprints of the toes in dusty places. At middle and lower altitudes the species is active year round at 37° F. or higher; those in the high mountains hibernate in winter. For mating the toads resort to ponds where the males (having no large vocal pouches) utter low tremulous notes like those of goslings. Breeding in the lowlands is from March to May, but is delayed until early summer at high elevations. The male grasps the female in the armpits, and the small black eggs (up to 16500) emerge in two long gelatinous strings. Fertilization is external. A dozen pairs may spawn in one pool. The small black tadpoles grow and transform from June in the lowlands to late August in the High Sierra.

7. Western Spadefoot

8. Western Toad

male

10. Pacific Treefrog

female

9. Yosemite Toad

14. Leopard Frog

Foothill

Mountain

12. Yellow-legged Frogs

11. Red-legged Frog

13. Bullfrog

236

Plate 45. Amphibians

A-9. Yosemite Toad. *Bufo canorus* (pl. 45). H. & B. 1¾"–3"; resembles Western Toad but space between eyes usually less than width of upper eyelid, and space between (parotoid) glands on shoulder less than width of gland; sexes unlike: ♂ smaller, back and sides olive-green, with minute black spots edged with whitish; ♀ larger, back and sides with irregular sharp-edged patches of black rimmed with white; dark brown warts in dark patches. Under surface whitish in both. Distr. High Sierra, 6500–10000+ ft., from near Sonora Pass s. to Kaiser Pass; commonly in wet meadows.

Being a truly "boreal" toad, this species does not emerge from hibernation until April or May when snow-melt water is coursing through the meadows. Shortly thereafter the males enter pools and begin calling—10 to 20 mellow ventriloquial notes as a prelude to breeding. The eggs, 1500 to 2000 per female, are laid in May and June. The small tadpoles resemble those of the Western Toad but evidently winter over and transform the next year. After spawning the toads live in damp surface retreats but all disappear by September or October to avoid freezing winter temperatures.

A-10. Pacific Treefrog. *Hyla regilla* (pl. 45). H. & B. 1" to 2"; tips of toes with enlarged pads; hind foot well webbed; side of head with black stripe from snout through and beyond eye (or armpit); body color variable and changeable—green, brown, reddish, tan, gray, or black; often with dark T- or Y-shaped mark on head. Distr. Across Sierra from Great Valley to Great Basin and to 11000+ ft. elevation.

The smallest of local tailless amphibians is this tree toad. It is widespread in the Sierra and on the Pacific Coast from British Columbia to Nevada and Lower California. Adults shelter in rock crevices, under bark, in rodent burrows, on streamside vegetation, under culverts, and in buildings—with no preference for trees. In one place or another it spawns from January to May or June. In water the male inflates his dusky throat pouch and utters a loud *krĕck-ĕk* at 1-second intervals for long periods. When numbers are present, the chorus is deafening. Females lay the eggs in loose irregular clusters with soft, sticky jelly attaching to grass blades and stems. The tadpoles grow and transform in midsummer at lower elevations.

A-11. Red-legged Frog. *Rana aurora* (pl. 45). H. & B. 2½"–5"; eardrum ⅔ or more size of eye; skin smooth or slightly rough; a low ridge (dorsolateral fold) on each side of back from eye to end of body; upper surface brownish to olive with fuzzy-margined dark spots pale at center; limbs blotched with blackish; pale streak on upper jaw from below eye to shoulder; under surface pale; hind parts, including legs, reddish in life. Distr. Western foothills s. to Eldorado Co.; in permanent ponds, lakes, reservoirs, and quiet pools along streams.

This rather uncommon and wary frog is so weak-voiced that it is found only by persons who search for it. Toward the end of winter its eggs, 2000–4000, are deposited in a sticky mass attached to vegetation in water up to 6" deep. Each egg is covered by 3 jelly coats, the outermost ⅓" in diameter. Most of the larvae transform by mid-summer, the young frogs being slightly over 1" long. The food is largely of insects caught in or near the water.

A-12. Yellow-legged Frogs. *Rana boylei* and *muscosa* (pl. 45). H. & B. to 3"; eardrum inconspicuous, ⅔ or less diameter of eye; folds along back inconspicuous or none; upper surface with many small rough tubercles; color of upper surface blackish, brownish, grayish, or greenish, with some irregular dark spots; under surface whitish with yellow on hinder part and hind legs. DISTR. From Foothill belt into Subalpine belt; along streams or in lakes.

Two kinds of Yellow-legged Frogs inhabit the Sierra. The Foothill species (*R. boylei*) lives in foothill streams on the western slope and also along the east base of the range north to near Mono Lake. It spawns in streams after the high-water stage is past, from late March to early May. The 900–1000 eggs, about ¼" in diameter, are in firm jelly, resembling a cluster of grapes, and attached to rocks in shallow flowing water. They transform into frogs about 1" long during July and August. The Mountain species (*R. muscosa*) has a more pointed nose, shorter hind leg, rather smooth eardrum, and when alive, an odor of garlic! It occurs from near Mt. Whitney (at 11500 ft.) to slightly beyond Lake Tahoe, mostly above 7000 ft. Its smaller egg masses (100–350 eggs) are laid in mountain lakes and waters of slow streams during June or July. Because of low water temperatures and a short summer, the larvae overwinter (probably in water under ice) and transform when about 1 year old. Both species remain close to water at all times.

A-13. Bullfrog. *Rana catesbeiana* (pl. 45). H. & B. to 8"; eardrum conspicuous, size of eye (♀) or larger (♂); no folds on back; skin rather smooth; upper surface greenish or grayish brown, sometimes with brownish spots; dark crossbars often on hind legs; under surface whitish to cream, often yellowish on chin and hinder parts. DISTR. Great Valley and some foothill areas; in lakes, reservoirs, margins of larger streams, and irrigation ditches.

The bullfrog of eastern North America was introduced into California about 1905–1915 and now is common in many permanent waters, especially those with muddy bottoms. It is highly aquatic and seldom goes far onto the shore. Its food is varied: many kinds of insects, earthworms, snails, small fish, frogs and larvae, small snakes, birds, and mammals. In late spring the loud deep-pitched calls, *jug-o'-rum,* etc., are a prelude to breeding, in June or July. The egg mass (10000–20000 eggs) may be a yard in diameter. The larvae spend a year or more before becoming young frogs about 2" long. California law sets a limit of 24 per day or 48 per week when bullfrogs are sought for eating.

A-14. Leopard Frog. *Rana pipiens* (pl. 45). H. & B. 2¼″–4″; skin smooth with 2 folds on back from eye to end of body; upper surface green, brown, or gray with conspicuous oval spots of dark brown or black, each sharply outlined in lighter color; under surface cream to whitish, yellowing behind. DISTR. Along e. side of Sierra where introduced at Lake Tahoe, Fallen Leaf Lake, etc.; lives in marshes and wet meadows.

Most of North America is occupied by this frog, but it reaches only the eastern border of California. No other species uses so wide a variety of habitats. It will forage at some distance from water but if disturbed makes off rapidly, often in zigzag course by jumps of up to 6 feet. Its voice is low and guttural, of long and short notes. The eggs are in firm clusters, about 3″ by 6″, attached to marsh vegetation.

20. REPTILES

Turtles, lizards, and snakes are "cold-blooded" (variable-temperatured) and must avoid extremes of heat and cold. Their bodies are covered with dry horny skin whereby they can live in dry situations. The shell of a turtle is covered with horny plates separated by furrows. On lizards and snakes there are many small scales in the skin. Each scale on the back and sides in some species has a low lengthwise keel; those on the under surface usually are flat and smooth. The under surface on lizards has many small scales, but on our snakes there is a single row of broad scales below on the body and 1 (or 2) rows beneath on the tail. The outer covering of dry skin ordinarily is molted one or more times each year. On most lizards it comes off in pieces, whereas on snakes (and a few lizards) it loosens around the mouth and the animal crawls out of the old covering, leaving the "slough" in one piece. Turtles eat some plant material and carrion but lizards and snakes are predatory, taking live prey according to their size. The rattlesnake is the only poisonous Sierran reptile.

Abbreviations: H. & B., head and body length; T., tail length; T.L. total length; ♂, male; ♀, female.

R-1. Western Pond Turtle. *Clemmys marmorata* (pl. 46). Body enclosed in a shell (to 6″ long in adults) of firmly joined bones covered with a few rows of large horny plates; upper part (carapace) arched, lower part (plastron) flat; head, tail, and legs covered with scales, and all these parts can be drawn into the shell; color olive-brown above, yellowish below, variously patterned with dark markings. DISTR. Ponds and quiet streams of Great Valley and Foothill belt.

This is the only turtle native to interior California. It is highly aquatic, basking on rocks or logs in and near water, but submerging at the hint of danger. The food includes aquatic plants, insects, and carrion. At some time from May to August the adult female leaves

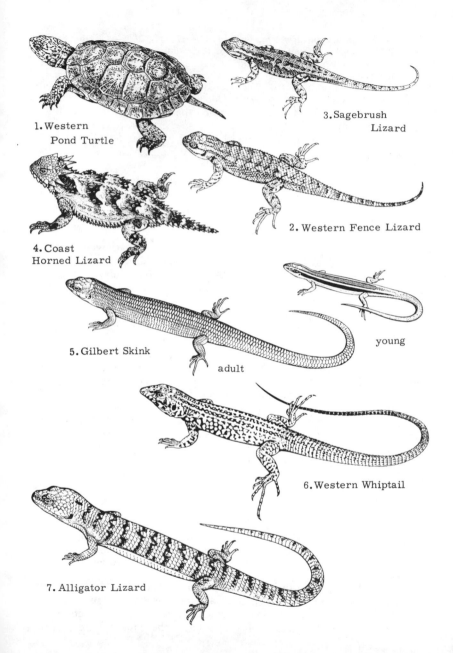

1. Western
   Pond Turtle

3. Sagebrush
   Lizard

4. Coast
   Horned Lizard

2. Western Fence Lizard

5. Gilbert Skink

young

adult

6. Western Whiptail

7. Alligator Lizard

Plate 46. Reptiles

the water and uses her claws and feet to dig a small hole in a stream bank or hillside often some distance from the home pond or stream. Here she lays 5 to 11 hard-shelled eggs and covers them with soil. The young hatch in about 2 months and go to the water. From about November until February all the turtles hibernate in mud beneath the water.

R-2. Western Fence Lizard. *Sceloporus occidentalis* (pl. 46). H. & B. 2¼"–3¾", T. 3½"–5"; body and tail rounded; scales on upper surface projecting, pointed, and overlapping, each with keel, 35 to 51 in row from last plate on head to line across back of thighs; scales on under surface smaller, smooth, overlapping; scales on back of thigh keeled; body above blackish, dark brown, or gray with lengthwise rows of blackish spots; under surface whitish with some dark marks; hind surface of thighs yellow to orange; throat and sides of belly blue in ♂ (belly all blue in high mts.); ♀ with lesser or no blue. Distr. From Great Valley across Sierra to Great Basin on rocks, trees, wooden fences, and buildings.

Commonest and most easily seen of all our reptiles is the Western Fence Lizard because when active it lives mostly on surfaces above the ground. From April to October it is abroad during the warmer daylight hours at the lower altitudes, and for a lesser season in the High Sierra. The cold season is spent in hibernation within logs or below ground, beyond the reach of frost. Its food includes a variety of insects and spiders. The male often flattens his sides and raises the skin of the throat, thereby displaying his blue markings—possibly as an intimidation to another male invading his territory. When courting he does the same, and bobs up and down. A female lays 5 to 15 soft-shelled eggs (mid-May to mid-July) in damp, well-aerated soil and covers them with loose earth. The young hatch in about 2 months, to forage and grow somewhat before hibernating.

R-3. Sagebrush Lizard. *Sceloporus graciosus* (pl. 46). H. & B. 2"–2½", T. 2½"; resembles fence lizard but scales smaller (to ¹⁄₁₆") and those on back of thigh most or all smooth; above greenish to brownish gray, below whitish; usually with rust color behind foreleg or on sides; throat and sides of belly pale blue. Distr. On both slopes mainly in Lodgepole–fir belt, chiefly on ground near rocks or logs.

The little Sagebrush Lizard (not confined to sagebrush in the Sierra) lives mostly on the ground but goes up on boulders or logs and occasionally on trees. It is common around mountain chaparral thickets. In the Yosemite region it is found abroad from late May until mid-October. As food it uses many kinds of small insects, ticks, scorpions, and snails. In late June or July the female lays 3 to 4 (2–7) eggs, which hatch between August and October.

R-4. Coast Horned Lizard. *Phrynosoma coronatum* (pl. 46). H. & B. to 3½", T. to 1½"; body flat, broad; head armored and bearing sharp spines (horns) at rear; back with many fine granular scales and scattered larger pointed and keeled scales; similar large scales along sides of body and tail; under surface smooth-scaled; above yellowish or reddish with about 4 pairs of large blackish marks bordered behind by white; below yellowish, dusky-spotted. DISTR. Great Valley and into Foothill belt of w. slope on open sandy ground.

This small flat lizard (or "horned toad") lives entirely on the ground. It takes shelter in burrows or crevices or by burying itself shallowly in sand. Its food is small insects. In early summer the female lays 6 to 16 eggs and the young hatch about 2 months later, being about 1⅛" in head-and-body length. A paler species (*P. platyrhinos*) inhabits the Great Basin.

R-5. Gilbert Skink. *Eumeces gilberti* (pl. 46). H. & B. to 4½", T. to 6⅜"; body and tail evenly tapered to end; scales smooth, flat, thin, round-edged, overlapped; legs short, scarcely longer than body diameter. Adult: Head coppery red, tail pinkish red, body olive-brown above, bluish green on sides, pale beneath. Young: Head and body dark brown, 2 sharp yellowish stripes along back, under surface gray, tail blue. DISTR. W. slope from Foothill belt into open Yellow Pine belt, occasionally higher; on ground in grass or leafy debris.

Both the blue-tailed young and reddish-tailed adult are so smooth they can slip through one's finger as if oiled. If a skink is picked up or attacked, the tail breaks off readily and continues to wriggle—a counterattraction as the animal escapes. This lizard is secretive, finding shelter under logs or rocks and living mostly on the ground amid surface cover, but may forage over logs or on low rock walls. It is most active in late afternoon from March to June. When moving rapidly (to avoid capture) it progresses by snake-like wriggling of the body, but it uses the small legs and feet when stalking prey—mostly insects. In summer the female lays 8 or 9 eggs in spaces under rocks or below ground.

R-6. Western Whiptail. *Cnemidophorus tigris* (pl. 46). H. & B. to 4", T. to 10", twice or more length of body; body, and especially tail, slender, legs stout, the hind pair large; back and sides with fine bead-like scales; under surface with 8 rows of squarish scales; tail ringed with keeled scales. Body blackish with lengthwise pale stripes (young) or small buff to white spots (adult); legs and sides of head dark-blotched; under surface white or warm tan, scales dark-edged. DISTR. Edge of Great Valley into Yellow Pine belt on open, dry, sandy, gravelly, or rocky areas.

Swiftest of local lizards is the Whiptail, which may be glimpsed as it dashes across a foothill road. It starts suddenly, runs 50 or 100 feet, sometimes on the hind legs, and stops abruptly, often behind a bush or rock. The main power is in the stout hind legs; the long tail is a counterbalance and "rudder." When foraging the Whiptail makes short jerky advances and often extends its long forked tongue. If pursued it may take shelter in a rodent burrow. The prey is of insects, spiders, and scorpions, sometimes dug out of the ground. Females lay 8 or 9 eggs, during the summer season.

R-7. Alligator Lizards. Genus *Gerrhonotus* (pl. 46). H. & B. 3½″–6″, T. (uninjured) to 2x head and body; head bluntly triangular, big in old adult; body slender, parallel-sided, a *flexible fold with granular skin along each side;* tail long, tapered to tip; legs and feet small; body scales squarish, in grid pattern, those on back and sides keeled, in 14 or 16 rows; belly scales flat. Upper surface brown or olive, with dark markings; under surface gray to yellowish. DISTR. Western foothills to Subalpine belt, on ground in grass, under brush, and around rocks or logs.

This lizard is active by day and dusk and, although essentially terrestrial, it can climb and even swim. The "diamond" head leads many people to infer that the animal is poisonous, but it is not. If taken in hand it is aggressive and may twist and pinch a finger, but the fine teeth rarely draw blood; the captor, however, may be smeared with excrement. When undisturbed the lizard walks slowly, but if excited wriggles the body to aid the small legs and feet in travel. While foraging the long forked tongue is protruded in search of the insects, spiders, and small lizards or snakes used for food. The side folds of skin enable the body to swell when filled by a meal or with eggs. The tail breaks easily and often regenerates rather completely.

The Southern Alligator Lizard (*G. multicarinatus*) of the Foothill belt usually has 16 rows of scales and dark crossbars on the back. The female lays 6 to 20 eggs between June and early August; the young (H. & B. 1¼″) hatch in 50 or more days. The Northern species (*G. coeruleus*) lives from the Yellow Pine belt into the Subalpine belt. It is smaller and normally has 14 rows of scales, and the dark markings are not in distinct crossbars. The female retains her eggs through development and produces 6 or 7 living young.

R-8. Rubber Boa. *Charina bottae* (pl. 47). T.L. to 28″; body stout, of nearly uniform diameter (no neck); tail short, blunt-ended; scales smooth, shiny, 35+ rows around middle of body; top of head with large scale between eyes; a short spine (vestige of leg) projects slightly at each side of vent in males. Color tan to greenish brown above, yellowish below. DISTR. Mainly in Yellow Pine belt in loose soil.

Our small native boa has a blunt tail and sometimes is called two-headed snake. It is chiefly active at dusk and night on the ground, but can both climb and swim. It shelters in damp places under rocks, logs, or boards on the ground, often near streams. Taken in hand it is docile and may coil in the form of a ball, when the "rubbery" folds of loose skin become evident. It hunts small mammals and reptiles, which are killed by constriction. The 3 or 4 young are born alive.

R-9. Garter Snakes. Genus *Thamnophis* (pl. 47). T.L. (adults) 24″ to about 48″; neck usually distinct; body slender, tail tapered to sharp tip; scales on back and sides of body and tail, each with keel, 19 or 21 rows on mid-body; upper surface blackish or grayish and with either yellow line along back and pale line on either side, or with many light spots on back (but no large blotches or crossbands); under surface pale green or grayish. Distr. Great Valley to Great Basin, few in High Sierra; in or near water, marshes, or grasslands, some in dry places.

Commonest of serpents in the Sierra are the garter snakes, often called water snakes. On open ground they travel slowly, but faster in grassland. Some swim readily by sidewise looping of the body and can dive. They are active by day and at dusk, even later in warm places. At high elevations they are abroad from late May into October and longer in the lowlands. If handled they often discharge foul-smelling fluid from anal scent glands, and also excrement. The young are born alive in broods of 10 to 20, sometimes more. Three kinds are present. The Common Garter Snake (*T. sirtalis*) lives in or near ponds and streams, eating both land and water animals. It has 19 scale rows at mid-body, usually 7 scales on the upper lip, and a yellow midline stripe. The Western Garter Snake (*T. elegans*) has 23 scale rows and usually 8 scales on the upper lip; it is represented by two different types. The *terrestrial* form lives mainly on land, feeding on slugs, land salamanders, and mice but rarely on fish. It has a yellow back stripe, and scale no. 6 on the upper lip is squarish. The *aquatic* form uses water for escape, and it feeds on fishes, amphibians, and water insects. Its back has light spots (but no stripe), and scale no. 6 on the upper lip is higher than wide.

R-10. Western Ringneck Snake. *Diadophis amabilis* (pl. 47). T.L. to 15″, body diameter ⁵⁄₁₆″, size of a pencil; scales on back small, smooth, in 15 (17) rows; upper surface uniform olive to slate; *neck collar pale yellow or reddish;* under surface orange to red with fine black dots. Distr. Foothill and Yellow Pine belts in humid spots under rocks, logs, or boards.

When caught, this pretty little snake usually coils the tail in a tight spiral and turns belly uppermost. Its food includes treefrogs, salamanders, small lizards or snakes, worms, and maybe insects. Females produce 2 or 3 eggs, which hatch in about 6 weeks.

R-11. Racer. *Coluber constrictor* (pl. 47). T.L. 30″–54″, body slender, tail tapered to fine tip; scales on back smooth, 17 rows. Adult uniform olive-brown above, greenish or bluish on sides, plain yellow below; young blotched with brown to blackish saddle marks or spots. Distr. Foothill and Yellow Pine belts, mainly in grassland.

The fast-moving Racers, relatives of the eastern blacksnake, forage with the head and neck held above the ground; while mainly terrestrial, they climb readily. Despite the species name "constrictor," they catch prey and hold it down by a loop of the body. The food includes insects, toads, frogs, reptiles, birds and their eggs, and small rodents. The white leathery-shelled eggs, 1 or 2 dozen, are laid in early summer under stones or logs, or in moist soil. About 2 months later they hatch, the young being 8–12 inches long. No other western snake shows such differences in coloration between young and adults.

R-12. Striped Racer. *Masticophis lateralis* (pl. 47). T.L. to 48″ (even 60″); slender, tail pointed; scales smooth, 17 rows; upper surface dark brown to black with narrow yellowish line along each side. DISTR. Mainly in Foothill belt.

The active Striped Racer travels well on the ground but also is adept at climbing over bushes and in trees. Its prey includes frogs, lizards, snakes (including rattlesnakes), birds, and rodents. When birds are nesting, this racer seeks out nests to swallow the eggs or young. A commotion among small birds in foothill oaks at this season often centers on such robbing. The few eggs are laid in late spring.

R-13. Gopher Snake. *Pituophis catenifer* (pl. 47). T.L. to about 60″, body stout, scales keeled (smooth on lower sides), 29+ rows; tail tapered; ground color buff with large squarish or oval "saddle marks" of black or brown, and smaller dark spots on sides. DISTR. Great Valley into Yellow Pine belt, mainly in grasslands or open areas.

The large "Bull" Snake often remains motionless when approached, but if aroused it can travel at fair speed. When cornered it will coil the body, draw back, spread the head (somewhat like that of a rattlesnake), fill its lungs, and then lunge and hiss at the intruder. In dry leaves the tail may vibrate, imitating faintly the rattler's warning. If held, it may bite a finger but do no other damage. The Gopher Snake can climb trees to hunt bird nests, and it can dig in loose soil. It finds shelter under rocks, logs, or boards and in rodent burrows. Mice, rats, squirrels, pocket gophers, rabbits, birds to the size of quail, and occasionally lizards are eaten. Mating occurs in spring or early summer; the eggs average 6–7 (3–12) per clutch and require about 70 days until hatching. Emerging young are up to 16 inches long.

R-14. Common Kingsnake. *Lampropeltis getulus* (pl. 47). T.L. to 42″, body to 1″ in diameter; scales smooth, 23 (or 25) rows; coloration brownish black with narrow yellow or creamy white rings brokenly encircling body. DISTR. Mainly in Foothill belt on shaded ground.

This seemingly quiet reptile (formerly called Boyle Kingsnake) can pursue and capture other snakes, including rattlesnakes, being largely immune to the venom of the latter. Besides snakes it also eats lizards, birds and their eggs, mice, and pocket gophers, all of which it kills by constriction. It is active by day and at dusk, and while mainly terrestrial can climb to seek young birds and eggs. Its 6 to 12 eggs are laid in summer and require about 70 days to hatch.

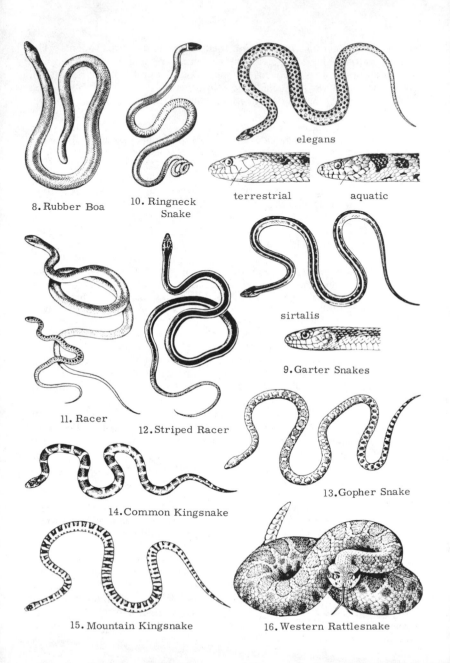

8. Rubber Boa

10. Ringneck Snake

elegans

terrestrial   aquatic

11. Racer

12. Striped Racer

sirtalis

9. Garter Snakes

13. Gopher Snake

14. Common Kingsnake

15. Mountain Kingsnake

16. Western Rattlesnake

Plate 47. Reptiles

R-15. California Mountain Kingsnake. *Lampropeltis zonata* (pl. 47). T.L. to 30", body of moderate size, scales smooth, 21–23 rows. Coloration bright, in bands of black, white (or cream), and red, each white band between 2 of black. DISTR. Yellow Pine belt, in forest.

Most beautiful of Sierran reptiles is this snake, which is marked with three contrasting colors. Formerly it was called Coral Kingsnake because its color pattern somewhat resembles that of the poisonous Coral Snake (not found in California). It is quiet, somewhat secretive, and not common. Its food includes skinks and small rodents, prey being killed by constriction. Captives have eaten other snakes.

R-16. Western Rattlesnake. *Crotalus viridis* (pl. 47). T.L. to 60", girth to 5", body heavy, head broad, bluntly triangular, neck distinct, *tail ending in jointed horny rattle;* head scales many, small; body scales large, keeled, 23–27 rows; pupil of eye elliptical; body yellowish or grayish brown with series of large dark brown or black blotches along back, 2 rows of small dark spots on sides. TRACK. broad, much curved. DISTR. Great Valley into Lodgepole–fir belt, also on e. side (none in Lake Tahoe Basin); several records in s. Sierra at 9000–10000 ft., one at 11000 ft., commonest in western foothills; found in grasslands, brushy areas, rock outcrops, and along trails.

Our only *poisonous* reptile, the Rattlesnake, is the subject of much misinformation and folklore. Its hazard to man is not great. The chance of meeting one in the Sierra is slight (except during spring in the foothills). Persistent efforts at killing rattlers in mountain communities, around summer resorts, and elsewhere have reduced their numbers. Of the thousands of visitors in the mountains every summer, very few ever see a Rattlesnake. Anyone on foot away from settlements *may* meet one. To avoid any danger it is well, therefore, to glance occasionally at the trail ahead, to look on the other side of a log or rock before jumping over, and not to put hands on a ledge above one's head where it is impossible to see over the top.

The Rattlesnake, like other "cold-blooded" animals, has no internal heat regulation; it adjusts the body temperature by moving between warm and cool sites. In cooler weather (Oct.-March) in the foothills it hibernates in a frost-free burrow or rock crevice, emerging when the air reaches about 70° F., and is out by day from about April into June. During the heat of summer, however, when exposure to direct sun would be quickly fatal, it is usually abroad between dusk and dawn. At higher elevations hibernation is longer, and the snakes are on the surface mainly during the warmer daytime hours.

Unlike most other snakes the Rattlesnake is slow, even lethargic. Often it lies in a warm spot on a rock outcrop or beside a trail, waiting for prey. If come upon quietly it may remain motionless except to flick the slender forked tongue out and back (which assists its sense of smell). Again it will glide slowly away. When the snake feels that it is cornered it will coil, in preparation for striking.

The Rattlesnake feeds mainly on ground squirrels, other rodents, and the smaller rabbits, together with some birds and lizards. As a guide in striking at prey (and enemies) it has on either side of the snout, between nostril and eye, a small pit containing a delicate heat-sensory structure by which it detects the presence of a warm-blooded mammal or bird. Other prey evidently is located by sight.

The jointed horny rattle on the tail can be vibrated rapidly to buzz, somewhat like a cicada. It is usually but not always sounded when the snake is approached. All snakes shed the outer horny covering of the skin at intervals. In other species this slips off the tapered tail. The end of a Rattlesnake's tail is blunt with a constriction. At molt the old horny covering at the end remains loosely attached to the new growth within. Successive molts (commonly 2 or 3 per year) result in a chain of loosely attached segments. The number of segments, if the first small "button" is present, indicates the number of molts, not years of age; commonly there are 8 to 10, exceptionally up to 22.

Mating occurs in the spring. The eggs remain in the female's body until the young are fully developed. They appear late in summer, 6–7 (1–14) in a brood, and are under 12 inches long when hatched.

The venom apparatus includes 2 long, sharp, hollow teeth or fangs (like hypodermic needles) hinged inside the roof of the mouth. A small duct from a poison gland connects to each fang. The venom serves to kill prey and to protect against enemies. In the presence of either the snake places the fore part of its body in an S-shaped curve, holds the tail vertically, and vibrates the rattle. To "strike" the mouth opens widely (nearly 180°), the fangs are erected, and the head lunges forward. The fangs penetrate the victim's flesh, the snake's lower jaw rises to grip, and venom is injected. Then the head is pulled backward, withdrawing the fangs. This all happens in an instant. A rattler rarely strikes more than half its total length, usually less, and seldom more than 12 inches above the ground. It cannot "jump" at prey or enemy. High leather boots usually are adequate protection against snake bite.

In the event someone is bitten: (1) Put the patient down and keep the part bitten absolutely quiet; (2) apply a tourniquet above the wound to limit the flow of blood and lymph toward the heart; release it for a few seconds every 15 or 20 minutes and then retighten; (3) send for a physician *at once;* (4) seek for a supply of antivenin; and (5) do not give any alcoholic stimulant. Employees of the Forest Service, National Park Service, or public utility corporations and many counselors at summer camps have instructions and sometimes materials to deal with Rattlesnake bite.

21. BIRDS

The feathers of birds insulate the body, provide the smooth exterior contours, and contain the pigments responsible for coloration. Large feathers of the wings make flight possible, and those of the tail serve for steering and gliding (fig. 18). These "warm-blooded" creatures have body temperatures higher than mammals, whereby their senses are acute and their reactions speedy. Most species are active by day.

The songs and calls, used for communication between individuals, are distinctive for each species. They are useful to students seeking to find and identify birds. Other useful features are the mannerisms in flight or perched, and the kind of environment occupied. Beginning students depend largely on coloration, but experienced persons use voice, mannerisms, and habitat more in identification. Success in observing birds requires that one be quiet and remain motionless or move slowly. "Squeaking" by noisily kissing one's hand is useful in attracting some species for closer view.

Bird species are segregated ecologically like other animals—on or near water, in grassland, shrubbery, etc. Those living in trees may be further divided as trunk-, twig-, or foliage-foragers (fig. 19). Locations for nests are similarly diversified.

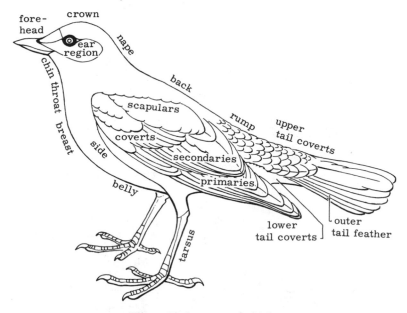

Figure 18. Structure of a bird.

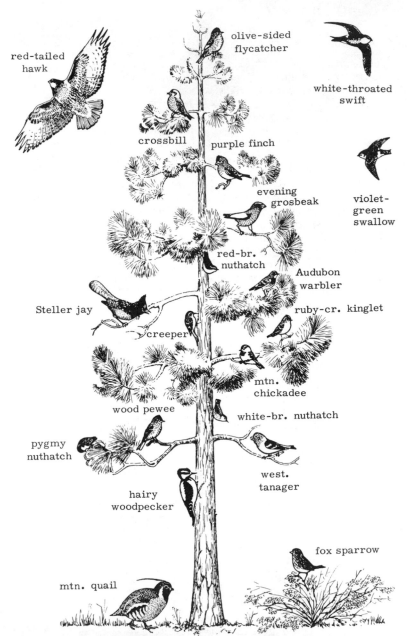

red-tailed hawk

olive-sided flycatcher

white-throated swift

crossbill

purple finch

evening grosbeak

violet-green swallow

red-br. nuthatch

Audubon warbler

Steller jay

ruby-cr. kinglet

creeper

mtn. chickadee

wood pewee

white-br. nuthatch

pygmy nuthatch

west. tanager

hairy woodpecker

fox sparrow

mtn. quail

Figure 19. Forage places (habitats) of some Sierran birds.

Abbreviations: T.L., total length; T., tail, base to tip; ♂, male; ♀, female; Ad., adult; Im., immature. Seasonal status: R., resident throughout year; V., visitant; S.V., summer visitant, arrives in spring, nests, and departs late summer or autumn; W.V., winter visitant, arrives in autumn and departs in spring; Tr., transient, present only while en route between summer and winter ranges; C.V., casual visitant, appearing irregularly (some lowland species visit higher altitudes after nesting).

B-1. Common Loon. *Gavia immer* (pl. 48). T.L. to 36"; size of small goose; head, neck, and back black, streaked and spotted with white; under parts white. VOICE. A long *oo-ah'-ii* and "laughter"-like notes; seldom heard in winter. DISTR. Rare V. on open waters.

The loon formerly nested and may still do so on a few lakes in the northern Sierra. In the water its body is low, mostly submerged. When frightened it dives instantly and can swim far under the surface. It winters on lowland waters and the seacoast.

B-2. Eared Grebe. *Podiceps caspicus.* T.L. 12"; size of small duck; body plump, neck and bill slender, tail not evident; above brownish black, below silvery white; a white patch on spread wing. Summer Ad.: Head and breast slate, a buffy tuft (ear) behind each eye, side of body chestnut. DISTR. S.V. to lakes on e. side from Mono Co. n.; visits lakes in Sierra.

Scattered flocks of this grebe appear in spring on Mono Lake. The birds sit low in the water with neck vertical and head horizontal; they dive at the least disturbance. Pairs later nest on other small lakes in northeastern California.

B-3. Pied-billed Grebe. *Podilymbus podiceps* (pl. 48). T.L. to 15"; smaller than coot (B-25). Ad. (breeding): Crown, hind neck, and back blackish, sides brownish, under parts mottled white, black patch on throat, bill pale, crossed with mid-band of black. Ad. (winter): Upper parts brown, no black on throat or bill. No white on wing. VOICE. A cuckoo-like *cuck-cuck-cuck . . . cow-cow;* alarm call, *toot, toot.* NEST. Near tules; a floating pile of decayed plants; eggs 5–8, dull bluish white, 1¾" x 1¼". DISTR. Occasional on quiet waters of lower altitudes.

When floating this little grebe shows a narrow head and thick arched neck. It lunges forward to dive but can disappear quietly by sinking. Its food includes small fishes and aquatic insects and plants.

B-4. White Pelican. *Pelecanus erythrorhynchus.* T.L. to 70", spread to 96"; huge, with large yellow bill and throat pouch; body all white, wing primaries black. DISTR. S.V. to Lake Tahoe and other lakes.

The pelican rides high in the water, its great bill held close to the breast. It fishes while floating by quick thrusts of the bill. When startled the bird rises noisily, striking the water with both wings and feet. Once aloft it alternates several slow wingbeats with a long glide. Flocks fly

Table 5. Sierra Birds Grouped by Environments

IN OPEN AIR	MARSHES	GRASSLAND
11. Turkey Vulture	8–10. Ducks	19. Marsh Hawk
15. Red-tailed Hawk	25. American Coot	21. Sparrow Hawk
16. Swainson Hawk	122. Yellow-headed	26. Killdeer
17. Golden Eagle	Blackbird	31. Mourning Dove
18. Bald Eagle	123. Red-winged	37. Burrowing Owl
42. Poorwill	Blackbird	49. Red-shafted
43. Common Night-	124. Tricolored	Flicker
hawk	Blackbird	60. Western Kingbird
44. White-throated	155. Song Sparrow	67. Horned Lark
Swift		74. Yellow-billed
68. Violet-green		Magpie
Swallow	STREAMSIDE PLANTS	76. Common Crow
69. Tree Swallow		95. American Robin
70. Barn Swallow	46. Rufous Hum-	98. Western Bluebird
71. Cliff Swallow	mingbird	99. Mtn. Bluebird
75. Raven	47. Calliope	105. Loggerhead
	Hummingbird	Shrike
OPEN WATER	53. Yellow-bellied	106. European
	Sapsucker	Starling
1. Common Loon	56. Downy Wood-	121. Western
2. Eared Grebe	pecker	Meadowlark
3. Pied-billed Grebe	64a. West. Flycatcher	126. Brewer Blackbird
4. White Pelican	64b. Traill Flycatcher	134. California Linnet
5. Double-crested	97. Swainson Thrush	143a. Savannah
Cormorant	109. Warbling Vireo	Sparrow
7. Canada Goose	112. Yellow Warbler	143b. Grasshopper
8–10. Ducks	116. Tolmie Warbler	Sparrow
20. Osprey	117. Yellowthroat	145. Lark Sparrow
25. American Coot	118. Yellow-breasted	
28. Wilson Phalarope	Chat	BRUSH OR CHAPARRAL
29. California Gull	119. Pileolated	
	Warbler	23. California Quail
WATER MARGINS	123. Red-winged	24. Mountain Quail
	Blackbird	32. Roadrunner
6. Great Blue Heron	125. Bullock Oriole	42. Poorwill
other herons	127. Brown-headed	61. Ash-throated
25. American Coot	Cowbird	Flycatcher
26. Killdeer	129. Black-headed	86. Wrentit
27. Spotted	Grosbeak	90. Bewick Wren
Sandpiper	130. Lazuli Bunting	94. Calif. Thrasher
48. Belted Kingfisher	138. Goldfinch	110. Orange-crowned
62. Black Phoebe	141. Rufous-sided	Warbler
87. Water Ouzel	Towhee	116. Tolmie Warbler
	151. White-crowned	140. Green-tailed
MARSHES	Sparrow	Towhee
	155. Song Sparrow	141. Rufous-sided
6. Great Blue Heron		Towhee
other herons		

Table 5. Sierra Birds Grouped by Environments (*Continued*)

BRUSH OR CHAPARRAL	OPEN WOODLAND	FOREST OR WOODS
146. Rufous-crowned Sparrow	149. Chipping Sparrow	108. Solitary Vireo
147a. Bell Sparrow		113. Audubon Warbler
151. White-crowned Sparrow	**FOREST OR WOODS**	114. Black-throated Gray Warbler
152. Golden-crowned Sparrow	12. Goshawk	115. Hermit Warbler
153. Fox Sparrow	13. Sharp-shinned Hawk	128. Western Tanager
	14. Cooper Hawk	129. Black-headed Grosbeak
OPEN WOODLAND	22. Dusky Grouse	131. Evening Grosbeak
31. Mourning Dove	30. Band-tailed Pigeon	132. Purple Finch
45. Anna Hummingbird	49. Red-s. Flicker	133. Cassin Finch
49. Red-s. Flicker	50. Pileated Woodpecker	135. Pine Grosbeak
51. California Woodpecker	53. Yellow-bellied Sapsucker	137. Pine Siskin
52. Lewis Woodpecker	54. Williamson Sapsucker	139. Red Crossbill
56. Downy Woodpecker	55. Hairy Woodpecker	148. Junco
57. Nuttall Woodpecker	58. White-headed Woodpecker	149. Chipping Sparrow
61. Ash-throated Flycatcher	59. Three-toed Woodpecker	
66. Wood Pewee	64. Small Flycatchers	**MEADOWS**
73. Scrub Jay	65. Olive-sided Flycatcher	21. Sparrow Hawk
74. Magpie	66. Wood Pewee	95. American Robin
76. Common Crow	72. Steller Jay	99. Mtn. Bluebird
80. Plain Titmouse	78. Clark Nutcracker	126. Brewer Blackbird
81. Common Bushtit	79. Mtn. Chickadee	133. Cassin Finch
82. White-breasted Nuthatch	82. White-breasted Nuthatch	151. White-crowned Sparrow
88. House Wren	83. Red-breasted Nuthatch	154. Lincoln Sparrow
93. Mockingbird	84. Pygmy Nuthatch	
95. American Robin	85. Brown Creeper	**ROCKY PLACES**
98. Western Bluebird	89. Winter Wren	78. Clark Nutcracker
101. Western Gnatcatcher	95. American Robin	91. Canyon Wren
104. Cedar Waxwing	96. Hermit Thrush	92. Rock Wren
107. Hutton Vireo	100. Townsend Solitaire	136. Gray-crowned Rosy Finch
111. Calaveras Warbler	102. Golden-crowned Kinglet	
125. Bullock Oriole	103. Ruby-crowned Kinglet	**SAGEBRUSH**
134. California Linnet		63. Say Phoebe
138. Goldfinch		64e. Gray Flycatcher
142. Brown Towhee		74. Black-b. Magpie
		77. Piñon Jay
		144. Vesper Sparrow
		147b. Sage Sparrow
		150. Brewer Sparrow

in line or irregular V-formation, spiraling to rise over a mountain. Those nesting on lakes in Nevada occasionally appear on large Sierran waters.

B-5. Double-crested Cormorant. *Phalacrocorax auritus.* T.L. to 36″; bill, head, neck, and body slender; plumage black; small throat pouch orange; bill yellow-sided. DISTR. Occasional S.V. on n. Sierran lakes.

On the water the fish-seeking cormorant rides low, its neck upright and the bill tilted slightly upward. In flight the wings beat rapidly, the tail is evident, and the neck slants upward. Cormorants from nesting colonies on Great Basin lakes appear, mostly singly, on some Sierran waters.

B-6. Great Blue Heron. *Ardea herodias* (pl. 48). Ht. about 48″, spread to 72″; head white on top, black on sides; back, wings, and tail grayish blue; ends of wings black; neck pale gray; under parts streaked black and white; legs long and bare. VOICE. A loud, harsh croak, repeated. NEST. Mostly in colonies; a crude platform of sticks, usually high in an open tree near water; eggs 3–6, dull greenish blue, 2½″–1⅞″. DISTR. Common R. in Great Valley and lower open foothills; C.V. (except winter) higher in Sierra.

In flight the blue color, slow flapping of the large broad wings, and trailing long legs make identification of this heron easy. Either standing or flying the neck is crooked (whereas that of a crane is extended). The Great Blue may appear along any open water, marsh, or meadow, wading in the shallows or stalking slowly over grassland in search of food. The slender bill, 4½ to 6 inches long, is an effective pincer, serving to grasp a fish in water, a frog on the bank, or even a mouse in dry grassland—all of which serve as food.

Several other herons may be found in the margins of the Sierra. The small Green Heron (*Butorides virescens;* T.L. 16″–18″) lives and nests in willow thickets bordering slow-moving west slope streams of the foothill region. The head is black-topped, the back and wings grayish green, the neck and shoulders reddish brown, and the under surface grayish.

The Black-crowned Night Heron (*Nycticorax nycticorax;* T.L. 23″– 26″) roosts by day in dense streamside thickets at the edge of the Great Valley and hunts after dark, when its coarse *squawk* may often be heard. Two or 3 slender white plumes extend from the black head to the mid-back, the wings and body are light gray, and the under parts whitish.

The American Bittern (*Botarus lentiginosus;* ht. 22″) is less than half the size of the Great Blue Heron. Its plumage is streaked with light and dark brown, resembling dead stems of tules among which the bird commonly hides. The species has nested at June Lake and other waters bordered by thickets of cat-tails or tules.

1.Common Loon

3.Pied-billed Grebe

6.Great Blue Heron

7. Canada Goose

8. Mallard

9.Wood Duck

10.Common Merganser

Plate 48. Birds   255

B-7. Canada Goose. *Branta canadensis* (pl. 48). T.L. 35″–43″; head and neck black with broad white chin band; back brown, under surface gray, tail black, area under tail white. VOICE. A deep 2-part *ka-honk*. NEST. On ground (some on hay piles), of grass and twigs lined with down; eggs 4–10, dull white, 3⅜″ x 2¼″. DISTR. Sparse S.V. on e. slope from June Lake n.; W.V. in Great Valley.

Wild geese are wary at all seasons, whether floating on water or standing or foraging on shore. This "honker" formerly nested commonly on many east side lakes from Tahoe northward, and some may still do so. The young gray goslings swim under care of the parents until able to fly. By the end of summer adults and immatures band together and fly in V-shaped flocks. In winter, geese of this and other species live on grasslands and grainfields of the Sacramento Valley.

B-8. Mallard. *Anas platyrhynchos* (pl. 48). T.L. 20″–25″; like domestic duck but smaller; legs and feet orange-red; wing patch blue, edged with white. Ad. ♂ : Head and neck glossy green with narrow white neck ring, breast chestnut, back and belly pale gray, tail with up-curled feathers, bill greenish yellow. Ad. ♀ : Mottled brown, lighter below, feathers pale-edged; a dark line through eye; bill orange and dusky. VOICE. Of ♀ loud *quack, quack . . .* ; ♂ softer-voiced. NEST. On ground near water (or on dry land), of grasses, reeds, and down; eggs 8–12, greenish or grayish buff, 2¼″ x 1⅝″. DISTR. C.V. on quiet waters on both sides of Sierra and on lakes at middle altitudes.

The common Mallard may appear at times on almost any lake or smooth stream, particularly those margined with aquatic plants. Some of the birds probably nest occasionally in secluded sites on such waters on either side of the mountains. Like other river ducks it is a surface feeder and never dives; often it "tips up" to reach plants under shallow water.

B-9. Wood Duck. *Aix sponsa* (pl. 48). T.L. 17″–20″. Ad. ♂ : Top of head shiny green with violet crest, patch at eye and chin white, back brown, wings black, purple, and white, breast chestnut, under parts white. Ad. ♀ : Eye patch white, upper parts and breast brown, throat and belly white. VOICE of ♀ *wher-eek*. NEST. In tree hole at 6–30 ft., lined with down; eggs 10–15, ivory, 2″ x 1½″. DISTR. Great Valley and Foothill belt along quiet tree-bordered waters.

Unlike its relatives, the Wood Duck lives at all times on ponds or slow-moving streams that are well screened or arched over by willows, cottonwoods, oaks, and waterside vines where it is hidden from view. It nests in a rotted-out cavity or flicker hole in a tree, usually one over water. The young, some hours or a day after hatching, flutter down and join the mother on the water. Acorns are commonly used for food. Winter flocks of 15 or more Wood Ducks formerly lived on beaver ponds.

B-10. Common Merganser. *Mergus merganser* (pl. 48). T.L. 21"–27"; bill long, slender, reddish; back of head with short crest; feet reddish. Ad. ♂: Head and neck glossy green, upper back black, lower back and tail gray, neck, much of wings, and under surface white. Ad. ♀ and Im.: Head and neck reddish brown, but throat white, back and tail gray, wings black with white patch, under parts white. NEST. In hollow tree or on ground, lined with grasses, roots, and down; eggs 6–17, ivory, 2½" x 1¾". DISTR. S.V. in Yellow Pine and Lodgepole–fir belts, on forest-margined lakes or swift streams from upper Kern R. n.

This fish duck may be expected in summer on the more remote waters. The slender bill bears horny "teeth" and a hooked tip, useful for catching the various kinds of fishes taken for food. It dives and swims readily under the surface when searching for prey. Over the years broods of mergansers have been reported at many places in the Sierra. Trout fishermen consider the bird a competitor, but its numbers are small and the total effect is slight.

The small Harlequin Duck (*Histrionicus histrionicus*) has nested rarely on swift streams of the Yellow Pine belt and higher from Tuolumne to Madera County. The adult male is dark slate blue with white patches on head, body, and wings and a white collar; the female is dull dark brown with a white patch on each cheek and ear region. The species winters on the central California seacoast.

Other ducks that may be seen at times on lakes and reservoirs are the Bald-pate (top of head white in ♂), Pintail (long-necked), Shoveler or Spoonbill (broad-billed), and either of 2 small Teals, the Cinnamon (♂ chestnut brown) and Green-winged (♂ with green wing band).

B-11. Turkey Vulture. *Cathartes aura* (pl. 49). T.L. 30", T. 12", spread 72"; plumage dull black, lower surface of hinder part of wings grayish; head naked, red. NEST. In hole of cliff, no lining; eggs 2, white, brown-blotched, 3" x 2". DISTR. Common in Great Valley and Foothill belt, mostly as S.V.

Turkey "buzzards" soar overhead with their large wings tilted upward. Whenever the air is warm they circle and spiral on upwelling currents with little change in the set of wings or tail. The individuals usually are spaced out, perhaps one per square mile, scanning the ground for any dead animals—ground squirrel, rabbit, horse, or cow. When one sees such food it glides down, rocking sideways while descending. Other vultures are attracted by this signal and soon converge toward the site. A large carcass may bring a dozen or more to tear off and devour the carrion. In morning and evening and on dull days the buzzards perch on open trees in hunched posture with the head between the shoulders. During migration they often are in loose flocks.

The huge California Condor (*Gymnogyps californianus*) formerly occurred sparingly in the Sequoia National Park region. Its wings have large white areas below at the front; the spread is nearly 10 feet.

12. Goshawk

11. Turkey Vulture

13. Sharp-shinned Hawk

14. Cooper Hawk

15. Red-tailed Hawk

16. Swainson Hawk

258

Plate 49. Birds

B-12. Goshawk. *Astur atricapillus* (pl. 49). T.L. 22″, T. 10″–12″; size of Red-tailed Hawk (B-15) but more slender, wings shorter, rounded, tail longer, narrower. Ad.: Above dark slate, below white with fine black cross-bars. Im.: Above dark brown, below white with dark brown streaks. VOICE. Loud, short *kak, kak, kak,* or *kee-ar.* NEST. In trees at 20–60 ft., a shallow twig platform; eggs 3–4, bluish white, 2⅜″ x 1¾″. DISTR. Rare R. in Lodge-pole–fir belt forest.

The three speedy "bullet" or bird hawks are the large Goshawk, medium Cooper Hawk, and small Sharp-shinned Hawk; all have broad rounded wings and narrow tails. As in other hawks and eagles, fe-males are larger than males. In the open these hawks alternate a few quick wing strokes with short circling flight, but when pursuing prey they dart swiftly through trees and shrubbery. The Goshawk of the fir belt catches some grouse, other birds, squirrels, and chipmunks. At lower elevations in winter it may kill farm poultry. Bird victims are plucked before being eaten.

B-13. Sharp-shinned Hawk. *Accipiter striatulus* (pl. 49). T.L. 10″–14″, T. 6″–8¾″; size between robin and pigeon; spread wings rounded, tail nar-row, square-ended, crossbarred above, grayish beneath. Ad.: Above dark bluish gray, below finely crossbarred with white and dark. Im.: Above brown, below white with brown streaks. VOICE (near nest). A high *kee-ki-ki.* NEST. In trees at 10–40 ft., a low platform of twigs; eggs 4–5, bluish white, brown-blotched, 1½″ x 1¼″. DISTR. S.V. in Yellow Pine and Lodgepole–fir belts; W.V. below heavy snow; in forest or amid trees.

If the little Sharp-shin chances on a group of small birds feeding and chattering in shrubbery, they immediately "freeze" motionless and silent, the better to escape capture, although one may be taken. The prey is usually of linnet or warbler size but occasionally a blue jay is caught.

B-14. Cooper Hawk. *Accipiter cooperi* (pl. 49). T.L. 14″–20″, T. 8″–9½″; slightly smaller than crow; resembles Sharp-shinned Hawk, about twice the bulk, and tail rounded at end. VOICE. Adult, a harsh *kluk, kluk, kluk;* a clear *swēē′-ew;* of young, *quick, quick, quick.* . . . NEST. A stick platform well up in trees; eggs 4–5, bluish white, buff-spotted, 2″ x 1½″. DISTR. R. mostly in Foothill and Yellow Pine belts, in open woodland, often near streams.

This mid-sized "bird hawk" is marked by its round-ended tail. It circles in the open more than the Sharp-shin, yet can be secretive. Like other hawks, and owls, it tears and swallows large pieces of prey. After digestion of a meal, the bones, feathers, and hair are formed into a pellet and regurgitated. Pellets from below a nest in Yosemite Valley had remains of chipmunk, red-shafted flicker, Steller jay, robin, tanager, warblers, and towhees.

B-15. Red-tailed Hawk. *Buteo jamaicensis* (pl. 49). T.L. 19″–25″, T. 8½″–10½″, spread 48″–56″; size of Turkey Vulture (B-11); wings broad, tail broad, short, fan-shaped in flight. Above dark brown, tail bright reddish in adults; below dark brown to white in different individuals. VOICE. A shrill long whistle, *squee-oo*. NEST. A bulky twig platform well up in trees or on cliffs; eggs 2–3, dull white, brown-spotted, 2⅜" x 1⅞". DISTR. R. over most of Sierra and margins, in summer up to 12000 ft.

Singly or in pairs, Red-tails circle and glide high in open air as they watch for squirrels or rabbits on the ground. When prey is sighted, the hawk swoops and strikes with its large sharp claws. The larger animals are torn apart and eaten where killed, but smaller ones are carried off to a tree perch. Like other large flesh-eating birds, a Red-tail may gorge a large meal that will suffice for several days. When not hunting, the hawk will perch high in a dead or live tree where it has a wide view. If disturbed it leaps off, beats strongly with the big wings, and soon begins to soar. Hunters mistakenly call this the "chicken hawk" and shoot it on sight, but the species is highly beneficial.

B-16. Swainson Hawk. *Buteo swainsoni* (pl. 49). T.L. 20"–22", T. 8½"–10", spread to 56"; resembles Red-tailed Hawk but slightly smaller, chin whitish, breast often dark, wings more pointed, their undersides pale at front and dark at rear, tail never red. VOICE. Like Red-tail's but clearer, prolonged. NEST. A stick platform in trees; eggs 2–4, bluish or greenish white, brown-spotted, 2¼" x 1¾". DISTR. Sparse S.V. in Foothill belt and on plains e. of Sierra; on grasslands near scattered trees; visits high mountain meadows in late summer.

This migrant soaring hawk, once common on open lands bordering the Sierra, has declined in numbers. It arrives in March and April and nests in lowland sites. Then some individuals move to mountain meadows before the hawks, often in open flocks, go south out of California in September and October. Grasshoppers and small rodents are the chief food.

B-17. Golden Eagle. *Aquila chrysaetos* (pl. 50). T.L. 30"–40", T. 14"–15", spread 80"–90"; plumage dark brown, paler (golden brown) on head; base of tail below and patch on outer part of wing whitish (except old Ad.). VOICE. A single loud cry, sometimes repeated. NEST. High in large trees or on cliffs, a large pile of sticks and twigs, lined with grass; eggs 2, dull creamy white with brown spots, 2⅞" x 2¼". DISTR. R. in Foothill and Yellow Pine belts of w. slope; C.V. in summer up to 13000 ft., and along e. slope; over hills and grasslands.

The Golden Eagle of the hills and mountains exceeds all other resident Sierran birds in size. It soars skillfully with the wings stretched horizontally and at times goes so high as to become a mere speck in the sky despite its 7-foot spread. More commonly it nests in the foothills but some occupy crags in higher parts of the southern Sierra. Its principal food is like that of the buteo hawks—ground squirrels and rabbits. Many persons believe this eagle is powerful enough to kill and carry lambs of domestic sheep, but evidence is scant or none. There

17.
Golden Eagle

19. Marsh Hawk

21. Sparrow Hawk

18. Bald Eagle

20. Osprey

Plate 50. Birds

261

are several reports from Sequoia National Park of efforts by eagles to take young deer fawns and one instance of an eagle actually carrying a very young one.

B-18. Bald Eagle. *Haliaetus leucocephalus* (pl. 50). T.L. 31″–40″, T. 12″–15″, spread to 96″; body blackish, head and tail white in adults. DISTR. Uncommon V. or migrant to large lakes.

The big white-headed eagle, emblem of the United States, lives about lakes and large rivers and is a fishing bird. It has nested in high trees about some lakes in northeastern California and may still do so. Individuals occasionally are seen over some of the bigger open Sierran waters.

B-19. Marsh Hawk. *Circus cyaneus* (pl. 50). T.L. 18″–24″, T. 8¾″–10½″; a moderately small hawk with slender crossbarred tail and narrow but round-ended wings; rump white. Ad. ♂ : Pale bluish gray above, white below. Ad. ♀ and Im.: Dark brown above, paler and streaked below. NEST. On ground, of dried grasses, etc.; eggs 5, dull bluish white, 1¾″ x 1⅜″. DISTR. R. in Great Valley and lower w. slope; C.V. on e. side; lives over marshes and grasslands.

The Marsh Hawk alternates a few wingbeats with a short glide but does not circle. Often it skims close over grassland with the wings tilted slightly upward, tilting and turning as it searches for the small rodents and insects sought for food.

B-20. Osprey. *Pandion haliaetus* (pl. 50). T.L. 21″–25″, T. 7″–10″, spread to 65″, long-winged; above blackish brown, most of head and under surface whitish; dark "wrist" spot on each wing, tail black-ended. VOICE. A shrill *kee, kee* and a low *kak, kak*. NEST. Near water in broken-topped trees at up to 100 ft., of large sticks, often bulky; eggs 3, creamy with brown blotches, 2⅜″ x 1¾″. DISTR. C.V. on waters of n. Sierra.

The "fish hawk" lives about water. In flight the front edge of each wing is slightly bent. When seeking food the bird often hovers over the water with feet dangling, then plunges feet first to capture fish. It has nested commonly at Eagle Lake east of Mt. Lassen.

B-21. Sparrow Hawk. *Falco sparverius* (pl. 50). T.L. 9″–12″, T. 4¼″–5¼″; our smallest hawk, body slightly larger than robin; wings pointed and long, tail slender; 2 vertical black bars on side of head below eye, top of head, back, and most of tail rusty red, under surface white. Ad. ♂ : Wings blue at base, tail with one black band and white tip. Ad. ♀ : Wings rusty brown, tail with several narrow black bars. VOICE. A shrill *kill-y kill-y*, repeated. NEST. In holes in trees or rock ledges; eggs 4–5, creamy, brown-dotted, 1⅜″ x 1⅛″. DISTR. R., commonest in Great Valley but in summer up into Subalpine belt, chiefly about grasslands and meadows.

Misnamed "Sparrow" Hawk, this little falcon is the smallest, commonest, and least wary of all our hawks. It perches on poles, wires, or open trees near grasslands. In the air its flight is swift, with many quick turns, and the bird often hovers for several seconds on rapidly beating wings. At nesting time it sometimes goes high in the air and then pitches down on set wings until near the ground. Occasionally a pair will pester a shrike or large hawk, perhaps in defense of their forage area. Small rodents and grasshoppers are the principal food; few small birds are eaten.

B-22. Dusky or Blue Grouse. *Dendragapus obscurus* (pl. 51). T.L. 20″–23″, T. 8″; form fowl-like, larger than quail; plumage dark bluish gray with fine lighter markings; tail square-ended with pale band across dark tip. VOICE. Of ♂ in nesting season a deep wooden *unt, wunt, wunt, tu-wunt, wunt, wunt;* ♀ clucks at chicks, alarm *kuk, kuk.* NEST. On ground, a slight depression lined slightly with grasses, leaves, and feathers; eggs 7–10, pinkish buff, brown-spotted, 1⅞″ x 1⅜″. DISTR. R. mostly in Lodgepole–fir and upper Yellow Pine belts, among conifers.

This grouse lives year-long in the conifer forests, where its main food, needle tips of pines and firs, is always available. The dense body plumage and feathered legs protect against the cold of winter. In spring and early summer males perch solitarily 60 feet or more up on tree limbs and hoot at short intervals for hours; inflated neck sacs, covered by bare yellow skin, serve as resonators to make the sound far-carrying. The females, on the ground, incubate and bring off their chick-like broods by June or early July. Males then in small groups move upslope, followed later by the hens and young. The summer diet includes several kinds of berries. All usually return before winter. Goshawks and martens are their chief enemies.

B-23. California Quail. *Lophortyx californica* (pl. 51). T.L. 9½″–11″, T. 4½″; crown of head with short black top-knot curving forward; body plump; back tail and wings plain grayish brown, breast clear blue-gray, belly white or buff with patch of chestnut, sides cross-marked with black; face of ♂ black, rimmed with white. VOICE. Assembly call, "come-right′-here"; disturbance call an explosive *whit, whit,* repeated; of lone male, a loud *kyark.* NEST. On ground in slight depression with sparse grass lining; eggs 12–16, ivory with light brown spots, 1¼″ x 1⁵⁄₁₆″. DISTR. Common R. of Great Valley and Foothill belt in streamside thickets or under chaparral.

Interrupted shrubby cover, margined by scattered herbaceous plants, is preferred habitat for this common lowland quail. Only in nesting season are the birds in pairs, the male on guard while the female incubates. The downy chicks leave the nest at once, in care of both parents, and within 2 weeks are fledged enough to fly. Later in summer family groups merge into larger flocks that forage and live together, roosting at night in oaks or other dense-foliaged trees or shrubs. Quail run rapidly on the ground. When frightened they flush with whirring wings and sail into escape cover. Their food is mostly of seeds and some leafy materials with a few berries and insects. Wildcats, foxes, coyotes, and Cooper Hawks are common enemies.

22. Dusky Grouse

24. Mountain Quail

23. California Quail

25. Amer. Coot

26. Killdeer

29. California Gull

27. Spotted Sandpiper

264

Plate 51. Birds

B-24. Mountain Quail. *Oreortyx picta* (pl. 51). T.L. 10½″–12″, T. 3″–3¼″; a long slender black plume on head; throat and side of head chestnut; streak below eye white; head, upper back, and breast bluish gray; rest of back, tail, and wings brown; sides chestnut with white and black bars; belly whitish. VOICE. Of ♂ a single *quēē-ark,* at intervals; alarm call *ca-ca-ca-ca,* or *gup-gup,* repeated. NEST. On ground under brush, lined with pine needles or grasses; eggs 10–12, buff, no spots, 1⅜″ x 1″. DISTR. R. in Yellow Pine and Lodgepole–fir belts of w. slope; in latter belt and below on e. slope; on brushy areas in scattered forest.

The picturesque Mountain Quail is larger but less common than its lowland relative and not always easy to find or see. The birds forage quietly in sheltered places and when disturbed are apt to run and hide rather than flying. Pairing begins by early April, and the nesting season is from mid-May into July. When downy broods are out the parents utter various low clucking and whining notes and some harsher calls. A few insects are eaten early in summer, but seeds of grasses and herbs and berries of various shrubs are the staple foods. By early autumn the quail are in small flocks and begin to move downslope, to winter below the level of heavy snow.

B-25. American Coot. *Fulica americana* (pl. 51). T.L. 13″–16″, size of small duck; bill narrow, white; front toes lobed; head and neck black, rest of body dark slate, a white V under tail. VOICE. An explosive *pulque, pulque,* repeated; also a harsh *kerk.* NEST. In marshes, often exposed, a pile of tules or sedges; eggs 8–12, buff with dark dots, 1⅞″ x 1¼″. DISTR. R. on slower waters of Foothill belt, C.V. elsewhere.

The familiar dark-colored Mud Hen may appear on any quiet lowland stream or pond margined with aquatic vegetation. Afloat, its head bobs fore-and-aft in keeping with strokes of the lobed feet. If disturbed it paddles toward open water. When forced to fly it "runs" on the surface with much splashing by both wings and feet before rising into the air. Coots eat both plant and animal materials. They variously reach for plants on the water surface, dive for deeper morsels, or go ashore to nip off vegetation there. The downy young take to the water soon after hatching; they are black with patches of crinkly hairlike feathers of bright orange. In winter Coots often live in large flocks.

B-26. Killdeer. *Charadrius vociferus* (pl. 51). T.L. 9½″–10½″, T. 3½″–4″; a plover, size of robin; above pale brown, rump tawny, forehead and under surface white, two black bands on breast. VOICE. A loud shrill *kill-dee,* often repeated. NEST. On dry ground or gravel, sometimes near water, shallow, bare or scantily lined; eggs 4, pear-shaped, buff, dark-blotched, 1⁷⁄₁₆″ x 1″. DISTR. Common R. in Great Valley and Foothill belt; C.V. to mountain meadows and e. slope; on wet grasslands and water margins.

Singly or in small groups the Killdeer is the most widespread shorebird or wader. It runs rapidly, bobbing upwards at frequent intervals. When startled it flies off to circle and call noisily. The speckled eggs and scant nest lining are difficult to see against most backgrounds. The same is true of the downy chicks marked with broken patterns of black, brown, and white. A parent bird when approached will run quietly away from nest or young before flying. Killdeers eat insects and small aquatic animals.

B-27. Spotted Sandpiper. *Actitis macularia* (pl. 51). T.L. 7″–8″; smaller than robin; above pale brown, below white with round black spots in summer; spread wing shows a narrow white band; tail short. VOICE. A clear *peet-tweet-tweet*. NEST. On wet meadow or gravel, scant lining of grasses or none; eggs 4, pear-shaped, buff, darkly blotched, 1¼″ x ⅞″. DISTR. S.V. at any altitude on open sandy or pebbly lake or stream shores.

The pale brown and white body, inch-long bill, and incessant bobbing of the hind parts mark this little freshwater sandpiper. As it walks the head moves fore-and-aft in unison with the feet. On taking to flight it makes an arc over the water to some more distant shore; after the first few strokes the wings are held spread, curving downward and moving only at the tips. The bird forages in the shallows or on the shore close to water, picking up small aquatic animals or insects for food. It is seen singly or in pairs and does not flock.

B-28. Wilson Phalarope. *Steganopus tricolor*. T.L. 8¼″–10″; size of robin, but head, neck, and bill slender. Ad. ♀ (spring): Top of head, hind neck, and back pale gray, sides of head and neck black and cinnamon, base of tail white, breast tawny, chin and belly white. Ad. ♂ (spring): Duller, no cinnamon. Ad. and Im. (fall): Upper surface pale gray. NEST. In marsh or grass, shallow, sparse grass lining; eggs 4, pear-shaped, buff with dark blotches, 1¼″ x 1⁵⁄₁₆″. DISTR. S.V. (May-late Sept.) along e. base of Sierra s. to Bishop, in marshes and on lakes.

In spring and autumn many of these small slender birds appear on Mono Lake. They forage along the shore or ride on the water and turn from side to side, using the needle-like bill to pick food from the surface. This species nests beside lakes of the Great Basin. Among phalaropes the differences between sexes are reversed. The female is larger and brighter-colored than the male—who incubates the eggs.

Besides the shorebirds described (nos. 26–28) other species regularly pass in migration both east and west of the mountains—snipe, sandpipers, avocets, and stilts—and some visit waters in the Sierra.

B-29. California Gull. *Larus californicus* (pl. 51). T.L. 20″–23″. A medium-sized gull. Ad.: Head, neck, tail, and under surface white, back pale gray, wings black-ended; bill yellow, dark-banded near tip, with orange spot on lower mandible (jaw); legs and feet greenish yellow. Im.: Mixed dark and light brown. VOICE. A high *kyarr*, or repeated *kee-kee-kee*. NEST. On ground of islands in lakes, scant lining of grasses, twigs, or feathers; eggs 3, buff-gray, blotched with dark brown, 2⅝″ x 1¾″. DISTR. Common S.V. on Mono Lake; C.V. to lakes in n. Sierra.

Great Basin lakes are the summer home of the California Gull. In former years up to 1000 pairs nested on Paoha Island in Mono Lake, and there were other large colonies on lakes in Nevada and Utah. Adults often visit Lake Tahoe (perhaps from Pyramid Lake), and a few go less often to other Sierran lakes, even at 10000 feet. On the water the gull rides high, with wing tips crossed over the back; in the air the long pointed wings sweep in graceful arcs or are spread as the bird circles or glides. The similar-appearing Ring-billed Gull (with yellow legs) occasionally visits mountain lakes.

Terns may appear on lakes of the northern Sierra in summer. They are more slender than gulls with long narrow wings and forked tails. Terns fly gracefully, change direction quickly, often hover, and plunge into the water to catch small fishes. The Forster Tern (*Sterna forsteri;* T.L. 14″–15″) is white with a black crown and pale gray back and wings. The smaller Black Tern (*Chlidonias niger;* T.L. 10″) is black on the head, neck, and under surface and dark ashy gray on the back, wings, and tail.

B-30. Band-tailed Pigeon. *Columba fasciata* (pl. 53). T.L. 15″–16″, T. 6″–6½″; size and form of domestic pigeon; above bluish gray, below pinkish brown; tail with dark band across middle, square-ended; back of neck with white ring. VOICE. A deep *wuh'-woo,* repeated. NEST. Usually in oaks at 8–40 ft.; a loose, bulky stick platform; eggs 1, seldom 2, pointed, white, 1½″ × 1⅛″. DISTR. Common S.V. in Yellow Pine belt and W.V. in Foothill belt, occasionally higher, mostly in or near oaks.

Our native pigeon of the West usually lives in flocks. Pairs often nest close together and join others while feeding. Its general behavior is much like that of the domestic bird, clapping the wings when starting to fly and cooing intermittently while perched. Flocks tend to remain hidden in foliage but may sun themselves on bare branches or rocks. Acorns are staple food, together with berries of manzanita, toyon, choke-cherry and coffeeberry; grain in fields is eaten when available. The Band-tail has nested from Plumas County to Tulare County.

B-31. Mourning Dove. *Zenaidura macroura* (pl. 53). T.L. 11″–13″, T. 5¾″–6½″; smaller than domestic pigeon; above olive-brown, below pale brown, breast pink, end of tail V-shaped and white-edged. VOICE. A mellow, *ah-coo', roo, coo.* NEST. On tree branch, bush, or ground, a crude twig platform; eggs 2, white, 1⅛″ x ¾″. DISTR. Common R. in Great Valley and Foothill belt, in summer on e. slope and occasionally at higher elevations; in open woodland or chaparral mixed with grassland.

Mourning Doves in swift whistling flight are common over the western lowlands and foothills. They perch on fences, overhead wires, or open-branched trees, feed on the ground, and seek drinking water morning and evening. When walking their gait is slightly angular and the head bobs to and fro with each step. The food is entirely of seeds gleaned on the ground. Doves nest through a long season, from March to July or later. The young are fed a special material (pigeon milk) formed in the parent's gullet. Through much of the year the birds are in pairs, but in winter they live in loose flocks ranging widely in search of food.

B-32. Roadrunner. *Geococcyx californianus* (pl. 53). T.L. 20"–24", T. 11½"–12", bill 1¾"–2"; body size of small chicken but tail very long; legs and feet stout; plumage pale brown, feathers of back dark-centered, tail mostly black with white spot at end of each feather, head blackish with a slight crest. VOICE. Series of low notes descending in pitch, *cŏŏ, cŏŏ, cŏŏ,* . . . ; bill is clicked when excited. NEST. In bushes or low trees, a stick platform; eggs 3–5, white, 1½" x 1⅛". DISTR. Sparse R. in Great Valley (near river bottom thickets) and Foothill belt (in open chaparral).

The running "ground cuckoo" of the arid West must be sought around dry shrubby cover of the foothills or valley edges. When flushed it will run, then hop or fly to a low perch and stand while raising and lowering both the head crest and tail. It is a skillful, aggressive hunter and has a varied diet—lizards, snakes, tarantulas, crickets, grasshoppers, mice, and small birds.

B-33. Barn Owl. *Tyto alba* (pl. 52). A medium-sized owl, T.L. 15" or more, spread 45 inches; face heart-shaped, no ear tufts, eyes small, dark; upper surface light golden brown, under surface white, face white, rimmed with brown. VOICE. A single long rasping *sksch;* also a rapid *click, click, click,* . . . . NEST. In hole of tree, cliff, or earth bank, unlined; eggs 5–7, white, 1¾" x 1¼". DISTR. R. on w. slope from Great Valley into foothills and edge of Yellow Pine belt wherever roosting shelter and grasslands are present.

Originally this owl roosted and nested in cavities of cliffs, gullies, or large trees. Now it also uses barns, attics, and old-fashioned steeples. Dense-foliaged trees often serve for daytime shelter. If disturbed it will fly off, even in strong sunlight, and find another retreat. The flight of this and other owls is silent because of the very soft plumage. At dusk the Barn Owl goes hunting over grasslands or alfalfa fields inhabited by its prey—small rodents. These are grasped and killed by the sharp claws, torn into a few small pieces, and swallowed. Digestion removes the flesh, and then the residue of hair and bones is regurgitated as an oblong pellet. By gathering pellets below a roost and identifying their contents (skulls, teeth, and bones) we learn the owl's diet. Besides small mice, many pocket gophers are taken. Sometimes these are almost the only rodents captured, a help to farmers and gardeners. Evidently gophers are seized as they forage outside the burrows after dark. The names monkey-faced owl and golden owl sometimes are used for this species because of the shape of its face and color of plumage.

36. Pygmy Owl

34.
Screech Owl

41. Saw-whet Owl

40.
Long-eared Owl

35.
Great
Horned
Owl

33.
Barn Owl

38. Spotted Owl

39. Great Gray Owl

Allan Brooks.

37. Burrowing Owl

Plate 52. Birds   269

B-34. Screech Owl. *Otus asio* (pl. 52). Small, T.L. 9″. Head flat-topped, with ear tufts; plumage streaked with dark and light gray, resembling oak tree bark, eyes yellow. VOICE. Low-toned mellow quavering notes in rapid series; single clucking notes when adults and young forage together. NEST. In tree cavities; eggs 4–5, white, 1⅜″ x 1¼″. DISTR. R. in Foothill belt, especially amid oaks or river bottom trees.

The quavering call of this small owl is a characteristic night sound in the foothill oak region. In the Sierra it seems less common than elsewhere in California. Its food is largely of insects.

B-35. Great Horned Owl. *Bubo virginianus* (pl. 52). Large, T.L. to 20″, spread to 52″; head flat-topped with large ear tufts, eyes yellow; plumage mixed dark and light brown, back streaked, under surface barred, throat whitish. VOICE. A deep *whuh-whoo, whoo-whoo.* NEST. In hole in cliff or deserted nest of large hawk, crow, or magpie; eggs 2–3, white, 2⅛″ x 1¾″. DISTR. R. on both slopes up to Subalpine belt; in woods.

From dusk until dawn the deep hooting of this owl may be heard wherever there are open woods or streamside timber, except in the higher altitudes. As dusk approaches it perches well up on a dead or open-topped tree to watch and listen for prey. Each individual has a territory over which it presides and hunts, excluding others of its own sex and species; hooting evidently helps to define this area. Calling may begin by 4:30 P.M. in December but not until 7 P.M. or later in midsummer, and may also be heard during a day of heavy clouds. As dawn approaches the owl seeks a dense-foliaged tree as daytime shelter. Rabbits, wood rats, some lesser rodents, and a few birds, including smaller owls, are taken as food.

B-36. Pygmy Owl. *Glaucidium gnoma* (pl. 52). Smallest Sierran owl, T.L. to 7″, spread 14½″; head round (no tufts), eyes yellow; plumage grayish brown above with small white spots, under surface white with blackish streaks. VOICE. A single mellow *whoot,* repeated at intervals; a long trill followed by hoots: *too-too-too . . . too-too-whoot-whoot.* NEST. At 6–75 ft. usually in old woodpecker holes near meadows; eggs 3–4, white, 1⅜″ x 1″. DISTR. R. in Yellow Pine belt of w. slope.

Unlike most other owls, the Pygmy calls and is active by day. It lives mainly amid the denser conifers, where it can hide when not foraging. Small birds recognize this owl as an enemy; when one is located they congregate and flutter, uttering distress notes. Once in winter 15 ruby-crowned kinglets and 2 plain titmice were about one owl, and again 50 juncos were similarly engaged. A person's whistled imitation of the owl's voice may attract a Pygmy—and also small birds. The young are fed lizards, plucked small birds, and mice; later they catch grasshoppers. Adults take chipmunks and lesser rodents, and birds in summer. After a meal the owl may perch high in the open while grooming.

B-37. Burrowing Owl. *Speotyto cunicularia* (pl. 52). Small; T.L. 9"–11", T. to 3½"; head rounded, no ear tufts; legs long; plumage mixed light brown and white; eyes yellow. VOICE. A mellow *cuck-oo,* repeated at dusk in spring. NEST. In burrow of ground squirrel or badger; eggs 6–11, white, 1¼" x 1". DISTR. R. in Great Valley or foothills and Great Basin, in flat or rolling grasslands.

The pale, round-headed "billy owl" or "ground owl" may be seen by day on level or rolling grassy areas, standing near the mammal burrow it uses for shelter, or sometimes on a nearby fence post. It bobs down and up at intervals and may give the soft two-syllabled call. Young in the nest utter a rasping hiss, remindful of the rattle-snake's buzz. The food is mainly of insects, but includes mammals, small reptiles, toads, and birds. Some insects are caught while flying at night.

B-38. Spotted Owl. *Strix occidentalis* (pl. 52). Medium-sized, T.L. 19", head rounded, no ear tufts, eyes dark; plumage brown with many contrasted white spots in crosswise rows. VOICE. Varied, often barking notes, *whŭ, whŭ, whŭ,* like those of small dog. NEST. In cavity of cliff or tree; eggs 2–3, white, 2" x 1⅝". DISTR. R. in Yellow Pine belt of west slope, in forest.

Walking in the woods at dusk one may hear the barking voice of this owl and occasionally glimpse its rounded head. In daytime the repeated insistent calls of a gray squirrel, or of kinglets, warblers, and jays may lead an observer to a Spotted Owl perched motionless in a dense tree. One foothill rancher enjoyed a pair of Spotted Owls near his home because of their varied calls in early evening. Wood rats, white-footed mice, and grasshoppers are included in the food.

B-39. Great Gray Owl. *Strix nebulosa* (pl. 52). Largest Sierran owl, T.L. to 23", spread to 54"; head big, round, no ear tufts; eyes yellow; plumage grayish brown, dully streaked with white. VOICE. A single deep *whoo* at irregular intervals. DISTR. Sparse R. s. to Madera Co. at 3200–7900 ft. in coniferous forest.

This big owl of the Eurasian and American Arctic occurs sparingly in the northern Rockies and Sierra Nevada. Most of the Sierra records are in the Lodgepole–fir belt of the Yosemite region, where evidence of nesting was obtained. It seems to be active by day, so bird students should watch and listen in deep woods for a large, dark round-headed owl with deep voice.

B-40. Long-eared Owl. *Asio otus* (pl. 52). Medium-sized, T.L. to 16", head and face round, 2 long tufts on top above eyes; above brownish black, mottled, below pale brown, striped; eyes yellow. VOICE. Varied; a long mellow *hoot,* repeated; also cat-like calls. NEST. Uses old nest of crow, magpie, or hawk in tree; eggs 4–5, white, oval, 1½" x 1¼". DISTR. On both slopes below Lodgepole–fir belt, near streams.

Meadowlands near streamside trees are the preferred habitat of this owl. Meadow mice and deer mice, some other rodents, and a few birds are taken for food. Nesting is in late April or May, and by June family groups may be found by day in willow thickets.

B-41. Saw-whet Owl. *Aegolius acadicus* (pl. 52). Larger than Pygmy Owl, T.L. to 8½"; head round, no tufts; eyes yellow; above cinnamon-brown, below white with brown streaks. VOICE. A rasping call, repeated; a bell-like note. DISTR. Uncommon on both slopes in conifer forest.

There are only scattered records of this species in the Sierra. Elsewhere it is known to nest in old woodpecker holes and feed mostly on small rodents. The call is heard mainly in the nesting season.

B-42. Poorwill. *Phalaenoptilus nuttalli.* T.L. 8", T. 3¾", body size of robin; head broad, eyes large, bill and feet small; feathers soft, owl-like; throat and band under end of tail white, plumage otherwise mixed black, gray, and brown. VOICE. A mellow, *poor-will-o,* repeated; a soft *quirt* in flight. NEST. Eggs laid on bare ground, 2, pinkish, 1" x ¾". DISTR. Common S.V. in chaparral of Foothill belt, also along e. base of Sierra in sagebrush.

When darkness falls the Poorwill takes wing and weaves in irregular course close above the ground and shrubbery. Its mouth is as broad as the head and fringed with bristles, a gaping trap that serves to gather the flying insects used for food. By day the bird rests quietly on the ground under a bush; the variegated plumage blends with surface objects, making it difficult to see. The young remain on the site where hatched until able to fly.

B-43. Common Nighthawk. *Chordeiles minor* (pl. 53). T.L. 8½", T. 4½", body of robin size; mouth broad; wings long and slender, reach beyond tail when folded; plumage barred or spotted with brown, gray, black, and white; chin, patch on outer part of each wing, and bar near end of tail (♂ only), white. VOICE. *Pee-nt* or *pee'-ark,* 1- or 2-syllabled. NEST. Eggs on bare ground or rock, 2, creamy, 1³⁄₁₆" x ⅞". DISTR. S.V. in Lodgepole–fir and Subalpine belts, also in Sagebrush belt on e. side.

Nighthawks begin to hunt flying insects at sundown, do some foraging at night, and continue into the morning on cloudy days or when the young need food. In pursuing prey they fly high and can turn quickly. At times one will dive from a height, with the wings in V-shape, until near the ground; as it turns upward a booming "whoof" is produced by vibration of the wing tips. In midday the nighthawk perches lengthwise on a tree limb or log. The Lesser or Texas Nighthawk (*C. acutipennis*) occurs in summer at the edge of the Great Valley; its voice is low and purring, and the bird forages near the ground and shrubs.

B-44. White-throated Swift. *Aeronautes saxatilis* (pl. 54). T.L. 6¾", T. 2⅔", swallow-like but wings longer, slenderer, tail longer; black except for white on throat, midbreast, and sides of rump. VOICE. Rapid shrill twittering notes. NEST. In cliff cavities, saucer-shaped, of feathers or twigs "glued" to rock; eggs 3–6, white, $1\frac{1}{16}''$ x $\frac{9}{16}''$. DISTR. S.V. locally on w. slope up into Yellow Pine belt.

Swifts forage high in the air, often in loose companies, alternately on level course, climbing by rapid fluttering flight, or diving at tremendous speed as they pursue flying insects. They differ from swallows in having a crossbow outline because of the backward-curving wings. Swifts are abroad from early morning until dusk. They never alight on the ground or a perch but roost and nest only in crevices of cliffs usually inaccessible to other animals. Two other swifts occur on the west slope. The smaller Vaux Swift (*Chaetura vauxi*) lacks white on the flanks. The larger Black Swift (*Nephoecetes niger*) is all black, has a broad tail and a more swallow-like flight.

B-45. Anna Hummingbird. *Calypte anna.* T.L. $3\frac{1}{2}''$; back and rump metallic green; below dusky, green-tinged; ♂ with head, chin, and throat iridescent rose-red. VOICE. Of perched ♂ a high *zeezy-zeezy* . . . ; of feeding ♀ a low *tsup*. NEST. In trees or shrubs a cup $1\frac{3}{4}''$ dia. felted of mosses and lichens and lined with plant down; eggs 2, white, $\frac{1}{2}''$ x $\frac{3}{8}''$. DISTR. Common R. in Foothill belt, in mixed woodland and chaparral; C.V. upslope in summer.

This largest of local hummingbirds uses both wild and garden flowers for nectar. On occasion it visits sapsucker drillings to take the tree sap. When such supplies lessen it hovers around golden oaks to catch minute insects on the leaves. In summer some individuals go into the Yellow Pine belt or higher to feed in flowers that blossom at that season. After the mating period, early in the year, the female does all the work of nest building, incubation, and feeding the young.

B-46. Rufous Hummingbird. *Selasphorus rufus.* T.L. $3\frac{1}{2}''$. Ad. ♂ : Above bright reddish brown; chin and throat iridescent coppery red, bordered below by white; under surface rufous brown. Ad. ♀ : Back bronzy green; sides of body and base of tail rufous-tinged. VOICE. A high *zee,* often repeated. DISTR. Tr. along lower w. slope in spring and in higher altitudes during summer.

The Rufous Hummingbird moves north in spring along the foothills when flowers there are blossoming and afford nectar for its food. It nests north of California, but returning males appear at higher elevations by early July. Later in that month females and immatures arrive. From then into September the species may be expected around any area of mountain flowers. Individuals then often take up "feeding territories," each vigorously defended against intruding hummers. Migrants have been seen traveling southward above timberline.

B-47. Calliope Hummingbird. *Stellula calliope* (pl. 53). T.L. $2\frac{3}{4}''$–$3\frac{1}{2}''$, smallest local hummingbird. Ad. ♂ : Throat with long slender iridescent lavender feathers; above light green, below white, sides buffy. Ad. ♀ and Im.: Above bronze-green, below grayish white, buff-tinged. VOICE. In pursuit, a faint *tweez-e-zeet-zee*. NEST. In trees at 9–75 ft., on twigs, dia. about 1¼", of plant down and lichens; eggs 2, white, ½" x ⅓". DISTR. Common S.V. in upper Yellow Pine and Lodgepole–fir belts at 4000–9000 ft.

The diminutive Calliope Hummingbird comes in April or May, probably along the lower slopes, nests in the main forest belt, and departs southward in July or August by way of the higher mountains. It thus takes advantage of the seasonal shift in blossoming flowers upslope as the year advances. Both coniferous and deciduous trees serve for roosting and nesting. Flowers of currant, gooseberry, manzanitas, paintbrush, and pentstemon are commonly visited for nectar.

B-48. Belted Kingfisher. *Megaceryle alcyon* (pl. 53). T.L. 11"–14½", T. 4"; head big with loose crest, bill stout, tail small; above blue, below white; neck collar white; breast band blue; below this on ♀ a 2nd band of rusty brown extended on sides. VOICE. A loud rattle. NEST. Near water on vertical sand or clay bank in 3–6 ft. tunnel; eggs 3–6, white, 1¾" x 1⅜". DISTR. Common about streams and lakes through much of Sierra, withdrawing from higher frozen waters in winter.

Sooner or later the Kingfisher's rattling call may be heard on most waters. The bird perches briefly on some bare branch or snag, then moves on over the water or circles among trees. Its prey is of large aquatic insects and small fishes usually caught by a direct plunge; sometimes the bird hovers on beating wings while searching. Fishermen deem the Kingfisher a competitor and enemy, in consequence of which many of the birds are shot. Decline in abundance of fish, however, is more a matter of human fishing pressure and the Kingfisher is only a minor element.

B-49. Red-shafted Flicker. *Colaptes cafer* (col. pl. 19). T.L. 13", T. 5"; larger than robin; above brown, narrowly barred with black; below grayish with many black dots and a black bar on breast; rump white; wings and tail show dull red in flight. VOICE. Varied; a loud *claip* or *klee-ap;* in spring a rolling monotonous *kuk, kuk, kuk,* . . . ; when 2 flickers meet, *yuck-a, yuck-a,* . . . ; drums a rapid tattoo on resonant wood. NEST. Excavated hole 2" dia., in tree or stub often at 8–25 ft.; eggs 5–12, shiny white, 1⅛" x 1¹³⁄₁₆". DISTR. Common R. from Great Valley to Great Basin, to above 10500 ft.; in winter below level of heavy snow.

The Flicker, like other woodpeckers, has a stout pointed bill, long extensible tongue, the toes 2 in front and 2 behind with sharp curved claws, and tail feathers with stiff shafts and pointed tips. It clings upright on trees and uses the bill to dig for insect larvae within the wood. For nesting a gourd-shaped hole is dug in some tree trunk. Unlike other woodpeckers the Flicker also forages on the ground for ants or grasshoppers and seeks berries on various kinds of bushes. Its flight is strong and direct, with infrequent wingbeats; upon alighting it may

32. Roadrunner

30.
Band-tailed Pigeon

31.
Mourning
Dove

43. Common Nighthawk

50.
Pileated Woodpecker

47.
Calliope Hummingbird

54.
Williamson
Sapsucker
male

48.
Belted Kingfisher

Plate 53. Birds

275

perch on a branch, bow deeply several times, and utter its explosive *klee-ap*. In autumn several Flickers often can be seen within a few yards of one another on the ground under trees; the local population then may include migrants from farther north. Like other woodpeckers, Flickers sleep in holes at night, and in winter they often drill under the eaves of lowland buildings for such shelter.

B-50. Pileated Woodpecker. *Dryocopus pileatus* (pl. 53). T.L. 15"–19", T. 7". Far the largest Sierran woodpecker; body black; pointed crest on head bright red; wing with large white area forward on under surface and smaller white patch on outer side. Voice. A loud low-pitched *kuk, kuk, . . .* in slow and irregular series. Nest. In hole well up in tree; eggs 3–4, white, 1⅝" x 1⅝". Distr. Common R. in upper Yellow Pine and Lodgepole–fir belts on w. slope.

The big Pileated lives mainly on fir trees, digging carpenter ants and large beetle larvae from dead wood for food. When at work the noise is like that of someone pounding with a hammer; its head can sweep an 8-inch arc and chips may be thrown fully 2 feet. The excavations often are several inches wide and some are as long as a person's forearm. The nest cavity is 6 inches in diameter by 18 inches deep and the entrance 3 or 4 inches across. In flight the head is drawn back, the wings beat continuously, and the course is direct.

B-51. California Woodpecker. *Melanerpes formicivorus* (col. pl. 19, fig. 20). T.L. 9", T. 3"–4"; near size of robin; chin, back, and wings shiny black; forehead, rump, belly, and patch on wings (in flight), white; crown red; throat and sides of head yellowish; red crown on ♀ preceded by black band. Voice. A nasal *ya'-kup, ya'-kup, ya'-kup;* also *krra'-ka, krra'-ka.* Nest. Hole in tree or pole, at 10–30 ft.; eggs 4–5, white, 1" x ¾". Distr. Common R. in Foothill belt and locally in Great Valley and Yellow Pine belt, in oaks.

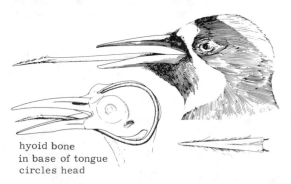

hyoid bone
in base of tongue
circles head

Figure 20. Head and tongue of California Woodpecker. The long tongue is enclosed in a muscular sheath around the back of the skull, and can be extended well beyond the bill to pull a grub from a hole in wood—aided by bristles on the tip of the tongue.

Unlike some of its shy forest-dwelling relatives, the California or Acorn Woodpecker is easy to see and hear, almost always in or near oaks, and often in groups of 2, 3, or more. On a tree or pole it clings with the head out and tail in against the support; it hitches upward moving the head and tail alternately in and out. Acorns are its habitual food. When oaks are producing the bird carries an acorn to a limb or pole, pecks off the shell, and eats the contents. During the season of plenty, acorns are stored for future use. The woodpecker drills a hole in a tree or post of a size to fit each acorn gathered, which then is tamped firmly into place. On two well-stocked trees the pits ranged from 3 to 40 feet above ground and by estimate one held over 2300 and another 10500 acorns. For this habit the Spanish Californian called the bird *el carpintero*. Besides acorns, this species sometimes goes fly-catching for insects that pass in the air near a tree. The species is further notable because an extra adult or pair may assist the parents in rearing their brood.

B-52. Lewis Woodpecker. *Asyndesmus lewisi* (col. pl. 19). T.L. 11″, T. 4½″, slightly larger than robin, wings long for a woodpecker. Above greenish black, belly rose-red, breast and neck collar grayish white. NEST. In tree holes; eggs 5–9, white, 1″ x ¾″. DISTR. Of irregular occurrence, seasonally and altitudinally; in scattered timber.

The Lewis Woodpecker is a wanderer, apt to be seen anywhere in the Sierra except dense forests. It may nest in a locality one year, then be only a winter visitant or entirely absent. In some degree it depends on acorns as food, but also it may frequent a burn with standing dead trunks containing beetle larvae. In flight the long wings beat continuously, resulting in a crow-like flight different from that of other woodpeckers. This mannerism and the distinctive coloration make identification easy.

B-53. Yellow-bellied Sapsucker. *Sphyrapicus varius* (col. pl. 19). T.L. 9″, T. 3¼″, smaller than robin; whole head, throat, and breast crimson red; back and wings black, with white spots; rump and stripe along edge of wing white; belly yellowish. VOICE. A single low *chŭrr*. NEST. In hole dug in tree; eggs 5–6, pinkish white, 1⅚″ x 11⁄16″. DISTR. Common S.V. in Yellow Pine belt and in lower Lodgepole–fir belt on both slopes; W.V. to w. slope foothills and valleys; inhabits mixed woodlands and forests.

Sapsuckers are woodpeckers that feed on tree sap and soft wood (bast and cambium). This bird, often named Red-breasted Sapsucker, works mainly on deciduous trees—willow, cottonwood, aspen, oak, and apple —but sometimes on pines or incense cedar. It drills small holes, wider than high, in horizontal rows on trunks or limbs. The pits extend through the bark to the cambium on the outermost growing wood. Sap flows from the wounds, and the bird revisits the site at intervals, using its brush-like tongue to take the sticky fluid and any insects caught.

(Small birds may also patronize the drillings.) Repeated rows of holes drilled below the first series, sometimes in subsequent years, yield grill-like patterns. Occasional trees are completely girdled, attacked by insects or fungus, and eventually killed. This sapsucker seldom calls, and its pecking is done quietly.

B-54. Williamson Sapsucker. *Sphryapicus thyroideus* (pl. 53). T.L. 9½", T. 3⅕"; near size of robin. Ad. ♂ : Black; rump and large patch on fore-part of wing white; small white stripes behind eye and back from bill; chin spot red; belly yellow. Ad. ♀ : Head and throat brown, chest black, belly yellow, rump white, rest of plumage barred with black and pale brown. VOICE. A weak *whang*. NEST. In hole in tree stub; eggs 5–6, white, 1⁵⁄₁₆" x ⅝". DISTR. R. mainly in Lodgepole–fir belt on both slopes; some stray lower and higher in autumn; in conifer woods.

Unlike other woodpeckers, the male and female of this sapsucker are markedly unlike in color, and the young differ somewhat from the adults. The species lives in the higher coniferous forests, foraging mostly on the lodgepole pine but also on firs, Jeffrey pine, hemlock, and occasionally aspen. The pits made through the bark to obtain sap are scarcely larger than the bird's bill. They are in irregularly horizontal rows but never completely encircle the trunk. One 60-foot lodgepole had 26 rows of punctures all made in one season. This pine reacts to the drilling by later producing a swollen ring in the wood beneath each row; the resulting scar-like growths can be seen on many living and dead lodgepoles. In winter, when sap movement is scant, the Williamson Sapsucker, a year-long resident, probably finds dormant insects or larvae hidden in bark crevices.

B-55. Hairy Woodpecker. *Dendrocopus villosus* (col. pl. 19). T.L. 10½", T. 3¾"; about size of robin; above black, side of head with 2 white bars, middle of back white, and wings with white dots; below white, including outer tail feathers; ♂ has narrow red arc on back of head. VOICE. A single sharp *speenk*. NEST. In hole dug in tree; eggs 3–6, white, 1" x ¾". DISTR. R. mostly in Yellow Pine and Lodgepole–fir belts, some in belts above and below; inhabits partly open or burned forest, also deciduous trees along streams.

The Hairy Woodpecker occurs widely in forests but nowhere is common, at least in summer. It digs or flakes off bark to find insect larvae, more often in dying or dead trees where these are common. In spring when courting, the male frequently utters a staccato run of notes, *spenk-ter-ter-ter*, and drums on a resonant tree. Young just out of the nest may call noisily, but in other seasons this species is rather quiet.

B-56. Downy Woodpecker. *Dendrocopus pubescens* (col. pl. 19). T.L. 6½", T. 2½"; between junco and robin in size; coloration like Hairy Woodpecker (B-55) except white outer tail feathers barred with black. VOICE. A short high-pitched trill, descending in pitch. NEST. In hole in tree at 10–25 ft.; eggs 4–5, white, ¾″ x ⁹⁄₁₆″. DISTR. Sparse R. from Great Valley into Yellow Pine belt; in willows, cottonwoods, or apple trees mostly near streams.

Smallest of Sierran woodpeckers and much like the preceding species is the little Downy, which favors streamside softwood trees. It is not common, seldom calls, and each individual seems to have a restricted range. Once a bird is located it can usually be found repeatedly in the same forage area. The Downy makes small irregularly placed pits in bark when digging out insects for food. Trees or branches well advanced in decay are used to dig holes for nesting or night shelter.

B-57. Nuttall Woodpecker. *Dendrocopus nuttallii.* T.L. 7″, T. 2¾″; only slightly larger than Downy Woodpecker; head black with 2 white stripes on side; black wings, sides, and outer tail feathers barred or spotted white and black; under surface white; ♂ with red on back of head. VOICE. A short rattling trill. NEST. A hole in tree; eggs 3–6, white, ⅞″ x ⅝″. DISTR. Common R. in Foothill belt, mainly in oaks.

Among the foothill oaks one often hears a brief rattling call that draws attention to its maker, the little Nuttall Woodpecker. In the air its wings beat a few strokes and then close, whereupon the bird swoops downward; its course is deeply undulating when going between trees. In foraging it hitches upward on dry or dead limbs, pecking and digging out boring insects for food. Besides oak trees it also gives attention to digger pines, streamside cottonwoods, and even apple trees in orchards. In the latter places Nuttall and Downy Woodpeckers may be near one another.

B-58. White-headed Woodpecker. *Dendrocopus albolarvatus* (col. pl. 19). T.L. 9″, T. 4″; less than size of robin; plumage all black except white head and neck and white patch on wing (best seen in flight); ♂ with red arc on back of head. VOICE. A high sharp *wiek*, repeated when excited. NEST. In hole, often in dead tree stub at 5–15 ft.; eggs 3–7, white, 1″ x ¾″. DISTR. Common in Yellow Pine and lower Lodgepole–fir belts; in conifer forest.

No woodpecker is so readily identified as the "whitehead," which often perches within easy view and in some places is fairly common. It forages mostly on living pines and firs, but seldom on lodgepole pines. For nesting it uses upright stubs of dead trees that are hard on the outside but soft within. By pecking out innumerable short splinters a gourd-shaped cavity is dug, the entrance 1½–2 inches in diameter and the interior 3–4 inches across by 12–16 inches deep. The eggs and later the young, naked at hatching, rest on a lining of chips or rotted wood which is kept clean by the parents. Both adults forage and bring food at short intervals so that the young become fledged and ready to emerge within a couple of weeks. Over the years the many holes of this and other woodpeckers serve chickadees, nuthatches, and perhaps pygmy owls and flying squirrels for nests or shelters.

B-59. Black-backed Three-toed Woodpecker. *Picoides arcticus* (col. pl. 19). T.L. 9½"–10", T. 3⅖"; smaller than robin; above black, below white; sides of body and lower surface of wings barred with black and white; crown of ♂ golden yellow. VOICE. A single low *week* or *tup*. NEST. In hole in tree or stump; eggs 4, white, ⅞" x ⅝". DISTR. Sparse R. in Lodgepole–fir and Subalpine belts; in conifer forest.

This is a rather uncommon "boreal" woodpecker that has its southern limit in the Sierra of Tulare County. It lives year round in forests of lodgepole pine and red fir. Except when drilling for food or drumming during the courting season, it is quiet and may escape notice.

B-60. Western Kingbird. *Tyrannus verticalis* (pl. 54). T.L. 8"–9½", T. 3¾"; smaller than robin; head broad; upper surface and breast light gray, throat paler, belly yellow, wings brown, tail black with white margin on outermost feathers; crown of ♂ with concealed red. VOICE. A sharp *whit,* and loud harsh bickering calls. NEST. Dia. to 6", of grasses and weed stems, in trees or bushes, even on fence posts; eggs 3–5, creamy, brown-blotched, 1" x ¾". DISTR. Common S.V. along both sides of Sierra in dry open places with scattered trees, poles, or posts for lookouts.

This Kingbird, like any flycatcher, sits on an exposed perch and watches for flying insects with frequent turns of the head. When one passes near, the bird darts out and snaps it in the bill, then resumes watching from the same or another perch. This species also catches grasshoppers on the ground. Kingbirds arrive in April or May and live in more open areas than other flycatchers. They resent intrusion of their territories and will take after an approaching crow, heron, or owl, hovering and pecking at the larger bird while uttering harsh cries. If a person approaches a Kingbird nest the parents, sometimes joined by other pairs, will flutter overhead, voicing their protest, and the male may flash his red crown feathers. After the nesting season some Kingbirds wander into the mountains for a while, but all depart southward by August or September.

B-61. Ash-throated Flycatcher. *Myiarchus cinerascens* (pl. 54). T.L. 8¼", T. 4"; head with blunt crest, body slender, tail long; head and back grayish brown; closed wing with 2 dull white bars; breast light gray; belly white, yellow-tinged; spread wings and tail show reddish brown. VOICE. A throaty *ker* or *ker-cherr'* of descending pitch; song a loud rolling *tŭck'a-roo,* often repeated at short intervals. NEST. In holes of trees or stumps, lined with grass, rootlets, feathers, and often cast snake skin; eggs 4–5, creamy, with fine dark lines or spots, ⅞" x ⅝". DISTR. Common S.V. at lower altitudes on both slopes; over brushlands with occasional trees.

The slender form, slight crest, long tail, and rather upright posture make the Ash-throat easy to recognize. It is the only flycatcher that patrols the chaparral areas, where it forages low over the shrubbery. Unlike others of its kind, the bird makes frequent changes of position and hunts over a relatively large area. Being a hole nester, it must live

44. White-throated Swift

60. Western Kingbird

61. Ash-throated Flycatcher

62. Black Phoebe

65. Olive-sided Flycatcher

64. Small Flycatcher

67. Horned Lark

66. Wood Pewee

Plate 54. Birds

in places having occasional trees with decay cavities or woodpecker holes where the eggs can be incubated and the young reared.

B-62. Black Phoebe. *Sayornis nigricans* (pl. 54). T.L. 6½", T. 3⅔"; head with low crest; plumage black except for white on belly. VOICE. A single plaintive *pser,* the song 2 pairs of similar notes, with alternate rising and falling inflection. NEST. On ledge of rock or flat surface in a building, a cup made of mud pellets mixed with grass; eggs 3–5, white, ¾" x 9⁄16". DISTR. On w. side from Great Valley to lower edge of Yellow Pine belt; along rock-bordered streams or around old buildings near water.

The Black Phoebe is our only resident flycatcher, able to find insect food at all seasons. In spring it must be near water to obtain mud for nest making. Then it forages over a stream or pool and even takes insects from the water surface. In winter the bird occurs more widely, sometimes living around farmyards. This phoebe commonly sits in exposed places, on streamside rocks, on bare branches or twigs, and on the roofs of small buildings, but in the heat of summer it seeks shady perches. Because of its special nesting needs it is of less uniform occurrence than many other birds, although man-made bridges and buildings have increased the places where it can live.

B-63. Say Phoebe. *Sayornis saya.* T.L. 8", T. 3½"; size and form of Black Phoebe; top of head dark brown; back grayish brown; tail blackish; throat and breast brownish gray, belly cinnamon. VOICE. A long plaintive *pee-ur.* DISTR. S.V. locally along e. base of Sierra; strays after nesting season, and some as W.V. in Foothill belt.

This brownish phoebe nests and forages over the Great Basin sagebrush in summer. In winter it appears in the western foothills of the Sierra, perching on rocky outcrops and earth bluffs.

B-64. Small Flycatchers. Genus *Empidonax* (pl. 54). T.L. 5"–6", smaller than junco; bill small, flattish; a white ring around eye; 2 dull white bars on wing; different species are olive-green to ashy gray above, and yellowish to gray below.

Five species of these little flycatchers visit the Sierra for the summer. They are similar in size, with some differences in color. Each has rather different calls, and for nesting each occupies a particular habitat (see below). In late summer, however, some stray elsewhere, even to high altitudes, before migrating southward. The Western and Traill Flycatchers are fairly distinctive as to color and voice, but specimens are needed to identify the others precisely. Their eggs are much alike. All these species have the usual habits of perching in rather upright posture while watching for passing prey, flicking the tail at intervals, and darting on short circling flight to capture insects.

a. Western Flycatcher. *E. difficilis.* Above olive-green, below yellowish. VOICE. A clear whistled call, *swee'p;* song a shrill *see'rip, sip, see'rip,* repeated. NEST. In low trees or stumps or on ledges; a cup of rootlets, moss, etc.; eggs 3–4, dull white, ⅝″ x ½″. DISTR. S.V. in Yellow Pine belt on w. slope; in canyon bottoms among incense cedars and alders near streams.

b. Traill Flycatcher. *E. trailli.* Above brownish gray, below pale gray to whitish. VOICE. A soft but distinct *whit'*, sometimes repeated 2 or 3 times; song *wheet-p'teer* often repeated. NEST. Low in willows; cup-like, of grasses and plant fibers. DISTR. S.V. from western lowlands into Yellow Pine belt and locally on e. slope; lives in dense willow thickets.

c. Dusky Flycatcher. *E. oberholseri.* Above grayish brown, below yellowish gray. VOICE. Call, *pit,* or *swee'pit;* song lisping, *see'pit, wurt'zel, see'pit, swer'zel,* etc. NEST. Low in small trees or shrubs at 15 ft. or less; of plant and bark fibers. DISTR. Common S.V. on both slopes in Lodgepole–fir belt and adjacent areas; mostly over brush patches perching at 10–30 ft. in nearby trees. (Formerly called Wright Flycatcher, *E. wrighti.*)

d. Hammond Flycatcher. *E. hammondi.* Coloration much like *c.* VOICE. A weak *pit;* song *see'wit, psēēt, swĕrz,* etc. NEST. On horizontal limb at 15 ft. or higher, of plant fibers. DISTR. S.V. from Tulare Co. n. on w. slope; in dense forests of Red Fir, Lodgepole Pine, etc.; perches at 20–100 ft.

e. Gray Flycatcher. *E. wrighti.* Resembles *c,* but grayer above. VOICE. Call a sharp *whit;* song of 2 phrases, a strong *chi-wip* and faint *cheep* in varied combination. NEST. In high sagebrush; a deep cup of grasses, etc. DISTR. S.V. on e. slope from Inyo Co. n. in sagebrush belt, sometimes near forest edge. (Formerly called *E. griseus.*)

B-65. Olive-sided Flycatcher. *Nuttallornis borealis* (pl. 54). T.L. 7½″, T. 3″, a large flycatcher, with big head and short tail; plumage olive-brown above and on sides, middle of whole lower surface yellowish white, flanks white. VOICE. Call a soft *puck,* 2 or 3 times, mostly at evening; song a loud *wher, whee', whew.* NEST. Usually in conifers at 60–70 ft., of twigs, leaflets, and moss; eggs 3–4, creamy with brown blotches, ⅞″ x ⅝″. DISTR. Common S.V. in Yellow Pine and Lodgepole–fir belts of w. slope; lives high in conifers; Tr. in lower elevations on both slopes.

In mid-May this flycatcher may be noted while en route along both sides of the Sierra to its summer home area in the main conifer forest. When established for nesting it perches in the treetops, greeting the earliest dawn with the 3-syllabled song sounding like "oh see'view," and giving at dusk the softer triple call note. Pairs sometimes flutter about the nest and give voice to kingbird-like bickerings, but usually only the simpler voicings are to be heard. This is the only flycatcher with white flank marks. It departs by the end of August.

B-66. Wood Pewee. *Contopus sordidulus* (pl. 54). T.L. 6½″, T. 2¾″, of junco size; above and on sides plain dark brown, middle of under surface yellowish white; no special white markings. VOICE. A throaty *bzew.* NEST. On horizontal limb at 15–40 ft., a well-formed cup of plant fibers and grasses; eggs 3, white, brown-blotched, ¾″ x 9/16″. DISTR. Common S.V. from Foothill belt into Lodgepole–fir belt of w. slope and comparable areas of e. slope; in open forest or woodland.

The Wood Pewee is the commonest and most widely occurring of Sierran flycatchers and is the plainest in garb, with no special white markings. During May it migrates in numbers through the lower altitudes and soon is settled for the summer. Perches on twigs 15 to 40 feet above ground, often in exposed places, are occupied in open forest of many sorts. Its monotonous droning call begins with the first hint of daylight and often is almost the last of bird voices at dusk. Nesting begins in May and continues until the end of July, when some broods are to be seen. By mid-September all the pewees have gone southward.

B-67. Horned Lark. *Eremophila alpestris* (pl. 54). T.L. 6½″–7″, T. 2¾″, larger than linnet (B-134), much smaller than Meadowlark (B-121); above light brown, outer tail feathers black (white-edged), below whitish; bar across forehead, stripe from bill to eye, and band on breast, black; ♂ with short black "horn" (of feathers) above each eye. VOICE. Call a faint high *see* or *see-tle;* song a tinkling *teet, toot, teet-teetle-eetle-ettle* when bird circles in air. NEST. On open ground in scant cover, a depression lined with grasses; eggs 2–5, gray-green, with brown blotches, ¾″ x ⁹⁄₁₆″. DISTR. On plains areas w. and e. of Sierra and in some flat valleys from Truckee R. north; inhabits open sparse grassland.

Wide open areas with sparse surface vegetation are the home of this lark. It walks with a slight sidewise swaying of the body and fore-and-aft movement of the head. If disturbed, this changes to a gliding run when the pale feathering blends closely with the ground color. Horned larks commonly are in loose flocks; even in the nesting season several pairs will often join temporarily. On taking to flight the birds may scatter, then wheel about and come together again near the place from which they started. Their food is mostly of seeds picked from the ground, a little green vegetation, and some insects.

B-68. Violet-green Swallow. *Tachycineta thalassina* (pl. 55). T.L. 4¾″–5½″, T. 2″, body smaller than linnet or junco (B-148); wings long, pointed, when closed extend 1″ beyond short slightly notched tail; above bronzy green, violet on rump; sides of head and rump and all lower surface white. VOICE. A plaintive *tsee,* sometimes repeated. NEST. In cavities of trees, cliffs, or buildings, lined with grasses and feathers; eggs 4–5, white, ¾″ x ½″. DISTR. Common S.V. in Foothill and Yellow Pine belts of w. slope, also along e. base of Sierra.

Far the commoner swallow with a white under surface is the Violet-green, which summers over the lower parts of both the east and west slopes. Often it forages much higher in the air than other swallows and may sometimes be seen near White-throated Swifts (B-44), when the differences in form and manner of flight between swallow and swift are evident. For nesting the Violet-green uses either natural cavities or woodpecker holes in trees or small crevices in cliffs, so that many sites are available. The species is present from late April into September.

B-69. Tree Swallow. *Iridoprocne bicolor.* T.L. 5″–6¼″, T. 2½″, size of linnet; tail nearly square-ended; above black with blue iridescence, below

71. Cliff Swallow

70. Barn Swallow

68. Violet-green Swallow

73. Scrub Jay

74. Yellow-billed Magpie

72. Steller Jay

78. Clark Nutcracker

86. Wrentit

Plate 55. Birds

white. VOICE. A faint *seet,* sometimes repeated as a twitter. NEST. In holes in trees or buildings, lined with grasses and feathers; eggs 4–6, white, ¾" x ½". DISTR. Sparse S.V. at w. and e. edges of Sierra; often near standing water.

This rather uncommon swallow lacks the white rump marks of the Violet-green. It lives near quiet water, perching often on exposed twigs of the tree in which the nest cavity is located.

B-70. Barn Swallow. *Hirundo rustica* (pl. 55). T.L. to 7¾", T. to 4⅓", body size of linnet but wings longer and narrower, tail long and deeply forked; above shiny dark blue, forehead and under surface reddish brown; breast with bluish band, often incomplete. VOICE. Series of twittering notes, both musical and throaty. NEST. On flat beams or ledges in buildings or under bridges; an open cup of mud, grass, and feathers; eggs 4–5, white with brown spots, ¾" x ⁹⁄₁₆". DISTR. Common S.V. locally on w. side into edge of Yellow Pine belt and along e. base of Sierra; near water where nesting sites are present.

Barn Swallows, in pairs or small groups, may be present in summer wherever shelving places for solitary nests occur near water. When one perches on a twig or wire, the pointed tips of the two wings and two long outermost tail feathers are evident. In flight this swallow is graceful in appearance because of the slender forked tail. The species is present from March until mid-September and in late summer may appear in upmountain localities.

B-71. Cliff Swallow. *Petrochelidon pyrrhonota* (pl. 55). T.L. 5"–6", T. 2⅛", size of linnet, wings long and narrow, tail short, squarish; forehead creamy white, back, wings, and tail black-appearing, rump pale brown, cheeks and chin reddish brown, throat patch blue-black, under parts light gray. VOICE. While feeding, a low *shurr;* when disturbed at nest, a plaintive *kleer,* repeated; song "squeaky" notes. NEST. In colonies, on rough cliffs, or under eaves of buildings; spherical with narrow-necked opening, of mud pellets; eggs 3–6, creamy with brown spots, ¾" x ⁹⁄₁₆". DISTR. Common S.V. at lower altitudes both e. and w. of Sierra, locally where nest colonies can be built; forages in open.

This highly colonial swallow originally made nests on cliffs but now commonly uses rough-surfaced buildings, crowding a dozen to a hundred on some favorable site. Each nest is made of great numbers of mud pellets gathered singly at some water margin. The narrowed roundish entrance at the top leads into an expanded chamber provided with slight fibrous lining. Nests are safe from most enemies, but the birds will fly about and utter complaining cries if a person approaches a colony. On the west slope adults arrive in March but nesting is delayed until early May. By then flying insects are more abundant, so that they can alternate feeding with nest building, incubation, and caring for the young.

B-72. Steller Jay. *Cyanocitta stelleri* (pl. 55). T.L. 12″–13″, T. 5⅓″–6⅓″; head crested, tail slightly rounded, wings short, rounded; head, crest, and fore parts blackish; wings, tail, and rest of body deep blue; wings and tail crossed with narrow black bars; young more blackish, fluffy. VOICE. A loud harsh *ksch, kschak,* or *glook,* each in 3's; a whistled *skwee-oo;* a low crackling *ker-r-r-r;* a "squeaky wheelbarrow" note; rarely a faint whisper song. NEST. In conifers at 8–40 ft., dia. to 12″, of twigs with mud, lined with needles or grass; eggs 3–5, greenish with olive-brown spots, 1¼″ x ⅞″. DISTR. R. in Yellow Pine and Lodgepole–fir belts; some at lower levels in winter; mainly in conifer woods.

The noisy crested Steller Jay is mostly solitary, in pairs while nesting, but gathers in numbers to vocalize around an owl or other unusual subject. Much of its time is spent in trees, where it ascends from branch to branch "like going up a staircase," perching at a high lookout, then gliding on spread wings and tail to the base of another tree. It forages on the ground but less than the lowland jay. The birds are quiet and stealthy while nesting but noisy again when broods are awing. The diet is varied: seeds, nuts, and acorns; insects and other small animals; and food gleaned at camps and resorts. In nesting season they sometimes take eggs or young of small birds; a jay or two near such a nest often brings complaining calls from various lesser birds nearby.

B-73. Scrub or California Jay. *Aphelocoma coerulescens* (pl. 55). T.L. 12″, T. 5¾″, body size of robin but tail longer, wider, rounded at end; no crest; head, neck, wings, and tail blue, back grayish brown, under surface grayish white with incomplete blue collar on breast. VOICE. Varied; a mildly harsh *kwish,* 3 to 5 times; a single softer *kschu-ee;* a guttural *krr′r′r′r′* by pairs or groups, etc. NEST. In low trees or shrubs at 3–40 ft., of long twigs, lined with rootlets or hair; eggs 4–6, green with darker green dots or buff with red dots, 1⅛″ x 1³⁄₁₆″. DISTR. Abundant R. in Foothill belt, streamside trees of Great Valley, and edge of Yellow Pine belt; sparse R. on e. side in piñons and junipers.

This avian busybody of the foothill oaks is easy to see and hear. Often it perches alertly with feet spread, head up, and tail level or tilted upward; again it will sit motionless for minutes with the tail hanging vertically. Being bold and curious, it watches all local events and is quick to dash off in noisy flight and investigate. If an owl or other predator is sighted, the bird's excited calls promptly bring other jays to the spot. The varied "vocabulary" evidently is meaningful to others of the species. In the spring season, however, the pairs are silent and secretive within their nesting areas. Then they eat insects, and eggs or young of small birds as found. Otherwise acorns are a staple diet. Besides those eaten, the jays bury many acorns singly in the soil; some are later recovered and eaten, but others remain to sprout and grow.

B-74. Magpie. Genus *Pica* (pl. 55). T.L. 16″–20″, T. 8″–12″, much larger than jays, tail long, tapered; plumage black except for abruptly white belly and large patch on rear of each wing (shown in flight). Voice. Varied, harsh or soft; *qua, qua,* 2–6 times. Nest. In trees at up to 50 ft., of twigs, roofed, to 24″ dia., with side entrance; eggs 5–8, grayish green with olive-brown spots, 1¼″ x ⅞″. Distr. Common R. locally along bases of both slopes of Sierra.

Magpies are gregarious, living where trees (or bushes) for roosting and nesting are near open grasslands or fields where the birds can find insects or seeds for food. On the ground they either walk or hop, the tail usually horizontal. The talkative Yellow-billed Magpie (*Pica nuttalli*) lives in the Great Valley and some open spots in the western foothills. The quieter Black-billed (*P. pica*) occurs in the Great Basin in open valleys with trees or large bushes. Physically the two differ only in color of bill.

B-75. Common Raven. *Corvus corax.* T.L. 22″–26½″, T. 9⅘″, spread to 54″; wings long, pointed, tail large, wedge-shaped; plumage glossy black. Voice. A deep throaty *croak.* Nest. On cliffs; of sticks with lined depression; eggs 5–6, green, brown-spotted, 2″ x 1⁵⁄₁₆″. Distr. Occasional C. V. in high s. Sierra, mainly in summer.

The Raven is as large as a Red-tailed Hawk (B-15). In flight it may alternately flap and soar, holding the wings horizontally. The tail is wedge-shaped or slightly rounded, not square as in a Crow. Singly or in small groups Ravens may appear in the southern Sierra at almost any season.

B-76. Common Crow. *Corvus brachyrhynchos.* T.L. 16″–20″, T. 7″, tail square-ended; plumage glossy black. Voice. A loud harsh *caw* or *karr.* Nest. In trees, often hidden; a large cup of twigs lined with bark strips or grasses; eggs 5–6, green, brown-blotched, 1⅝″ x 1⅛″. Distr. Common R. locally in Great Valley and edge of foothills, rare C. V. at Mono Lake.

Crows are not of uniform occurrence. Flocks live in certain areas over the years, but other places that seem of equal character are unoccupied. For foraging the birds require open flat country where both insects and various plant foods are available year-long. For nesting they seek substantial trees fairly resistant to swaying by wind. In winter they use groves of densely spaced trees where members of a large flock can roost close together.

B-77. Piñon Jay. *Gymnorhinus cyanocephala.* T.L. 10″–11¾″, T. 4⅘″; larger than robin; tail shorter than body; above uniform pale dull blue, below lighter; no crest or special markings. Voice. A high nasal *kä'-e,* singly or repeated. Nest. In piñons or junipers, at 10–50 ft.; of twigs, with deep felted cup; eggs 4–5, bluish white with fine dots or streaks, 1⅛″ x ⅞″. Distr. Common R. locally along entire e. base of Sierra; in piñons or junipers and sagebrush; C. V. in fall or winter on w. slope.

The Piñon Jay, unlike other jays, is gregarious and even nests in colonies. At all seasons the birds live and forage in loose flocks of 4 to 40 or more. Nuts of piñon and other pines are preferred food throughout the year, supplemented with grasshoppers and other insects while feeding young. Except in the breeding season, the flocks wander widely in the Great Basin and some are apt to appear on the west slope. Members of a feeding flock indulge in much "conversational" calling.

B-78. Clark Nutcracker. *Nucifraga columbiana* (pl. 55). T.L. 12"–13", T. 4"–5", larger than robin; head and body light gray; wing black with large white patch at rear margin; tail white except black central feathers. VOICE. A harsh nasal cawing, *kayr* or *kra-a,* often prolonged, repeated irregularly; softer calls by young. NEST. In conifers at 8 to 40 ft., of twigs and bark; eggs 2–3, pale green, sparingly flecked, 1¼" x 1⅝₆". DISTR. Common R. in High Sierra (mostly above 9000 ft.); C.V. at lower altitudes in winter; in treetops of open forest and on ground.

The Nutcracker (Clark crow or "camp robber") is the most conspicuous bird of upper sun-drenched slopes. It seeks prominent lookouts in the tops of conifers, does much "restless" flying, calling loudly and often. Nesting begins in snowbound March, nestlings are fed in April or May, and fully fledged young accompany their parents by June. Thereafter Nutcrackers live in straggling companies. The staple diet is of pine nuts picked or pried out of cones. Other food includes seeds, carrion, and insects. Nutcrackers take some flying insects in the manner of a flycatcher. The birds also glean tidbits of food in camps or at high mountain resorts.

B-79. Mountain Chickadee. *Parus gambeli* (col. pl. 20). T.L. 5"–5½", T. 2½", smaller than junco; top and back of head, whole chin, and throat black; side of head and stripe above eye white; body gray. VOICE. Song, *tee-tee, too-too;* call, a wheezy *chick-a-dee-dee,* or *chee-chee-chee;* alarm, a sharp *tsik-a.* NEST. In tree cavities or old woodpecker holes; eggs 5–8, white, ⅝" x ½". DISTR. R. from Yellow Pine to Subalpine belt, mainly in open woods.

The ever active and acrobatic little chickadees spend most daylight hours scanning the outer foliage and twigs of conifers and oaks for their minute insect food, often hanging inverted to do so. Their foraging is mostly within 50 feet of the ground, sometimes in shrubs or tree cavities, but rarely on the ground. In April or May each pair chooses a small territory, looks into many recesses, and usually selects a nest hole 2–10 ft. aboveground, often one dug by a woodpecker. The bottom is felted with mammal hair or feathers. The female incubates persistently, being fed by the male. After the broods are abroad, chickadees form loose bands of their own kind or with other small birds. During the winter they drift slowly through the trees, feeding and calling often to keep in touch with one another. Suet, bacon, or butter hung up near a cabin will often attract chickadees.

The Chestnut-backed Chickadee (*P. rufescens*) has been reported in Sequoia National Park.

B-80. Plain Titmouse. *Parus inornatus* (pl. 56). T.L. 5"–5½", T. 2½"; smaller than junco or linnet; head with erect tapered crest; plain grayisli brown above, pale gray below. VOICE. In spring a sharp *peet'-o,* 3–5 times in quick succession; also a wheezy chickadee-like call. NEST. In natural cavities or woodpecker holes in trees; eggs 6–8, white, sometimes reddish-spotted, ⅝" x ½". DISTR. Common R. in Foothill belt, in oak woodlands.

This somber-garbed relative of the chickadees is lively and pert. The crest is habitually erect and the tail usually in line with the back. It forages, upright or inverted, mainly in the outer foliage of oaks, sometimes in pines, and occasionally in brush. The male's shrill repeated song is a feature of foothill woodlands at nesting time. Broods accompany the parents for a few weeks after emerging; thereafter titmice live mostly in pairs. The food, of minute insects, is gleaned from twigs, leaves, and crevices.

B-81. Common Bushtit. *Psaltriparus minimus* (pl. 56). T.L. 4"–4½", T. 2⅛"; ⅓ size of linnet, tail longer than body; plain gray, paler below, head cap brownish. VOICE. A low *pst, pst,* variously inflected. NEST. Usually in oaks; a gourd-like sac 8"–9" long, entrance at side near top, woven of spider web, mosses, lichens, plant down, etc.; eggs 5–7, white, 9/16" x 7/16". DISTR. Common R. in Foothill belt, C.V. in late summer or fall upslope; inhabits foliage of oaks and tall shrubs.

The Bushtit is little larger than a hummingbird. Except when nesting it lives in loose flocks of 10 to 25. The roving band works slowly through the foliage, each member independent but giving frequent faint calls to keep in touch with its associates. The birds perch upright or inverted while scanning leaves for the minute insects taken as food. If a hawk or other enemy is sighted, all the birds freeze motionless and utter a special "confusion chorus" note. Unlike the related chickadee and titmouse, the Bushtit builds its own nest, a felted sac hung in an oak. Its interior is shaped like a woodpecker hole.

B-82. White-breasted Nuthatch. *Sitta carolinensis* (col. pl. 20). T.L. 5"–6", T. 2", size of junco, tail short; top of head and back of neck black, back and middle of tail bluish gray; cheeks and under surface white, outer tail feathers black, white-spotted. VOICE. Call a nasal *hank;* song *cher-wer,* repeated. NEST. In old woodpecker hole or decay cavity, lined with hair, feathers, or leaves; eggs 5–9, white, brown-spotted at large end, ¾" x 9/16". DISTR. Common R. in Foothill belt; some in Lodgepole–fir belt, except in winter; also S.V. on e. slope; lives low on trunks and large branches of both conifers and deciduous trees.

This nuthatch is the largest of our 3 species. It usually forages within 20 ft. or less of the ground, on rough-barked trees, most commonly on oaks but also on some conifers. By use of the stout, curved claws it hitches either upward or downward, not using the tail for support. The sturdy bill serves variously to probe for insects, to open nuts on occasion, and to enlarge a nest hole. The bird scans crevices and holes for its food, exceptionally catching insects in flight. The single call is uttered at irregular intervals. For nesting this species often uses a hole within 10 or 15 ft. of the ground.

B-83. Red-breasted Nuthatch. *Sitta canadensis* (col. pl. 20). T.L. 4″–4¾″, T. 1⅖″, half size of junco, tail short; top and side of head black in ♂ (slaty in ♀), white line over eye and black line through eye, back bluish gray, below reddish brown. VOICE. A high nasal *nă* or *wĕh,* singly at intervals, but repeated quickly when disturbed. NEST. In hole of tree at 5–40 ft., with soft lining; eggs 4–7, white, brown-spotted, ⁹⁄₁₆″ x ⁷⁄₁₆″. DISTR. Common S.V. in Lodgepole–fir belt, some in Yellow Pine and Subalpine belts; usually high on conifers; W.V. at lower altitudes.

In summer this nuthatch usually stays well up in big conifers but occasionally visits the base of a tree. Its clear, far-carrying call suggests a child's trumpet or elfin horn. If disturbed by the presence of a jay or other marauder, the bird sounds its notes in quick sequence, sometimes for several minutes. The food probably is of small insects gleaned from bark. It prefers to excavate a new nest hole each year and sometimes smears pitch around the entrance. In winter at lower elevations it forages on smaller trees.

B-84. Pygmy Nuthatch. *Sitta pygmaea* (col. pl. 20). T.L. 3⅖″–4½″, half size of junco; tail short; top and sides of head grayish brown; back bluish gray, below pale buff. VOICE. Chattering notes, *sŭp, sŭp′,* etc., by members of flock. NEST. In hole of tree, lined with hair, feathers, etc.; eggs 4–9, white, brown-dotted, ⁹⁄₁₆″ x ⁷⁄₁₆″. DISTR. Sparse R. of Yellow Pine belt on w. slope and in Jeffrey pines of e. slope; in open forest of large conifers.

This nuthatch, the size of the preceding species, is less common. Save when nesting it lives in small flocks that forage among the conifer needles and on the small outermost twigs in the manner of chickadees. When a flock is moving there is a babel of small voices, but while foraging the notes are few. The little birds commonly work at 75 ft. or more above ground.

B-85. Brown Creeper. *Certhia familiaris* (col. pl. 20). T.L. 5″–5¾″, T. 2½″, less than half size of junco, tail feathers stiff, pointed at tip, bill slender, curved; above dark brown, streaked with white, below dull white. VOICE. Call a longish *see;* song *see′, see′, se-teetle-te, see′.* NEST. Behind loosened piece of tree bark within 15 ft. of ground; of bark strips, twigs, feathers, etc.; eggs 4–8, white, reddish dots at large end, ⁹⁄₁₆″ x ⁷⁄₁₆″. DISTR. Common R. in Yellow Pine and Lodgepole–fir belts of w. slope; C.V. higher and on e. slope in late summer; occasional W.V. on lower w. slope; inhabits dense mature coniferous forest.

The little brown-streaked Creeper is not easy to find on the trunk of a large tree unless the observer is guided by its wiry call note. The bird clings to the rough bark surface with its delicate curved claws and presses the pointed tail feathers inward for support. From the base of a tree it hitches for some distance, then flits to another tree and starts a new ascent. It always moves upward or in spiral course, never turning sideways or heading downward like a nuthatch. A Creeper seems to forage without rest, scanning bark crevices for the tiny insects and spiders used as food. In spring a nest often may be found by seeing a parent fly directly to the site.

B-86. Wrentit. *Chamaea fasciata* (pl. 55). T.L. 6½″, T. 3¼″–3½″, body size of linnet but tail longer than body and slender; above grayish brown, below paler, throat with faint dusky streaks. VOICE. Song clear, whistled, on one pitch, *pit, pit, pit-tr-r-r-r-r*, starting slowly, ending as a trill; call a subdued ratchety *krrr*. NEST. In shrubs at 18″–24″, or trees to 15 ft.; a deep cup of cobweb and bark fibers with incurved edge and fine lining; eggs 4, pale greenish, ¾″ x ⁹⁄₁₆″. DISTR. Common R. of Foothill belt in chaparral or low trees.

This uniquely Californian bird always carries its slender tail up at an angle to the back. It lives *within* the chaparral, 5 ft. or less above the ground, rarely appearing outside the leaf crown and seldom going into trees. To see the bird an observer should sit under the brush and "screep," which may bring one or two Wrentits close to investigate; then the white iris is visible. Pairs are spaced out and resident on their territories of ½ to 2½ acres, which they defend against others of the species throughout the year. Adults eat insects and berries. The parents alternate in incubating and feeding the young. After nesting a few Wrentits stray upward into brush-lined valleys of the Yellow Pine belt.

B-87. Water Ouzel or Dipper. *Cinclus mexicanus* (pl. 56). T.L. 7″–8½″, T. 2″, body size of robin, tail very short; all plumage dark slate gray; a small white spot on upper eyelid. VOICE. Call a short *bzēēt*, singly or in rapid series; ♂ has elaborate varied song. NEST. On rocks near or over rushing water, of moss, entrance on side; eggs 3–6, white, 1″ x ¾″. DISTR. Common throughout conifer forest belt on both slopes at 2000–11000 ft.; lives along cold, swift, permanent streams, occasionally on lake shores.

This is our only "song" bird that lives solely on perennial cascading streams. The dense feathering that sheds water is its only aquatic adaptation, the feet being unwebbed. When perched on a midstream rock, the Ouzel bobs down and up every few seconds. It flies along a winding stream course, keeping close over the water and uttering the short call repeatedly. To feed, the bird forages in the shallows or plunges right into the water, where it can walk on the bottom while searching for aquatic insects. The Ouzel is a yearlong resident wherever streams remain unfrozen during winter, up into the Lodgepole–fir belt. Its song may be heard at almost any season, being most impressive in winter when other bird voices are few. The nest is usually placed where moistened by spray, even behind a waterfall, so that its mossy exterior remains green so long as used.

80.
Plain Titmouse

81.
Common
Bushtit

92.
Rock Wren

91. Canyon Wren

90. Bewick Wren

88.
House Wren

89.
Winter Wren

87.
Water Ouzel

94.
California
Thrasher

Plate 56. Birds   293

B-88. House Wren. *Troglodytes aedon* (pl. 56). T.L. 4½"–5¼", T. 2", much smaller than junco, bill slender; above brown, paler below, no contrasted markings. VOICE. Call a scolding *schee;* song of ♂ rapid, bubbling. NEST. In hole of tree or building, large for the bird, of twigs lined with soft materials; eggs 6–8, white, thickly brown-dotted, ⅝" x ½". DISTR. Common S.V. in Foothill belt of w. slope; also on e. side in aspens and lower conifer forest; forages in brush but nests in tree holes; C.V. in late summer higher in Sierra; a few as W.V. low on w. slope.

House Wrens arrive on the west slope by late April and a little later on the east side. Thenceforth, for a month or so, the bubbling song of males is one of the most frequent of avian voices. The birds usually forage low in thickets or chaparral but need a tree cavity, a space in some building, or a box in which to nest. Any extra interior space is filled with coarse twigs until the entrance is small; then a smoother lining is added. After the broods are fully fledged some of these wrens wander upslope, occasionally toward timberline.

B-89. Winter Wren. *Troglodytes troglodytes* (pl. 56). T.L. 4", T. 1¼", our smallest wren, half size of junco, tail very short; plumage dark reddish brown, a pale line over eye. VOICE. Call *tschĕp,* often 2 times quickly; song high-pitched, varied, rapid. NEST. Usually near water in cranny of stump or root tangle; of twigs and moss; eggs 4–7, white, brown-dotted, ⅝" x ⁷⁄₁₆". DISTR. Sparse R. on w. slope in Yellow Pine belt (Butte to Tulare Co.) and on e. slope in conifer forest s. to Mammoth; in damp canyons amid exposed tree roots and woody debris.

Smallest of local wrens, this dark reddish species must be sought in moist, shady sites. It twists about, bobbing frequently, and skips from perch to perch, holding the tail cocked up at a sharp angle. It favors dark recesses under overhanging banks or logs, and amid downed branches. In consequence an observer usually has only glimpses. The rapid, squeaky song is sometimes heard in winter as well as in the spring nesting season.

B-90. Bewick Wren. *Thyromanes bewickii* (pl. 56). T.L. 5"–5½", T. 2⅓"; about junco size, tail nearly length of body; above plain dull brown, below ashy white; a conspicuous white line over eye; outer tail feathers tipped with grayish white. VOICE. Call a hoarse *tserk;* also a soft *chee-chee-* . . . ; song lively, sibilant, ending *seet, seet, seet, tsee.* NEST. In cavity of tree or trash pile mostly filled with twigs or plant stems, lined with hair, feathers, or grasses; eggs 5–7, white, brown-spotted, ⅝" x ½". DISTR. Common R. in Foothill belt of w. slope; lives more in mixed brush than trees.

Chaparral and other shrubby hillside vegetation are the home of the rather pale-colored Bewick Wren. The birds are scattered, so that 6 or less may be heard in a half-day trip during the late spring. A foraging bird on the ground holds the tail up, but a singing male lets it droop. Both songs and calls are varied, so that an observer must study at length to learn them.

B-91. Canyon Wren. *Catherpes mexicanus* (pl. 56). T.L. 5½″–5¾″, T. 2″–2⅕″, bill ¾″ slender, slightly curved; more than half size of linnet; color rich reddish brown, throat and breast pure white; upper surface with fine black and white dots, tail with 4 or 5 narrow black bars. VOICE. Call a short *bzert;* song about 10 loud clear notes, descending in pitch and slowing at end. NEST. Near stream in rock crevices or building, of twigs felted over with moss or other soft materials; eggs 5–6, white with brown dots, ¾″ x ½″. DISTR. Fairly common R. in Foothill belt, edging into bordering areas; about crannies in rock walls or rock slides, often near water.

Anyone who visits a rock-walled foothill valley during the spring is likely to hear the loud clear song of this wren, but the bird may not be near. Typically it inhabits rather barren canyons but sometimes lives about wooden cabins and then can be watched at close range. Its color is striking—a pure white throat and reddish back. The bird hops in zigzag path on bent legs; every few seconds it slowly raises and then quickly depresses the body. When foraging it prowls into all manner of crevices in search of insects. The nest has a smoother exterior than that of other wrens.

B-92. Rock Wren. *Salpinctes obsoletus* (pl. 56). T.L. 5⅛″–6⅛″, T. 2¼″, nearly the size of linnet; bill long, slender; above light grayish brown, below whitish, a pale line over eye, breast flecked with dusky, tail with light tip and subterminal black bar. VOICE. Call a clear tinkling trill; song of clear and burred notes varied in pitch, *chr, chr, chr, ter, ter, ter, eche, eche* . . . NEST. In cliff cranny or tunnel end, of twigs or grasses with approach runway of rock scrap or pebbles; eggs 5–6, white, brown-dotted, ¾″ x 9⁄16″. DISTR. Common R. from Great Valley to Great Basin and up to 10500 ft.; in winter below heavy snow; lives on rock outcrops or rock slides, also in dry earth walls of gullies.

This large pale-colored wren lives among bare broken rocks or on earth bluffs anywhere from the lowlands to Sierran summits. Often it appears on the highland granite domes or rock slides. The bird has a long bill and claws, short legs, and a flattish head and body fitting it to prowl into crevices when searching for food. It is ever active, turning from side to side, bobbing frequently, and uttering the trilled call at short intervals. The varied song is to be heard during the spring months.

B-93. Mockingbird. *Mimus polyglottos.* T.L. 9″–11″, T. 5″; size of robin but more slender, tail long, rounded at end; above plain dark gray, below white; in flight shows large white patch on wing and white margin on tail. VOICE. Song varied, resembles calls of some other birds; call a harsh *chuck*. NEST. In thick bushes or trees; bulky, of twigs, with soft lining; eggs 3–6, bluish or greenish white, brown-blotched, 1″ x ¾″. DISTR. Sparse R. at low altitudes on w. slope and in some Great Valley towns; lives in scattered trees.

The Mockingbird now is a conspicuous resident in many lowland cities of central and southern California. Originally it was probably native in the scattered Blue Oak belt below the chaparral where it still lives in small numbers. The bird is in song through the year except at the end of summer when molting. Its "vocabulary" includes modified songs and calls of Linnet, Meadowlark, Shrike, California Jay, Plain Titmouse, and other local associates.

B-94. California Thrasher. *Toxostoma redivivum* (pl. 56). T.L. 11½"–13", T. 5"–5¾", size of robin but tail long, equaling body; bill slender, curved, 1" long; plumage plain brown, paler beneath, chin whitish. Voice. Call a low *chuck;* song lengthy, of chuckling notes, whistles, etc., in irregular sequence. NEST. In shrubs or low trees; a rough bowl of twigs with smooth lining; eggs 2–4, blue with brown dots, 1³⁄₁₆" x ¹³⁄₁₆". DISTR. Moderately common R. of Foothill belt in mixed chaparral.

The thrasher is adapted by structure and habits for life in the chaparral. The short round wings and long tail are suited to brief flights with frequent turning, and the plain brown plumage is inconspicuous. On its stout legs and feet, with tail cocked up, the bird can run and dodge under the brush cover to escape observation and enemies. Only for singing does it emerge to perch on a tall shrub or small tree, mostly in morning and toward evening in the spring. No two songs seem alike, being a varied array of notes, deep and rich, whistled, or chuckling. The population is never large, perhaps a pair or two per quarter section.

B-95. American Robin. *Turdus migratorius* (pl. 57). T.L. 10"–11", T. 3⅕"–4¾"; above dark slate, head and tail blackish; below rich reddish brown, chin and area under tail white. VOICE. Song of 4 or more loud caroling notes on same pitch with rising and falling inflection; calls various: *tuk, tuk,* 1 or several times, shrill when excited; also a squealing *wi'eh.* NEST. In trees at 4–75 ft. usually on horizontal branch (or shelf in building) to 4" high x 6"–7" dia., of grass stems, pine needles, etc., mixed with mud; eggs 4–5 (3–6), deep blue, 1⅛" x ¹³⁄₁₆". DISTR. Common S.V. from w. border of Yellow Pine belt across Sierra into edge of Great Basin, in forest bordering moist grassland; also W.V. in Great Valley and Foothill belt, sometimes higher, foraging in berry-producing plants.

The familiar red-breasted Robin is common and widespread (hence a useful size reference for many other birds). Males average slightly darker and larger than females; their bills are almost clear yellow in summer. From late April through summer the birds are in pairs, busy with nesting. Then the male's song is heard, especially from dawn into early morning and toward sundown. The nest is formed of grasses and needles with many pellets of mud gathered singly and pressed into the structure to make a rigid cup. When the mud has dried, the eggs are laid and incubation begins. In this season and while feeding young, the adults forage singly in damp grassland. Each stands, watches, and listens. If nothing is detected it runs a few steps and stands again. When a larva, insect, or worm is located, the bird bends over and grasps the prey. The spotted young emerge from late May until the end of July, being later in high altitudes, and some parents may rear sec-

97. Swainson Thrush

100. Townsend Solitaire

96. Hermit Thrush

95. Robin

99. Mountain Bluebird

105. Loggerhead Shrike

104. Cedar Waxwing

106. Starling

Plate 57. Birds

297

ond broods. After the molt old and young gather in flocks which roam together and winter at lower elevations. When grassland animals become scarce or unavailable, the Robin flocks feed on berries of many plants —elder, juniper, choke-cherry, toyon, mistletoe, and others. With the development of lawns and irrigated farms, Robins have taken to nesting in several towns of the Great Valley and other lowland areas.

B-96. Hermit Thrush. *Hylocichla guttata* (pl. 57). T.L. 6″–7″, T. 2⅗″–3″, larger than junco; above plain brown but tail reddish brown, breast buffy, sides grayish, belly white, lower throat, breast, and sides with round black spots, eye ring and band on wing (seen in flight) buff. VOICE. Call a soft *tup* or *chuck* 1 or 2 times, occasionally a harsh *tschee;* song clear, musical, of spaced phrases each of 3 to 6 notes, varying in pitch. NEST. In low tree; of twigs, bark shreds, and grasses, scantily lined; eggs 3–5, blue with brown spots, ⅞″ x ⅝″. DISTR. Common S.V. on both slopes in Lodgepole–fir belt and bordering areas at 3700–11000 ft.; also W.V. on w. slope below heavy snow; inhabits glades and ravines under shady cover.

This quiet, reclusive relative of the Robin lives on or near the ground under leaf canopy. Every few seconds it twitches the wings, when the tail is raised and then slowly lowered. These mannerisms and the rufous tail distinguish this thrush from the Swainson Thrush (B-97). In foraging the Hermit hops a few steps, quickly flicks pieces of leafy debris aside with its bill, and gazes intently at the cleared spot to find insects for food. The nesting season song is exhalted music to human ears—slow-cadenced, rising and falling in pitch, varied, and not continuous. The summer birds are present from May into August; others from the Northwest and Alaska are winter visitants from mid-October into April.

B-97. Swainson or Russet-backed Thrush. *Hylocichla ustulata* (pl. 57). T.L. 6⅘″–7⅔″, T. 2⅘″–3⅓″, about twice size of junco; above plain brown, breast buffy with triangular dark brown spots, belly white; eye ring and concealed bar in wing buff. VOICE. Call a liquid *what* or *whoit,* a harsher *chee-wr-r;* song of 2–4 clear notes, then an equal number slurred, rising in pitch, the last finely drawn out. NEST. In shrub or small tree at 4–5 ft., of plant and grass stems or bark shreds, with mud; eggs 3–5, bluish green with reddish brown spots, ⅞″ x ⅝″. DISTR. S.V. on w. slope in Foothill and Yellow Pine belts and on e. slope in willow thickets; inhabits trees and shrubs near streams or moist meadows.

These thrushes appear as transients in the foothills during the latter part of May and by early June are in song on their nesting grounds in damp sheltered cover. The males often sing from perches well up in trees and may be in voice during the day as well as in the morning and evening. Young reared in the mud-reinforced nests may be emerging by late June.

B-98. Western Bluebird. *Sialia mexicana.* T.L. 6½″–7⅛″, T. 2¾″, larger than linnet. Ad. ♂: Above mostly dark blue, chin and throat same, breast, sides of body, and middle of back chestnut brown, belly grayish. Ad. ♀:

Duller, upper surface and throat grayish blue, breast and sides pale brown. VOICE. Call a soft *kew,* also a harsh *che-check;* song (uncommon), repeated soft calls. NEST. In tree cavity or woodpecker hole; eggs 3–8, pale bluish green, ⅞" x ⅝". DISTR. Common R. in Foothill and lower Yellow Pine belts of w. slope; also on e. side s. to Lake Tahoe; summers about oaks, winters around berry-producing plants.

In spring and early summer pairs of these bluebirds live about oak trees over grasslands. While watching for insects, they occupy open perches offering a wide view. Some prey is caught in flight and some, including grasshoppers, is taken on the ground. After nesting, the birds are in loose flocks of varying size. When disturbed they fly off scatteringly high in the air, calling frequently. Until the next spring season they wander widely, concentrating wherever their favorite food—mistletoe berries—can be found.

B-99. Mountain Bluebird. *Sialia currucoides* (pl. 57). T.L. 7", T. 2⅖", half again size of junco. Ad. ♂ : Above clear pale blue, lighter on breast, belly white. Ad. ♀ : Above pale grayish blue, brighter on rump and tail; below grayish buff, belly whitish. Young: Breast mottled. VOICE. Call a weak *terp.* NEST. In woodpecker hole or other tree cavity; eggs 4–8, bluish white, ⅞" x ⅝". DISTR. Common S.V. across Sierra mostly at 8000–12000 ft.; around open short grassland.

This pale-colored Bluebird summers in the High Sierra about meadows and grass patches. Perches on rocks or tree stubs are used when watching for insects. Often the bird will hover on beating wings at 10 to 20 ft. in the air, while scanning the ground for food. The species arrives in May and has been seen until late September at high altitudes. It winters scatteringly in the San Joaquin Valley.

B-100. Townsend Solitaire. *Myadestes townsendi* (pl. 57). T.L. 8"–8½", T. 4"–4½", body larger than junco, tail long; plumage gray, slightly paler below, tail white-edged, middle of wing pale buff in flight, narrow eye ring, white. VOICE. Call a metallic *clink,* occasionally a harsh *chack;* song elaborate, somewhat like that of Black-headed Grosbeak (B-129). NEST. At base of tree or in crevice of earth bank; of twigs and needles; eggs 3–5, bluish white, brown-spotted, 1¾6" x ⅝". DISTR. S.V. from upper Yellow Pine belt into Subalpine belt on openly forested areas; W.V. on w. slope from Foothill belt to middle altitudes where berry crops are available.

The Solitaire, a member of the thrush family, has a varied, intermittent song of clear full notes, some suggestive of a mockingbird or thrasher. Summer songs, morning or evening, come from high in the conifers, but in fall or early winter the birds sing from lower in junipers or oaks and during midday. While singing a bird may flutter upward several feet, then drop back to its perch. The bell-like call resembles a note of the California ground squirrel. The straggling, loose nest is placed on the ground. In warm weather the bird eats insects, catching many in flight, but in autumn and winter it seeks berries of juniper, mistletoe, toyon, manzanita, and the like.

B-101. Western Gnatcatcher. *Polioptila caerulea.* T.L. 4″–5½″, T. 2⅛″; about ⅓ size of junco, tail equaling body, bill slender; top of head and back bluish gray, tail black margined with white, below pale gray. Forehead of ♂ black. VOICE. Call a weak *chee-e;* song high-pitched, wheezy *cheu, chee, chree,* of 3–6 notes. NEST. In oaks at about 10 ft., a small cup of grass covered with lichen or spider web; eggs 4–5, pale greenish or bluish, brown-spotted, ⁹⁄₁₆″ x ⁷⁄₁₆″. DISTR. Common S.V. in Foothill belt on w. slope in oak woodland.

The dainty blue-gray Gnatcatcher, unlike the kinglets, nests in the hot blue oak belt of the western foothills. From April until early fall it twitches about, showing the long black and white tail as it hunts in foliage and small twigs for minute insects. At nesting time each pair lives within a hundred-yard radius of the nest tree, but when the young are fledged family parties range more widely. Some stray upmountain in late summer before migrating southward.

B-102. Golden-crowned Kinglet. *Regulus satrapa* (col. pl. 20). T.L. 4″, T. 1¾″, scarcely ⅓ size of junco, tail shorter than body; above olive-green, below whitish, a white stripe over eye with black border above; crown orange and yellow (♂) or yellow (♀), 1 or 2 light bars on wing. VOICE. High-pitched, wiry *tse, tse-tse,* etc., song longer than calls. NEST. Hidden in fir foliage, a cup of mosses, lichens, spider web, etc.; eggs 8–9, creamy with brown spots, ⁹⁄₁₆″ x ⁷⁄₁₆″. DISTR. Fairly common S.V. in higher Yellow Pine and Lodgepole–fir belts of w. slope; also W.V. in Yellow Pine and Foothill belts; inhabits denser foliage of firs and other trees.

Faint lisping calls from among the terminal tufts of needles or leaves are the bird watcher's clue to locating these kinglets. Save when pairs are nesting, they travel in groups of 5 or 6, hopping and fluttering as they glean little insects from twigs and leaves. Their color matches the foliage except when a favorable view permits one to see the brilliant crown patch. The calls closely resemble parts of the male's spring song, being given more rapidly than those of the Brown Creeper (B-85).

B-103. Ruby-crowned Kinglet. *Regulus calendula* (col. pl. 20). T.L. 4″–4½″, T. 1¾″, about ⅓ size of junco; above grayish green, below buffy white, eye ring dull white, wing with 1 or 2 light bars; ♂ has concealed crown patch of bright red, exposed occasionally. VOICE. Call a ratchety *che,* given 2 to many times; summer distress call *yer-rup,* repeated; song resembling *see, see, see, oh, oh, oh, cheerily, cheerily, cheerily,* the last 3 notes loudly whistled. NEST. On conifer branch, often high, a bulky cup of soft material; eggs 5–11, white, brown-spotted, ⁹⁄₁₆″ x ⁷⁄₁₆″. DISTR. Common S.V. in Lodgepole–fir belt and bordering areas at 4000–10000 ft. in conifer forests; common W.V. in trees of foothills and lowlands.

The Ruby-crown, although of small size, has a clear, far-carrying song. It may be heard in the lowlands during late spring, throughout nesting time in the forest, and sometimes in autumn. This kinglet forages solitarily in the terminal foliage of conifers and in oaks, and may dart out to catch flying insects. In winter it hunts in leafless willows or alders and occasionally drops down to search plants on the ground. When one of these birds discovers an owl perched in a tree, its repeated insistent calls often attract others of the species to flutter about and join in a complaining chorus. The summer *yer-rup* often announces jays prowling near a kinglet nest.

B-104. Cedar Waxwing. *Bombycilla cedrorum* (pl. 57). T.L. 6½″–7½″, T. 2⅖″, slightly larger than junco, head crested, tail small, plumage sleek; chin, bill, and streak through eye black, above grayish brown, tail yellow-tipped, breast cinnamon, belly yellow; some shorter feathers on wing with waxy red tips. Voice. A faint high-pitched *zee,* often repeated. Distr. Sparse, irregular W.V. on both slopes at lower elevations; in berry-producing trees or shrubs.

Compact flocks of 15 to 50 Waxwings fly low overhead and perch close together in the upper parts of trees. When feeding, the birds flutter and cling to small branches and occasionally voice their shrill rattly notes. Their diet is of berries on mistletoe, toyon, and ornamental shrubs.

B-105. Loggerhead Shrike. *Lanius ludovicianus* (pl. 57). T.L. 8″–10″, T. 3¾″–4½″, size between junco and robin; above bluish gray, below white, stripe through eye black, wing black showing broad white patch in flight, tail black centrally but end and margins white. Voice. Call a harsh *skree,* often repeated; a somewhat varied spring song. Nest. In trees at moderate height, bulky but compact, of twigs, etc., felted with hair or feathers; eggs 5–7, grayish or greenish white, brown-speckled, 1″ x ¾″. Distr. Common R. in Great Valley, few in Foothill belt or along e. base of Sierra; in open where exposed perches are available.

The Shrike is a stocky songbird with hooked bill that is predaceous, feeding on grasshoppers, crickets, ground beetles and similar insects, some mice, and occasional small birds. It lives solitarily except when nesting and perches at 4 to 15 ft. on exposed tree limbs, wires, or posts to watch the open ground beneath for prey. When changing position it flies low over the ground, then *up* onto a new lookout.

B-106. European Starling. *Sturnus vulgaris* (pl. 57). T.L. 7½″–8½″, T. 2¾″, size of blackbird but short-tailed and chunky, bill long, slender. Ad. (spring): Black with greenish gloss, bill yellow. Ad. (winter): Black, finely speckled with buff or white, bill black. Voice. A clear whistle; several guttural and chattering notes; song varied, including notes of other birds. Nest. In cavities of trees, cliffs, or buildings; irregular, of grasses, etc.; eggs 5–7, slightly glossy, pale blue to whitish, 1¼″ x ⅞″. Distr. Introduced 1872–1896 in eastern states and now spread across North America; inhabits open farms, pastures, lawns, etc.

The Starling, an undesirable alien, began appearing in California during the 1940's and is increasing in numbers. Unlike native black-birds it has a short tail and zigzag walk and flies by alternately flapping and sailing, often with great speed. Elsewhere it has taken over tree cavities used for nesting by bluebirds, titmouses, and chickadees and may do the same here. It feeds on insects, wild and cultivated fruits, and grains.

B-107. Hutton Vireo. *Vireo huttoni.* T.L. 4¼"–4¾", T. 2", about ½ size of junco; plumage greenish olive, slightly paler below, spot between bill and eye, partial eye ring, and 2 bars on wing whitish. Voice. Call low, harsh; song drawling, *zree, zree, zree.* Nest. In oak, hung from small forked branch, mainly of moss; eggs 4, white, brown-dotted, ¾" x ½". Distr. Fairly common R. in Foothill and lower Yellow Pine belts of w. slope; in live and golden oaks.

This vireo resembles a Ruby-crowned Kinglet (B-103) in coloration but is more deliberate in movements. Of our vireos it is the greenest in coloration. The Hutton lives and nests in the evergreen oaks of the lower west slope.

B-108. Solitary Vireo. *Vireo solitarius* (pl. 58). T.L. 5"–5⅔", T. 2⅛", about ¾ bulk of junco, tail short; above grayish green, below whitish, line from bill to eye, eye ring, and 2 bars on wing white. Voice. Call a harsh *chē,* repeated; song *quēē'up, tsēēr,* notes separate, alternately rising and falling. Nest. In oak or conifer at 5–30 ft.; a basket lashed in twig crotch, of plant fibers, exterior decorated with petals, spider web, etc.; eggs 3–5, white, few dark spots, ¾" x 7⁄16". Distr. Common S.V. in Yellow Pine and lower Lodgepole–fir belts; in oak and conifer forests.

During April and May, these vireos are migrants through foothill woodlands before they settle for nesting in the main conifer belt. At the end of summer some wander higher before departing southward. In the nesting period they inhabit oaks and conifers on dryish slopes but may also live in mature cottonwoods or alders. This bird, known also as Cassin Vireo, keeps to open places under the leaf crown, and its movements are rather deliberate. The song season may continue until late in July.

B-109. Warbling Vireo. *Vireo gilvus* (pl. 58). T.L. 4¾"–5⅖", T. 2"–2⅓", ⅔ size of junco, tail shorter than body; above grayish green, below grayish white, a light line over eye. Voice. Call a throaty *zree;* song a sustained warbling with continued repetition. Nest. In tree, hung in small crotch; of plant fibers and bark strips; eggs 3–5, white, with dark brown dots, ¾" x ½". Distr. Common S.V. on w. slope from Foothill to Lodgepole–fir belt, also on e. slope; mostly in deciduous trees near streams.

In spring and early summer the voluble warbling song of this vireo is a major part of the bird chorus in many stream borders. It is likely to be heard in midday, when other species are quiet, and the male even sings when incubating. This is the commonest of local vireos. It usually forages and sings well up in the trees, although the nest may be lower.

B-110. Orange-crowned Warbler. *Vermivora celata* (col. pl. 21). T.L. 4⅔", T. 2", ½ size of junco; above dull greenish, below greenish yellow. Voice.

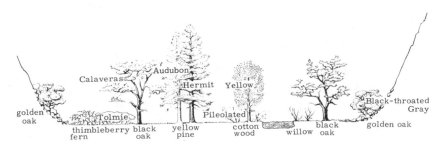

Figure 21. Ecological segregation of Wood Warblers in Yosemite Valley during the nesting season. Habitats are named below. Each warbler has a separate forage niche and does not compete with the others.

Call *chit* or *tsip;* song rapid, a weak tinny trill rising and then falling in pitch at end. NEST. On ground of shaded hillside; of grasses and plant fibers; eggs 3–6, white, heavily speckled with dark brown, ⅝″ x ½″. DISTR. Sparse S.V. in Foothill and Yellow Pine belts of w. slope, and low along e. base of Sierra; lives in shaded inner foliage of trees and shrubs or chaparral.

This and the other warblers (nos. 111–119) are solitary birds, of quick active movements and temperament which forage for insects mostly within the shelter of leafy vegetation. Each of the 10 species uses a separate environment so that they do not compete with one another (fig. 21). The Orange-crown is a bird of shrubbery and open woods. It is plain-colored with no contrasted markings, and the male's concealed crown patch of orange is rarely seen. The bird usually forages at 30 feet or lower and nests on the ground.

B-111. Calaveras or Nashville Warbler. *Vermivora ruficapilla* (col. pl. 21). T.L. 4¾″, T. 2″, ½ size of junco; above olive-green, below yellow, head and neck (except throat) gray, eye ring white, crown of ♂ chestnut. VOICE. Call *tseep* or *tsip;* song 4 or 5 rapid shrill notes, then 3 or 4 lower, *tsirp, tsirp, tsirp, tsirp, sup, sup, sup, sup.* NEST. On ground; well made of bark strips and grasses with fine lining; eggs 4–5, cream, with small or large spots of reddish brown, ⅝″ x ½″. DISTR. Common S.V. in Yellow Pine belt of w. slope; forages mostly in oaks or maples, commonly at 25–40 ft.

The light grayish head, white eye ring, and yellow under parts distinguish this species from other tree-foraging warblers in the Sierra. The birds are not always easy to see against the light green foliage of early summer, and they occasionally forage up to 70 feet above ground. Besides oaks and maples they may visit Douglas firs. The Calaveras arrives in May and after nesting may linger at higher altitudes until mid-September.

B-112. Yellow Warbler. *Dendroica petechia* (col. pl. 21). T.L. 4⅛″–5¼″, T. 2″, ½ size of junco; essentially all yellow, greenish yellow above, ♂

streaked below with chestnut. VOICE. Call a loud *tsip;* song high, shrill, 4 or 5 separate notes and a series of shorter ones. NEST. In bushes or low trees; a compact woven cup of gray weed bark and fine grasses with soft lining; eggs 3–4, white to pale green or gray with largish spots of dark brown, $^{11}\!/_{16}$″ x ½″. DISTR. Common S.V. on both slopes below Lodgepole–fir belt, in streamside deciduous trees.

This "summer yellow bird" often is common, up to 20 having been noted in a 4-hour census. Its clear sharp song is heard from late April to early July in waterside willows, cottonwoods, and alders. The species forages and sings at up to 40 feet above ground, but usually places its nest below 15 feet.

B-113. Audubon Warbler. *Dendroica auduboni* (col. pl. 21). Smaller than junco; T.L. 4¾″–5¼″; T. 2⅜″; *rump always yellow* (except young), chin usually yellow; tail broad, with white bar near end. Ad. ♂ (summer): back bluish gray, streaked with black; breast black; crown, chin, and sides of breast yellow. Ad. ♀ (summer): Like ♂ but breast mottled gray and black. Ad. and Im. (winter): Brownish above and below, little or no black on breast. VOICE. Song a mellow, tinkling, *turly, urly, urly, urly, urly, i-ci;* call a sharp *tsip.* NEST. Usually in conifers, at 9–50 ft., bulky, of bark and needles, lined with feathers; eggs 3–5, greenish white with black, brown, or lilac spots, $^{11}\!/_{16}$″ x $^{9}\!/_{16}$″. DISTR. S.V. in Yellow Pine to Subalpine belts on both slopes at 3000–10000 ft., chiefly in conifers; W.V. in Foothill belt and lower valleys.

The Audubon Warbler is the largest, commonest, and most widespread of Sierran warblers in summer, throughout the conifer forest. From autumn until spring it abounds below the snow line in broadleaved trees of town and country, even foraging on the ground. In trees it hunts small insects in the outer foliage, changing location often by short semicircular flights *out beyond* the leafage, and may catch flying insects there. In winter it takes small fruits. Except when pairs are nesting, these warblers are in scattering groups, sometimes with bluebirds, juncos, or other small birds. The Audubon has 7 or 8 plumages according to age, sex, or season, from grayish down in nestlings and streaked body feathering in juveniles out of the nest to the bright male breeding plumage.

B-114. Black-throated Gray Warbler. *Dendroica nigrescens* (col. pl. 21). T.L. 4⅔″–5⅔″, T. 2″, ½ size of junco; head, chin, and throat black (♂, mixed with white in ♀), a white line over eye and another from bill along side of throat, back bluish gray, tail with broad white margins, 2 light bars on wing, under surface white, sides streaked with black. VOICE. Call a low *chit;* song a drawling *wēē′zy, wēē′zy, wēē′zy, wēē′zy, wĕr.* NEST. Low in bush or at 25–50 ft. in conifers; a deep loose cup of plant fibers, grass, and moss; eggs 3–5, creamy, brown-blotched, ⅝″ x ½″. DISTR. Fairly common S.V. on w. slope in upper Foothill belt and Yellow Pine belt; mainly in golden oaks.

The crown and upper foliage of evergreen golden oaks are the usual forage areas of this rather slow-moving warbler. Although strikingly patterned, its coloration is disruptive among the sunlit leaves so that the bird is not always easy to see. It arrives in April, and young may be out of the nest early in June; some individuals remain until September or October.

B-115. Hermit Warbler. *Dendroica occidentalis* (col. pl. 21). T.L. 5", T. 2¼", ½ size of junco. Ad. ♂ : Head yellow, chin black; back bluish gray, black-streaked; tail black centrally but white-margined; 2 light bars on wing. Ad. ♀ & Im.: Head dull yellow, crown black-mottled, chin whitish, dusky-spotted. VOICE. Call a moderate *tchip;* song *ter'ley, ter'ley, ter'ley, sic', sic'.* NEST. In fir on branch, at 15 ft. or more; compact, of twigs, moss, and plant down; eggs 3–5, white, heavily brown- and gray-spotted, ⅝" x ½". DISTR. Varying S.V. in Yellow Pine and Lodgepole–fir belts; in fairly dense pine and fir forests.

This bird occupies coniferous forests at middle altitudes. There it may be in association with the wider-ranging Audubon Warbler. The song is more rapid than that of the Black-throated Gray but not so clear as that of the Audubon Warbler. It usually forages at 20 feet or more above ground on flat spreading branches of firs and pines.

B-116. Tolmie or MacGillivray Warbler. *Oporornis tolmiei* (col. pl. 21). T.L. 4¾"–5½", T. 2", about ⅔ size of junco; head, neck, and breast gray (darkest in Ad. ♂), eyelids white, above plain dull green, below yellow. VOICE. Call a loud *tchip;* song 3–5 clear separate notes, then several shorter ones close together, *sir-pit', sir-pit', sir-pit', syr, sip, sip.* NEST. Low in a bush; of coarse and fine grass; eggs 3–5, dull white blotched with dark brown, ¾" x ⁹⁄₁₆". DISTR. Common S.V. on both slopes in Yellow Pine and lower Lodgepole–fir belts; in dense, low shrubbery over damp ground.

Unlike the tree-dwelling warblers, this species lives in thickets of cherry, thimbleberry, ceanothus, bracken, and similar plants, but it seldom invades chaparral. The birds forage within about 4 feet of the ground and stay within the shrub cover, being more often heard than seen. Some males go up into low trees to sing, but others sing and forage within thickets. Nests are commonly within 30 inches of the ground. When one is found, it is easy to observe the course of incubation and rearing until the young depart.

B-117. Yellowthroat. *Geothlypis trichas* (col. pl. 21). T.L. 4¾"–5¾", T. 2¼", about ½ size of junco; back and tail yellowish brown, below yellow (♂) or yellowish white (♀), face and forehead of ♂ black, bordered above by white. VOICE. Call a sharp but hoarse *tchack;* song *witch'et-y, witch'et-y,* 3–4 times slowly but insistently. NEST. Low in weeds, tules, etc., of grasses, lined; eggs 3–4, white with blackish streaks and grayish dots, ⅔" x ½". DISTR. Common locally along base of Sierra, R. along w. slope and S.V. on e. side in low dense vegetation close to water.

The Yellowthroat lives within 6 feet of the ground, where there is continuous shielding vegetation such as cat-tails, tules, willow thickets, or blackberry vines. Under this the bird forages and nests. It may sometimes be "squeaked" out for a glimpse, but usually the observer must be content with hearing the calls and song.

B-118. Yellow-breasted Chat. *Icteria virens.* T.L. 7"–8", T. 3½", slightly larger than junco, tail equaling body; above plain greenish brown, throat and breast yellow, belly white, eyelid and stripe over eye white. VOICE. Calls and song varied, whistles and chuckling notes, some imitations of other birds. NEST. In bush or small tree; 6"–7" dia., loosely woven of grasses and plant stems; eggs 3–5, white, spotted with reddish brown and gray, ⅞" x ⅝". DISTR. Local S.V. along w. base of Sierra; in dense streamside thickets.

Largest and most vocal of local warblers is the Chat, which summers in lowland riparian growths, sometimes in company with the Yellowthroat. It is rather slow of movement and its calls and songs are varied, unlike the set themes of other warblers. The songs may be heard before daybreak and after dusk and even when other birds are quiet in the afternoon heat or at midnight. When singing it often jumps into the air and then flutters down with drooping wings and tail.

B-119. Wilson Warbler. *Wilsonia pusilla* (col. pl. 21). T.L. 4¼"–5⅛", T. 2"–2⅕", ½ size of junco; head with black cap (smaller on ♀), above yellowish green, forehead and under surface yellow. VOICE. Call a throaty *tchĕp;* song flat-toned, *chi, chi, chi, . . . chit, chit* louder and faster at end. NEST. In low bushes or on ground; rather bulky, of mosses or grasses with small lined cup; eggs 4–6, white, with reddish brown spots, ⅝" x ⁷⁄₁₆". DISTR. Spring Tr. along both bases of Sierra and S.V. in Lodgepole–fir belt of w. slope; in thickets over damp ground near streams or lakes.

The black-capped (pileolated) Warbler forages mostly within 6 feet of the ground in thickets of willow, creek dogwood, and other moisture-loving plants. In summer up to 8 pairs per mile may be found in the plant cover along some streams. This warbler often captures flying insects. Its song is sharp and staccato. The subspecies that nests in the Sierra arrives early in May, nests in June, and visits the higher altitudes until mid-September. Another, northern subspecies migrates northward along both bases of the mountains in May.

B-120. House Sparrow. *Passer domesticus.* T.L. 5½"–6¼", T. 2⅖", size of junco but chunkier. Ad. ♂: Crown gray, upper surface brown, streaked with black; cheek chestnut, middle of throat and much of breast black, below grayish white. Ad. ♀ and Im.: Head grayish brown, no black chin or throat, otherwise like ♂. VOICE. Call a harsh *chis-sick;* song irregular, not melodious. NEST. In branches of a tree or stuffed into a cavity, a bulky sphere of grass, etc., lined with feathers, entrance on side; eggs 3–7, white, heavy with gray-brown marks, ⅞" x ⁹⁄₁₆". DISTR. Introduced from Europe, in Calif. since 1871; mostly in towns along bases of Sierra.

The alien English or House Sparrow became abundant in "horse-and-buggy" days over the Great Valley and survives in many communities.

Only occasionally does it venture above the foothill country. At all seasons it lives in loose flocks. Males in fresh autumn plumage are white on the chin; the black appears over winter with wear of the feathers.

B-121. Western Meadowlark. *Sturnella neglecta* (pl. 58). T.L. 10″–11″, T. 3″, body chunky, bill, legs, and feet stout, wings and tail short; above brown, black-streaked; head with 3 pale stripes: over crown and above each eye; tail white-margined; below yellow, breast with black crescent. Voice. Calls: a clear whistle, a short *chuck'*, a throaty *chr-r-r-r*; song clear, rolling, melodious, 8–12 notes. Nest. On weedy ground, of dried grasses, often with scant "dome," and approach runway; eggs 3–7, white with brown and gray spots, 1⅛″ x 1¹⁄₁₆″. Distr. Common R. in Great Valley and on clearings of Foothill belt; also along e. base of Sierra; in grasslands.

The melodious voice of the Western Meadowlark at nesting time is a pleasing element in open areas on both sides of the Sierra. Males sing while perched on trees, rocks, wires, or posts, and sometimes on the wing. When foraging the birds walk on the ground, taking both insects and seeds. In fall and winter Meadowlarks live in loose roving flocks of 10 to 75 birds which are less closely knit than those of blackbirds.

B-122. Yellow-headed Blackbird. *Xanthocephalus xanthocephalus* (pl. 58). T.L. 9″–11″, T. 3¾″. Ad. ♂ : Larger than robin, head, neck, and breast yellow, wing patch white, plumage otherwise dull black. Ad. ♀ : Slightly smaller, head, chin, and breast dull yellow, body dark brown, unstreaked. Voice. Call low-pitched *kluck* or *cack*, varied; song a series of low harsh notes. Nest. In tules or weeds at 1–3 ft. over water, a tall woven basket of reeds or grasses; eggs 3–5, grayish or greenish white, heavily brown-spotted, 1″ x ¾″. Distr. Irregular S.V. in n. Sierra and areas w. and e. of mts., in cattail or tule marshes; irregular W.V. in Great Valley on open grasslands.

Nesting Yellow-heads utter an amazing array of calls sounding like *gurrl, yewi*, or *cut-that-aout*, and the song has been compared to the noise of a rusty gate hinge. Nests are placed scatteringly in marsh vegetation with enough water below to discourage land predators. Some pairs begin early, and others delay their nesting until early summer. In winter the birds sometimes are in flocks with other kinds of blackbirds.

B-123. Red-winged Blackbird. *Agelaius phoeniceus* (pl. 58). T.L. 7½″–8½″, T. 3″, smaller than robin. Ad. ♂ : All black except for red patch with buff border, at bend of wing. Ad. ♀ : Smaller; above brownish black, a light stripe over crown and one over each eye, below heavily streaked with dark brown. Voice. Call in flocks a sharp *chăck*, of ♂ near nest *tee'-urr;* song *tong-leur'-lee*, slightly trilled at end. Nest. In cat-tails or tules near water or in dense moist weeds, a woven cup of reeds, grasses, or plant bark, lashed to upright stems; eggs 4–5, bluish green, brown-blotched, 1″ x ¾″. Distr. Common S.V. or R. locally below Lodgepole–fir belt on both slopes; in moist or swampy places.

In spring the Red-wings are spaced out in marshes or wet swales, each pair living in and defending a small territory. The male in courting

108.
Solitary Vireo

109. Warbling Vireo

121.
Western
Meadowlark

123.
Red-winged
Blackbird

126.
Brewer
Blackbird

122.
Yellow-headed Blackbird

125. Bullock Oriole

128.
Western Tanager

Plate 58. Birds

display has his feathers fluffed out, tail spread, wings drooping, and the red epaulets raised. Commonly he clings to an upright stem, giving the on-guard call *tee'urr* at intervals. Meanwhile the smaller and duller female is busy close by at the nest. On the west slope nesting is spread from April into June. At other seasons the Red-wings are in flocks of up to several hundred and then range widely over pastures and grasslands.

B-124. Tricolored Blackbird. *Agelaius tricolor.* T.L. 8½″–9″, T. 3⅔″, resembles Red-winged Blackbird but red wing patch of ♂ bordered by white bar. VOICE. Call a harsh *chĕck;* song a scolding *ĕskŏw-ĕskēō.* NEST. In close colonies in dense thickets of tules, cat-tails, or weeds; a stout basket of grasses and reeds; eggs 4, pale green, with blackish marks, 1⅛″ x ¾″. DISTR. Local R. in Great Valley and Foothill belt, in or near marshy areas.

This blackbird, restricted to California, differs from the Red-wing in several ways. The birds are gregarious at all seasons, they nest in dense colonies, are quite direct in flight, and often keep near the ground when awing. The male's song is brief and unmusical.

B-125. Bullock Oriole. *Icterus bullockii* (pl. 58). T.L. 8″, T. 3½″, smaller than robin. Ad. ♂ : Crown, chin, back, and middle of tail black, side of head and neck, rump, and whole lower surface orange, large wing patch white, outer tail feathers yellow. Ad ♀ and Im.: Above grayish brown, sides of head and breast yellow, belly whitish, wing with 2 white bars, tail yellowish when spread. VOICE. Call of ♂ a clear *klēēk,* a harsh *cha-cha-cha* . . . ; song *hip'-kip-y-ty-hoy'-hoy* rapid, accented. Of ♀ : simple harsh notes. NEST. In trees at 6–40 ft.; a hanging pouch to 9″ long of woven plant fibers or horsehair; eggs 3–6, gray white, with scrawling blackish lines, 1″ x ⅝″. DISTR. Common S.V. in Great Valley and Foothill belt of w. slope and along e. base of mts.; in oaks, cottonwoods, etc.

No foothill bird is more brilliant than the male of this oriole—orange, black, and white—as glimpsed in flight or in the trees. The birds arrive on the west side in late March or early April. Soon they are building their airy "hang nests" (which often survive into the next winter). They forage for insects and fruits in the trees and take others on the ground. Males precede the females in both arrival and departure, which is in late summer.

B-126. Brewer Blackbird. *Euphagus cyanocephalus* (pl. 58). T.L. 8¾″– 10¼″, T. 3⅘″–4½″, slightly smaller than robin. Ad. ♂ : Shiny black, iris white. Ad. ♀ and Im.: Dull brownish black, iris dark brown. VOICE. Call (♂ and ♀) a harsh *tchick;* "song" a wheezy *tseur* or *tshēē.* NEST. Usually in tree at moderate height (often in colonies); of twigs and grasses firmed with mud; eggs 3–7, greenish gray, brown-spotted, 1″ x ¾″. DISTR. Common R. at lower altitudes on both slopes, nests to 7300 ft. on w. slope and invades mts. to timberline in summer; forages on grasslands.

The Brewer is the commonest and most wide-ranging of our blackbirds. The females and young are never streaked like those of other species. The nests are usually in trees but occasionally close to the ground or even in bushes, and noisily defended against invaders. Both parents feed the brood, often walking close together over grassland when seeking insects or worms, then flying directly to the nest. Most nesting is below 4000 feet but after the broods are fledged the adults and young, in small groups, move up to forage on mountain meadows, and some remain there into October. Lowland winter flocks may include hundreds of individuals.

B-127. Brown-headed Cowbird. *Molothrus ater.* T.L. 7″–7½″, T. 2⅘″, smaller than ♀ Red-wing, bill short, sparrow-like. Ad. ♂: Shiny black except head and breast dull brown. Ad. ♀: Dull brown, paler and faintly streaked below. VOICE. Chattering notes; of ♂ a sharp whistle; song a gurgling *glu-glu-glēē*. DISTR. R. at lower levels w. and e. of mts., in streamside vegetation and pastures.

Bird students dislike the cowbird because it avoids nesting and the female lays her eggs singly in the nests of small songbirds. Incubated with the owner's eggs, the hatchling cowbird takes a major share of the food brought by the foster parents and may evict one or more of the rightful nestlings. When grown the young "alien" departs to join other cowbirds.

B-128. Western Tanager. *Piranga ludoviciana* (pl. 58). T.L. 6¾″–7¾″, T. 3¼″–3½″, smaller than robin. Ad. ♂: Head red, wings, upper back, and tail black, rest of body yellow. Ad. ♀: Above dull yellowish brown, below dull yellow. VOICE. Call a hoarse *chĕr'tig* or *chēē'-tik,* repeated; song a drawling *chĕr'-wĕr,* 3 to many times. NEST. On horizontal branch of pine or fir, in foliage; of needles, twigs, or plant stems, lined; eggs 3–5, blue, brown-spotted, ⅞″ x ⅝″. DISTR. Common S.V. in Yellow Pine and Lodgepole–fir belts of w. slope, scarcer on e. side; in open forest.

Tanagers migrate through the foothills in May and settle for summer in open forest areas above, where they remain until mid-September. The birds are deliberate in movement, and not shy, sometimes coming to the ground or tables in a camp. The male, although bright-colored, is not always easy to see when in foliage. The female builds the nest and incubates, but both parents feed the young. Early in the summer insects are the chief food, but later berry crops attract the tanagers, sometimes in small flocks, before they migrate.

B-129. Black-headed Grosbeak. *Pheucticus melanocephalus* (pl. 59). T.L. 7½″–8⅘″, T. 3⅖″–3⅘″, smaller than robin, bill short, conical. Ad. ♂: Above mostly black; neck collar, rump, and under surface orange-brown; wing with 2 bars and large patch of white; end of tail white-spotted. Ad. ♀: Above dull brown, streaked with black; a light stripe over crown and 1 above each eye; wing with 2 white bars; breast light brown, belly yellow. VOICE. Call (♂ and ♀) a sharp *spick;* song a rolling, musical, rapid warble

129.
Black-headed Grosbeak

130.
Lazuli Bunting

131.
Evening Grosbeak

138.
Common Goldfinch

139. Red Crossbill

137. Pine Siskin

140.   Green-tailed Towhee

141.
Rufous-sided
Towhee

Plate 59. Birds   311

of ascending and descending notes. NEST. Usually near streams in low trees or bushes; bulky, loose-woven, shallow, of twigs or plant stems; eggs 3–4, bluish green, brown-spotted, 1 3⁄16" x 3⁄4". DISTR. Abundant S.V. on both slopes, in Foothill and Yellow Pine belts on w. side; in streamside trees and open forest.

The rich warbling song of the Black-headed Grosbeak is a large element of the spring bird chorus. Males are singing on arrival in April and continue into July, sometimes on the wing, and also when incubating on the nest. Singing "females" probably are males not in completely adult plumage. The species prefers open woods, usually near water, and forages much in crown foliage. Nests are commonly within 12 feet of the ground. Some broods emerge in late May and a few late in July.

B-130. Lazuli Bunting. *Passerina amoena* (pl. 59). T.L. 5"–6¼", T. 2⅛"–2⅖", smaller than junco, tail short. Ad. ♂ : Head, throat, back, and rump light blue; breastband tawny; rest of under parts white; tail and wings blackish brown, 1 (or 2) white wing bars. Ad. ♀ and Im.: Above dull dark brown, below pale brown, belly whitish. VOICE. Call (♂ and ♀) a weak *tsip,* song long, rapid, of short phrases high, low, then high in pitch. NEST. At 4 ft. or less, usually in weeds or bushes, made of leafy grasses, finely lined, and lashed to a support stem or crotch; eggs 3–4, pale bluish green, rarely speckled, 3⁄4" x ½". DISTR. Common S.V. at lower altitudes on both slopes, esp. in Foothill belt; in low plants along ravines near streams.

The sky-blue male of this finch perches on tall bushes or low trees to sing, which it does persistently through much of the day. The dull-colored female remains more in tangled undergrowth. Both forage within weedy or shrubby cover, and the nest is in that sort of shelter. The birds begin arriving by mid-May and the last depart late in September.

B-131. Evening Grosbeak. *Hesperiphona vespertina* (pl. 59). T.L. 7"–8½", T. 2¾"–3⅕", a large chunky sparrow, smaller than robin; bill stout, conical; end of tail notched. Ad. ♂ : Body brownish yellow; crown, wings, and tail black; a large white wing patch; forehead and stripe over eye yellow. Ad. ♀ and Im.: Brownish gray, darkest on head; belly whitish; wings and tail black, white-spotted. VOICE. Call a shrill *plēē-ēk;* song 3 loud high notes given slowly, *zer-r-p, zir-r-p, prili-p.* NEST. In trees at moderate height, of twigs and rootlets, lined; eggs 3–4, pale greenish blue, sparse dark marks, 7⁄8" x 5⁄8". DISTR. Irregular S.V. in Yellow Pine and Lodgepole–fir belts, on both slopes; mainly in dense pine or fir forests; also irregular W.V. in lowlands w. of mts.

The Evening Grosbeak is a large finch, contrastingly patterned but a poor songster. The sharp call is unmistakable. The birds are variable in occurrence—sometimes locally common, in small groups, again scarce or absent. They forage both high in trees and on the ground. Buds of various trees and some berries are included in their diet.

B-132. Purple Finch. *Carpodacus pupurens* (col. pl. 22). T.L. 6″–6½″, T. 2½″, size of junco (B-148), tail short, notched at end. Ad. ♂: Crown, rump, chin, and breast purplish red; belly whitish, unstreaked; rest of plumage dark brown tinged with red. Ad. ♀: Above grayish brown (olive-tinged) streaked with dusky brown, below whitish, broadly streaked with dark brown; a dark patch behind eye. Voice. Call (♂ and ♀), a sharp *pert;* song a short rapid rolling warble. Nest. In tree at 5–40 ft. on a branch, out from trunk; a well-made cup of twigs, mosses, and grasses; eggs 4–5, pale bluish green, with gray or black streaks, 1¾6″ x ⁹⁄₁₆″. Distr. Common S.V. mainly in Yellow Pine belt of w. slope in conifers and oaks; W.V. in Foothill belt.

There are 3 tree-dwelling Sierran finches in which the males are reddish on crown, breast, and rump but the females streaked and without red. The Cassin Finch inhabits the higher forests, the Purple Finch the Yellow Pine belt, and the Linnet the foothills and lowland valleys. The Purple Finch's song is short and rolling without the squeals of the Linnet's song, and it is heard through a shorter season. This species forages in terminal foliage of trees and bushes, sometimes on the ground, eating buds, catkins, and berries. When wintering at the lower elevations it may be in flocks of up to 15 birds.

B-133. Cassin Finch. *Carpodacus cassini* (col. pl. 22). T.L. 6½″–7″, T. 2¾″, slightly larger than junco or purple finch; tail notched at end. Ad. ♂: Crown bright crimson, rump and breast pale pink; back, wings, and tail dark brown, dusky-streaked and reddish-tinged; belly whitish. Ad. ♀ and Im.: Above grayish (to greenish yellow), streaked with dusky brown, below whitish, sharply streaked with dusky brown. Voice. Call 1 or 2 syllables; song resembles that of Linnet. Nest. In pine at 10–80 ft. among needles at end of branch; of twigs, grasses, and bark strips; eggs 4–5, bluish green, gray to black spots, 1¾6″ x ⁹⁄₁₆″. Distr. Common R. in Lodgepole–fir and Subalpine belts on both slopes and up to 10500 ft.; in open forest and about meadows.

The Cassin Finch, largest of the red finches, lives yearlong in the High Sierra, seldom descending much in winter. The male's song is more varied than in the Purple Finch, with both well-rounded notes and some Linnet-like squeals. The birds alternate between treetop positions and the ground. Buds seem a favorite item of diet. When not nesting these finches are in small flocks of up to a dozen.

B-134. California Linnet or House Finch. *Carpodacus mexicanus* (col. pl. 22). T.L. 5½″–6″, T. 2¼″–2½″, size of junco, tail square-ended. Ad. ♂: Forehead, line over eye, rump, chin, and breast crimson; belly whitish, streaked sharply with brown; back, wings, and tail brownish. Ad. ♀: Above grayish brown (no red), below whitish streaked with brown. Voice. Call *chee-ep,* rising in pitch at end; song varied, bubbling, and long, with squeaking notes. Nest. Usually low, in tree, bush, cliff crevice, or vine on a house; a sturdy cup of grasses or other stringy material; eggs 4–5, pale bluish green, few dark spots at large end, ¾″ x ½″. Distr. Abundant R. in Great

Valley and Foothill belt (locally higher) on w. slope and S.V.(?) along e. side of mts.; in scattered trees amid grassland and near water.

Of all native birds the Linnet is most adapted as a "house finch." Pairs often nest in vines on dwellings. At other seasons the birds live in small or large flocks that frequent fields and grasslands. When frightened, they take off in the open on high circling flights before descending again. They eat seeds of grasses and small herbaceous plants, thistles, and some wild berries. They also relish the fruits and berries of orchards and gardens, often doing much damage. In new plumage the red feathers on males are white-edged, but these margins wear off over winter so that the birds become brighter colored by nesting time.

B-135. Pine Grosbeak. *Pinicola enucleator.* T.L. 8"–8½", T. 3¾", slightly smaller than robin; plumage dark gray. Ad. ♂: Pinkish red on head, breast, and rump. Ad. ♀ and Im.: Dull yellow on crown and rump. VOICE. Call a loud clear *woit-leek,* repeated. NEST. In conifer at 16–35 ft. out on a branch; a frail twig platform, grass-lined; eggs 3, greenish blue, with dark spots, 1" x ¾". DISTR. Sparse R. in High Sierra, Plumas Co. to Fresno Co., at 4700–10000 ft.; in open subalpine forest near meadows.

This relatively uncommon and plain-colored finch is a strict resident of the higher mountains. It has been found where alpine hemlocks and associated trees grow. Needle buds, fir and hemlock seeds, and berries of high-altitude shrubs are included in its food.

B-136. Gray-crowned Rosy Finch. *Leucosticte tephrocotis* (col. pl. 22). T.L. 5¾"–6¾", T. 3", larger than junco; body deep brown, feathers rosy-edged on forepart of wing, rump, tail, and sides; crown black, back and sides of head gray; ♀ duller than ♂. VOICE. Calls *zee'o, hootititeet;* song high-pitched, chirping, varied. NEST. In niche of cliff or under a rock; thick-walled, of mosses and dried grasses; eggs 4–5, white, ⅞" x ⅝". DISTR. Locally common R. in Alpine belt from peaks w. of Lake Tahoe to Olancha Peak, Tulare Co., at 9500–14000+ ft.; about cliffs and talus near snowbanks and alpine turf; in winter some descend to e. slope Sagebrush belt.

The alpine bird of the Sierra Nevada is the Rosy Finch or Leucosticte that lives in bleak places above timberline. There the birds forage and nest, retreating eastward downslope perhaps only in the severest weather. In summer they find seeds of sedges and some frozen insects at the melting edges of snowbanks and take similar food from small patches of green turf near lakes. They also catch flying insects. The adult diet is mostly of plant materials, but young receive a high proportion of animal food. There is a protective "snow mask" of specialized feathers over the nostrils. Leucostictes live in small flocks, up to a dozen or more, which fly and wheel in the open over their rugged homeland.

B-137. Pine Siskin. *Spinus pinus* (pl. 59). T.L. 4½"–¼", T. 1⅞", size of junco but tail short, deeply notched; plumage streaked brown and dull white, middle of wing and whole base of tail show yellow in flight. VOICE. Call a plaintive *swe-ah'* higher-pitched at end; also a throaty "watch-winding" *zwe-e-e-e-et,* ending strongly and abruptly; song twittering, goldfinch-like. NEST. Usually in conifer on a spreading branch, of twigs, plant fibers, and moss; eggs 3–4, pale bluish green, lightly dotted at large end, $^{11}\!/_{16}''$ x $\frac{1}{2}''$. DISTR. Common S.V. in Yellow Pine to Subalpine belts on both slopes, in conifers; W.V. at lower altitudes.

This duller, high-mountain relative of the goldfinches lives from spring to fall in the mountain coniferous forest but winters at lower levels. Much of the year the birds are in small to large flocks. In flight each member rises and drops independently, yet the flock remains compact. Often the Siskins leave high perches to fly in wide circles, then return almost to the same places. The food includes tender buds of conifers and black oak and the catkins of alders and willows. In late summer they seek ripening seeds of sunflower-like plants near the ground.

B-138. Common Goldfinch. *Spinus tristis* (pl. 59). T.L. 5″, T. 1¾″, ½ size of junco. Summer: Ad. ♂ : Body bright canary yellow; forehead black; wings black, white-barred; tail black, white centrally at end; Ad. ♀ : Dull greenish brown, white of ♂ dulled. Winter ♂ and ♀ : Above brown, below grayish brown, wings and tail as in summer. VOICE. Flight call *ti-dee-di-di;* song lively, varied. NEST. In tree or shrub at 5–15 ft., lashed in a crotch; of plant fibers, compact; eggs 4–5, plain pale green, ⅝″ x ½″. DISTR. Common R. in Great Valley, fewer in Foothill belt of w. slope; often around willow thickets.

Three species of goldfinches live along the western edge of the Sierra. Save when paired for nesting they are commonly in small flocks. Their flight is undulating—a few wing strokes and the bird rises, then swoops down with wings closed; members of a flock rise and fall independently of one another. The male Common Goldfinch is truly a wild canary in its yellow and black summer coat. This species favors willow thickets and nests late, well into summer. It forages for buds and seeds in tree-tops but also drops down to seek seeds of thistles and other composites.

The Green-backed Goldfinch (*S. psaltria*) is the smallest but commonest of the three local goldfinches. The male is dark greenish above with crown, wings, and tail black; in flight it shows white in a wing patch and at the base of the tail. The female is dull greenish brown above and dull white below, with smaller white markings. This species lives from the Great Valley into the Yellow Pine belt and also along the east base of the Sierra. It frequents openings between scattered trees or bushes, feeding in weed patches.

The Lawrence Goldfinch (*S. lawrencei*) is a scarce resident, mainly in the Foothill belt. The male has a black chin, and yellow on throat, rump, and wing bars; the light area on the tail is midway between base and tip. The female lacks the black but has yellow on her wings.

B-139. Red Crossbill. *Loxia curvirostra* (pl. 59). T.L. 5½"–6¼", T. 2½", chunky-bodied, larger than junco; bill heavy, mandibles curved, crossed near tip. Ad. ♂ : Red on under surface, head and rump, wings and tail dusky brown. Ad. ♀ : Above dull greenish gray, yellowish below and on rump. VOICE. Call *sŭp, sŭp, sŭp;* song warbling. NEST. In pine among needles near end of a limb; of twigs, grass, and moss; eggs 3–4, greenish white, few spots, ⅞" x ⅝". DISTR. Moderate R. from Yellow Pine belt to Subalpine belt on both slopes, in conifers.

The Crossbill's peculiar mandibles serve to pry between the scales of a cone and extract the seeds which are much used as food. Yet on the ground the birds can glean food by spreading the jaws and using the tongue. Males old enough to mate vary in color from greenish yellow or orange to bright red. Most often the Crossbills stay high in the trees, where frequent calls give indication of their presence as they forage or fly. Small flocks may visit lowland localities in winter.

B-140. Green-tailed Towhee. *Chlorura chlorura* (pl. 59). T.L. 7"–7½", T. 3½"–3¾", smaller than robin; crown bright chestnut, above greenish brown, wings and tail dull yellowish green, throat white, bordered by black stripes, breast ashy, belly whitish, under tail coverts buffy. VOICE. Call cat-like, *me-u* or a longer *mee-a-yew;* song wheezy, *eet-ter-te-te-te-si-si-si-seur.* NEST. Low in shrub, bulky, of needles, twigs, grasses well lined; eggs 3–4, bluish white, with red and gray spots, 1³⁄₁₆" x ⅝". DISTR. Common S.V. in Lodgepole–fir belt on both slopes, lower on e. side; in shrubs, usually snow brush, sagebrush, or bitterbrush.

The sprightly Green-tailed Towhee, with its cat-like call, is less common than the Fox Sparrow (B-153) on the west slope but more abundant among the sagebrush and bitterbrush east of the mountains. It arrives early in May and may remain until early October. Nesting occurs in late May and June, and by late July the streaked-breasted young are much in evidence. It forages like a Fox Sparrow under shrubby cover and takes shelter there when disturbed.

B-141. Rufous-sided Towhee. *Pipilo erythrothalmus* (pl. 59). T.L. 8½"–9½", T. 4¼", size between junco and robin, tail equaling body. Ad. ♂ : Upper surface and fore part of body black, small white spots on wings and larger ones of white at end of tail, sides reddish brown, belly white; iris red. Ad. ♀ : Like ♂ but head brownish black. Im.: Above dark brown, below pale brown and streaked. VOICE. Call cat-like, a long *zuee,* slightly varied; song trilled, *tu-wheeze.* NEST. Usually on ground, of grasses and bark strips, lined; eggs 3–4, white or tinted, finely marked with reddish brown, ⅞" x 1¹⁄₁₆". DISTR. Common R. mainly in Foothill belt and edges of adjacent belts on w. slope; also along e. side of mts.; on ground under brush.

Brushy thickets, usually near a small stream, are the home of this contrastingly marked Towhee. There it scratches industriously in the ground litter, kicking backward with both feet as it searches for food, mostly of seeds. The tail is usually held up at an angle with the back. In spring the males, toward evening, go into the tops of bushes or low trees and repeat their monotonous short songs. The streaked young are abroad by July, and in late summer and autumn some of the towhees range upmountain, but return as snow and cold weather arrive.

B-142. Brown Towhee. *Pipilo fuscus* (pl. 60). T.L. 8½"–9", T. 4½", length of robin but body smaller, tail long; almost uniform brown, under tail coverts bright reddish brown, throat dusky-streaked. Voice. Call a loud *cheep,* also squealing notes by a pair; song a quick series of *cheep* notes, more rapid at end. Nest. In bush or tree at 3–8 ft., a bulky well-made cup of plant fibers finely lined; eggs 3–4, pale bluish green sparingly spotted, 1" x ¾". Distr. Common R. mainly in Foothill belt of w. slope, around thickets.

Brown Towhees forage on open areas of sparse grassland, about foothill gardens, and on road margins, always near shrubs or small trees into which they can fly to safety. When startled into flight they may give the sharp call repeatedly. The long tail is closed and straight out while on the ground but is widely spread for steering when the bird dodges around shrubs or trees. Nesting begins in April and finishes by the end of June. Unlike many other foothill birds this towhee is resident throughout the year, never wandering upslope.

B-143a. Savannah Sparrow. *Passerculus sandwichensis* (col. pl. 23). T.L. 5", T. 2⅕", smaller than junco; tail short; above streaked with black and brown, below white narrowly streaked with dark brown on sides of throat and breast, a whitish stripe over crown and one (often yellow) over each eye. Voice. Call a weak *seet;* song 2 or 3 short chirps followed by a buzzing trill. Nest. In grassland or pasture, on ground; of grasses and horsehair; eggs 4–5, greenish or bluish white, spotted with brown, ¾" x ½". Distr. Common S.V. in Great Basin and larger valleys of n. Sierra (subspecies *nevadensis*); also W.V. (northern races) along w. base of Sierra; inhabits grassland.

This bird lives in grassland or savannah at all times, finding its food and placing its nest there. Individuals sometimes perch on bushes, rocks, or low fences, but then drop down and disappear into the sheltering grass. The birds summering on the east side are present from late April until mid-September.

The Grasshopper Sparrow (B-143b; *Ammodramus savannarum;* col. pl. 23) is smaller than the Savannah Sparrow, with a short tail, black and chestnut back, buffy unstreaked under surface, and a blackish crown with 3 pale stripes. It is a sparse resident of irregular occurrence; it keeps to the ground in grass and has a buzzy, insect-like song.

B-144. Vesper Sparrow. *Pooecetes gramineus* (pl. 60). T.L. 6"–6¾", T. 2½", near size of junco; above streaked with brown and black, below whitish with narrow brown streaks on breast and sides; outermost tail feather on each side mostly white; bend of wing chestnut. Voice. Song 2–3 clear notes, 2 higher, then buzzy trills. Nest. In depression on ground, of grasses, rootlets, etc.; eggs 4–5, white with reddish brown marks, ⅞" x ⅝". Distr. Common S.V. e. of mts. and in s. High Sierra, in grass and sagebrush; also W.V. (another subspecies) in Great Valley, on open ground with short vegetation.

The Vesper Sparrow is marked by its white-edged tail and habit of frequenting more open grassland than Savannah Sparrows. The males perch on sagebrush to sing, but otherwise the species stays mostly on the ground.

B-145. Lark Sparrow. *Chondestes grammacus* (pl. 60). T.L. 6½″–7¼″, T. 3″, larger than junco, tail rounded when spread; crown and ear region chestnut, a light stripe over crown and over each eye, cheek white with 3 black lines backward from bill, back brown, black-streaked, tail black centrally bounded by white, under surface of body pure white with round black spot on breast. VOICE. Call a weak *seep;* song low-toned, varied, many buzzing notes or trills, long-continued. NEST. On ground under grass clump (loosely formed) or in bush or tree; a cup of grasses and twigs, lined; eggs 4–5, whitish, with dark lines, 1¾₁₆″ x ⅝″. DISTR. Common R. on w. slope mainly in Foothill belt; local S.V. e. of mts.; in grasslands with scattered small trees.

Grassland with fences, poles, or scattered trees is the Lark Sparrow's domain. Its rounded, white-margined tail is spread when the bird rises from the ground and sometimes while perched. The varied, wheezy song may last for a minute or more and is to be heard throughout the day in spring. Nesting begins late in May. During fall and winter small flocks roam the countryside, foraging on the ground, going into trees if disturbed, and then sometimes flying off in the open to more distant perches.

B-146. Rufous-crowned Sparrow. *Aimophila ruficeps* (col. pl. 23). T.L. 5½″–5¾″, T. 2⅗″; size of junco but tail and wings shorter; crown reddish brown; above grayish brown, rufous-streaked; chin whitish with narrow black border on each side; below grayish buff. VOICE. Call a slow, nasal *dear, dear, dear;* song weak, somewhat like that of Lazuli Bunting (B-130). NEST. On ground, of stems and grasses, lined; eggs 4–5, white, ¾″ x ⅝″. DISTR. Local R. in Foothill belt on w. slope on dry hillsides with scattered small shrubs.

Open dwarf chaparral mixed with grass is the habitat of this little sparrow. It avoids broad expanses of chaparral. The male's song is seldom heard, but the plaintive calls are given rather frequently.

B-147. Bell Sparrow. *Amphispiza belli.* T.L. 5″–6″, T. 2⅔″; size of junco or linnet (B-134); head (except chin) gray; above dull brown; below white with dark breast spot; eye ring, dot between bill and eye, and cheek stripe white. VOICE. Call a faint *seet;* song tinkling, *inksely-inksely-inksely-ser.* NEST. At 1–2½ ft. up in shrub, a cup of plant stems lined with flower heads; eggs 3–4, pale bluish with reddish-brown marks, ¾″ x ⁹₁₆″. DISTR. Sparse R. on w. slope Foothill belt, Eldorado to Mariposa Co. in adenostoma chaparral; S.V. on e. slope in Sierra Co., about Mono Lake, and s. in Sagebrush belt.

142.
Brown Towhee

144.
Vesper Sparrow

145.
Lark Sparrow

148. Junco

154.
Lincoln
Sparrow

153. Fox Sparrow

155. Song Sparrow

Plate 60. Birds

319

Two races of this sparrow inhabit opposite sides of the Sierra, the darker (B-147a; col. pl. 23) in the west slope greasewood or chamise chaparral and the more grayish form, the Sage Sparrow (B-147b; col. pl. 23), amid sagebrush on the east. The birds are in pairs or at most in family groups and seldom appear outside the shrubby cover.

B-148. Junco. *Junco oreganus* (pl. 60). T.L. 5½"–6", T. 2½"; a small sparrow; head, neck, and breast black (intense in ♂, grayish in ♀ and im.); back and wings plain dark brown; tail black except 2 outer feathers on each side white; belly white; bill pinkish. VOICE. Call a weak *seep* or sharp *tsick;* song a rapid, quavering metallic trill of 1–3 seconds, *eetle, eetle, eetle.* . . . NEST. Sunk in ground, about 3" x 3"; thick-walled, of stems, dried grass, and moss, finely lined; eggs 3–5, pinkish to bluish white, marked with reddish brown and gray, ¾" x ⅝". DISTR. Common S.V. in Yellow Pine to Subalpine belts on both slopes in open conifer woods; also common W.V. on w. slope below heavy snow (sparse on e. slope).

The commonest summer bird in the Sierra is the Junco. It gleans seed on the ground under open forest, hopping in zigzag course, often flashing the white tail margins. When flushed it flies to a nearby tree or shrub, hops through the branches, and then may go to another tree. Nesting begins in May when males perch above ground to sing. Young emerge from late June into August, so some pairs may renest or rear second broods. Nests are often near meadow margins or open creek banks, sometimes beside logs, occasionally in the open. The juvenile birds are streaked above and below but by autumn are immatures with dark "cowl" and unstreaked body. Family parties of late summer merge into the loose flocks that wander until the next spring. Some remain in the lower forest where snow does not persist, and others go to the foothills and lowlands.

B-149. Chipping Sparrow. *Spizella passerina* (col. pl. 23). T.L. 5"–5½", T. 2½"; smaller than junco; crown bright rufous; a black line through eye and white line over eye; above brown, black-streaked; below plain ashy white (streaked in juveniles). VOICE. Call a weak *tseet;* song a cicada-like monotonous buzz lasting a few seconds. NEST. In shrubs or low trees at 2–12 ft.; of plant stems, grasses, and rootlets, finely lined with hair; eggs 3–5, bluish green, with brownish black marks, ⅔" x ½". DISTR. Common S.V. from Great Valley nearly to timberline and on e. slope; usually in clear areas near small trees.

Chipping Sparrows may be present from April to late September, in any altitude, wherever smooth bare or grassy ground is close to small trees. This is the "niche" one seeks for a camp so these rather fearless little birds are often close about human visitors. They are active from dawn to dusk, even in midday heat, scanning the surface for food. Their nesting begins late in April at lower elevations and continues into July in the High Sierra. Then family groups are in evidence until migration.

B-150. Brewer Sparrow. *Spizella breweri* (col. pl. 23). T.L. 5″, T. 2½″; resembles Chipping Sparrow but paler, crown finely streaked and no line over eye. VOICE. Call a weak *tseet;* song canary-like. NEST. Low in sage or other bushes; compact, of twigs, stems, and rootlets, lined; eggs 3–4, pale bluish green, reddish-spotted, ⅔″ x ½″. DISTR. Common S.V. on e. slope in Sagebrush belt; occasional spring migrant in Foothill belt.

This dull-garbed relative of the Chipping Sparrow matches in coloration the Great Basin sagebrush, in which it is perhaps the commonest bird. Some occur in sagebrush high on the east slope. In early autumn, before the southward migration, they are abundant about Mono Lake.

The Black-chinned Sparrow (*S. atrogularis*), about the size of a Chipping Sparrow, frequents mixed foothill chaparral from Mariposa County southward on the west slope. It has a black chin and reddish brown back; the head, neck, and under parts are plain dark gray.

B-151. White-crowned Sparrow. *Zonotrichia leucophrys* (col. pl. 23). T.L. 5¾″–7″, T. 3″; larger than junco; crown with 3 white and 4 black stripes alternating (light and dark brown on Im.); above gray, streaked with brown; tail plain brown; 2 rows of white spots on closed wing; below grayish white, unstreaked. VOICE. Call a sharp *peenk* or faint *seep;* song clear, plaintive *we chēē' ah wē-ē-ē-ē ah.* NEST. On ground or up to 3 ft. in shrub; of plant stems, bark shreds, etc., lined with fine grass; eggs 3–5, pale bluish green, brown-spotted, ⅞″ x ⅔″. DISTR. Common S.V. in Subalpine belt, locally in Lodgepole–fir belt, from Plumas Co. s.; about willow thickets in meadows (*a.* Mountain White-crown, *Z. l. oriantha*); also common W.V. below heavy snow on both slopes in and near shrubbery (*b.* Gambel Sparrow. *Z. l. gambeli*). Lower white stripe on head in *a* starts at eye, in *b* from base of bill.

White-crowned Sparrows are present somewhere in the Sierra at all seasons, the mountain race from May through September at high altitudes and the Gambel Sparrow from mid-September until early May on the lower slopes, east and west. The birds forage on level grasslands near bushes, into which they dart when frightened. The summer population lives about shrubby willow thickets that serve as escape cover, song perches, and nesting sites.

B-152. Golden-crowned Sparrow. *Zonotrichia atricapilla* (col. pl. 23). T.L. 6″–7″, T. 3⅓″; larger than junco; crown of Ad. golden yellow, margined with black (dull brown in Im.); above dull brown, black-streaked; below pale grayish brown; 2 rows of white spots on wing. VOICE. Call 1-syllabled; song 3 clear whistled notes descending in pitch, like *oh dear me.* DISTR. Common W.V. on w. slope in Foothill belt and Great Valley; in or near thickets.

The slightly larger Golden-crowns share lowland and foothill thickets with Gambel Sparrows from October to May. On their arrival in autumn, some Golden-crowns visit shrubbery in the Yellow Pine and Lodgepole–fir belts but go downslope when snow comes.

B-153. Fox Sparrow. *Passerella iliaca* (pl. 60). T.L. 6¼″–7¼, T. 3½″; chunky, size between robin and junco; above uniform dark brown, of reddish or grayish cast; wings and tail tinged with foxy red; below white with bold triangular black spots most numerous on breast. Voice. Call a single loud *chink;* song clear, melodious, 2 loud notes, *wee, chee,* and a trill. Nest. At 8″–24″ or higher in snow brush or other shrub; a loose exterior of twigs lined with pine needles and hair; eggs 3–4, pale greenish marked with reddish brown, ⅞″ x ⅔″. Distr. Common S.V. in Lodgepole–fir belt on both slopes (2 subspecies); also migrant and W.V. in Foothill and Yellow Pine belts (other subspecies); in and near thick shrubs.

The sprightly Fox Sparrow summers in thickets of snowbrush and other mountain chaparral. The birds live and forage on the ground, near or under brush. They jump and scratch backward with both feet, showering debris and making holes 2 or 3 inches wide to obtain seeds for food. When an observer approaches they are adept at circling within the shrubbery or flying off near the ground to hide in another bush. Males perch on high twigs of bushes or low branches of trees to sing their clear lay. The nests are well hidden. The summer birds arrive in May and depart by September, but are replaced by members of several northern races that come as winter visitants. Some of these go well up into the mountains until snow drives them downslope.

B-154. Lincoln Sparrow. *Melospiza lincolni* (pl. 60). T.L. 5″–6″, T. 2″–2½″; smaller than junco; above brown or olive streaked with black; chin and belly white; sides and buffy chest band narrowly black streaked. Voice. Call a low *sip;* song rapid, gurgling, *zee, zee, zee, ti-ter-r-r-r-r-r.* Nest. On grass tuft in swampy ground; a cup woven of grasses; eggs 4–5, pale, bluish green with reddish brown marks, ⅔″ x ½″. Distr. Moderate S.V. in Lodgepole–fir belt and parts of adjacent belts; also W.V. on lower w. slope mainly in Foothill belt; in wet meadows or tall grass with willows.

In summer this sparrow lives in places used by White-crowned Sparrows but is reclusive, keeping under cover of the damp vegetation when foraging or singing. The nesting population arrives by mid-May but by the end of July is no·longer seen or heard. Birds of a race from the north winter on the west slope.

B-155. Song Sparrow. *Melospiza melodia* (pl. 60). T.L. 5″–6½″, T. 2⅔″, larger than junco; above dark brown or gray, below white, all surfaces black-streaked; a pale stripe over crown and one over each eye; a dark spot on breast. Voice. Call a low, blurred *tchunk;* song variable, usually 3 short notes, *cheet, cheet, cheet,* a longer note, then a trill. Nest. On ground, in bush or low tree; of slender twigs, plant stems, and grasses; eggs 3–4, greenish white, spotted with reddish brown, 1¾₁₆″ x ⅝″. Distr. Moderate S.V. on e. side s. to Owens Valley; also R. along lower w. slope at edge of Great Valley; in grass or shrubbery near water.

The streaked Song Sparrow carries its tail up at an angle with the back. It is active and quick-moving, much like a wren. It lives in pairs or singly, never in flocks, in damp places or near water, but comes into view oftener than the related Lincoln Sparrow. The song may be heard beyond the nesting season. The grayish Modoc Song Sparrow nests on the east side in summer, and some individuals of that race winter on the lower west slope. Two resident dark-colored races of the Great Valley occur in the foothills, and still other subspecies from the north appear there in winter.

22. MAMMALS

Mammals, the four-footed animals or quadrupeds, are "warm-blooded" with a regulated body temperature about that of mankind. In consequence they can be rather independent of environmental temperatures. Many avoid temperature extremes by using a shelter in caves, hollow trees, or in the ground; often the nest is of insulating plant fibers. The body is insulated by the *pelage* or covering of hairs. Commonly these are of two types, longer and stouter *guard hairs* that resist wear, and the softer, shorter *under fur* that protects against heat loss. Pigments in the hair provide the external color. All species produce living young nourished after birth by milk from the female's mammary glands. At birth the young are either naked, blind, and helpless (rabbits, squirrels, other rodents, carnivores) or fully haired, with eyes open, and able to get about (hares, deer). Mammals have acute senses of smell, hearing, and sight; many species have sensory hairs on the head (vibrissae or "whiskers" and others) that provide touch sensations from objects in the environment as the animal moves about. Most mammals are active only by night, but their presence is marked by tracks (fig. 22), droppings, nests, and other "signs" (fig. 23). To overcome winter food shortage some species migrate (bats, deer), and others hibernate in a long winter sleep at reduced body temperature (squirrels, chipmunks).

Abbreviations: H.&B., head and body length from tip of nose to base of tail; T., tail, from base to end of bony vertebrae; H.F., hind foot length including claws; E., ear, from crown of head; wt., weight, in ounces (oz.) or pounds (lbs.); ♂, male; ♀, female.

M-1. Shrews. Genus *Sorex* (pl. 61). H.&B. to 3″, T. to 2″; smaller than house mouse. Snout slender, tapered; teeth pointed, black-tipped; eyes and ears small; all feet delicate; pelage short, dense, smooth, uniform brown above, lighter (to whitish) below. DISTR. From upper edge of foothills across Sierra to e. base; some in wet places near streams or in meadows, others in drier sites.

Shrews, smallest of the mammals, are secretive, rarely being seen and leaving little evidence of their presence. They forage in moist places, amid grass or leaves, under logs or stones, and in burrows of mice or moles. Some venture into dry chaparral or among rocks. Between periods of profound slumber they dart about rapidly, twitching their

2. Mole

3. Bat

1. Shrew

4. Cony

8. Cottontail

9. Brush Rabbit

7. Black-tailed Jackrabbit

10. Aplodontia

Plate 61. Mammals

noses and hunting mainly by scent or touch, occasionally giving high-pitched squeaks. Like their relatives, the moles, they feed on insects, worms, and animal flesh, sometimes plant materials. One of these voracious "micro-carnivores" will eat flesh equaling its weight in a day. Mice in traps set by naturalists often are consumed overnight by shrews, leaving only skin and bones. A distinctive musky odor makes shrews distasteful to most hawks and owls, so few are eaten. Little is known about shrew home life. In the Sierra, young are produced from May to August, 2 to 6 (or more) per litter, naked and minute at birth but maturing rapidly. Few shrews survive a second winter. Six or more species inhabit the Sierra Nevada, some of local occurrence and others of wide distribution there and elsewhere. Precise identification requires skins and skulls for study by a trained mammalogist.

The water shrew (*Sorex palustris*), largest of local species, has a tail as long as its body (3"). The hind toes are closely fringed with hairs, and the pelage is water-resistant. It lives in or near rapid mountain streams, is abroad by day, is often seen by fishermen, and is eaten by trout. It not only swims and dives but can walk on the bottom and even on the water surface!

M-2 Mole. *Scapanus latimanus* (pl. 61, figs. 23, 24). H.&B. 4½", T. 1½". Body cylindrical; snout long, tapered; fore feet lateral with broad fleshy palms, 5 heavy claws; no eyes or ears visible; pelage short, velvety, silvery black or grayish; tail scantily haired. SIGN. Low ridges (mole runs) on surface and irregularly conical mounds (mole hills). DISTR. From Great Valley across Sierra, locally, up to 9500 ft.; in soil of river bottoms, humus of forest, and in dryish meadows.

The mole lives in the ground. When hunting food it "swims" or pushes through soft soil an inch or so below the surface by use of its broad fore feet and claws. This makes a low rounded ridge over the animal's temporary shallow subway. These irregular runs, often yards in length, may be retraveled after a few hours or days as the mole searches for food: earthworms, insects or their larvae, other small animals, and some seeds. Deeper permanent burrows also are dug, with an enlarged nest chamber. The excavated soil is pushed up in frequent short vertical tunnels onto the surface to become conical mole hills. The last load of soil remains as a central core—like the plug in a quiescent volcano. Moles are active throughout the year, moving up- or downslope to live in moderately moist soil. The young, 2 to 4 or 5 per litter, are born in spring.

M-3. Bats. Order CHIROPTERA (pl. 61). Small mammals, form delicate, H.&B. 1½"–3", T. 1½"–2½", spread 8"–15½"; wings formed of thin webs of skin between bones of arm and 2nd to 5th fingers on each "hand"; 1st digit free, with claw; also a web between hind legs and tail; mouth wide; ears large, paper-thin; hind toes with sharp curved claws; pelage dense, uniformly colored, usually brownish. DISTR. From Great Valley to Great Basin.

Our only flying mammals are the bats or "flitter mice" that emerge at dusk to catch night-flying insects for food. Their seemingly erratic flights are purposeful—in pursuit of prey. When hunting, bats emit short bursts of supersonic sound (to 50 bursts per second at frequencies of 50000 cycles or higher); these echo back from the diminutive prey to the bats' highly sensitive ears, somewhat in the manner of man-made radar. By this guidance the insects are located and caught.

Of nine or more species of bats inhabiting the Sierra Nevada, some hunt close to the ground between trees and shrubs or over clearings, others at heights of 25 to 50 feet within the forest, and the free-tailed bat of the foothills forages out in the open. During the day bats, singly or in groups, hang up by their hind claws in dark crevices in trees or rocks, some in caves, and some in buildings. The young, one or two per female, are born in early summer. When small they may cling to the mother while she forages but later remain in the roost until they can fly. In winter, when insects are scarce, some species hibernate and others migrate to warmer places. Identification of bats requires specimens in hand to compare with detailed technical descriptions—see "References" (p. 358).

M-4. Cony. *Ochotona princeps* (pl. 61). H.&B. 6″–7″, T. about ½″; resembles small guinea pig; body short, face and ears rounded; fore and hind legs small, about equal; tail not evident; pelage pale gray with reddish overcast; soles haired except ends of toes. SIGN. Piles of vegetation cut green and cured as hay in shelter under rocks; droppings flat, rabbit-like, dia. ⅛″, in groups on lookouts; also whitish urine stains on rocks. VOICE. A high nasal *check-ick*, uttered once or repeated for 10–15 seconds. DISTR. Mainly in Subalpine belt, occasionally higher or lower, at 7700–12000 ft.; lives in rock slides.

The cony, pika, or rock rabbit, distant alpine relative of the true rabbits, lives solitarily in high mountain talus and rock slides, sometimes in a density of 6 per acre. Midday travelers often hear the cony's nasal bleating and by careful searching may see one or more. The animal's day begins when the air is well warmed and ends before the chill of evening. It is active, however, in winter, under the snow blanketing its domain. When not foraging the cony perches on a backward-slanting rock with good outlook and overhead protection, whence it can scramble to safety. These lookout posts are dotted with the diminutive droppings and whitened by urine stains. For food the cony cuts stems, up to 3 ft. long, of plants growing near rock slides and carries these in its mouth into shelters under overhanging rocks, where it becomes dried. Sometimes a cubic yard of this "hay" is gathered in the winter "barn" (fig. 23). Marmots, bushy-tailed wood rats, ground squirrels, and chipmunks are associates of the cony, and its main enemies are weasels and martens. The 3 or 4 young are born between May and September.

M-5. White-tailed Jackrabbit. *Lepus townsendi.* H.&B. 18″–22″, T. 3½″, E. to 6″, wt. 5–8 lbs. Form of Black-tailed Jackrabbit but larger and heavier; brownish gray in summer, all white in winter except black ear tips; feet and tail well furred, always white; tail white both above and below. SIGN. Flattened spherical droppings, dia. ½″. DISTR. High Sierra from Mt. Whitney region n., to 12000 ft. near timberline; also on flat areas e. of mountains.

Largest of the hares in western mountains and northern plains, the White-tail is uncommon in the Sierra. It lives in open or semiopen places but is active at late dusk and into the night, hence is rarely seen. Its "eye shine" to a flashlight or headlight is fiery red, more brilliant than in the Black-tail. Groups of droppings under bushy mats of white-bark pine and similar cover indicate that these sites serve for shelter by day or during winter storms. The young, 2 or 3 per litter, are born from late spring into summer.

M-6. Snowshoe Hare or Rabbit. *Lepus americanus.* H.&B. 13″–18″, T. 1½″–2 ″, E. 3½″–4″, wt. 2–4 lbs. Of rabbit form, bigger than Cottontail, feet large; upper surface darkish brown in summer, all white in winter (ear tips dusky); under parts and lower surface of tail always white. DISTR. N. from Lake Tahoe region at high elevations, in forest areas; also at Pine Crest, Tuolumne Co.

The Snowshoe or Varying Hare (white in winter, brown in summer) ranges from the far American Arctic south into the Rockies and northern Sierra Nevada. Here it lives amid streamside alders and willows, in dense thickets of young conifers, and under ceanothus-manzanita chaparral—plant cover equivalent to that occupied by the Brush Rabbit (M-9) at lower altitudes. The Snowshoe shelters by day in a shallow "form" under protective vegetation, going out to forage at dusk, by night, or in early morning. It eats grasses, herbs, and shrubs, together with bark of some deciduous trees in winter. The young average 3 to 4 per litter, are born in spring and able to forage when about 2 weeks old.

M-7. Black-tailed Jackrabbit. *Lepus californicus* (pl. 61). H.&B. 18″–19″, T. 2¼″–3½″, E. 5½″–6½″, wt. 3–7 lbs. Of rabbit form but racy in build; above pale yellowish brown, ticked with black; under surface pale buff to white; top of tail black. SIGN. Tracks (fig. 22) oval, front 1½″, hind 2½″; droppings flattened spheres, dia. ⅜″; "forms" (resting places) on ground under bushes; trails straight, narrow, through grass in open. DISTR. Great Valley and Foothill belt on w. side, mainly in unobstructed grassland but some in openings amid chaparral; also in flatter open areas e. of Sierra.

The long-eared hare of the American West was named "jackass rabbit" by the pioneers, in contrast to the shorter-eared Cottontails. Unlike the latter, this animal lives in the open, makes off overland if alarmed (never hiding in shrubbery or burrows), and bears fully formed young.

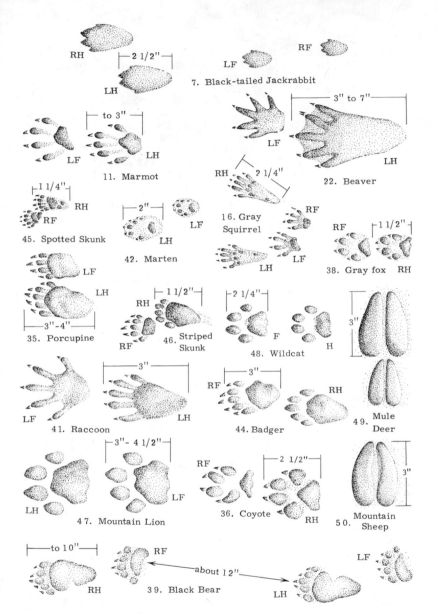

Figure 22. Mammal tracks. (Adapted in part from W. H. Burt and R. P. Grossenheider, 1964, A Field Guide to the Mammals. 2d edition. Boston, Houghton Mifflin Co.)

2a. Mole ridge

2b. Mole mound

17. Chickaree middens

19. Pocket Gopher earth cores

22. Beaver cutting--aspen

26. Nest of Dusky-footed Wood Rat

4. Cony haypile

35. Porcupine gnawing

39. Black Bear scratches

Figure 23. The work of mammals.

When foraging it makes short hops, keeping the soles of the hind feet on the ground and the ears erect. If frightened, it lays the ears back and leaps 2 to 3 yards at a bound, touching only the toes. Jackrabbits are active toward dusk, at night, and in the earlier morning. Midday each rests in a sheltered form under a bush, where there is clear view all about to watch for enemies—coyotes, eagles, or large hawks, and also dogs and hunters. The food is of grasses, herbs, and stems and leaves of shrubs. Alfalfa, grains, and other crops also are relished and often damaged. In consequence, there has been unending destruction of "jacks," so that the population today is a small fraction of that around 1900. Jackrabbits carry a disease, tularemia, transmissible to man. Young, 4 or 5 per litter, are produced through most of the year. The newborn are about 6 inches long, fully haired, with eyes open, and 2-inch ears.

M-8. Cottontail. *Sylvilagus audubonii* or *nuttallii* (pl. 61). H.&B. 12"–15", T. 2", E. 2½"–3½", wt. about 2 lbs. Smaller than jackrabbit or domestic rabbit; ear about length of head; upper surface of body yellowish brown with blackish overwash; under surface and tops of hind feet white; tail cottony white beneath. Sign. Droppings flattened spheres, dia. ¼". Distr. Great Valley and valley bottoms of foothills on w. slope (*S. audubonii*); also in valleys e. of Sierra in flatter areas (*S. nuttallii*); inhabits brushy places near grasslands.

Cottontails are common where grassy forage places are bordered by shrub and vine growths that afford escape shelter. Less often they live on open grassy hillsides and use remodeled ground squirrel burrows for hiding and nesting. They forage in the early morning, disappear during midday, and are abroad again toward evening or even late afternoon in glades shaded from direct sunshine. In favorable pasturage 2, 3, or more may be seen close together, and they sometimes venture out 25 feet or so from the sheltering thickets. At the hint of danger they go for safety, displaying the cottony-white tail at each bound. The blind, nearly naked young, about 6 per litter, are born in spring and early summer. The nest is lined with fur from the female's body, and placed in a short burrow or in a secluded surface depression.

M-9. Brush Rabbit. *Sylvilagus bachmani* (pl. 61). H.&B. 10"–12½", T. 1"–1½", E. 2½"–3", wt. 1–1½ lbs. Ear shorter than head, half as broad as long; body above dark brown, heavily washed with black giving deep gray effect; below grayish white; under side of tail partly white. Sign. Droppings, flattened spheres, dia. ¼"; runways under brushy cover. Distr. Foothill belt of w. slope to 4000 ft., mostly under chaparral.

The little "blue" Brush Rabbit, about half the weight of a Cottontail, is abroad in early morning and toward dusk. It seldom ventures far from the sheltering shrubs, and each individual has a restricted home range. Sometimes, when come upon, the animal will "freeze" immobile. Then, if it senses danger, it takes a few quick hops and disappears into the chaparral, with which its coat blends in color. The food includes grasses and herbs during the spring but also includes stems of ceanothus and other shrubs. The litter of 2 to 5 is born in spring.

M-10. Aplodontia. *Aplodontia rufa* (pl. 61). H.&B. 11"–14", T. 1"–1½"; wt. 2–3 lbs. Body stocky, limbs short, front claws long; head blunt, eyes and ears small; pelage dense, short, erect, blackish brown above, grayish below. SIGN. Surface runways and underground tunnels 6"–7" (to 10") dia., with many openings, under shrubbery near small streams; much fresh-cut vegetation or bark on ground, also nearby bushes or trees pruned of small twigs. DISTR. Locally in Lodgepole–fir and Subalpine belts on both slopes at about 6000–11000 ft.; mostly nocturnal, some activity on cloudy days.

Aplodontia looks like an oversized tailless meadow mouse. It is a relict rodent, of wider occurrence in the geological past, now living only from southern British Columbia to Sequoia National Park. Although often called "mountain beaver," it is no beaver, and most of the population inhabits Pacific Coast lowlands (south to Marin County). In the Sierra its burrows and runways are near small streams bordered by willow, creek dogwood, fern thickets, and other riparian plants. The burrows are extensive with many entrances, often damp, and kept clean. Most kinds of plants near the burrows are cut for food, often in excess amount, and piles of this green fodder may be seen near or in the damp or wet tunnels. Aplodontias sometimes climb shrubs or small trees to cut little twigs for food or nest making. The animals seem sociable but not gregarious. The young, usually 3 or 4, are born in spring and become full sized by late summer.

M-11. Yellow-bellied Marmot. *Marmota flaviventris* (pl. 62). H.&B. 14"–18", T. 5"–8", wt. to 7+ lbs. Body stout, legs and feet small; upper surface yellowish brown grizzled with white; face blackish; a narrow white band before eyes; sides of neck and under surface buffy. VOICE. A loud sharp whistle, *sirk,* sometimes repeated. SIGN. Burrows 5"–6" dia. under large rocks or at bases of trees; blackish droppings to ½" dia., long, pointed at one end. DISTR. Lodgepole–fir belt to above timberline at 6200–12000 ft.; in or near meadows with rock outcrops or boulders for shelter.

Largest of the ground squirrel tribe is the Marmot, often called woodchuck or groundhog, that lives around upper Sierran meadows. It emerges lean in spring—April or May—when snow is still present and feeds avidly by day on grasses or other meadow vegetation, becoming layered with fat by September or October before returning to hibernation. During the warmer daylight hours it alternates foraging and resting on a rock that commands a wide view. Such lookouts are marked by many droppings. When danger threatens, its loud whistle is sounded and the animal runs for its burrow. The dens are under rock piles or tree roots where neither man nor carnivores can dig; hence the tunnels and nest places are unknown. The 3 to 8 young are born early in spring and able to go about on the surface by July.

M-12. Belding Ground Squirrel. *Citellus beldingi* (pl. 62). Size of house rat; H.&B. 7″–8½″, tail 2¼″–3″, wt. 7–10 oz. Body light yellowish brown, with broad patch of bright reddish brown along back. VOICE. Call of 5–8 shrill, short whistles, *seek,* in quick succession; female with young utters a single note, *e-chert!* SIGN. Burrows usually in flat ground, dia. about 2″. DISTR. Higher central Sierra Nevada from Independence Lake s. to Long Valley, Mono Co., and Coyote Flat, Inyo Co., at 6500 to 11800 ft.; mainly in meadowlands, occasionally on dry slopes.

This "picket-pin" ground squirrel of the higher Sierra grasslands often is locally abundant. Travelers approaching a meadow usually are announced by repeated shrill piping whistles relayed from one squirrel to another. Any that are out in the grasslands then usually run toward their burrows and often stand upright on hind feet and tail to look about for the impending danger. The species feeds mainly on grass and grass seeds and does not climb. Adults emerge in March, possibly earlier, while there is still much snow. The young, averaging about 8, appear from mid-May onward according to altitude. When half-grown they emerge to live about the mouth of the parent burrow, gradually learning to forage for themselves. By late September or early October, all the population is in hibernation.

M-13. California Ground Squirrel. *Citellus beecheyi* (pl. 62). H.&B. 9″–10¾″, tail 6″–7½″, wt. 1–1½ lbs. Body dull yellowish brown ticked with black and white hair ends, sides of neck and shoulders grizzled white with dark brown patch between, plain buff below. VOICE. A sharp metallic clink. SIGN. Burrows to 4½″ dia.; also runways about 3″ wide through grass. DISTR. From Great Valley up to 8200 ft. on w. slope; also on e. slope from about 8000 ft. downward; commonest on plains and open foothills, fewer in Yellow Pine belt; mainly in open situations.

The lowland "digger" ground squirrels, once enormously abundant, have been far reduced by control to protect crops and pastures. They are still present scatteringly well into the Sierra. The burrows, in hillsides where possible, extend many feet and may be two yards or more in depth. These serve for safety retreats, hibernation, food storage, and rearing of young. The tunnels also afford shelter for toads, various snakes, burrowing owls, skunks, and other animals. Grasslands often show trails where the squirrels travel repeatedly between their burrows and feeding places. This species, like other ground squirrels and the chipmunks (but not the tree squirrels or marmot), has thin inner cheek pouches for carrying food or nest material. In spring the squirrels eat some green vegetation, but most of the year they depend on seeds of grasses and low herbs. They dig some bulbs and at times climb into oaks for acorns. The annual brood, averaging 5 or 6, appears from April into June, and the young become independent by late summer. Individuals living above the snowline hibernate in winter, and some in the lowlands "go to sleep" (estivate) from late summer until about January or February.

14. Golden-mantled Ground Squirrel

18. Flying Squirrel

12. Belding Ground Squirrel

17. Chickaree

11. Marmot

13. Calif. Ground Squirrel

16. Calif. Gray Squirrel

19. Pocket Gopher

21. Kangaroo Rat

Plate 62. Mammals

M-14. Golden-mantled Ground Squirrel. *Citellus lateralis* (pl. 62). About ⅔ size of house rat, tail half length of head and body. H.&B. 5¾"–7½", T. 2½"–4", wt. 4–8 oz. Head and neck all yellowish or coppery red, back grizzled brown, each side with broad white stripe bordered black, under surface pale gray to whitish; tail black centrally, buffy at margin. Sign. Burrows 2"–2½" dia. usually near rocks or logs. Distr. Mainly in Lodge-pole–fir and Subalpine belts, lower on e. slope, at 6000–11800 ft.; lives on forest floor, around chaparral and meadow margins, and on steep rocky slopes.

The "copperhead" is the commonest and often the tamest of Sierran ground squirrels, larger than any chipmunk but smaller than the other ground squirrels. It rarely stands up on its hind feet and only occasionally gives a sharp warning call. Squirrels at campgrounds or lunch places often will gather food, sometimes from a person's hand, until the cheek pouches bulge. This material may be eaten, carried into the burrow, or quickly buried in a shallow surface excavation. Only occasional burrow entrances are seen, and the tunnels probably do not extend far into the ground. The food is mostly a mixture of plant materials. Adults may emerge from hibernation by early April, and the young, 2 to 6 per litter, are born in June and July, appearing above ground when they are quarter- to half-grown. Some do not enter hibernation until mid-October; at lower elevations occasional adults may be abroad in winter. Enemies include the weasel, mountain coyote, and hawks.

M-15. Chipmunks. Genus *Eutamias* (col. pl. 24). Small, marked with alternate dark and light stripes, 9 along back, 5 on each cheek; a whitish spot behind each ear; sides yellowish to reddish brown, under surface whitish, tail flat, brush-like, with hairs on sides.

Eight species of chipmunks live in the Sierra Nevada, but no more than 2 (rarely 3) in the same locality. Identification of individuals often is possible by carefully noting the size, color, area of occurrence, kind of environment occupied, and voice.

a. Alpine Chipmunk. *E. alpinus.* H.&B. 4", T. 2½"–3", wt. to 1⅖ oz.; *smallest* and *palest,* sides pale buff, tail buffy edged. Distr. Mt. Conness, Tuolumne Co., to Olancha Peak, Tulare Co., 7600–12600 ft.; Subalpine and Alpine belts, among rocks or fallen timber, essentially terrestrial (rarely in trees). Voice. A low wiry *sweet,* repeated; a slow *whit;* a low chuckle.

b. Sagebrush Chipmunk. *E. minimus.* H.&B. 4⅛"–4⅜", T. 3", wt. to 1⅖ oz.; small, pale, *grayish.* Distr. Only on e. side in Sagebrush belt, 6400–10500 ft.; on ground or among bushes. Voice. A high *tsew;* also a rapid *chip,* repeated.

c. Mono Chipmunk. *E. amoenus.* H.&B. 4¼"–5", T. 3"–3⅜", wt. to 1¾ oz.; sides light brown. Distr. E. slope, Plumas Co. to Mammoth Pass, 4400–9400 ft. (on w. slope to Cisco); in open conifer forests around chaparral, logs, and rocks, mostly terrestrial. Voice. Like Lodgepole Chipmunk.

d. Montane Chipmunk. *E. quadrivittatus.* H.&B. 5", T. 3⅝", pale-colored, crown of head and shoulders *gray,* stripes on back sharply contrasted, sides tawny. DISTR. Near crest in s. Sierra, Mammoth Lakes to Cottonwood Lakes, 8500–11000 ft.; on exposed slopes near pine trees.

e. LODGEPOLE CHIPMUNK. *E. speciosus.* H.&B. 4½"–5", T. 3¼"–3¾", wt. to 2⅓ oz.; medium-sized, and *brightest-colored,* sides bright reddish brown, *white* stripes on head and back. DISTR. On both slopes from Lassen Peak to Bullfrog Lake, Fresno Co., and Little Cottonwood Creek, Inyo Co., at 5200–8500 ft. (north) to 5000–11000 ft. (south); Lodgepole–fir and Subalpine belts, on ground about logs or rocks but near trees which it climbs (to 40+ ft.) to escape. VOICE. A high *whisk,* repeated; a shrill *tsew;* a rapid *pst-pst-pst-a-kū* when frightened and retreating.

f. ALLEN CHIPMUNK. *E. townsendi.* H.&B. 5¼"–6", T. 4"–4⅜", wt. to 3¾ oz.; dull, *grayish.* DISTR. From Mt. Lassen s. to Shaver Lake, Fresno Co., at 3300–9000 ft. mainly in Lodgepole–fir belt, in thickets and around logs, occasionally climbs to 50 ft. VOICE. Like Long-eared Chipmunk.

g. LONG-EARED CHIPMUNK. *E. quadrimaculatus.* H.&B. 5¼"–6", T. 3⅜"–4", wt. to 3⅔ oz.; *ruddy brown,* ear taller, with larger white spot behind. DISTR. Greenville, Plumas Co., s. to Bass Lake, Madera Co., and e. to Woodfords, Alpine Co., at 3200–7500 ft., in upper Yellow Pine and Lodgepole–fir belts, around brush patches or logs, in open forest, rarely a few feet up in trees. VOICE. A sharp *psst,* usually single; a hollow *bock,* at intervals.

h. MERRIAM CHIPMUNK. *E. merriami.* H.&B. 5"–5¾", T. 4⅜"–4⅞", wt. to 2⅝ oz.; large, *dullest-colored.* DISTR. W. slope, Tuolumne Co., to Tulare Co., 940–6200 ft., e. slope n. to Onion Valley, Inyo Co., 8500 ft.; mostly in Foothill and lower Yellow Pine belts (also among piñon pine), in chaparral and brush, climbs trees readily. VOICE. A high *whisk;* a low *bock,* repeated; also sputtering notes.

The colorful little chipmunks are busy every sunny day from spring until early autumn. Much of their activity is in finding food during the summer's plenty to store against times of scarcity. Like the related ground squirrels, each has a pair of thin internal cheek pouches used to carry seeds, nuts, or berries. Their fore feet serve well as hands to gather and manipulate food and for digging. Some food is eaten as found, some taken into the underground burrow, and some buried on the surface. The chipmunk digs a small pit as deep as its head, discharges the contents of the pouches, fills the excavation, and pats down the surface. In springtime there are many "pugholes" where buried food has been removed. Besides getting food and caring for young, chipmunks find time for much that seems like play, when one will pursue another round and about over logs and stumps. The burrow serves for escape shelter, for sleeping, for rearing the young, and, in the higher altitudes, for hibernation. Chipmunk burrows, unlike those of ground squirrels, are usually hidden; few have been found and excavated by naturalists. Some nests have been discovered in decaying stumps. The foods have been learned by examining the contents of cheek pouches of chipmunks taken as scientific specimens. They include seeds of pines and other conifers, shrubs such as ceanothus, many wildflowers, grasses, and sedges, and occasional fungi. Some insects may be eaten. The pouches of one chipmunk were loaded with 20 Jeffrey pine seeds, and another had 1169 mixed small seeds. At the lower altitudes, east and west, young are born by May or earlier but higher up they arrive into July. Broods commonly are 3 to 6, and young are abroad within a month. Chipmunks are the prey of snakes, hawks, weasels, and other carnivores.

M-16. California Gray Squirrel. *Sciurus griseus* (pl. 62). Large and slender, tail with conspicuous "brush." H.&B. 10″–11½″, tail 9½″–11″, E. to 1½″ high, wt. 1½–2 lbs. Body uniform gray with slight pepper and salt effect, under surface pure white, tail gray margined with white. VOICE. A hoarse rough coughing, usually in slow series. SIGN. Remains of pine cones cut open to obtain seeds; bulky outside nests high in conifers. DISTR. Foothill and Yellow Pine belts of w. slope, from 400–500 to 6000 ft.

The gray squirrel is slender but strong-muscled with a long broadly haired tail that serves as counterbalance and rudder. Sharp claws on all toes help in clinging to irregularities in tree bark when climbing. Its gait is bounding, using the fore and hind legs in pairs; on a flat area it can leap up to 4 feet at a jump. It runs easily on overhead branches and crosses between adjacent trees where branches overlap. The animal is active throughout the year, remaining hidden only during bad weather. It builds outdoor globular stick nests to 18 inches in diameter with a central lined cavity; they are placed at heights up to 75 feet, mainly in conifers. Rotted holes in oaks also are lined to serve for shelter. The principal food is pine seeds and oak acorns, available over a long season. Lacking cheek pouches this squirrel must consume its food mainly where found. Pine cones are cut and sometimes opened on a convenient branch above ground. Otherwise the cone is allowed to drop; then the squirrel descends and cuts off the scales one by one to get at the seeds. Many acorns are buried against future need; the squirrels later locate some by smell and eat them when food is scarce. Those not recovered may sprout and start new oaks. The young number 2 to 4 per brood and are born in the spring, appearing in early summer when about half-grown. The gray squirrel population has fluctuated from year to year for unknown reasons.

M-17. Sierra Chickaree. *Tamiasciurus douglasii* (pl. 62). About size of house rat, H.&B. 7⅜″–8¼″, T. 4⅜″–5½″, E. to 1″ tall, wt. 7¾–10½ oz. Upper surface dark brown with reddish tinge along back and black line low on each side, under surface white or buffy, tail blackish with silvery hair tips. VOICE. A prolonged whinnying of high notes, 4–5 per second; also a short explosive *quer'-o*, often repeated. SIGN. Green cones of fir and pine cut and dropped under trees; remains of cones with scales removed to obtain seeds. DISTR. Throughout Lodgepole–fir and Subalpine belts, at 5000–11000 ft., some in Yellow Pine belt, especially in winter.

The sprightly talkative Chickaree or Red Squirrel of the higher forests lives more in trees than does its gray counterpart. It gallops up tree trunks and when on the ground; but moves the feet separately when on branches or descending. If a person sits quietly and "squeaks" he can often attract a chickaree for a close view, when it will call repeatedly, jump, and flick its tail. This squirrel is active all winter, save in severe storms, and bounds readily over the snow. From autumn until spring it eats seeds of fir, pine, and even the big tree. It cuts and drops many green cones, then descends to cache them beside logs or rocks near its home trees; one squirrel had nearly 500 stowed in a 50 x 50-foot area. Chilled under winter snow, the seeds remain palatable until eaten. When feeding, the squirrel sits on the ground, a log, or a rock where it can watch for enemies. Holding a cone in its "hands," it cuts off the scales, one by one, and shucks and eats the seeds, leaving only the ragged core (fig. 23). The Chickaree's nest is usually hidden in a pine or fir tree cavity some feet above ground and lined with grass, small twigs, or other soft materials. The young, born mainly in June and July, average about 5 per litter. Hawks and weasels are the principal enemies.

M-18. Northern Flying Squirrel. *Glaucomys sabrinus* (pl. 62). H.&B. 5½"–6½", T. 4½"–5¾", wt. 3–6 oz. About ⅔ size of house rat; body flattened, a fur-covered membrane along each side between legs; head rounded, eyes large, ears moderate; tail broad, flat, heavily furred; pelage dense, silky, gray above, dull white below. Voice. A low *whurr*. Distr. Yellow Pine and Lodgepole–fir belts of w. slope at 3000–8100 ft., in black oaks and red firs.

This nocturnal squirrel runs up a tree, spreads its legs with their connecting skin webs, and silently glides down through the air for as much as 100 feet. Just before alighting it bends the broad tail upward to act like a rudder, so that the squirrel lands upright on its feet on the base of another tree—with an audible thump. It does not fly. The silky pelage makes for silent gliding when owls are abroad, and the big eyes are efficient for nighttime vision. Some foraging is done on the ground. By day this squirrel shelters in cavities of black oaks or red firs, sometimes in woodpecker holes, using shredded bark for an insulated nest. There is indirect evidence that flying squirrels may be nearly as common as red squirrels or ground squirrels. The food probably includes nuts, seeds, tree buds, insects, fungi, and some animal flesh, as these squirrels are often caught in meat-baited traps set for carnivores. Litters vary from 2 to 6 and are born mainly in June and July, but half-grown young have been found late in October.

M-19. Pocket Gophers. Genus *Thomomys* (pl. 62). Form sturdy, H.&B. 6"–8", T. 3"–4", wt. to 6 oz.; a large external fur-lined cheek pouch at each side of mouth; 2 pairs of slender cutting teeth (incisors) project beyond lips; eyes and ears small; fore claws long, slender; tail short, slender, sparsely haired; pelage short, smooth, light to dark brown, paler below. Sign. Scattered low, rounded mounds of loose earth. Distr. Common throughout

Sierra up to timberline, most often around meadows and in soft soil of open forest, none in dense woods or bare rocky areas.

Signs of Pocket Gophers—their surface mounds—are common, but the animals are seldom seen. Each lives separately in an extensive irregular tunnel system about 2 inches in diameter at 6 to 18 inches underground, and rarely emerges. To extend the tunnel a short lateral is dug to the surface, excavated soil is pushed out, and then the opening is closed; farther on another lateral and mound are made. The gopher digs with its fore feet, cuts roots with the incisor teeth, and scrapes the loosened material backward. Then (having narrow "hips"), it turns about in place and pushes the soil out the lateral by using the forefeet and chin. A mound usually is fan-like because successive loads are pushed in radiating pattern from the tunnel mouth. At one side, a lower circular area marks the last earth from the lateral that closed the entrance. Mole hills (see M-2), by contrast, are "erupted" from below and are of irregular form (fig. 24).

When winter snow covers the land at higher altitudes, the gopher forces its way up and makes snow tunnels, paralleling the ground surface, into which excavated soil can be packed. The spring melt leaves this material as long, branched "gopher cores" lying on the ground and over small rocks or low bushes (fig. 23). Cores persist until washed apart by heavy rains. In high altitudes some gophers in autumn move into drying meadows, but with the spring thaw they tunnel upslope to drier sites.

From spring to autumn a gopher makes short vertical holes, crops vegetation around the edge, and then fills the hole level with the surface. At dusk occasional gophers come on top of the ground and may go 100 feet from the opened burrow in search of food; they may also do so after dark. The food is of green vegetation, roots, and bulbs, carried in the cheek pouches. Some is stored in enlarged chambers of the tunnel system for use in times of scarcity. The nest cavity,

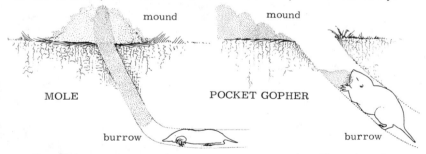

Figure 24. Burrowing methods of mole and pocket gopher. The mole pushes excavated soil up through a mound, but the pocket gopher puts the soil out through a hole temporarily opened on the surface.

6 to 8 inches in diameter, is filled with shredded plant fibers, crinkled like excelsior. This makes an insulated sleeping compartment and serves to shelter the annual brood of 5 or 6 young. Weasels and snakes kill gophers in the tunnels, badgers and coyotes dig them out of the nests, and owls catch some abroad at night. On cultivated lands gophers damage useful plants but on the wild lands of the Sierra their burrowing is an agency of soil formation and erosion, helping to make meadows. The tunnels serve as shelter for some small mammals, amphibians, and insects.

Several species of gophers occupy parts of the Sierra—lowlands, foothills, middle and high altitudes—only one kind in each area. They differ in size, color, and other details but are alike in habits.

M-20. Pocket Mice. Genus *Perognathus*. Body size of house mouse; H.&B. 2½"–3½", T. 2½"–5", H.F. ¾"–1", wt. to 1 oz.; a fur-lined pouch at each side of mouth; fore legs and feet small, hind feet and tail long; pelage yellowish brown above, white beneath. SIGN. Holes ¾"–1¼" dia. closed by day, under bushes. DISTR. Along base of both slopes of Sierra in sandy or soft soil.

Pocket Mice, like the related Kangaroo Rats, spend the day in their burrows and forage at night. They hop on the long hind feet, using the tail for balance. When undisturbed their jumps are short, but if alarmed they bound rapidly in 3-foot leaps. Their food is of small seeds, gathered by the little front feet and carried in the cheek pouches. The annual brood of 2 to 6 is born in May or June on the west slope but slightly later on the east side. The larger, spiny-haired *P. californicus* occupies the foothill chaparral almost to the yellow pine forest; *P. inornatus* lives in spare grasslands on soft soil margining the Great Valley, and *P. parvus* on the east slope is among the sagebrush at 4000–8000 ft. elevation. The latter two are smaller and silky-coated.

M-21. Kangaroo Rats. Genus *Dipodomys* (pl. 62). H.&B. 3¾"–5½", T. 6"–7½", H.F. 1½"–1¾", wt. 1½–3 oz.; a large, external fur-lined cheek pouch at each side of mouth; ear small, flat on head; fore feet small, hind legs and feet long; tail longer than body, with tuft at end; pelage silky, above sandy brown, light or dark, with white stripe across each thigh, under surface white. SIGN. Burrows about 2" dia. in loose soil near bases of bushes, entrance filled by day with soft earth; tracks, paired impressions of hind feet with long heel print, in series 7"–36" apart, tail track interrupted. DISTR. Margin of Great Valley and into western foothills; also along e. base of Sierra; in sandy ground.

The Kangaroo Rat of the arid Southwest leaps with its long hind legs and feet, using the tail as a stabilizer and support. When frightened it makes repeated jumps of 3 feet or more and disappears rapidly. The bounds are shorter when foraging at night. It feeds selectively on seeds of certain plants, using the small fore feet to stuff them into the cheek pouches. When a load is accumulated, the animal takes its food into the burrow for later use. Some seeds are buried in shallow surface pits and covered. Burrows are dug in soft sandy ground and may be complex, on more than one level; enlarged chambers serve for the nest and for food storage. The young, 2 to 4 per brood, are born in spring. One subspecies of *Dipodomys heermani* lives in the Great Valley and another in the foothills; *D. leucogenys* occurs at the east base of the Sierra south to Independence, and *D. merriami* beyond that town.

M-22. Beaver. *Castor canadensis* (pl. 63). Body stout, head blunt, tail flat, paddle-like, and scaly, hind feet webbed (fig. 22), pelage dense with long overhairs and plush-like under fur. H.&B. 24″–31″, T. 11½″–16½″, wt. 34–50 lbs. Coat rich golden brown, tail blackish. SIGN. Dams of brush and mud backing up water on streams to form ponds; "houses" of logs, twigs, and brush in ponds; toothmarks of gnawing on trees; burrows about 15″ dia. in banks of streams. DISTR. Local along some large rivers at edge of Great Valley and introduced a few places higher in Sierra; lives on slow-moving streams.

Beaver were native in waters of the Great Valley before the white man, but trapping soon decreased the population and only a few remain. This largest of our rodents lives beside and in the water. It builds dams to form ponds where it can avoid attack by large carnivores. The dams are made of logs and brush and the spaces between filled with mud. In the pond the animal constructs a house, often 4 or 5 ft. in diameter, with nest chambers inside reached by a tunnel from below the water surface. Beavers subsist mostly on the inner bark (cambium) of cottonwoods, aspens, and willows. These trees are cut by gnawing with the big incisor teeth (fig. 23). Some bark is removed in place, and smaller sections of the tree are dragged or floated to the pond and consumed there, after which the peeled wood is added to the dam. In the lowlands beavers often complicate farming practices by damming irrigation ditches. There is no shortage of food for them in these warm flooded lowland locations. In the higher Sierra, however, it is questionable whether the supply of aspen around the streams where they have been introduced will enable colonies to continue indefinitely.

M-23. Western Harvest Mouse. *Reithrodontomys megalotis.* Size and form of house mouse; H.&B. 2⅛″–3¼″, T. 2½″–3⅛″, H.F. ¾″, E. ½″, wt. ⅓ oz.; each upper incisor tooth with lengthwise groove; tail scantily haired. Pelage above buffy and black, below dull white; ear tawny-haired. DISTR. Great Valley and Foothill belt, mostly in grassland.

This little mouse is common in grassy or weedy places, often near water but sometimes on rocky slopes. It feeds on small seeds of local plants. The spherical nest is woven of shredded plant fibers, lined with fine grasses or down from willow or cottonwood. Elsewhere the nest is elevated in grass or bushes, but locally it is hidden in leafy ground debris. When disturbed the mouse utters a series of high-pitched squeals. Young are produced from April to October, usually 4 (1–7) per litter.

26. Dusky-footed
Wood Rat

30. Meadow Mouse

24. White-footed Mouse

32. Roof Rat

33. House Mouse

34. Jumping Mouse

31. Muskrat

35.
Porcupine

22. Beaver

Plate 63. Mammals

M-24. White-footed Mice. Genus *Peromyscus* (pl. 63). Medium-sized mice, feet and all under surface *pure white,* upper surface brown, pale or dark (bluish gray in young); eyes large, black; ears thin, relatively large; tail slender, well haired. Four species in Sierra Nevada.

a. DEER MOUSE. *P. maniculatus.* H.&B. 3″–4⅛″, T. 2″–3″, H.F. ¾″, E. ⅝″, wt. ½–⅔ oz. Smallest; tail shorter than head and body, white with dark stripe above; upper surface yellowish brown. DISTR. Across Sierra from Great Valley to Great Basin, 200–10200 ft. in all but Alpine belt and in most environments; mostly on ground; commonest Sierran mammal; breeds April-Oct., young 1–9, usually 3–4.

b. BRUSH MOUSE. *P. boylii.* H.&B. 3½″–4″, T. 3¾″–4⅓″, H.F. ⅞″, E. ¾″, wt. ¾–1¼ oz. Tail longer than head and body. DISTR. W. slope along entire Sierra, 200–8100 ft., Foothill and Yellow Pine belts, on wooded or brushy slopes with access to water; climbs rocks and trees; breeds Apr.-June, young 2–5.

c. BIG-EARED (PIÑON) MOUSE. *P. truei.* H.&B. 3¼″–4⅓″, T. 3⅔″–4⅓″, H.F. ⅞″–1″, E. ⅘″–1″, wt. ⅚–1⅖ oz. Tail equals head and body. DISTR. W. slope along Sierra to 2000 ft. in Foothill belt and on e. slope at higher altitudes amid piñon pines; in brushy and rocky places; breeds May-June, young 3–4.

d. CALIFORNIA MOUSE. *P. californicus.* H.&B. 4″–5″, T. 4⅝″–5⅓″, H.F. 1″–1⅛″, E. ⅘″–⅞″, wt. 1½–1¾ oz. Largest; tail longer than head and body. DISTR. W. slope, Mariposa to Tulare Co. in Foothill belt, among oaks or dense chaparral, often associated with wood rats; the least common species.

White-footed Mice are the commonest and most widespread of North American mammals. There are many species. The Deer Mouse occurs from Mexico to Quebec and Alaska. The four Sierran species are graded in size (see measurements), especially as to the ear and hind foot. The Deer Mouse is less than half the weight of the largest, the California Mouse. All four are in the Foothill belt, to which the Big-eared and California mice are restricted; the Brush Mouse continues through the Yellow Pine belt; and the Deer Mouse lives almost everywhere except above timberline. Being nocturnal and making no obvious trails or burrows, these little animals leave scant evidence, but when naturalists set lines of traps they usually catch more white-footed mice than all other kinds. Once in June on the east slope 30 traps in 4 nights took 66 Deer Mice and 10 other small rodents, evidence of a peak population. White-foots are most active in early hours of the night, but some retire only at dawn; they do not hibernate. Mostly they run on the ground while searching for their food, which includes seeds of grasses, herbs, and conifers, larvae or adult insects, and some fungi. Deer Mice are naked when born but soon become fully haired and mature rapidly. Some females only 5 weeks old are bearing embryos. The total life span is short. Mountain cabins when unoccupied and not adequately screened are often invaded by these mice; bedding and other fabrics are chewed to obtain nest material, and cereal foods are eaten. Because of their abundance, white-footed mice are common prey for snakes, owls, and mammalian carnivores.

M-25. Grasshopper Mice. Genus *Onychomys*. H.&B. 3½″–5″, T. 1½″–2½″, wt. to 2½ oz.; body stout, tail short, thick, tapered, well haired, white-tipped; pelage fine, dense, sharply bicolor, grayish or sandy brown above, white below. DISTR. E. of Sierra in sagebrush and sandy areas.

Most mice live on plant materials, but grasshopper mice eat insects, scorpions, and rodents—pocket mice, voles, or deer mice; they use seeds only when other food is scarce. They have keen senses, stalk and pounce on their prey, and kill by biting. They utter repeated high-pitched notes, audible at some distance, and lower barking notes. Young, 3 to 6, are born in spring to summer. These mice usually "borrow" the burrow of some other small rodent. The northern *O. leucogaster* ranges south to Mono County, and the southern *O. torridus* beyond that area.

M-26. Dusky-footed Wood Rat. *Neotoma fuscipes* (pl. 63). Size and form of house rat, but tail shorter than body; H.&B. 7¼″–8¼″, T. 6½″–7½″, wt. 7¼–8¾ oz. Ears large, rounded, finely haired; body pelage dense, soft, brownish gray with black hair tips; under surface of body and tail and top of feet white, base of feet dusky. SIGN. Neat houses 2 to 3 ft. high, rounded or conical, of twigs, leaves, wood scraps, etc. on ground under trees or brush, also in oaks at several feet above ground, or in rock crevices; droppings cylindrical, ⅜″ x ⅛″, on runways or about houses. DISTR. Foothill belt and edge of Yellow Pine belt (200–4600 ft.), amid trees or brush or among rocks.

The "trade rat" or "pack rat" carries various articles about, sometimes into cabins or camps, where it may exchange them for table utensils or other shiny objects. It is a good climber, mainly nocturnal, and hence rarely seen, but active throughout the year. The houses, one or more per rat, vary in form and composition, according to materials close by. Each contains one or more nest chambers connecting to runways that lead out onto or into the ground or nearby logs (fig. 23). The inhabitant usually forages within 25 yards of its home, eating fruits, berries, seeds, bark, leaves, herbs, and grasses. The young, 2 to 4 in a litter are born mostly from March to May and weaned in about two months.

M-27. Bushy-tailed Wood Rat. *Neotoma cinerea*. Larger than house rat or Dusky-footed Wood Rat; H.&B. 7″–9½″; T. 4¾″–7⅜″; wt. 9½–16¼ oz.; pelage long, dense, and soft, sandy brown above, darker on tail; feet and under surface of body and tail white; long hairs on sides of tail form a flat brush to 1″ wide. SIGN. Sparse accumulations of sticks and woody debris in rock crevices; droppings black, cylindrical, ½″ x ⅛″. DISTR. Higher Sierra Nevada, at 5000–13000 ft., in talus slides, rocky outcrops, or big weathered logs; mostly nocturnal.

This big wood rat lives near the conies in the rugged high country and evidently is active throughout the year. Its abode often has a musky odor from secretions of glands near the base of the tail. Like the lowland species, it trades and packs, sometimes to the dismay of campers and cabin dwellers in its territory. Its building tendencies are limited to casual accumulations of woody scraps, but there is likely a hidden insulated nest to offset the arctic chill of winter. The food is of fruits, nuts, and seeds, even bark, of local plants. From 3 to 5 young are produced in July; they grow rapidly, soon becoming full-sized.

M-28. Red-backed Mouse. *Clethrionomys occidentalis.* Like meadow mouse but middle of back reddish; H.&B. 4⅓″, T. 2″, wt. to 1 oz. DISTR. Plumas Co. n. in Yellow Pine belt, on forest floor.

Red-backed Mice live about logs and debris on the forest floor, mostly in damp places or near watercourses, occasionally in manzanita patches. No runways are evident. They are active all year, tunneling in snow during the winter. Green vegetation, some algae and fungi, and a few insects are eaten. Females containing 1 to 3 young have been taken from late March through April, and a few in November.

M-29. Lemming Mouse. *Phenacomys intermedius.* Resembles meadow mouse; H.&B. 4″, T. 1⅛″–1½″, wt. to 1 oz.; pelage ashy, brown-tinged above, whitish below; feet and tail pale ashy. DISTR. Pyramid Peak to Humphrey Basin, Fresno Co., chiefly in Subalpine belt, 7400–10800 ft.; in meadows and heather patches.

Only continued trapping will reveal the presence of this scarce vole-like mouse, which lives solitarily near red heather amid scattered lodgepole pines. Piles of droppings to 6 inches in diameter suggest places where the mice have wintered under the snow. Near these are cuttings, 1½ to 3 inches long, of heather, willow, and other plants, such as made by meadow mice.

M-30. Meadow Mice or Voles. Genus *Microtus* (pl. 63). H.&B. 4″–5½″, T. 1⅜″–2½″, wt. 1–2½ oz.; eyes small, ear buried in fur, pelage long, dense, and soft, above dark brown (sometimes reddish along back), below dark gray. SIGN. Runways 1″–1½″ wide cut in grass, with open holes to underground tunnels; droppings blackish, ⅜″ x ¼₆″. DISTR. Throughout Sierra locally, except Alpine belt, from Great Valley to Great Basin.

The California Meadow Mouse (*M. californicus*) lives in grasslands from the Great Valley through the western Foothill belt and also on the east slope in Mono and Inyo counties; the Mountain Meadow Mouse (*M. montanus*) occupies wet meadows from the Yellow Pine belt up to 11000 feet at timberline; and the Long-tailed Meadow Mouse (*M. longicaudus*) occurs in swamps and under streamside thickets in parts of the Yellow Pine belt and more commonly at higher elevations to 10700 feet.

The name meadow mice indicates that these small rodents usually live in damp green grassland. The California and Mountain species make small runways by clipping the vegetation close to the surface. In tall dense grass these paths are shielded from view above. The runways, strewn with grass cuttings and droppings, connect to holes, always open, of underground tunnels. An enlarged chamber, below ground, contains the globular nest of shredded plant fibers felted into a warm shelter. The mice are active day and night and do not hibernate. They consume large amounts of green watery vegetation, which is low in nutritive value. In the lowlands there are repeated broods, often at short intervals, through much of the year. Higher up the mice breed from April or May into September, usually having 3 to 7 per litter. The fast-breeding voles sometimes "erupt" in enormous numbers and strip the land of vegetation; then there is a population "crash" to a low level. Because of their abundance, meadow mice are caught by snakes, hawks, owls, herons, and many carnivorous mammals in the simple grass-mouse-predator chain. The Long-tailed Meadow Mouse does not regularly make and live in runways. It seems to range freely in damp and streamside locations.

The Sagebrush Vole (*Lagurus curtatus*), a short-tailed meadow mouse (H.&B. 3⅕"–4½", T. ¾"–1"), has dense lax pelage, ashy gray above and nearly white below. It occurs throughout the Great Basin, reaching the east base of the Sierra in Mono and Inyo counties in areas of sagebrush and rabbit brush. It eats herbaceous plants and sagebrush, and sometimes makes surface runways.

M-31. Muskrat. *Ondatra zibethica* (pl. 63). Large, tail narrow, higher than wide, and scaly; H.&B. 9½"–12", T. 7½"–10", E. small; wt. to 4 lbs.; coat dense, soft, dark brown, paler on under surface. Sign. Burrows to 7" in dia., usually under water, in ponds and slow streams; rounded "houses" of plant materials in quiet waters; tracks in mud; cut vegetation floating on water surface. Distr. In waters of Great Valley and lower foothills near growths of tule and cat-tail.

Muskrats were introduced west of the Sierra during the 1930's, and since have spread to many lowland waters. The animals live along marshy borders of lakes, streams, and irrigation ditches, digging burrows with underwater entrances in the banks, and sometimes building small "houses" in open water. The food is of underwater roots of cattails and other aquatic plants, and green vegetation from the shore. Broods of 5 to 7 are produced through much of the year. Muskrats are doing increasing damage to ditch banks, levees, and outlet boxes on irrigation structures. The number taken for fur does not seriously decrease the population.

M-32. Roof Rat. *Rattus rattus* (pl. 63). The typical rat; tail longer than head and body, scaly with few hairs; pelage coarse, many long overhairs; H.&B. 7"–8", T. 8"–10", E. 1", thin, nearly hairless, wt. to ½ lb. Above plain grayish brown, below uniform dull yellowish to whitish, feet dusky. Sign. Gnawings to 1½" in dia. in woodwork or cartons; chewings on food materials, clothing, and fabrics; droppings spindle-shaped, slender, to ⅜" long. Distr. Great Valley, Foothill belt, and into Yellow Pine belt, to 5000 ft., mainly about buildings.

This rat arrived in California with the gold rush and in time made its way into the interior and up the west slope of the Sierra, where it is found mainly in dwellings and barns. It is nocturnal and shy. Evidence of its presence usually is damage to food and clothing and droppings scattered where the rats have run. Now reported in only a few places, its numbers may increase as more people come to live on the lower west slope. There may be several broods per year, each of about 6 young.

M-33. House Mouse. *Mus musculus* (pl. 63). Small; tail slender, nearly hairless, scaly; H.&B. 3″–4″, T. 3″–3½″, E. ½″, wt. ½ oz. Coloration uniform, above dark grayish or yellowish brown, below plain dusky brown, buffy, or whitish. Sign. Holes to 1″ dia. in woodwork or food packages; irregular chewing on clothing or fabrics; droppings spindle-shaped, blackish, ⅟₁₆″ x ¼″. Distr. From Great Valley up w. slope to at least 4000 ft.; mostly in buildings, some in grassland.

The plain little House Mouse, an Old World alien, invaded America and California with the white man and has long been in settlements and on farms on the west slope of the Sierra. It is often unknowingly carried in baled hay, household goods, or bundles of clothing to new locations. While usually thought of as an inhabitant of buildings, in the lowlands it has reverted to a wild state and lives year round successfully in grasslands a mile or more from dwellings. Sometimes its numbers there equal the common native White-footed Mouse. Indoors it is a nuisance, eating many kinds of human food, scattering its droppings, and gnawing into packages, clothing, furniture, or cabinets. It breeds early and often, almost throughout the year, having broods averaging 5 or 6 at frequent intervals. The young mature quickly, and the life span is short.

M-34. Western Jumping Mouse. *Zapus princeps* (pl. 63). H.&B. 3¾″–4″, T. 4¾″–5½″, H.F. 1⅛″–1⅓″, E. 1″, wt. ⅔–⅞ oz.; a groove on front of each incisor tooth; front legs short, hind legs and feet long; tail exceeds head and body, scaly, few hairs; middle of back dark, sides yellow, below pure white, tail and feet dusky. Distr. Lodgepole–fir and Subalpine belts on both slopes at 5500–10000 ft., in wet meadows and grassy stream borders.

Like a Kangaroo Rat, the Jumping Mouse bounds on its long hind feet, covering 2 to 3 feet at each leap, and uses the tail for support and balance. Among streamside willows it makes zigzag jumps to avoid obstructions and seek shelter. It takes readily to water and swims well. Small grass seeds, fruits, and insects serve as food. The mouse digs small inconspicuous burrows but in summer makes nests hidden in surface vegetation. These are spherical, about 5 inches in diameter, of long, dry grass blades. One or two litters of 5 or 6 are born in summer.

M-35. American Porcupine. *Erethizon dorsatum* (pl. 63). H.&B. 20″–27″, T. 5″–12″, wt. 8–15 lbs. or more. Upper surface and sides of body and tail densely armed with pointed hollow quills up to 3″ long; yellow hairs between quills to 7″ long; winter fur black, 4″ long. SIGN. Paired incisor marks ¼″ wide on peeled trunks, mainly conifers (fig. 23); droppings bean-shaped, to 1″ x ⅜″, of undigested bark pulp; tracks (fig. 22) to 3″ long, toed-in. DISTR. Mainly in Yellow Pine and Lodgepole–fir belts in open forests at 4000–11000 ft. s. to Tulare Co.; occasionally in lower valleys of w. slope and on sagebrush plains of northeast.

This largest of terrestrial rodents is well protected. When alarmed it turns away, erects the quills, humps the body, and swings the stout tail laterally. If any quills touch an inquiring dog, wildcat, or person, the barbed tips lodge in the "enemy's" skin. The porcupine is active mainly at night. It climbs readily to eat the succulent inner bark, mainly of conifers in the West, but in spring takes some herbaceous plants on the ground. Its voice is a grunting or groaning *unh*. Individuals may rest or sleep aloft in trees but otherwise often shelter in rock slides. The single young is born in late spring, well haired, with its eyes open; its soft quills soon harden. Forest damage is slight with few "porkies" present, but moderate numbers may girdle and top many forest trees.

M-36. Mountain Coyote. *Canis latrans* (pl. 64). Size and form of large collie dog; H.&B. 30″–33″, T. 12″–15″; wt. 20 to 30 lbs. or more; E. to 4½″ long, pointed, held erect; tail bushy, dia. 4″, dark at tip; pelage long, gray to grayish brown, black stripe along back, under parts white; nose, ears, back, and legs reddish. VOICE. Loud high-pitched barking and wailing, mainly at night. SIGN. Dog-like; tracks (fig. 22) longer than wide, 2½″ x 2″, hind foot smaller, marks of claws show in soft soil; droppings to ¾″ in dia. DISTR. Throughout the Sierra; some from high mountains winter at lower levels; lives and hunts in open, usually singly.

Coyotes, our native "wild dogs," remain fairly common despite persistent efforts to reduce their numbers because of attacks on small livestock. People in remote high camps are often entertained by coyote "singing" at dawn or dusk—one often sounding like a chorus—and by occasional daytime glimpses of the animals. Coyotes are opportunists as to food. They dig out ground squirrels or pocket gophers, catch rabbits, mice, and grasshoppers, take occasional birds, and sometimes eat deer killed by mountain lions; they also eat carrion. Berries of manzanita, juniper, or other plants are eaten. For shelter they use a rock den, enlarge a rodent burrow, or dig their own. The young, 6 or 7 (3–11), are furred at birth and fed at the den by both parents, but by autumn scatter for independent life.

The Valley Coyote (*Canis ochropus*) lives in the western lowlands and foothills. It has a paler, less furry coat, larger ears, more slender snout, and smaller teeth than its mountain relative.

Of wolves in the Sierra, there are two old unverified reports. One, possibly an escaped alien captive, was killed in 1962 in Tulare County.

M-37. Red Fox. *Vulpes fulva.* Size of small collie; H.&B. 26″, T. 16″, bushy, white-tipped; E. 4″, pointed, black-tipped; coat rich reddish, under parts whitish; front legs blackish. VOICE. A bark, louder than that of Gray Fox. DISTR. Only in higher mountains; occasionally down to about 6000 ft. in winter.

Unlike their common eastern relatives, these foxes are scarce in the High Sierra, where they travel in and out of the sparse forest. They feed on White-tailed Jackrabbits, squirrels, chipmunks, mice, and some birds. In winter dense fur grows out between the toes, for easier travel on snow. Rocky dens presumably are used as shelter, where the young (3 to 9) are born about April.

M-38. Gray Fox. *Urocyon cinereoargenteus* (pl. 64). Form and size of small collie dog. H.&B. 22″–27″, T. 13″–16″, E. 3″; wt. 7–10 lbs. Body and tail iron gray with black stripe along middle; tail black-tipped; back of ears, sides, and legs yellowish brown; chin and belly white. SIGN. Tracks (fig. 22) about 1″, claw marks show in soft soil; droppings dog-like, dia. ½″. VOICE. A sharp bark and growling notes. DISTR. Foothill and Yellow Pine belts, in chaparral; solitary.

The principal home of this fox is the western slope, where it is the commonest carnivore; some individuals go into the forest above. The animal is active by day or night, trotting briskly under the shrubbery, across roadways, and into rocky places. It can climb trees, at least to escape danger. From August to early winter it may feed largely on manzanita or coffeeberries, then abundant; other plant material also is used. Animal food includes pocket gophers, mice, other rodents, rabbits, and some birds, even as large as quail. The young, averaging 4 per litter, are born in spring and under parental care about two months before becoming independent.

M-39. Black Bear. *Ursus americanus* (pl. 64). Large, males to 5 ft. long and 40 in. high at shoulder; tail 6″ or less; weight seldom over 300 lbs.; forefoot squarish (to 6½″ x 4″), hind foot triangular (to 9″ x 4½″); all 5 toes and claws of each foot usually show in tracks; pelage long, heavy, either glossy black or cinnamon brown. VOICE. Sniffs or snorts; a loud growl or bawl when scared or injured. SIGN. Irregular large blackish droppings; tracks in dusty places (fig. 22); scratches on trees (fig. 23). DISTR. Mainly in Yellow Pine and Lodgepole–fir belts at 1200–8500 ft., commoner on w. slope; inhabits forest floor or thickets, sheltering in caves, rock piles, or hollow trees.

This bear is the largest living Sierran carnivore. Some individuals are black and others cinnamon, each being of the same color throughout the year. Footprints in dusty places, the large irregular blackish droppings, and claw marks on trees are common evidence of its presence during summer and autumn. The bears themselves are often about campgrounds. Almost anything its paws can reach serves as food —small mammals or insects in nests, any flesh or carrion, garbage,

42. Marten

36. Mtn. Coyote

43. Long-tailed Weasel

40. Ring-tail

38. Gray Fox

41. Raccoon

39. Black Bear

44. Amer. Badger

Plate 64. Mammals

grasses, leaves, fruits, berries, and nuts. Bears usually acquire much fat in autumn, and some time after snow arrives they den up for a midwinter sleep that is less profound than the true hibernation of ground squirrels. In late winter the cubs are born, 2 or 3 of diminutive size (8 oz. or less), which are nursed in the den until able to go foraging with the mother. Both young and adults are adept climbers and may take to trees when disturbed. Some bears near summer homes or campgrounds become nuisances by learning to raid food supplies and garbage cans. *Do not feed bears; they can inflict severe injuries.*

The Grizzly Bear (*Ursus arctos*), emblem of California, originally inhabited the foothill oaks and chaparral and the lower forests of the Sierra. It was distinguished from the black bear by long front claws, a shoulder hump, grizzled coat, and larger size. Abounding during the gold rush, the Grizzly was rapidly reduced and the last living individual was seen during 1924 in Sequoia National Park (consult Storer, T. I., and L. P. Tevis, Jr., The California Grizzly. Berkeley and Los Angeles, Univ. of Calif. Press, 1955).

M-40. Ring-tail. *Bassariscus astutus* (pl. 64). H.&B. 14"–16", T. 14"–15", E. 1¾", rounded, wt. 2–2½ lbs. Muzzle tapered, body slender, legs short; tail long, bushy, with alternate black and white rings; body drab brown, paler below; a narrow black ring around eye, surrounded by white. SIGN. Track roundish, dia. 1"; droppings slender, irregular. VOICE. Adults bark, young make squeaking noises. DISTR. Foothill and lower Yellow Pine belts (rarely to 7200 ft.) in rocks or brush near water.

The Ring-tail, relative of the raccoon, is nocturnal and hence rarely seen, and its tracks are seldom in evidence. For daytime shelter it uses holes in oaks or other trees, small caves, spaces within rock piles, or old cabins. The long tail serves for balance in climbing and leaping on trees or rocks, at which the animal is agile. Its food includes white-footed mice, wood rats, other rodents, sparrows, and berries of manzanita, madrone, etc. The annual litter of 3 or 4 is born in May or June. Early settlers made it a pet to roam their cabins and keep down the mice, so it has been called miner's cat.

M-41. Raccoon. *Procyon lotor* (pl. 64). H.&B. 18"–24", T. 9"–12", wt. 9–18 lbs.; body robust, face with black mask bordered by white; E. 2"–2¼", rounded, white-edged; pelage dense, 1" long, yellowish or grayish brown with black-tipped guard hairs, paler beneath; tail bushy, 4–6 black rings alternating with yellowish white. TRACKS. "Hand-like" (fig. 22), front 1¾" long, hind 3" long. DISTR. Great Valley into Yellow Pine belt, mostly near water.

Many raccoons sleep by day in rotted-out cavities of trees, descending at night to forage on the ground or in water. Others den in rock piles or large burrows. Their tracks often show in streamside mud or sand, those of the front and hind foot commonly in pairs. Raccoons exceed bears in their varied diet—rodents and rabbits, birds, frogs, fishes, insects, other invertebrates, acorns, wild and cultivated fruits, berries, and grapes, besides carrion and cultivated grain and melons. When accessible, raccoons take nesting waterfowl or poultry on farms. The young, averaging 4 (3–7) are born in April or May. Raccoon pelts are commonly used for fur.

M-42. Marten. *Martes americana* (pl. 64). Size of small domestic cat but slender; ♂ H.&B. 14″–17″, T. 7″–9″, E. 1⅜″, rounded, T. bushy, dia. to 3″; ♀ smaller; ♂ and ♀ above plain brown, paler below with patch of orange or buff on throat; tail blackish toward tip. Distr. Mainly in Lodgepole–fir and Subalpine belts at 7000–10300 ft.; about rock slides in summer and autumn, otherwise in forest.

This medium-sized member of the weasel family is not common, mostly solitary, and rarely seen. It is an agile climber, taking shelter in tree cavities well above ground, and it hunts some food aloft. In winter the under surface of the feet is covered with hair, facilitating travel on snow. During the warmer months the marten hunts conies and rodents in rock slides but also captures ground squirrels, chipmunks, and sometimes grasshoppers. It also takes chickarees and birds, more often in winter. Mating occurs in summer but development of the embryos is suspended until midwinter, and the young (3; 1–5) are born in spring.

The Fisher (*Martes pennanti*), now rare in the Sierra, has the form of a heavy oversized weasel (H.&B. 20″–25″, T. 15″; wt. ♂, 8–10 lbs., ♀, 4–5½ lbs.). The nose, lower legs and feet, hind part of body, and all of the tail are black; the body otherwise is drab brown, becoming grayish on head and shoulders. In these mountains it lives in the Lodgepole–fir and upper Yellow Pine belts at about 5000–8000 feet, feeding on squirrels, other rodents, and birds. Heavy winter trapping of the Fisher for its fine fur has far reduced the population.

The Wolverine (*Gulo luscus*) has a bear-like head, heavy forelegs, arched back, and bushy tail (H.&B. 27″–29″, T. 8″–10″, wt. 17–34 lbs.). The body is brown with a broad yellowish stripe on each side from shoulder to rump; the face, feet, under surface, and end of tail are blackish, with the forehead and edges of the ears white. It formerly occurred from Lake Tahoe to Giant Forest and beyond Mt. Whitney, chiefly above 8000 feet; never common, it is now rare. The food includes various rodents and sometimes larger prey taken from bears or coyotes, together with carrion.

M-43. Long-tailed Weasel. *Mustela frenata* (pl. 64). H.&B. 9″–10½″, T. 4″–6″, wt. 8+ oz.; ♀ smaller; head short and tapered, neck, body, and tail long and slender, limbs short; in summer, upper parts including legs brown, under surface creamy yellow; in winter, white above and below; end of tail black at all seasons. DISTR. Across Sierra from Yellow Pine belt to edge of Sagebrush belt on e. slope, at 4000–10000 ft.; in old logs and under rock piles, sometimes under buildings.

The weasel is a fearless little carnivore, active at all seasons, and often abroad in daytime. Having a slender body it can seek squirrels or pocket gophers in their burrows and find other rodents in rock crevices. It can run up and down trees almost as easily as a tree squirrel. Both rodents and small birds are usual prey; these animals recognize the weasel as an enemy and give voice when one appears. Weasels breed in summer but embryo development is suspended until about March, and the 4 to 9 young are born a month later. The change to a white coat in winter makes the weasel almost invisible on snow.

The "Least" or Short-tailed Weasel (*Mustela erminea*), our smallest carnivore, is the size of a medium chipmunk, with slim body and short legs (♂, H.&B. 6½″, T. 2½″–3½″, wt. 2–3 oz.; ♀ smaller). In summer it is chocolate brown above and white below but becomes all white in winter except the black tail tip. It lives at the higher altitudes in the Tahoe and Yosemite regions, but being rare neither its full range nor local habits are known.

The Mink (*M. vison*) is mainly a lowland animal, but some live in the central and northern Sierra. It has the contours of a weasel but is larger (♂ H.&B. 12″–17″, T. 7″–9″, wt. 1¼–2¼ lbs.; ♀ smaller). The coat is dark brown, blackish at end of tail. It is highly aquatic and finds much of its food in water, but can travel and hunt on land, being mainly nocturnal. As prey it takes fishes, frogs, aquatic invertebrates, and some small mammals and birds.

M-44. American Badger. *Taxidea taxus* (pl. 64). ♂, H.&B. 24″–30″, T. 5″–6″, wt. 12–24 lbs.; ♀ smaller. Body robust, broad, flattish; legs short, stout; front claws 1″–1½″, nearly straight, heavy; head patched with black and white; body grayish yellow grizzled with white; narrow white stripe from nose over crown and along back; pelage long on sides; tail bushy; legs black. SIGN. Holes about 12″ dia. in ground; tracks (fig. 22) 2″ long, "toed in"; droppings 1″ dia., scarce. DISTR. In dry open country, irrespective of altitude, from Great Valley over Sierra and in Great Basin; solitary, partly diurnal.

The Badger in structure and habits is preëminently a digger with stoutly muscled fore parts, short sturdy legs, and heavy fore claws. Other carnivores hunt by sight and stealth, but the badger often senses (smells?) its prey—commonly ground squirrels or pocket gophers—in underground nests and rapidly digs them out. Other small animals and carrion are eaten. The badger also digs to escape a pursuing dog or man, to bury larger prey such as a rabbit until consumed, to make a sleeping place or nest chamber, and to bury its droppings. On the surface it can run with deceptive speed. Usually silent, it can hiss, growl, and grunt. If cornered it bites fiercely and may emit a strong scent from glands near the anus. The young, usually 2 (1–5), are born fully furred early in April and cared for by the mother until late summer. During old-time roundups, many a galloping cowboy was spilled and his mount broke a leg if it stepped into a badger hole.

M-45. Spotted Skunk. *Spilogale putorius* (pl. 65). Size of a medium ground squirrel; H.&B. 9″–12″, T. 5″–6″, wt. to 1½ lbs.; neck distinct, legs short; black with white spot on forehead, one below each ear, and four broken stripes on neck, back, and sides; tail bushy, with long white hairs at ends. SIGN. Odor! Tracks, H.F. to 1¼″ long, with marks of 5 toes, and pads (fig. 22). DISTR. On w. slope in Foothill and lower Yellow Pine belts to about 4000 ft.; also along e. base and into Lake Tahoe basin; in dry brushy or rocky uplands.

People often misname this animal the "civet cat" or "hydrophobia skunk" (but few are infected with rabies). The little creature is nocturnal, nimble, and a fair climber on fence posts, trees, and beams. At times it upends to stand and walk on the forefeet—in play, in anger, or before discharging scent. For shelter it uses hollow logs, crevices in rock heaps, burrows of other animals, and crannies under or in houses or farm buildings. The long, stout front claws are used in digging. The Spotted Skunk has a varied diet of many crickets and other insects, small rodents, birds, carrion, eggs, and some plant materials. The litter usually is about 4, born in April or May, and the young become full-sized in about 3 months.

M-46. Striped Skunk. *Mephitis mephitis* (pl. 65). About size of house cat; H.&B. 12″–17″, T. 10½″–13″, wt. to 8+ lbs.; head small, body stout, legs short, body pelage long, tail bushy (hairs to 5″ long); black, with narrow white line up forehead and large white area from back of head to shoulders, continuing as 2 white stripes to base of tail. SIGN. Odor! Tracks of 5 toes and claw marks on each foot, H.F. 1½″ long (fig. 22). DISTR. Common from Great Valley into Yellow Pine belt on w. slope; also along e. base of Sierra, including Lake Tahoe basin; in various environments.

The skunk goes foraging at dusk without fear of man or beast. It is "armed" with a defensive nauseating scent that can be sprayed from glands below the tail to a distance of several feet. The plume-like tail is somewhat of an indicator: if raised upright, an intruder should retire. The long fore claws aid in turning over stones when searching for food and to dig out insects in the ground, leaving small forage pits as evidence of such work. About half the food is of grasshoppers, beetles, and other surface-dwelling insects. This is supplemented by mice, pocket gophers, wood rats and squirrels, occasional reptiles and amphibians, berries of shrubs, and other plant materials. For shelter the skunk may take over a ground squirrel or badger burrow, use a hollow log or hole under a stump, a rock crevice, or a space under some deserted building. The young, about 5 per litter, are born in spring. Many

48. Wildcat

46. Striped Skunk

45. Spotted Skunk

47.
Mountain Lion

50.
Mountain Sheep

49.
Mule Deer

Plate 65. Mammals

skunks are killed by poisoned baits placed for coyotes or bobcats and thousands are trapped for fur, and yet the species remains common in many places.

M-47. Mountain Lion. *Felis concolor* (pl. 65). Form cat-like, size of mastiff dog, tail long and slender; H.&B. about 4 ft., T. 2½ ft.; wt. ♂ 84–165 lbs., ♀ 80–100 lbs.; above rich reddish brown, chin, throat, and middle of under surface white; outer sides of ear, nose, feet, and end of tail blackish. TRACKS. Cat-like, wider than long, 3″–4½″, hind edge of heel pad with 2 indentations (fig. 22). DISTR. On w. slope from upper Foothill belt into edge of Lodgepole–fir belt; in brushy and forested country.

Among local carnivores, the Mountain Lion (called cougar, panther, and puma) is second in size only to the black bear. It is large enough to attack man, like the big cats of other lands, but it almost never does so. Being quiet and secretive, it is seldom seen, even by people who live within its range. Mule Deer (M-49) are the favorite and principal food. The lion creeps stealthily within a short distance of a deer and then with a few quick bounds jumps on the quarry and strikes it down. Sometimes it eats much of the carcass, again only a small part, and may bury the remainder. When hunted by men with dogs, the lion takes to a tree. The dusky spotted kittens, usually 2 or 3, are born in March or April and live with the mother for much of the first year. Experience to date in the Sierra indicates there is no hazard to people from sleeping outdoors in the region occupied by this big cat.

M-48. Wildcat. *Lynx rufus* (pl. 65). H.&B. 25″–30″, T. 4″–6″, shoulder ht. 20″–23″, wt. 12–25 lbs.; pelage soft, deep; above light reddish brown in summer, gray in winter; under surface and inner sides of legs white, spotted or barred with black; ears black-tufted, black at tip and base; tail black-tipped, white below. TRACKS. Round, about 2″ dia., sole pad notched behind (fig. 22). DISTR. Common on w. slope, chiefly in Foothill and Yellow Pine belts; in brushland, rock slides, or timber.

The common name "bobcat" refers to the short tail of this species. Less shy than the mountain lion and often active by day, a Wildcat may be glimpsed as it bounds across a road and disappears in the brush. Usually silent, it can scream and yowl, during the mating season, louder than house cats. The animal can climb trees readily when in need of safety or when hunting the nest of some large bird. Rabbits and rodents make up most of the food, especially ground squirrels, wood rats, and pocket gophers. Some small birds are eaten, and a few quail. A Bobcat may kill deer that are impeded by deep snow. The young, commonly 3 (2–4), are born in spring in a den among rocks or at hollowed tree bases.

M-49. Mule Deer. *Odocoileus hemionus* (pl. 65). Adults 32″–42″ high at shoulder; occasional ♂ weighs 200 lbs.; E. large, 8″–9″ long to 4″ wide; T. slender near base, outer surface black, white beneath; adults uniform bright reddish brown in summer, grayish brown in winter; rump and throat whitish; young fawns reddish brown, spotted with white; antlers only in ♂, spike-like in 2nd summer, branched in older deer. SIGN. Tracks sheep-like, sharply pointed, varying with sex and age (fig. 22); droppings elliptical to ½" long, black. DISTR. Practically throughout Sierra in summer; in winter migrates to below heavy snow.

The thousands of people in the Sierra see only a few of the thousands of deer living there, so adept are these animals at hiding in brushy cover. Some deer live yearlong in the foothills and lower forests, but many migrate upslope with advancing spring greenery and a few later go almost to the crest. The return begins with the first storm bringing 6 to 12 inches of snow, commonly by mid-November. Winter concentrations on the west slope are near the lower border of yellow pines where the snow is 18 inches deep or less. Deer forage mostly in morning, late afternoon, and early evening; by day they bed down, often under sheltering bushes where there is a clear view of surroundings. The bed is a slight depression, 2 or 3 feet in diameter, sometimes scraped free of surface litter. The animals drink regularly, often traveling far in autumn when water is scarce. Deer eat a great variety of plants, browsing on shrubs and grazing on grass and herbs in meadows. Many bushes of ceanothus and other shrubs are trimmed of terminal branchlets and leaves. If local deer numbers are large, the bushes may show excessive use and be "pruned" in peculiar shapes by overbrowsing. Antlers begin growth on bucks in April and become mature by late summer, and the dried "velvet" (covering skin) is rubbed off by September. Bucks use their antlers contending with other males during the mating season or rut in early winter; the antlers are dropped by March. Fawns, commonly 2 per birth, appear in June; by early autumn their spots disappear with molt into the winter coat. Does and fawns commonly keep together until the next young are due. Native enemies are the mountain lion (M-47), which can kill deer of any age, and the coyote (M-36), which gets fawns and occasional older deer hampered by snow. Hunters shoot many deer annually under legal control, and an unknown number are removed by poachers. Some deer die of starvation, and some are lost through accidents.

M-50. Mountain Sheep. *Ovis canadensis* (pl. 65). Ht. at shoulder 3–3½ ft., wt. to 160 lbs.; coat gray or buffy brown with large whitish rump patch; hairs stiff, dense; horns permanent, on old males massive, spiraled back and outward often to full circle, on females small, erect, with slight backward curve. SIGN. Tracks to 3" long (fig. 22); droppings cylindrical to ½" long, slightly pointed at one end. DISTR. Originally from near Sonora Pass s. to Mt. Langley and Kaweah Mts.; in 1948 from near Convict Creek to Monache Meadows; in Alpine and Subalpine belts near crest on open areas.

Early travelers found bands of Mountain Sheep rather often along the Sierran crest, but meat hunters and herders of domestic sheep soon reduced the numbers. Despite complete legal protection there still is occasional poaching. In 1948 the population was estimated at under 400. The sheep inhabit high rocky areas, mostly above the mule deer, and have trails between feeding and bedding places and water supplies. Older rams live singly or in bands of 10 or more, females, yearlings, and lambs in groups to 15 or more. Low, sparse shrubby herbs, sedges, and grasses, including some roots, on gravelly slopes or meadows, are eaten. The sheep bed down in exposed sites; when frightened they run and jump for safety over rocky places. Mating is in late autumn, when rams fight by kicking and butting. Gestation is about 180 days, and lambs appear in May or June. Later they play much with one another and with their mothers. The principal losses are in winter when both young and adults become isolated by deep soft snow.

REFERENCES

There are many books and articles in both popular and scientific periodicals that deal with the Sierra Nevada and its geology and plant and animal life. The selected references included here contain much material to supplement the brief accounts possible in this handbook.

THE SIERRA NEVADA

Farquhar, F. P. 1965. History of the Sierra Nevada. Berkeley and Los Angeles, Univ. Calif. Press. xiv + 262 pp., illus. Mainly of human affairs.

Grinnell, Joseph, Joseph Dixon, and J. M. Linsdale. 1930. Vertebrate natural history of a section of northern California through the Lassen Peak region. Univ. Calif. Publ. Zool., vol. 35, v + 594 pp., 181 figs. Amphibians to mammals.

Grinnell, Joseph, and T. I. Storer. 1924. Animal life in the Yosemite. Berkeley, Univ. Calif. Press. xviii + 752 pp., 60 pls. (12 in color), 2 maps, 65 figs. Mammals to amphibians.

Hinds, N. E. A. 1952. Evolution of the California landscape. Calif. Dept. of Natural Resources, Bureau of Mines, Bull. 158, 240 pp., 2 maps, 156 figs. Geological history of Sierra Nevada, pp. 13–60.

Leconte, Joseph. 1971. A journal of ramblings through the High Sierras of California [in 1870]. New York, Sierra Club & Ballantine Books. xiv + 140 pp. (First published 1875.) Ten men on horseback rode from Oakland to Yosemite Valley, Lake Tahoe, and return.

Matthes, F. E. 1930. Geological history of the Yosemite Valley. U. S. Geol. Survey, Prof. Paper 160, vi + 137 pp., 52 pls., 38 figs.

Matthes, F. E. 1950a. The incomparable valley: a geological interpretation of the Yosemite. Edited by Fritiof Fryxell. Berkeley and Los Angeles, Univ. Calif. Press. xiii + 160 pp., 50 halftones, 2 maps, 11 figs.

Matthes, F. E. 1950b. Sequoia National Park. Edited by Fritiof Fryxell. Berkeley and Los Angeles, Univ. Calif. Press. x + 136 pp., 124 figs. Photos and interpretations of geology of southern High Sierra.

Schumacher, Genny (ed.). 1964. The Mammoth Lakes Sierra. A handbook for roadside and trail. San Francisco, Sierra Club. rev. ed. 147 pp., maps and illus.

Starr, W. W., Jr. 1967. Guide to the John Muir Trail and the High Sierra Region. 11th ed. San Francisco, Sierra Club. xii + 135 pp., map. Yosemite Valley to Mt. Whitney; trail built 1915–1938.

Sumner, Lowell, and J. S. Dixon. 1953. Birds and mammals of the Sierra Nevada . . . from Sequoia and Kings Canyon National Parks. Berkeley and Los Angeles, Univ. Calif. Press. xviii + 484 pp., 8 col. pls., 46 figs., 2 maps.

Wampler, Joseph, and W. F. Heald. 1960. High Sierra mountain wonderland. Berkeley, Joseph Wampler. vi + 122 pp., illus.

FUNGI

Krieger, L. C. C. 1947. The mushroom handbook. New York, Macmillan Co. 538 pp., 32 pls., 126 figs. Paperback. 1967. New York, Dover Publ. Co.

McKenny, Margaret. 1971. The savory mushroom. Revised by D. E. Stuntz. Seattle, Univ. Washington Press. xxi + 242 pp., 32 col. pls., 156 figs. (photos). Includes 156 species, identification, cookery.

LICHENS

Fink, Bruce. 1935. The lichen flora of the United States. Ann Arbor, Univ. Michigan Press. xii + 426 pp., 47 pls., 4 figs. Reprinted 1960.

MOSSES

Conrad, H. S. 1956. How to know the mosses and liverworts. Rev. ed. Dubuque, Iowa, Wm. C. Brown Co. ix + 226 pp., 3 pls., 442 figs.

FERNS, WILDFLOWERS, SHRUBS, AND TREES

Abrams, Leroy. 1926–1960. Illustrated flora of the Pacific States. Vol. 4 by Roxanna S. Ferris. Stanford, Stanford Univ. Press. 2790 pp., 6069 figs.

Hall, H. M., and C. C. Hall. 1912. A Yosemite flora. San Francisco, Paul Elder & Co. vii + 282 pp., illus.

Jepson, W. L. 1923. The trees of California. Berkeley, Sather Gate Bookshop. 240 pp., 124 figs.

Jepson, W. L. 1925. A manual of the flowering plants of California. Berkeley, Associated Students Store. 1238 pp., 1023 figs. Reprinted 1960. Berkeley and Los Angeles: Univ. Calif. Press.

Klyver, F. D. 1931. Major plant communities in a transect of the Sierra Nevada. . . . Ecology, 12:1–17, 2 figs. (maps). Lane's Bridge, Fresno Co., to near Round Valley, Mono Co.

McMinn, H. E. 1939. An illustrated manual of California shrubs. San Francisco, J. W. Stacey, Inc., and Berkeley, Univ. Calif. Press. xi + 689 pp., frontis., 775 figs. 2nd ed., 1951. Berkeley and Los Angeles: Univ. Calif. Press.

Munz, P. A., and D. D. Keck. 1959. A California flora. Berkeley and Los Angeles, Univ. Calif. Press. xii + 1682 pp., col. frontis., 134 figs.

Parsons, Mary E. 1907. The wild flowers of California. 3d edition. San Francisco, Cunningham et al. cvi + 419 pp., 250 + figs. Paperback 1966. New York, Dover Publ. Co. Scientific names updated by Roxanna S. Ferris.

Pasaterini, Samuel. 1963. Flora of our Sierran national parks—Yosemite, Sequoia and Kings Canyon. Tulare, Calif., Carl and Irving. 6 + 170 pp., 11 col. pls., 198 figs.

Rodin, R. J. [1960]. Ferns of the Sierra. Yosemite Nature Notes, 39(4): 44–124, 55 figs.

Smiley, F. J. 1921. A report upon the boreal flora of the Sierra Nevada of California. Univ. Calif. Publ. Botany, 9:1–423, 7 pls.

Sudworth, G. B. 1908. Forest trees of the Pacific Slope. U. S. Dept. Agric., Forest Service. 441 pp., 2 pls., 207 figs. Paperback. New York, Dover Publ. Co. Detailed distribution.

MISCELLANEOUS ANIMALS

Edmundson, W. T., editor. 1959. Ward and Whipple's Freshwater biology. 2nd ed. New York, John Wiley & Sons. xx + 1248 pp., illus. Keys and brief summaries on plants and invertebrate animals.

Keep, Josiah. 1935. West Coast shells. Revised by J. L. Bailey, Jr. Stanford, Stanford Univ. Press. x + 350 pp., 334 figs.

Pennak, R. W. 1953. Freshwater invertebrates of the United States. New York, Ronald Press Co. ix + 769 pp., 470 figs. Natural history and keys.

Pilsbry, H. A. 1939. Land Mollusca of North America (north of Mexico). Philadelphia Acad. Nat. Sci., Monograph 3, vol. 1: xvii + 994 + ix pp.; vol. 2: ix + 580 pp.; 1165 figs. total.

Storer, T. I., and R. L. Usinger. 1965. General zoology. 4th ed. New York, McGraw-Hill Book Co. viii + 741 pp., 550+ illus.

INSECTS

Chu, H. F. 1949. How to know the immature insects. Dubuque, Iowa, Wm. C. Brown Co. 234 pp., 631 figs.

Comstock, J. A. 1927. Butterflies of California. Los Angeles, published by author. 334 pp., 63 col. pls., 80+ figs. Includes 233 species of California and the Southwest, describing egg, larva, chrysalis, and food plants of many.

Essig, E. O. 1958. Insects and mites of western North America. Rev. ed. New York, Macmillan Co. xiii + 1050 pp., 766 figs.

Swain, R. B. 1948. The insect guide: orders and families of North American insects. Garden City, Doubleday & Co. xliii + 261 pp., 175 figs., some in color.

Usinger, R. L., editor. 1956. Aquatic insects of California. Berkeley and Los Angeles, Univ. Calif. Press. x + 508 pp., 502 figs.

FISHES

Evans, W. A., O. L. Wallis, and G. D. Gallison. 1961. Fishes of Yosemite National Park. Rev. ed. Yosemite Nature Notes, 23:1–30, 17 figs.

La Rivers, Ira. 1962. Fishes and fisheries of Nevada. Carson City, Nevada State Fish and Game Commission. 1–782 pp., 3 col. pls., 270 figs. Includes many fishes of the Sierra Nevada

Murphy, Garth. 1941. A key to the fishes of the Sacramento–San Joaquin Basin. Calif. Fish and Game, 27:165–171.

Wales, J. H. 1957. Trout of California. Sacramento, Calif. Dept. of Fish and Game. 56 pp., illus.

REPTILES AND AMPHIBIANS

Schmidt, K. P. 1953. A checklist of North American amphibians and reptiles [north of Mexico]. 6th ed. Chicago, American Society of Ichthyologists and Herpetologists. viii + 280 pp. Scientific and common names and distribution.

Stebbins, R. C. 1954. Amphibians and reptiles of western North America. New York, McGraw-Hill Book Co. xxii + 528 pp., 90 pls., 52 figs., many maps. Descriptions, distribution, habits, reproduction.

Stebbins, R. C. 1966. A field guide to western reptiles and amphibians. Boston, Houghton Mifflin Co. xiv + 279 pp., 569 figs. (185 in color). Identification and distribution (with maps).

BIRDS

Grinnell, Joseph, and A. H. Miller. 1944. The distribution of the birds of California. Pacific Coast Avifauna 27:1–608, 57 figs. (maps).

Hoffmann, Ralph. 1927. Birds of the Pacific States. Boston, Houghton Mifflin Co. xix + 353 pp., 10 col. pls., many figs. Identification and distribution.

Orr, R. T., and James Moffitt. 1971. Birds of the Lake Tahoe region. San Francisco, Calif. Academy of Sciences. lx + 150 pp., 1 col. pl., 15 figs. Historical account.

Peterson, R. T. 1961. A field guide to western birds. 2nd ed. Boston, Houghton Mifflin Co. xxvi + 366 pp., 60 pls. (36 color), some text figs.

Pough, R. H. 1957. Audubon western bird guide. Garden City, N. Y.: Doubleday & Co. xxxvi + 316 pp., 32 col. pls., many figs.

MAMMALS

Burt, W. H., and R. P. Grossenheider. 1964. A field guide to the mammals [of North America]. 2d ed. Boston, Houghton Mifflin Co. 284 pp., illus. many in color. Identification and distribution (with maps).

Grinnell, Joseph. 1933. Review of the recent mammal fauna of California. Univ. Calif. Publ. in Zoology, 40:71–234. Scientific and common names and distribution.

Grinnell, Joseph, J. S. Dixon, and J. M. Linsdale. 1937. Fur-bearing mammals of California. Berkeley, Univ. Calif. Press. 2 vols. xiv + 777 pp., 6 col. pls., 138 figs. Description, classification, habits, and relations to man.

Ingles, L. G. 1954. Mammals of California and its coastal waters. Rev. ed. Stanford, Stanford University Press. xiii + 396 pp., 46 pls., 24 pictorial keys, 95+ figs. Natural history, maps of range, keys for identification.

Murie, O. J. 1954. A field guide to animal tracks. Boston, Houghton Mifflin Co. xii + 374 pp., 196 figs. drawn by author.

Orr, R. T. 1949. Mammals of Lake Tahoe. San Francisco, California Academy of Sciences. ix + 127 pp., illus.

Palmer, R. S. 1954. The mammal guide mammals of North America north of Mexico. Garden City, Doubleday & Co. 384 pp., illus., many in color, tracks, distribution maps. Identification, habits, reproduction, economic status.

INDEX

Numbers refer to *pages;* the numbers of pages having black and white illustrations are in italics. However, color plates are referred to by *plate number* (as, cp. 10). For scientific names index references are given to the text page and also to the illustration page, where the plant or animal is referred to by its common name.

370 · *Index*